The Beekay Guide to 1000 Carp Waters

Compiled by
Kevin Maddocks
and
Peter Mohan

Acknowledgements

Beekay Publishers would like to thank all those people from many parts of the country who have so readily agreed to provide information to help with the compilation of this book.

We are especially grateful to John Wilson, the well-known angler and tackle dealer, of John's Tackle Den, 16 Bridewell Alley, Norwich, Norfolk, for permission to publish details based on his excellent book *Where to Fish in Norfolk and Suffolk*, published by Jarrold and Sons Ltd of Norwich, to Steve Bowers of 12 Machin Road, Erdington, Birmingham, and his friends of the Central Specimen Group who helped in connection with waters in the West Midlands, to Kevin Gulliford of Ebbw Vale who assisted with waters in Wales, and to Mr Beedom of Doncaster, Steve Francis, Neville Fickling, Len Gurd, Ann Pillinger, John Callaghan, Steve Cole, Bill Turner, Roger Emmet, Rupe Attwood, Adam Joste, Mick Sutton, Allan Parbery, Peter Stone, Mick Ellingworth, John Baron, Rory, of Southend Angling Centre and Mike of Bleak Hall Sports, Kempston, Bedford. We also thank all those who we hope will write to us in the future with corrections, amendments and additions for our fourth edition.

* County Maps
Please note that these maps are not to scale, nor are the locations indicated the exact geographical position of the place concerned. Where a number of places are very close to each other it was necessary to spread out the names over a wider area in order to make them legible.

**A
Waters which have the letter 'A' beside them have some form of accommodation connected with them, and so are particularly suitable for holidays; many of them for family holidays.

Cover picture: John Baker

Index compiled by Ann Pillinger

Withy Pool, Bedford Road, Henlow, Bedfordshire SG16 6EA.

ISBN 0 94767438 1

Produced by Dave Watson, Ascot, Berkshire. Tel: 0344 23844

Introduction

It has been said that the last thing left to do in carp fishing is to publish a list of carp waters and their locations, and this is what BK Publishers have tried to do with this book. We feel that the publication of this material ushers in a new era in carp fishing; one which is long overdue. The time has passed for one of the major factors in carp fishing to be the excessive secrecy which was a characteristic of the sport in past years.

In 1969, when the British Carp Study Group, the world's first large national organisation for carp anglers was founded, there were probably about 250 specialist carp anglers in the whole country; now there are reliably estimated to be around 50,000, many of whom, when they take up the sport each year in their thousands, demand every type of information about baits, methods and rigs, and also about locations of carp waters.

Secrecy

The older and more secretive carp anglers, who don't like the idea of a book of this kind, should remember that they are very much in the minority; most of today's carp anglers will welcome a book of this sort. We feel, too, that so will most carp anglers once they read the contents of the book. We have been very careful to omit all waters we know to be 'secret'; we have left out any waters, club or otherwise, where there are 'no publicity' rules; and we have omitted all waters where membership cannot be obtained. We even asked many carp anglers which waters they wanted to be left out of the book, and we did not include those waters!

Most of the waters listed are those which anyone can fish, and which were already known to many anglers. We don't feel that a listing in this book will substantially increase the number fishing any particular water; in fact, the number fishing your water may actually be reduced when readers learn about other waters from this book and go to fish them, thus 'spreading the load' better on waters throughout the country.

We are not in the business of giving away anglers' secrets and this has been carefully avoided in the book as far as possible. This book, the first ever Guide to Carp Waters, will have its critics, but we feel that like anything new it has now been accepted and has become as natural a part of the carp scene as any book on carp methods and tactics, and that all carp anglers will want to own a copy. Obviously, the book will be particularly helpful to the many thousands of anglers who take up specialist carp fishing every year, but we feel it will also be especially helpful to more experienced carp anglers who wish to try other waters, and we are sure that it will be of great help to the many who write to well known carp anglers regularly asking them for the names of waters they can fish whilst they are on holiday in different parts of the country.

Carp Waters

It must be noted by readers that many of the waters listed in this book are not really 'carp waters', if this is taken to mean waters containing mainly, or only, carp. In fact there are very few waters in the country which contain only carp, or where carp are very much in the majority. Most waters contain only some carp, and so many of these have been included in this book. We have listed many waters which contain few carp, because some carp anglers prefer to fish this type of water in the hope of big carp from an unrecognised water. So please don't expect most of the lakes listed to be packed with carp; they often aren't.

Quite a few of those 'secret' and 'no publicity' lakes which we have not been able to list in this book may come under the category of waters which contain mainly carp, and often big ones – which is the reason those who control the waters of this kind want to keep them quiet!

Organisation of the book

Some angling guides we have examined are so complex that they are difficult to use, and to avoid this we kept the layout of the book as simple as possible. The waters are classified into counties, which are arranged in alphabetical order, and the waters under each county name are also arranged in alphabetical order, with an index at the back of the book. The categories are listed for each water, and there are no abbreviations so there is nothing to look up; all the information you will need will be under the entry for the venue concerned.

We don't feel it appropriate for a book of this kind to include instructional articles or 'tips' on carp fishing. If you want this kind of material, obtain copies of a carp magazine, or we can strongly recommend the following books also published by BK Publishers: *Basic Carp Fishing* by Peter Mohan and *Carp Fever* by Kevin Maddocks, *Successful Angling Series Carp* by Rob Maylin, and *Big Water Carp* by Jim Gibbinson. All the information about baits, methods, tackle, flavours, bait recipes and rigs will be found in these four books.

Research

Readers (and reviewers!) should take careful note of the fact that it is **absolutely impossible** for a guide of this kind to be completely accurate.

The present revision took six months work, followed by three months to prepare and print the book. During this time, it is inevitable that many of the details listed have changed; in fact, we were making 'corrections of corrections' right up to the last minute, but it was obviously impossible to make corrections after the book had gone to print – and it takes three months at least to print a book, during which time some of the information in the book is obviously out of date, as waters change hands, or owners change fishing costs.

In addition, in January 1991 we wrote over **300** letters to people many of whom controlled waters listed in this book and only 80 replies were received – had the other 220 answered our letter, the book would undoubtedly be even more accurate.

Even some of our critics were of little help; they told us where we were wrong, but many didn't bother to send us the correct information, so that we could put it right!

If **you** can help, please contact us as soon as possible, so that we can make further corrections for the next edition in two years time.

Because of the obvious problems mentioned above, the Publishers can take no responsibility for any mistakes or omissions which may have occurred – all of our information is published in good faith, but it would have taken us many years to visit all the waters listed, in which case the book would never have been published, and some of the information supplied by others, may not necessarily be accurate.

We have done our best to make the information as accurate as possible, but had we taken any longer to check it even more carefully, more details would have become out of date!

Some of the categories such as whether a water is easy, moderate or difficult are subjective, and some anglers may not agree with us; we can only enter what in our judgement is correct.

We shall be happy to hear from readers if they have any criticism of the information provided, and especially if they would like to add any waters to the book which they think should be included. Just write to Beekay Publishers at the address given at the beginning of this book, if you wish to comment on any of the information given, or to add anything to the new edition.

Information

Please note the book is a 'guide' to carp waters. Exactly the same information is not included for every water, and any omissions are intentional. If you find that categories are omitted from some of the waters this was simply because we were not able to obtain the information in the case of that water to enable us to complete the category. If there was information which we were unable to obtain or which we weren't sure about, we simply left out that category.

In some cases we were able to find out very little about a water, but as long as we were able to give a rough idea of where it was, that it existed, and that it contained some carp, and that we could indicate in some way in which you could obtain permission to fish, then we thought it better to include the venue, and leave it to you to find out the rest of the information yourselves.

Revision

It is our intention to revise and to up-date the book every two years, or sooner, so any information you can provide for future editions will be gratefully received by the Publishers, and will enable us to keep this guide up to date. (See form on page 449)

Well-known Waters

Some readers may be surprised to find some of the well-known carp waters omitted from the list. As we have already said, we can see no point in listing waters which you cannot fish and other well-known waters have a publicity ban; there would be no point in including them, as this would only cause trouble for those lucky enough to be able to fish there. For this reason, some of the better known lakes have been left out.

Day Ticket Waters

In many cases, you can get permission to fish these waters in advance at the address given; if you can't, it might be worth going to the water and fishing. In many cases, there are bailiffs who will collect your money on the spot, although sometimes you may have to pay more if you buy a permit on the bank.

If it is stated that you must obtain a ticket in advance, it is advisable to do so, or you may be banned from fishing the water.

Club Waters

Clubs have some of the best carp waters in the country, but the carp angler may well have to share the water with non-carp anglers. It pays to try to get on with other anglers, whatever you may think of them. If you upset them too much, you may well find that the clubs start to ban carp anglers; this has already happened in some cases. We are in a minority on waters of this kind, so we should be careful how we behave.

We are sorry that so few good club carp waters are included in this guide. We know of many good club waters but it has not been found possible to include them because most of the clubs seem to be very shy of publicity.

To give some idea of the problems of compiling a guide of this kind, we wrote to more than 100 of the major clubs which we know have good carp fisheries, most containing carp of over 20lbs; some of these were clubs which advertise in the angling press for more members from time to time.

Less than 10% replied.

Syndicate Waters

Most syndicate waters have not been included because in many cases it is impossible to obtain membership. Those that are included are on the request of those in charge of the water. We have not put syndicate waters in without permission, and since these are always on private property readers should not go to these waters without permission. We know of a number of cases where anglers have lost their chance of getting into a syndicate water by walking round that water before being given permission to do so! Syndicate water locations are deliberately omitted to avoid unwelcome visitors. Please remember that a syndicate leader is under no obligation to offer membership to anyone; he is likely to be very choosy.

Using the Information Contained in this Book

Please remember to use this book as the 'guide' it is intended to be. Read the information on the water concerned and then try and find out as much more about it as you can, which will help you to be successful with your fishing here.

Don't expect every bit of information to be exactly accurate, although, as we have already said, we have tried to be as careful as possible about accuracy. However, waters change, often rapidly, and what was the best bait or method at the time of compilation may not be so by the time you get to the water. This applies to prices, of course, which may be altered at any time. It may even apply to the ownership or control of the water, which may have changed during the compilation or printing of this book, which has taken about a year. So please don't blame us if you go to a water listed and find that you can't fish it because control or other circumstances have changed since we listed it; just let us know how the circumstances have changed so that we can include the altered information in our next revision of this book. Club Secretaries change frequently, for example; those we have included were correct when we went to press.

Categories

Our categories are: Carp Only; Carp Water; Mixed Fishery; Few Carp. These are all self-explanatory, except perhaps the 'Carp Water' category, which in our judgement means that the water contains mainly carp.

BK Ratings

Our ratings are: Very Easy; Easy; Moderate; Fairly Hard; Difficult; Very Difficult; Super-Difficult.

As we have said earlier, these ratings are only our opinion; if you disagree, please let us know.

Carp Anglers' Behaviour

We do feel that a note in connection with this subject is appropriate in a book of this kind, especially as many people who control waters have told us that the behaviour of some carp anglers is giving cause for concern.

Do not leave litter of any kind — take it home with you, and be especially careful not to leave monofilament nylon line at the waterside; it can damage birds and animals. Leave the bank clean and tidy, and do nothing in any way to upset or annoy other anglers, those who own the waters, or those who may visit them. At a time when angling is under attack by many people, most of whom know nothing about the subject, be conservation conscious, and try to be a good example of an angler. Do not harm waterbirds, either directly or indirectly, keep to bye-laws, especially those which have been introduced in connection with the use of lead weights, shut all gates and do nothing to damage the banks or vegetation on the waters you fish.

Long-stay carp fishing is already causing carp anglers to be banned from some waters; if the 'float angler' can never get a place to fish because all the swims are occupied by carp anglers who live in bivvies and hardly ever leave the water, which is happening in some places, it won't be long before those who control waters start to ban this type of fishing. You have only yourself to blame if this happens. There are others to consider apart from yourself; others who have as much right to be on the water as you have, and if you spoil their fishing, they may soon be at a club meeting voting out your type of fishing!

Leaving baits out for long periods whilst you are away is another thing which has been getting carp anglers a bad name in some quarters; all of these points will only give extra help to those who are against angling, and we would urge our readers to avoid these bad aspects of modern carp fishing.

Rod Licences

It is an offence not to have the appropriate rod licences, and you may also break the rules of the water you are fishing if you don't obtain them. Even if you are one of those people who don't approve of rod licences you will certainly find that for the sake of a few pounds you can avoid all the problems concerned with prosecution if you get caught.

Water Authority licences can be bought from most tackle shops and the name of the Authority concerned is listed with each water. We are still using the divisional Water Authority names, but it should be remembered that all now come under the heading of the National Rivers Authority (N.R.A.). In most cases you need a licence for each rod you use, and the use of more than two rods is now banned in most areas.

In Conclusion

We hope you will find this book interesting and helpful. To help us keep up with changes which take place, we should be very interested to hear your comments and criticisms, or even occasionally a bit of praise if there is any due!

We also invite owners of commercial fisheries, day ticket or season ticket waters, or club waters, to send us details of their fisheries for inclusion in the next issue of this Guide; there is *no charge* for any insertion, although you may also take advertising space if you wish to do so – rates on application.

We hope later editions of the 'BK Guide to Carp Waters' will eventually list every carp water in the country which can be fished by the general angling public; with your co-operation we are sure this can be achieved.

Good fishing, and we hope you enjoy your time spent in the beautiful British countryside – or even on the slightly less attractive town waters!

COUNTY BOUNDARIES

1 TYNE AND WEAR
2 CLEVELAND
3 WEST YORKSHIRE
4 SOUTH YORKSHIRE
5 GREATER MANCHESTER
6 MERSEYSIDE
7 WEST MIDLANDS
8 BEDFORDSHIRE
9 BERKSHIRE
10 WEST GLAMORGAN
11 MID GLAMORGAN
12 SOUTH GLAMORGAN

Contents

The county designations used in this book are the most up to date: that is, those used since the boundary changes in 1974.

This means, for example, that there is now an East Sussex and a West Sussex, and that counties such as 'Middlesex' (now Greater London) and 'Worcestershire' (now Hereford and Worcester), no longer exist.

The waters in Ireland are all in the Irish Republic – we have not been able to track down any waters containing carp in Northern Ireland.

PARTRIDGE
OF REDDITCH

Quality Hooks made by British Hands

Size 4

Code **Z1 JACK HILTON CARP HOOKS.** Famous, sharp, strong and effective!
1/0, 1, 2, 4, 6, 8, 10, 12

Code **Z1AY THE BARBLESS** version of the Jack Hilton hooks.
1, 2, 4, 6, 8, 10

Size 4

Size 4

Code **Z2 PARTRIDGE RECORD BREAKER SPECIALIST HOOKS.** Strong offset bend, ideal for distance.
1/0, 1, 2, 4, 6, 8, 10, 12

Code **Z11 KEVIN MADDOCKS HAIR RIG HOOK.** Fine wire and out point with superb hooking qualities. Designed by Kevin for fishing with hair rigs.
4, 6, 8, 10, 12

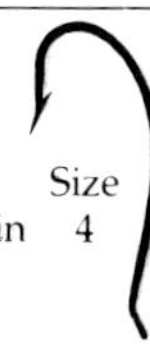
Size 4

Z12 KEVIN MADDOCKS OUTBARB SPECIMEN HOOKS
These hooks were developed as an all round specimen hook featuring the Outbarb. The position of the barb on the outside of the point helps both penetration of the hook on the strike and removal of the hook after landing the fish.
The offset bend helps hooking at a distance.
The hooks have the special Partridge "Flashpoints" and a black finish.
2, 4, 6, 8, 10

Size 4

GRS 13Z GREY SHADOW – Kevin Maddocks Cassien Carp Hooks –
These have our special NIFLOR finish and are Flashpointed. There are certain waters, such as Lake Cassien, where large fish and snags contrive to test tackle to the utmost limits. They have the same strength as the Jack Hilton hooks but all the fine hooking and holding features as the Kevin Maddocks Hair Rig hooks.
2, 4, 6, 8, 10

Size 4

Send for your free copy of our Carp Leaflet and a Partridge cloth badge.

Partridge of Redditch, Redditch, Worcestershire, B97 4JE.

AVON

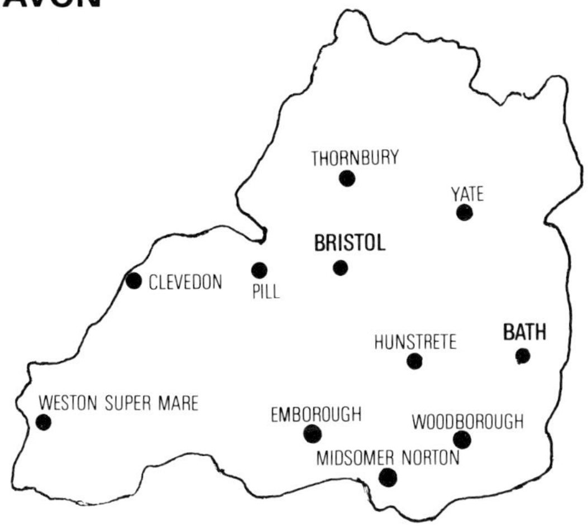

Bitterwell Lake

Location: Coalpit Heath, north Bristol
Type and Size: 2 acre pit
How to Find: About one mile from recreation ground at Coalpit Heath
Carp Stock: Heavily stocked, many small mirrors but occasional 20 caught
Category: Mixed Fishery
Other Species: Rudd, roach, tench, eels, small bream
Permits: Caravan on site (Mrs Scully, The Chalet, Bitterwell Lake, Coalpit Heath, Bristol)
Cost: £1.50 per rod per day
Baits/Methods: Normal carp methods and bait plus float fishing
Control: Council day and season ticket (Bristol Corporation)
Restrictions: No night fishing although occasional night fishing permission can be obtained. No loose feeding
W/A: Wessex
BK Rating: Moderate
Comments: Hard fished 'town' water, often shoulder to shoulder at weekends

Emborough Pond

Location: Ston Easton, near Midsomer Norton
Type and Size: 6 acre lake
How to Find: Off the A37 south of Bristol
Carp Stock: Some carp, mostly small commons
Category: Few Carp
Other Species: General coarse fish
Permits: Day tickets on bank. Information from I. Crudgington, 37 Broad Street, Bath (tackle shop)
Cost: On application
Control: Knowle Angling Centre
W/A: Wessex
Comments: 'Public' lake in attractive surroundings

Fishponds Lido

Location: Alcove Road, off Fishponds Road in the City of Bristol
Type and Size: Deep old pit of about an acre or less
How to Find: From the centre of Bristol find Fishponds Road and Alcove Road is less than a mile from the City Centre on the right. A path leads down to the lake.
Carp Stock: Probably about 60 carp which were put in, in two stockings. Fish from the earlier stocking have reached upper double figure size and some 20s.
Category: Mixed Fishery
Other Species: Roach, tench and perch
Permits: Season tickets from Fishponds Lido Angling Club, with a limited membership and a waiting list. Details and cost from the Secretary, Mr R Hole, 70 Pound Road, Kingswood, Bristol or from Veals Tackle, Bristol.
Restrictions: No night fishing
Control: Club
W/A: Wessex
BK Rating: Moderate
Comments: A town water surrounded by houses and with a floating restaurant on it yet the water contains 20lb carp, which shows these can be caught within a city.

Ham Green Lake

Location: Behind Ham Green Hospital, Pill, near Bristol
Type and Size: Dammed estate lake in two parts, about an acre each
How to Find: Take the A369 Bristol/Portishead road and turn right, signposted 'Ham Green and Pill'. Turn first right to Ham Green Hospital and continue down hill. Lake will be seen on the right.
Carp Stock: Not large numbers, perhaps 50 fish in both lakes. Commons to about 11lbs. Mirrors to about 16lbs. A well authenticated fish of 20lbs was caught in 1991.
Category: Mixed Fishery
Other Species: Roach, rudd, tench, pike, eels
Permits: On bank or Veals Tackle, Old Market, Bristol
Cost: On application
Control: Syndicate - Mr R Barnes, Withywood, Bristol
Baits/Methods: Normal carp methods and baits. Some surface fishing
BK Rating: Fairly Hard
W/A: Wessex
Comments: Heavily weeded and full of lilies. Upper part best.

Hunstrete Lake

Location: Village of Hunstrete, near Bath
Type and Size: Dammed estate lake of about 5 acres
How to Find: Take the main A4 Bath to Bristol road, and then the left fork (A368) at traffic lights at Newton St. Loe. After about 2 miles turn right towards Hunstrete and there is a path to the lake on the left, just before the village.
Carp Stock: Probably only about 20-30 fish, most of which are doubles. Two twenties reported caught in 1985. There might be as many as four 20's in the lake, and possibly a near 30.
Category: Few Carp
Other Species: Tench, roach, bream

Permits: Bathampton Angling Association; membership open at approximately £13.50 per season from the General Secretary, Dave Crookes, 25 Otago Terrace, Larkhall, Bath, Avon. Tel: Bath 27164. Limited tickets for Hunstrete Lake, details from Secretary.
Cost: Approximately £13.50 per season
Restrictions: No night fishing
Control: Club
BK Rating: Difficult
Baits/Methods: Advanced carp fishing rigs and baits necessary
W/A: Wessex
Comments: This is the lake named by Dick Walker in his literature as 'Lackey's Leap'. Fishing here with 'BB' Dick hooked one of the original commons, which now seem to have died out, and played it on very light tackle for an hour and 55 minutes, only to find it had the hook in its mouth and the line looped round a spine of the dorsal fin, which is perhaps why it fought so hard. Dick thought it was a 30, and the British record was then 26lbs; the fish actually weighed only 9¾lbs. There is a small syndicate on this water, details from the Secretary.

Hutton Pond

Location: Hutton Moor Road, Weston-super-Mare
Type and Size: Ballast pit of about 1½ acres
How to Find: Turn off the M5 motorway at the Weston-super-Mare exit and after about a mile find Hutton Moor Road on the left, shortly after the left hand Banwell turn. The pond will be found on the left after about 600 yards.
Carp Stock: A small number of mirrors most of which are lower doubles and are now quite old. Best known authenticated carp caught is 18¼lbs.
Category: Few Carp
Other Species: Bream, roach, rudd, tench
Permits: North Somerset Association of Anglers, permits approximately £12.50 as for Newtown Pond. Secretary: Mr R F Newton, 64 Clevedon Road, Tickenham, Clevedon, Avon. Club tickets also from local tackle dealers including Veals of Bristol, Old Market, Bristol.
BK Rating: Difficult, as there are not many carp
Control: Club
Baits/Methods: Good specialist methods needed as these fish have been caught quite a lot over the years. Some may still be taken on floating crust after dark or in the early morning. Normal carp boilies etc best on the bottom. Bream a problem on soft baits, hard boilies such as Maestros work well.
W/A: Wessex
Comments: Not a very pleasant little place, with a road on one side, a railway line across the north end, and a 'factory' on the opposite side to the road. This bank is out of bounds as the 'factory' is a Government institution of some kind. The lake is long and narrow and nearly all the carp are caught very close to the reeds on the 'factory' side; in fact, it is considered to be a waste of time to fish anywhere but within a metre of this farther reed hedge.

Newton Park

Location: Newton St. Loe, near Bath
Type and Size: 3½ acre shallow lake
Carp Stock: Recently stocked with 1,250lbs of carp - all small - from 4oz to 3lbs

Category: Carp Water
Other Species: Roach and perch
Permits: A members only water of Bathampton AA - tickets from local tackle shops
Secretary: D Crookes, 25 Otago Terrace, Larkhall, Bath
Control: Club
Restrictions: Barbless hooks; no keepnets; possibly no night fishing.
BK Rating: Very Easy
W/A: Wessex

Woodborough Park Lake

Location: Woodborough Court near Midsomer Norton
Type and Size: Dammed estate lake of about 2 acres
How to Find: Take the A367 Radstock road from Bath, and about two miles before Radstock you will see a left turn to Woodborough Court. Cars must be left in the car park on the right and it is about half a mile walk across fields to the lake.
Carp Stock: Well stocked with mirrors many of which are under 10lbs, but there are some doubles and the best reported is about 15lbs.
Category: Mixed Fishery
Other Species: Tench, roach and perch
Permits: This lake is on the same ticket as Hunstrete Lake, Bathampton Angling Association. Open membership from the General Secretary Dave Crookes, 25 Otago Terrace, Larkhall, Bath, Avon. Tel: 27164. In addition, only a few tickets are issued per day, and these must be obtained at a small extra cost from Crudgington Fishing Tackle, Bath or from Veals Fishing Tackle, Old Market, Bristol.
Cost: Approximately £13.50 per season plus a small daily payment
Restrictions: No night fishing; the dam is out of bounds
BK Rating: Easy
Baits/Methods: Normal carp fishing baits and methods; the carp used to take floating crust well and may still take mini-floaters.
W/A: Wessex
Comments: A very pleasant little water if you don't mind the walk. Since tickets are limited to four a day it can never get crowded. Bathampton AA now has another newly dug pond containing carp near Hunstrete; it is called 'Withy Pool' - our third water with that name!

BEDFORDSHIRE

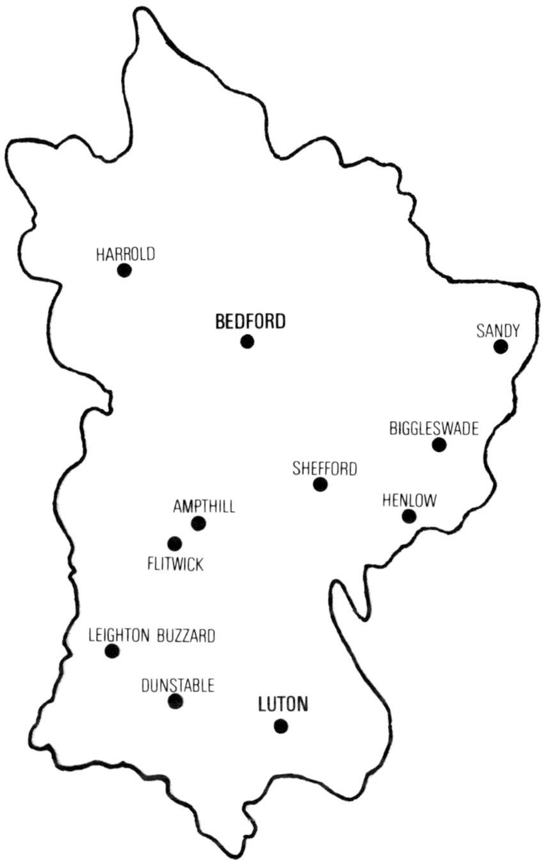

Airman Pit

Location: On the A600 Bedford road, between Withy Pool and Shefford
Type and Size: Brick pit of about 7 acres
How to Find: On the left hand side of the main A600 Hitchin to Bedford road between Kevin Maddocks' Withy Pool and the village of Shefford.
Carp Stock: Well stocked with small carp, a few doubles and one or two twenties.
Category: Carp Water
Other Species: Roach, rudd, tench, pike, catfish, perch
Permits: Seasonal from Shefford and District AA. Secretary: Mrs M Rose, 120 High Street, Stotfold, Hitchin, Herts. Tel: 0462 733373; or from Chris's Tackle Box, Henlow Camp, Beds
Cost: £24 per season
Control: Club
W/A: Anglian
BK Rating: Easy
Comments: There is another pit containing many carp on the same ticket

Arlesey Lake

Location: Church End, Arlesey, near Hitchin
Type and Size: Very deep, old brick pit of about 12 acres
How to Find: Turn right going north on the A600 (Hitchin to Bedford road) at Henlow Camp, then right again at A507 junction - lake is alongside railway line on right.
Carp Stock: About 100 carp to 30lbs. Plenty of upper doubles and some good twenties.
Category: Mixed Fishery
Other Species: Perch, tench, roach, pike, catfish
Permits: D Beatham, Etonbury Farm, Stotfold Road, Arlesey SG16 6XB. Tel: 0462 731709.
Cost: On application
Control: Syndicate
BK Rating: Moderate
W/A: Anglian
Comments: Famous as the lake where the late Richard Walker invented the Arlesey Bomb for fishing for the big perch at long range in 40ft of water. The lake is now being filled in and the fishing is not so pleasurable.

Beckerings Park Farm Reservoir

Location: Steppingly, near Flitwick, just to the left of the A418 Flitwick-Millbrook road
Type and Size: Small reservoir
Carp Stock: Stocked in 1990 with 25 doubles including 7 carp over 20lbs
Category: Mixed Fishery
Other Species: Tench, roach and bream
Permits: Members only water of Luton and District AC. Secretary: G Buss, 1 Easthill Road, Houghton Regis, Dunstable, Beds LU5 5EQ. Tel: Dunstable 862452. Permits can be obtained from local tackle shops, especially Leslie's of Luton.
Control: Club
Restrictions: Members only
BK Rating: Moderate
W/A: Anglian

Bedford Boating Lake

Location: Alongside the River Great Ouse, Bedford Embankment
Type and Size: Public town lake of about 2 acres
Carp Stock: Occasional carp reported, including a 20lb common in July 1991
Category: Few Carp
Other Species: Roach, dace, bream, perch and pike
Permits: None necessary - free fishing. Anglian W/A licence required for each rod.
BK Rating: Difficult
W/A: Anglian
Comments: Busy town boating lake not known for its carp, but it does contain one or two good fish; lots of people and water birds. In August 1991 a famous match angler caught a 4lb terrapin here, which bit its captor - so anything could happen in this public lake.

Blue Lagoon

Location:	On the Beds./Herts. border near Arlesey
Type and Size:	60 foot deep chalk pit of over 30 acres
Carp Stock:	Not many carp, but there are some big ones - a 37lb leather was caught in 1989 and at least one other 30 in 1990
Category:	Few Carp
Other Species:	Big pike, tench, bream, rudd, roach, perch and chub
Permits:	24 hour day tickets on bank, and also season tickets
Cost:	Day tickets about £2 per day
BK Rating:	Difficult
W/A:	Anglian
Comments:	A true big fish water, with most fish caught in shallow water close in.

Blunham L-Shaped Lake

Location:	Blunham, between Sandy on the A1 and Bedford (A603)
Type and Size:	Long, narrow gravel pit of 5 acres
How to Find:	Turn off the A1 at Sandy and go to Blunham
Carp Stock:	Quite well stocked to upper twenties
Category:	Mixed Fishery
Other Species:	Tench, roach, rudd, bream, perch
Permits:	Season tickets from Blunham Angling Club, and local tackle shops.
Cost:	£15 per season
Control:	Club - Secretary: G Palmer, Tel: 02302 3959
BK Rating:	Difficult
W/A:	Anglian

Blunham Pits

Location:	Blunham, just off the A1 at Sandy, near Biggleswade
Type and Size:	2 lakes of 6 and 7 acres, both gravel pits, and a stretch of the River Ivel
How to Find:	Turn off the A1 at Sandy, and the lakes will be seen near Blunham
Carp Stock:	Muddy Lake - good head of doubles and a few twenties to over 30lbs. Clear Lake - good head of doubles and a few twenties.
Category:	Muddy - Carp Water; Clear - Mixed Fishery
Other Species:	Tench, roach, rudd, pike and perch
Permits:	Chettle and Sons Angling Club (syndicate). Often vacancies from Mr Twell, Maperton Lodge, Station Road, Raunds, Northants. Tel: 0993 622007
Cost:	Approximately £45 per person
Control:	Syndicate
BK Rating:	Moderate
W/A:	Anglian
Comments:	Plenty of good carp in the River Ivel as well as in the pits.

Elstow Pits

Location:	Just off the A6 at Elstow near Bedford
Type and Size:	Brick pit of 30 acres plus
How to Find:	The pit will be seen on the right hand side of the A6 road going south from Bedford, near the village of Elstow
Carp Stock:	Well stocked with carp to 30lbs, with plenty of good doubles and 20's.
Category:	Carp Water
Other Species:	Roach, rudd, tench, bream, pike

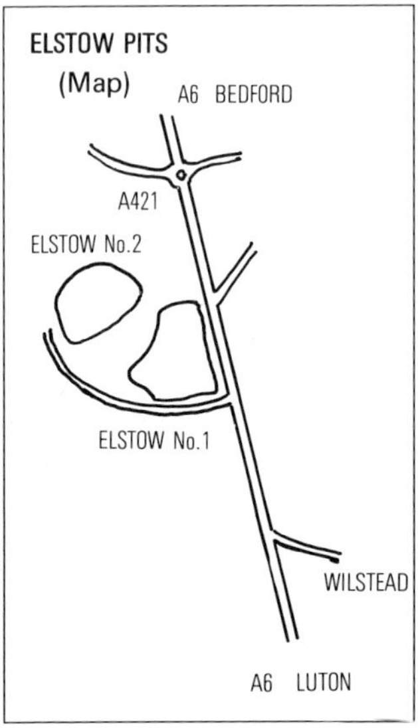

Permits: Syndicate only from Linear Fisheries, 2 Northcroft, Shenley Lodge, Milton Keynes MK5 7BE (Vacancies)

Cost: Approximately £150 a season

Control: Linear Fisheries, Tel: 0908 607577

BK Rating: Moderate

Restrictions: No day tickets - season (syndicate) in advance only

W/A: Anglian

Comments: One of the best upper doubles and 20's waters. A big water with good carp fishing, although the fish can be hard to find. Normal carp fishing methods and baits. Regulars estimate there are 50-100 twenties in this

Elstow Pit, Bedford a Linear Fisheries syndicate water which contains nearly 100 twenties

lake. There is a second large pit on the site, which is included in the membership. This contains a small number (perhaps only 20) really big fish, most of which are 20's, with the best caught a 33 pounder in 1991.

Felmersham Gravel Pits

Location: Felmersham, off the A6 between Bedford and Rushden, and about 7 miles north of Bedford
Type and Size: Two quite large gravel pits
Carp Stock: Well stocked with carp to about 10lbs
Category: Mixed Fishery
Other Species: Tench
Permits: Luton and District AA. Secretary: S R Branch, 3 Holmbrook Avenue, Luton, Beds. Members only.
Cost: About £12.50 per season
Control: Club
BK Rating: Moderate
W/A: Anglian

Green Lagoon

Location: Beds/Herts border near Arlesey
Type and Size: Three acre chalk pit, up to 30ft deep
Carp Stock: Fairly well stocked with carp to low twenties
Category: Mixed Fishery
Other Species: Large bream, tench, perch, pike and roach
Permits: 24 hour day ticket on bank; season tickets
Cost: About £2 per day
BK Rating: Moderate
W/A: Anglian
Comments: Heavily fished, with difficult access.

Harrold-Odell Country Park

Location: 10 miles north west of Bedford
Type and Size: Matured gravel pit of about 7 acres
How to Find: The Country Park is signposted (5 miles) to the left of the A6 between Bedford and Rushden, shortly after the Falcon Inn
Carp Stock: Some carp, numbers and size not known
Category: Mixed Fishery
Other Species: Pike, roach, rudd, perch, tench and bream
Permits: The water is controlled by Harrold Working Mens AC. Tel: 0933 55696 (Cliff Roberts)
Control: Club
Restrictions: Members only. Probably no night fishing
W/A: Anglian
Comments: A pleasant lake, but in a busy country park with Nature Reserve. Details, refreshments etc on site. There is another much larger lake opposite, where there are certainly fish, and possibly carp, and we understand that there may later be public fishing in this one also. For information contact Bedfordshire Leisure Services Dept, Beds County Council, County Hall, Cauldwell Street, Bedford. Tel: 0234 63222.

Houghton Regis Quarry

Location: Houghton Road, Dunstable
Type and Size: 11 acre chalk pit
How to Find: At the end of the main street in Dunstable going towards Leighton Buzzard; turn right at the roundabout towards Houghton Regis, and the pit is on the left.
Carp Stock: About 200 carp; the best caught to date is 23lbs, plenty of low doubles, but most fish between 9 and 11lbs.
Category: Mixed Fishery
Other Species: Roach, bream, tench and pike
Permits: Members only, Dunstable and District AC. Enquire in local tackle shops
Cost: Low cost for season tickets
Control: Club
Restrictions: Special permission needed for night fishing; members only
BK Rating: Moderate
W/A: Thames

Kempston Hardwick

Location: Kempston Hardwick village, near Bedford
Type and Size: 4 pits, about 30 acres
How to Find: Take the Ampthill road from Bedford, and the lake is opposite the Chimney Corner public house in Kempston Hardwick
Carp Stock: This is a recently stocked water with a reasonable head of carp to lower doubles. Carp are reported to be growing well. Carp to 20lbs plus.
Category: Mixed Fishery
Other Species: Tench, roach, bream, perch and pike
Permits: Enquire locally, or tackle shops in Bedford
Control: Not known at time of going to press
BK Rating: Moderate
W/A: Anglian
Comments: Also Brogborough Lake, carp to 24lbs.

Oldfield

Location: Arlesey, near Hitchin
Type and Size: Two gravel pits of 6 and 4 acres in quiet countryside
Carp Stock: Very heavily stocked with good looking fish to mid-twenties
Category: Mixed Fishery
Other Species: Bream, tench, roach, rudd and perch
Permits: Syndicate membership from Bill Turner. Tel: 0462 482087
Control: Private
BK Rating: Very Easy
W/A: Anglian
Comments: The main lake has been the setting for several carp videos, including Carp Fever I and Carp from the Start I, featuring Kevin Maddocks who caught many good fish here.

Rackley Hills Pit

Location: Near the centre of Leighton Buzzard; Grovebury Road
Type and Size: Working sand pit of about 8 acres
How to Find: In Leighton Buzzard

Carp Stock: Small number of carp to 20lbs plus
Category: Few Carp
Other Species: Catfish to 35lbs
Permits: Seasonal from Leighton Buzzard Angling Club and selected tackle shops in the area. Secretary: B Smalley, 3 Isis Walk, Leighton Buzzard, Beds. Tel: 0525 852227.
Cost: £20 per season. Joint husband and wife £23. Juniors: £4. Senior citizens: £3.
Control: Club
BK Rating: Very Difficult, very few fish
Restrictions: Night fishing reserved for a selected few only
W/A: Anglian

Radwell Complex

Location: Between Milton Ernest and Sharnbrook
Type and Size: 4 pits, two of which are quite large
How to Find: These lakes can be seen from the A6, on the left hand side between Bedford and Rushden. Access is from a lane near the Swan public house in Radwell. To reach this village take a left turn off the A6 at Milton Ernest, cross the river and turn right just before the Swan
Carp Stock: All the pits contain carp to about 10lbs
Category: Mixed Fishery
Other Species: Tench, bream, roach, perch and pike
Permits: Vauxhall Motors AC. Season tickets from Leslie's of Luton, 89 Park Street, Luton. Tel: 0852 453542. Secretary: B Matthews, 88 Langford Drive, Luton Beds. Tel: Luton 419489.
Restrictions: Members only - no day tickets
Control: Club
BK Rating: Moderate
W/A: Anglian

Tingrith Manor Lake

Location: Village of Tingrith, near Toddington, Dunstable
How to Find: Leave the M1 at Toddington (junction 12) and take the road signposted 'Tingrith'
Type and Size: Estate lake of 5 acres
Carp Stock: Well stocked with commons to 10lbs. There are a few mirrors to upper doubles.
Category: Mixed Fishery
Other Species: Perch, roach, rudd, pike and catfish
Permits: Vauxhall Motors Angling Club. Season tickets from Leslie's Fishing Tackle, Luton. Secretary: B Matthews, 88 Langford Drive, Luton, Beds. Tel: Luton 419489.
Cost: On application
Control: Club
BK Rating: Moderate
W/A: Anglian
Baits/Methods: Normal carp fishing methods and baits; floating baits sometimes work well.

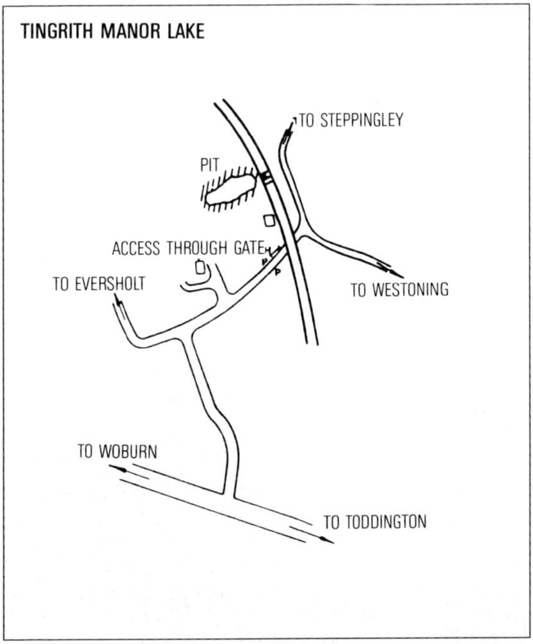

Peter Wilson with the Withy Pool lake record of 41 pounds

Peter Mohan with his personal best – a 33½ caught in August 1991 from Withy Pool on a KM Maestro Bird Spice boilie, using his favourite Mitchell reels and a Simpsons of Turnford KM1 rod.

Withy Pool A

Location: Bedford Road, Henlow Camp, Beds., SG16 6EA
Type and Size: Brick pit of 2½ acres and man-made lake of ¼ acre
How to Find: Take the A600 Hitchin to Bedford road going north, and the lake is on the left about 300 yards after the roundabout at Lower Stondon, about 4 miles from Hitchin
Category: Carp Water
Other Species: Catfish to 20lbs; pike, perch, roach, tench, bream, grass carp, orfe and koi carp to 10lbs.

Kevin Maddocks caught this 35 pounder from Withy Pool in February 1990, only two weeks after his 40 from Northants. Both fish were caught on Maestro Boilies straight from the packet!

Cost: On application
Permits: Fishing is only for those who rent one of the three caravans, apart from occasional vacancies in the small syndicate; no day tickets
Carp Stock: On application
Restrictions: No night fishing on main lake except for syndicate members
Control: Private: contact Kevin Maddocks at the above address. Tel: 0462 816960
BK Rating: Main lake - Difficult; small lake - Easy
W/A: Anglian
Comments: Contact the owners for free brochure on caravan and fishing holidays. Syndicate membership - waiting list. Small lake very heavily stocked with carp to over 20lbs, and lots of catfish; this lake can be night fished by those who stay in the caravans. Brand new building incorporating separate ladies and gents toilets and shower.

The main lake is a 100 year old clay pit which varies in depth from 4 to 25 feet. It contained 20lb carp in the '50's. Dick Walker fished it and Jack Hilton caught his first doubles from the water, which was formerly known as Cafe Pool and Maylin's Pool. Since Kevin and Brenda

Maddocks bought the property in 1985 it has become one of the best known small fisheries in the country for big carp – a fish under 20lbs from the main lake is very rare and more 30's are caught than 20's! In 1991 Withy Pool produced more than 20 thirty pound carp. The lake record currently stands at 41 pounds.

A lovely 20 pound plus common from the small lake at Withy Pool.

Woburn Sands

Location: Woburn Sands village, near Dunstable
Type and Size: Brick pit of 10 acres
How to Find: Take the A5 from Dunstable going north and turn off at Hockcliffe to Woburn Sands. Entrance is off the B557 road
Carp Stock: About 40 carp to 20lbs plus
Category: Mixed Fishery
Other Species: Roach, bream, tench, rudd, pike, catfish
Permits: Vauxhall Motors Angling Club. Season tickets only from Leslie's Tackle Shop, Luton. Secretary: B Matthews, 88 Langford Drive, Luton, Beds. Tel: Luton 419489
Cost: About £12 per season
Control: Club
BK Rating: Fairly Difficult
W/A: Anglian

Woburn Sands Syndicate

Location: Woburn Sands
Type and Size: 2 acre disused brick pit
Carp Stock: About 40 doubles and a few low twenties
Category: Carp Water
Other Species: Catfish and roach
Permits: Syndicate only – the Secretary, PO Box 885, Shenley Lodge, Milton Keynes MK5 7YU
Cost: On application
BK Rating: Moderate – the owner says that it's easy for good carp anglers, and difficult for those who are not so good! (I've only fished it once, and I had a blank, which shows what a useless carp angler I am! P.M.).
Restrictions: No long stay fishing
Control: Private
W/A: Anglian
Comments: A very pretty water, secluded and well protected; private property – do not visit without permission. Ideal for 'old fashioned' methods, such as stalking and float fishing.

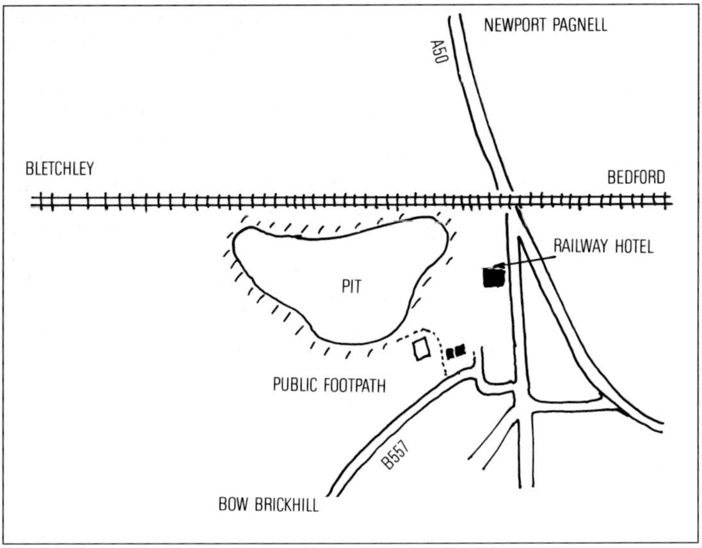

BERKSHIRE

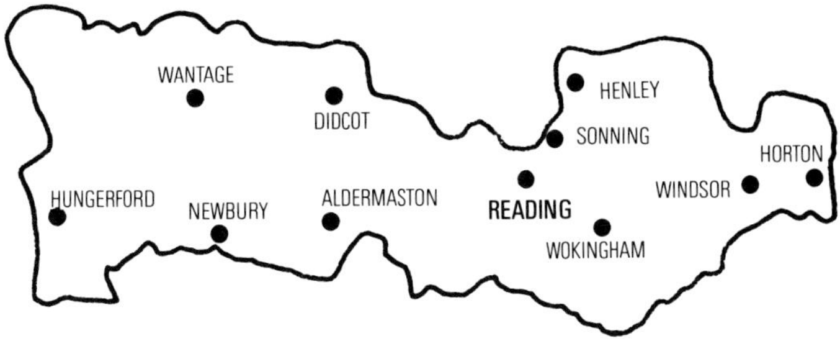

Aldermaston

Location: Paices Hill, Aldermaston, near Reading
Type and Size: 7 lakes of an acre or less, and one lake, No 6,of 3.8 acres. Gravel pits
How to Find: Take the M4 to the Theale turn off, and then A340 to Aldermaston. After Aldermaston the entrance is at the top of the hill on the right after the village.
Carp Stock: The Leisure Sport Guide describes the carp as 'numerous' in Lake 6, but only to about 8lbs. Some doubles were introduced into Lakes 2 and 3 in 1982-83, and best reported to date is 25lbs.
Category: Lake 6 - Carp Water. Other lakes are Mixed Fisheries
Permits: This is an LSAC 'Special Venue'. Season tickets and day tickets. Apply to Leisure Sport for an application form for a Special Venue. Thorpe Park, Staines Road, Chertsey, Surrey. Tel: Chertsey 64872. A limited number of Coverall Permits are issued for all 31 LSA new venues including the Special Venue waters. Two passport photographs required to be sent with the application form.
Cost: £25 per season; juniors/OAP/disabled - £12.50; Coverall Permits (31 venues) - £120 (juniors/OAP/disabled - £60). Day tickets - £2 (dawn to dusk only).
Restrictions: Usual rules - no camping, no fires, no radios. Night fishing allowed. Carp over 3lbs must not be retained.
BK Rating: Lake 6 - Easy; others - Moderate
Control: Leisure Sport
W/A: Thames
Comments: Day tickets from Youngs Garden Centre at site entrance.

Brimpton Lakes

Location: Shalford Bridge, near Aldermaston
Type and Size: Two large gravel pits
How to Find: Off the Brimpton-Woolhampton road
Category: Well stocked with carp, many of which are doubles
Category: Mixed Fishery
Permits: Reading and District AA. Secretary: D Capon, 61 Thame Road, Haddenham, Bucks HP17 8EP.
BK Rating: Moderate
Control: Club
W/A: Thames

Burghfield

Location: Pengewood Road, Pengewood, Burghfield
Type and Size: Lake 1 - 94 acres; Lake 2 - 5 acres; Lake 3 - 3 acres. Gravel pits
How to Find: Off the A4 from Reading to Southcote; Burghfield Road and the canal
Carp Stock: Carp to over 30lbs reported
Category: Few Carp
Other Species: General coarse fish
Permits: Leisure Sport Angling, Staines Road, Chertsey, Surrey. Tel: 0932 562633.
Cost: £24
BK Rating: Difficult
Control: Leisure Sport Angling Club
Restrictions: No bright lights
W/A: Thames
Comments: Night fishing is allowed.

Countryside Club

Location: Reading
Type and Size: Some lake carp fishing, details not known
Carp Stock: Well stocked with carp
Category: Mixed Fishery
Other Species: General coarse fish
Permits: Countryside, 109 Upper Woodcote Road, Caversham Heights, Reading.
Control: Private
BK Rating: Not known
W/A: Thames

Horton

Location: Stanwell Road, Horton, near Slough, Berks. Tel: 0753 684458
Type and Size: Church Pool - 14 acres; Boat Pool - 6 acres; former gravel pits
How to Find: Take junction 14 off the M25 and take the Poyle/Datchet road, and after roundabout take the first road on the left (Stanwell Road); the Horton Fishery entrance is on the left in one mile.
Carp Stock: Church Lake is well stocked with very big carp to 44lbs. There were already carp in this lake, a former trout fishery, but in 1991 when Longfield (Staines), a famous carp water, was closed and netted 57 big carp, all of which were twenties and thirties, with some doubles and two forties, were transferred to Church Lake, Horton and a number of 30's and 40's have been caught since. Other big fish will be put into this water, which must now rank as one of the top carp fisheries in the country.
Category: Mixed Fishery
Other Species: Grass carp to 16lbs, bream to 11½lbs, tench to 8¾lbs, pike, roach, perch and eels
Permits: Leisure Sport Angling, Thorpe Park, Staines Road, Chertsey, Surrey KT16 8PN. Tel: Chertsey 564872. This is an LSA 'Special Venue' and tickets may be hard to obtain.
Cost: £200 per season
Restrictions: Two rods only; 7 days stay only - after that you must leave for at least 24 hours. Members wishing to leave the fishery between 7am and 8pm are only allowed a 90 minute absence; no keepnets or sacks; no guests; 50 anglers only.

BK Rating: Difficult
W/A: Thames
Comments: There is a fisherman's lodge at Church Lake, open 24 hours a day, and two toilets in the car park. LSA rules and their bailiffs are very strict, and if you break the rules you will lose your membership. A 40½lb was caught in 1991.

Longmoor Lake

Location: California Country Park, Nine Mile Ride, Finchampstead, Wokingham
Type and Size: 6 acre lake
Carp Stock: Well stocked with carp to mid-twenties
Category: Mixed Fishery
Other Species: Pike, tench, perch, roach, rudd
Permits: Day and season tickets sold on lakeside
Cost: Adult Day - £2.00. Adult Season - £15.00.
Baits/Methods: Normal carp fishing bait and methods
Control: Council (Wokingham District Council)
Restrictions: No nut baits, barbless hooks, night fishing through a syndicate only, no fishing on paved frontage.
BK Rating: Moderate
W/A: Thames
Comments: Plenty of good carp averaging 15lb in this picturesque lake with several islands and lily beds.

Priory Water

Location: Near Windsor
Type and Size: Several gravel pits
How to Find: Just off the Wraysbury junction of the M25
Carp Stock: Priory - some good carp; Hythe Lagoon - some carp; Watts Pool - some carp
Category: Mixed Fisheries
Other Species: Mixed coarse fish
Permits: Head Bailiff: Brian Payne. Tel: 07842 50291 (day), 081-751 3445 (evening).
Cost: On application - about £12 per annum
BK Rating: Insufficient information
Control: Not known - try local tackle shops
W/A: Thames
Comments: Priory also used for sailing.

Sonning Eye Pit

Location: Off the A4155 Reading-Henley road at Sonning
Type and Size: Huge gravel pit
Carp Stock: Not many carp but said to be some big fish up to 40lbs
Category: Few Carp
Permits: Reading and District Angling Association. Secretary: D Capon, 61 Thame Road, Haddenham, Bucks HP17 8EP.
BK Rating: Very Difficult
Restrictions: No night fishing
Control: Club
W/A: Thames

South Lake/Redlands Lake

Location: Woodley, Reading
Type and Size: Lake of 50 acres
How to Find: Fairwater Road, behind The Thatchers public house
Carp Stock: Well stocked with carp to 25lb
Category: Mixed Fishery
Other Species: Tench, roach and bream
Permits: Mr Williams, South Lake Angling Society, 24 Duncan Road, Woodley, Reading.
BK Rating: Moderate
W/A: Thames
Restrictions: Only open to those living within 3 miles of Woodley.

White Swan Lake

Location: Dinton Pastures Country Park, Davis Street, Hurst, Wokingham
Type and Size: Open gravel pit of about 24 acres
Carp Stock: Well stocked with carp to upper twenties
Category: Mixed Fishery
Other Species: Pike, tench, perch, roach, rudd, chub, bream
Permits: Day and season tickets sold on lakeside
Cost: Adult Day - £2.00; Adult Season - £15.00.
Baits/Methods: Normal carp fishing bait and methods

Control: Council (Wokingham District Council)
Restrictions: No nut baits, night fishing through a syndicate only
BK Rating: Moderate to hard
W/A: Thames
Comments: Well stocked with carp, also holds tench to over 11lbs and pike to 34lb.

BUCKINGHAMSHIRE

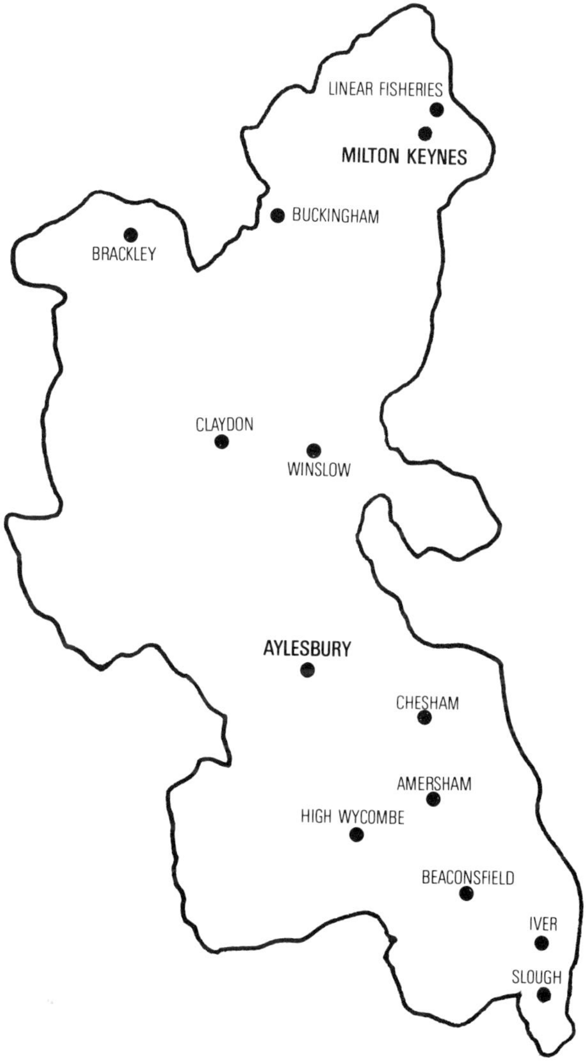

Alder Lake carp syndicate – a famous Linear Fisheries lake which produced 80 twenties in 1991

Alder and Poplar Lakes Carp Syndicate

Location: Linford Linear Fisheries, Little Linford Lane, Milton Keynes
Type and Size: Two gravel pits of 6 and 7 acres
How to Find: From junction 14 of the M1, turn right on the A409 towards Newport Pagnell, left at the first roundabout, right at the next roundabout and left again at the T-junction. In about 400 yards, turn right into Little Linford Lane. The entrance is on the left opposite the sailing club.
Carp Stock: Alder – mainly doubles to 29lbs; 100+ carp, 10% over 20lbs.
Poplar – very heavily stocked with carp to 19lbs.
Category: Carp Waters
Other Species: Annual netting removes other species to maintain the lakes as carp waters.
Permits: Linear Fisheries, Secretary: Len Gurd, Linear House, 2 Northcroft, Shenley Lodge, Milton Keynes, Bucks. Tel: 0908 607577. Syndicate season tickets only, no day tickets.
Cost: On application
BK Rating: Alder: Easy/Moderate. Poplar: Very Easy
Restrictions: No long stay fishing, 36 hour limit. Alternate Saturday and Sunday rotas. No sacking of carp. Bent hooks are banned.
Control: Linear Fisheries
W/A: Anglian
Baits/Methods: Usual carp fishing baits and methods. Carp in Poplar easy to catch on all baits and rigs.
Comments: This syndicate is already known as one of the country's best carp waters. Rules are strict so behaviour is good, and the waters are very well controlled by experienced carp anglers. These are two very pleasant mature lakes amid a big gravel pit complex. There are many trees and

bushes on both lakes and also numerous islands, bays and gravel bars. No retaining of carp. Membership of the rest of Linear is also available by season or day tickets from Len Gurd. There are 5 other lakes on the complex stocked with large fish of most species, including carp, and 3 miles of the River Ouse is included containing large barbel and other species. Linear Fisheries also has Elstow Pit, near Bedford, a top carp fishery with many doubles and twenties to 30lbs. Syndicate only - vacancies now - enquire from Secretary. Tel: 0908 607577 (9am-5pm). Both Poplar and Alder Lakes are featured in the 'Carp Fever' series of videos by Kevin Maddocks.

Gordon Owen with a 27-2 from one of the Linear Fisheries lakes at Linford

Amerden Pool

Location: Amerden Grove, near Slough
Type and Size: Small lake
How to Find: Take the laplow road from Slough and pass the Dumbell pub on your right. In 150 yds turn left at the garage, go under railway bridge, past sailing club, turn right and first right again, then follow track to lake.
Carp Stock: A small number of carp to 16lbs
Category: Few Carp
Other Species: Crucians, tench, rudd, roach and perch
Permits: Boyer Leisure, Farlows Lake, Ford Lane, Iver, Bucks. Tel: 0753 655909.
Cost: £35 per season, to include 4 other venues
Control: Boyer Leisure
Restrictions: Barbless hooks; no keepnets or carp sacks; do not go through the house entrance; do not disturb livestock on the farmland.
BK Rating: Difficult
W/A: Thames

Arboretum Specimen Syndicate Lake A

Location: Linford Linear Fisheries, Little Linford Lane, Milton Keynes
Type and Size: Mature gravel pit of 3 acres, stream fed
How to Find: As for Alder and Poplar Lakes, but pass the end of Little Linford Lane, go under the bridge and straight on at the mini-roundabout. Just after Linear Fisheries Rocla Lake, the entrance will be seen on the right. Car park is to the right of the entrance.
Carp Stock: 30+ fish from 10lbs to 30lbs, and some smaller fish
Category: Mixed Fishery
Other Species: Good head of tench to 6lbs+; bream to 8lbs+; big roach and rudd
Permits: Linear Fisheries. Secretary: Len Gurd, Linear House, 2 Northcroft, Shenley Lodge, Milton Keynes, Bucks. Tel: 0908 607577. Syndicate only.
Cost: On application
BK Rating: Moderate
Control: Linear Fisheries
Restrictions: No long stay fishing, 36 hours maximum. Alternate Saturday and Sunday rota. No sacking of carp.
W/A: Anglian
Comments: A most attractive lake with islands, backwaters, trees etc. Membership limited to 25, many of whom are not carp specialists; an ideal water for the specimen hunter. Self-catering houses. Tel: 0908 368220 (9am to 5pm).

Black Horse Lake A

Location: Linford Linear Fisheries, Little Linford Lane, Milton Keynes
Type and Size: Big open gravel pit of 25 acres
How to Find: From junction 14 of the M1, turn right on the A409 towards Newport Pagnell, left at the first roundabout, right at the next roundabout and left again at the T-junction. Go under the bridge, straight on at the small roundabout and turn right into the Linear Fisheries entrance. Car park on right.
Carp Stock: Holds some very large original carp caught to 32lbs. Stocked by Linear Fisheries with over 100 fast growing mirrors to double figures.
Category: Mixed Fishery
Other Species: Tench to 10lbs 3ozs; bream to 8lbs; pike to 30lbs; roach to 2½lbs; big eels
Permits: Season tickets (day only); day tickets; limited night syndicate vacancies. Linear Fisheries Secretary: Len Gurd, Linear House, 2 Northcroft, Shenley Lodge, Milton Keynes, Bucks. Tel: 0908 607577 or local tackle shops.
Cost: £3 per rod per day; £4 for 24 hour permits; £26 per daytime season; £35 for 24 hour season. Reductions for juniors, OAP and disabled.
BK Rating: Moderate
Control: Linear Fisheries
Restrictions: No night fishing except for night syndicate. No sacking of carp
W/A: Anglian
Comments: Large open gravel pit. Very rich water which produces big fish of all species. Carp stocked by Linear Fisheries put on 3lbs in the first year. Small number only of big original carp. Board sailing on this lake during the day. Self-catering houses. Tel: 0908 368220 (9am to 5pm)

Black Park

Location: Town of Iver
Type and Size: Park lake of about 7 acres
Carp Stock: Small number of carp to 28lbs
Category: Few Carp
Other Species: Pike and bream
Permits: Free fishing
Control: Council
BK Rating: Difficult
W/A: Thames
Comments: Refreshments etc. available on site.

Calves Lane Lake

Location: Love Hill Lane, off the B470 near Iver
Type and Size: Small lake
Carp Stock: Stocked in 1990 with 250 carp to 7lbs
Category: Mixed Fishery
Other Species: Roach, tench, perch and pike
Permits: Boyer Leisure, Farlows Lake, Iver Lane, Iver, Bucks SL0 9LL. Tel: 0753 655909. Season tickets to include 11 other waters.
Cost: £60 per season; £40 junior, £27.50 OAPs and disabled. It might be possible to obtain a single water permit at reduced price.
Control: William Boyers
Restrictions: No keepnets for carp; no groundbait.
BK Rating: Easy
W/A: Thames

Claydon Lake

Location: Middle Claydon, Winslow, near Leighton Buzzard
Type and Size: Estate lake of about 3 acres
How to Find: Take the A413 from Buckingham, and turn right to Middle Claydon just before the village of Winslow.
Carp Stock: Very heavily stocked with carp of 5-10lbs, with some doubles up to 20lbs. Mostly commons.
Category: Mixed Fishery
Other Species: Roach, rudd, bream, pike and very large catfish and zander
Permits: Season tickets for members only; Leighton Buzzard Angling Club, B Smalley, 3 Isis Walk, Leighton Buzzard, Beds. Tel: 0525 852227 or from Jim Brennan on the bank.
Cost: £20 adult, £23 husband and wife
Control: Club
BK Rating: Easy
Restrictions: No night fishing
W/A: Anglian
Comments: This lake is on an estate with a house once lived in by Florence Nightingale. It is a shallow, very open water. Cars must be parked by the roadside and it is more than half a mile's walk across a field to the lake. The water is famous for its catfish of over 30lbs, but there are plenty of carp also. The Leighton Buzzard Club has a number of other carp waters on the same ticket. An excellent water to gain experience on.

Common Pond

Location: Common near Gerrards Cross
Type and Size: One acre common land pond
Carp Stock: Fairly well stocked with carp including some doubles up to about 20lbs
Category: Mixed Fishery
Other Species: Roach and tench
Permits: Free fishing
Control: Local council
BK Rating: Easy
W/A: Thames

Furzton Lake

Location: Chaffron Way, Furzton, Milton Keynes
Type and Size: 40 acre man-made lake
How to Find: From junction 14 of the M1, take the A509 and turn right at the first roundabout. Follow this road (H5 Portway) for 6 miles to Watling Street roundabout, turn left and take the first right; then turn right at the second roundabout into Chaffron Way.
Carp Stock: Stocked in 1990 with about 1,400 carp, mirrors and commons, between 4lb and 14lb.
Category: Mixed Fishery
Other Species: Tench, rudd and perch
Permits: Day tickets from bailiff on bank
Control: Milton Keynes AA - membership from local tackle shops or from the Secretary, 107 Baccara Grove, Bletchley, Milton Keynes.
Restrictions: No fixed leads
BK Rating: Easy
W/A: Anglian
Comments: A new water, first opened in the 1990-91 season. Some areas out of bounds. Housing estate along one side.

Gayhurst Lakes

Location: Gayhurst Estate, near Newport Pagnell
Type and Size: Two pretty stream-fed estate lakes of 2 acres and one acre, both on the same stream, which runs from the larger lake to the small one
Carp Stock: The upper (larger) lake is very heavily stocked with carp to over 20lbs, although most are between 3lbs and 12lbs. The lower lake is said to contain some big carp but is so little fished that we have no records of catches.
Category: Carp Water
Other Species: Bream, roach and perch. Some pike in lower lake
Permits: Private syndicate water of Linear Fisheries, Linear House, 2 Northcroft, Shenley Lodge, Milton Keynes, Bucks MK5 7BE. Tel: 0908 607577 (24 hour Ansaphone).
Cost: £60 per season, and a £10 entry fee for Gayhurst Lakes. Enquire from the Secretary for prices and details of other Linear waters, including the Linear Fisheries Club with membership open to all.
Baits/Methods: Standard carp fishing methods; sweetcorn, luncheon meat and boilies all doing well.
Control: Linear Fisheries
Restrictions: Syndicate only - no day tickets. Membership in advance only. Alternate

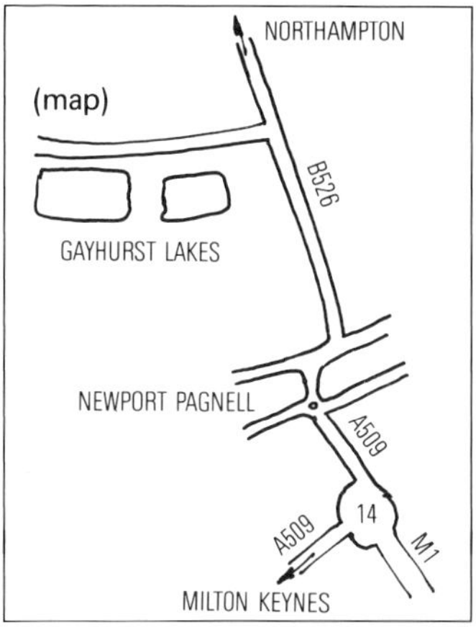

Saturday and Sunday rota to avoid weekend overcrowding. Small exclusive syndicate with limited membership, but vacancies at present.

BK Rating: Easy to Moderate
W/A: Anglian
Comments: Only Linear's second season controlling these lakes. They are on a beautiful and peaceful private estate in the grounds of a large mansion, and are surrounded by trees and bushes. Three carp of over 20lbs were reported from the water in the 1990 to 91 season, with a good number of doubles. Mirrors and commons. Frequent vacancies.

Haversham Lake

Location: The village of Haversham, near Milton Keynes
Type and Size: Big open gravel pit of more than 50 acres
How to Find: From Newport Pagnell take the Wolverton road and turn right down Little Linford Lane. Follow this past the other Linear waters to the T-junction, then turn left. In Haversham village, turn left down a rough track near the telephone booth
Carp Stock: Stocked by Linear with over 600 carp in 1986, and these fish are now being caught well into double figures, with the occasional 20 pounder.
Category: Mixed Fishery
Other Species: Pike to 26lbs, tench to over 8lbs+, perch over 3lbs, and roach over 2lbs. There are also some shoals of very large bream
Permits: Linear Fisheries Club, open to all: Linear House, 2 Northcroft, Shenley Lodge, Milton Keynes, Bucks., MK5 7BE. Tel: 0908 607577.
Cost: £25 per season (dawn to dusk); £35 per season, to include night fishing. Day tickets £3 per rod per day, 24 hour tickets at £4 per rod. Reductions for juniors/disabled/OAP's. Tickets must be purchased before fishing - £1 excess is charged by bailiffs to anyone fishing without a ticket.
Control: Linear Fisheries Club
Restrictions: Permits in advance only, or £1 excess charged by bailiffs on the bank
BK Rating: Moderate
W/A: Anglian
Comments: This big, rich water is expected to produce some huge carp within the

next few years, as they are growing very rapidly. Not heavily fished, and ideal for anyone who wants plenty of space. Price quoted above includes membership of Rocla Lake and Black Horse Lake and all other Linear Fisheries Club waters - details from Secretary as above.

Hyde Lane Reservoir

Location: Hyde Lane, Buckingham
Type and Size: Reservoir of about 40 acres
How to Find: Near Buckingham
Carp Stock: Not many carp, but some big fish to over 30 pounds
Category: Mixed Fishery
Other Species: A few catfish to over 25 pounds
Permits: Season tickets from local tackle shops
Cost: On application
Control: Club
BK Rating: Difficult
W/A: Thames

Lodge Lake

Location: Dansteed Way, Great Holm, Milton Keynes
Type and Size: Eight acre man-made lake divided by a central island
How to Find: Turn off the M1 at junction 14 and take the A509 to the first roundabout. Turn right into Portway and right again at the second roundabout into Brickhill Street. The left turn at the next roundabout will bring you into Dansteed Way and the lake will be seen on the left. Parking to the left of the lake in Bradwell Road.
Carp Stock: Very well stocked with about 1,500 carp to 22lbs - mirrors, commons and leathers
Category: Mixed Fishery
Other Species: Golden koi, crucians, roach, perch, bream, rudd and tench
Permits: Members only water of Milton Keynes AA (no day tickets). Membership open to all. Permits from local tackle shops or the Secretary, 107 Baccara Grove, Bletchley, Milton Keynes.
Control: Club
BK Rating: Easy
Baits/Methods: Usual carp fishing methods, although no fixed leads are allowed.
W/A: Anglian
Comments: Some areas are out of bounds and so cannot be fished.

Newport Pagnell Gravel Pits

Location: Newport Pagnell, off the Bedford Road
Type and Size: Eight small pits
Carp Stock: Most of the lakes contain carp, up to 20lbs in some of them
Category: Mixed Fishery
Other Species: Tench, pike, roach, perch and bream
Permits: Newport Pagnell Fishing Association. Secretary: R D Dorrill, 7 Bury Street, Newport Pagnell. Tel: 0909 610639.
Cost: About £12 per season
BK Rating: Moderate
W/A: Anglian

Red House Lake,
Linear Fisheries

Red House Lake

Location: Linford Linear Fisheries, Little Linford Lane, Milton Keynes
Type and Size: Gravel pit of 15 acres
How to Find: From junction 14 of the M1, turn right on the A409 towards Newport Pagnell, left at the next roundabout, right at the next roundabout, and left at the T-junction. Go under the bridge, straight across the small roundabout, and the Linear Fisheries entrance is about 400 yards on the right. There is also access from Little Linford Lane.
Carp Stock: Heavily stocked with carp to double figures by Linear in 1986/88. A few originals caught to 21lbs.
Category: Carp Water
Other Species: Bream to 8lbs; tench to 6½lbs; pike to 20lbs; roach and perch
Permits: Linear Fisheries Secretary: Len Gurd, Linear House, 2 Northcroft, Shenley Lodge, Milton Keynes, Bucks. Tel: 0908 607577. Seasonal (syndicate) only - frequent vacancies.
Cost: About £65 per season
BK Rating: Easy
Restrictions: No sacking of carp, no day tickets.
Control: Linear Fisheries
W/A: Anglian
Comments: Attractive, pleasant reed-fringed lake with a long promontory. Double figure carp were being caught here in the early 1980's. Linear Fisheries has Elstow Pit, near Bedford, a top carp fishery with many doubles and twenties to 30lbs. Syndicate only, vacancies now - enquire from Secretary.

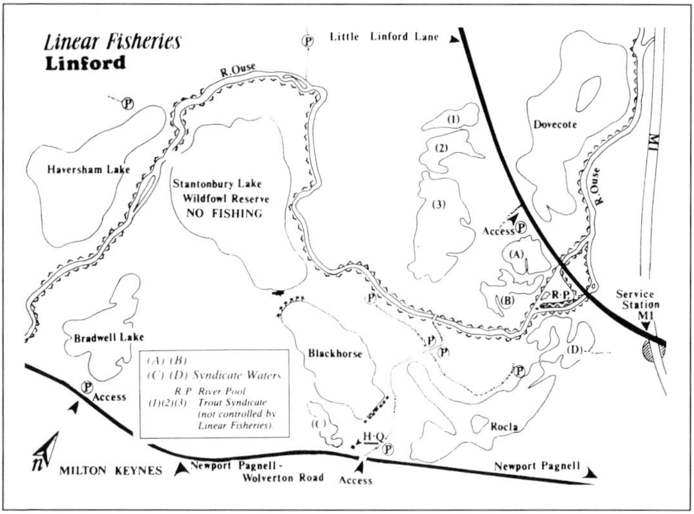

Rocla Lake A

Location: Linford Linear Fisheries, Little Linford Lane, Milton Keynes
Type and Size: Old matured gravel pit of 35 acres
How to Find: From junction 14 of the M1, turn right on the A409 towards Newport Pagnell, left at the first roundabout, right at the next roundabout and left at the T-junction. Go under the bridge, straight across the small roundabout and you will see Rocla on your right. The Linear Fisheries entrance and car parks are 400 yards on the right.
Carp Stock: Stocked by Linear with very large numbers of carp to double figures; many doubles to 20lbs caught.
Carp Stock: Mixed Fishery
Other Species: Bream to 8lbs; tench to 6½lbs; pike to 20lbs, roach and perch
Permits: Linear Fisheries Secretary: Len Gurd, Linear House, 2 Northcroft, Shenley Lodge, Milton Keynes, Bucks. Tel: 0908 607577.
Cost: £26 per season; £30 per 24 hour season ticket. Day tickets £3 per rod. Cost includes other Linear Fisheries waters.
BK Rating: Easy
Restrictions: No sacking of carp
Control: Linear Fisheries
W/A: Anglian
Comments: Another very attractive lake of irregular shape with trees and bushes. One large island which attracts the carp. Many bays and promontories. An angler had 21 carp in a day! Self-catering houses. Tel: 0908 368220 (9am to 5pm). This lake is featured in the 'Carp Fever' series of videos by Kevin Maddocks.

Snowberry Lake

Location: Bletchley, near Milton Keynes, just off the A5
Type and Size: Attractive 3 acre lake
Carp Stock: Well stocked with carp to upper twenties
Category: Mixed Fishery

Other Species: Tench, zander, roach, bream and crucians
Permits: Fourways Fisheries, Poplars Nursery, Harlington Road, Toddington, Dunstable LU5 6HE. Tel: 05255 5590.
Cost: £175 per season
Restrictions: No day tickets
BK Rating: Moderate
W/A: Thames
Comments: A very pleasant water, once controlled by the late Richard Walker.

Tiddenfoot Pit

Location: On the Leighton Buzzard ring road, Mentmore Road
Type and Size: Sand pit of 10 acres
How to Find: Near the town of Leighton Buzzard
Carp Stock: A small number of carp to about 24lbs
Category: Few Carp
Other Species: Catfish, bream, pike, roach, perch
Permits: Leighton Buzzard Angling Club. Secretary: B Smalley, 3 Isis Walk, Leighton Buzzard, Beds. Tel: 0525 852227.
Cost: £20 per season. Joint husband and wife £23.
Control: Club
BK Rating: Moderate
W/A: Anglian

Wolverton Lakes

Location: Stratford Road, Wolverton, Milton Keynes
Type and Size: Two small man-made lakes of about one acre
Carp Stock: About 100 mirrors and commons to 6lbs
Category: Mixed Fishery
Other Species: Crucians, tench, roach, perch
Permits: Members only water of Milton Keynes Angling Association (no day tickets). Membership is open to all - permits from local tackle shops or from the Secretary, 107 Baccara Grove, Bletchley, Milton Keynes.
Control: Club
Restrictions: Members only
W/A: Anglian
Comments: Small fish carp water, suitable for the non-carp specialist. Car park is at Wolverton Mill, opposite the footpath to the lakes.
BK Rating: Easy

CAMBRIDGESHIRE

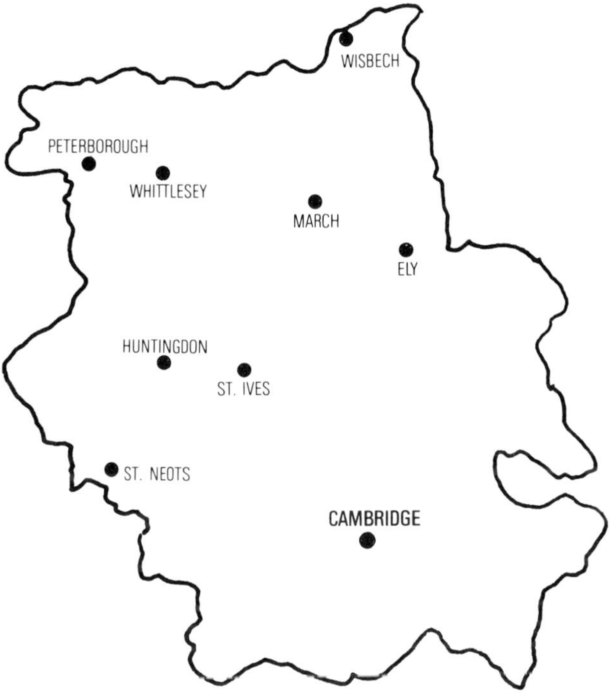

Barway Lake

Location: Barway, near Ely
Type and Size: 5 acre lake
Carp Stock: Well stocked with carp to 20lbs
Category: Mixed Fishery
Other Species: Tench, roach and crucians
Permits: P S and J M Randall. Tel: 0353 720052
Cost: Day tickets on application; 6am to dusk only.
Control: Private
BK Rating: Not known
Restrictions: No night fishing
W/A: Anglian

Brackhill Lake

Location: Earith between Huntingdon and Ely
Type and Size: 3 gravel pits
Carp Stock: Brackhill Lake said to contain 'a few' carp, has some to double figures. This complex is being developed as a carp fishery
Category: Few Carp
Other Species: Roach, perch, rudd, tench and bream
Permits: Enquire locally
Control: Private (ex A.R.C.)
BK Rating: Difficult
Restrictions: No night fishing
W/A: Anglian

Burnside Lake

Location: Old Blue Circle Cement Works, Coldhams Lane, Cambridge
Type and Size: 10 acre chalk quarry
Carp Stock: About 200 carp, between 7lbs and 15lbs
Category: Mixed Fishery
Other Species: Roach, rudd, bream, perch, chub and pike
Permits: Season tickets only from Cherry Hinton AC. Secretary: Mr Hobson, 25 Ivory Close, Cherry Hinton, Cambridgeshire.
Cost: £11 per season
Control: Club
Restrictions: No day tickets
BK Rating: Moderate
W/A: Anglian
Comments: The average depth of this quarry is about 25ft, with some areas 35ft deep. Most carp are caught in the margins or on floating or suspended baits because of the great depth.

Chawston Lake

Location: Chawston, near St. Neots
Type and Size: Gravel pit of about 8-10 acres
How to Find: One mile off A1 near St. Neots
Carp Stock: Quite well stocked with carp to 19-20lbs. Most are doubles of 10-14lbs
Category: Mixed Fishery
Other Species: General coarse fish
Permits: Chawston AC - tackle shop in St. Neots
Cost: On application
BK Rating: Moderate
Control: Club
W/A: Anglian
Comments: Fish to around 20lbs.

Chesterford Fisheries

Location: Great Chesterford, Saffron Walden
Type and Size: 3 lakes - 7 acres, 2 of 3 acres. Mature gravel pits
How to Find: Off M11, junction 9
Carp Stock: Chesterford Lake (7 acres) - 100 carp to 30lbs plus; Borough Lake - 40

Mark Churcher with a 27 pounder from Chesterford Fisheries

Borough Lake, Chesterford Fisheries; Paul Elsegood's excellent carp waters in Cambridgeshire

fish, doubles and twenties; Ickleton Lake - 100 plus doubles up to 18lbs, 3 thirties.

Category: Mixed Fisheries
Other Species: Big perch, roach, tench, pike
Permits: Season tickets only from Paul Elsegood, 2 Wentfords Cottages, Clare Road, Poslingford, Sudbury, Suffolk. Tel: 0787 277468.
Cost: £125
Control: Private
Restrictions: Fishing up to 10.30pm; and after 3am. No sacking.
BK Rating: Chesterford - Difficult for big fish. Borough - Difficult. Ickleton - Moderate.
W/A: Anglian
Comments: Do not visit water until you have contacted the owner. Tickets in advance only. No day tickets. Guest tickets for members. Cooking hut. Toilets. Club-type image.

Clearwaters Coarse Fishery

Location: Near Earith, which is not far from St. Ives
Type and Size: 13 acre lake, matured gravel pit
Carp Stock: Well stocked with carp to about 20lbs
Category: Carp Water
Other Species: Some other coarse fish, including tench
Permits: Season tickets in advance only - for details telephone 0582 853307, between 6pm and 9pm.
Control: Private
BK Rating: Moderate
W/A: Anglian

Decoy Lake

Location: Decoy Farm, Eastrea, Whittlesey, Peterborough
Type and Size: Gravel pit of about 3½ acres
How to Find: From Peterborough take the A605 to Whittlesey. Follow A605 towards March for 1½ miles, turn left opposite some white silos
Carp Stock: 11,000 small carp, up to 4lbs!
Category: Mixed Fishery
Other Species: Bream, tench, rudd, few roach
Permits: Club bookings and matches only; 10, 22 or 32 anglers only. From Peter Band on 0733 202230, or Tony Hudson on 0733 203428.
Cost: Approx £5 per peg for 6 hours fishing
BK Rating: Easy
Control: Private
Restrictions: Barbless hooks; keepnets supplied. No children. No night fishing.
W/A: Anglian
Comments: Spring fed water, specially stocked for match fishing. The 11,000 commons and mirrors were stocked at 7oz - 1lb, and some weigh 4lbs, after 6 months! No individual fishing - block bookings only. Enormous catches are routine. England International Ian Heaps, who regularly fishes the waters, says that he considers this the match fishing of the future, as heavily stocked carp match waters provide more sport for all. Something a bit different for our Guide - nearly 4,000 carp per acre!

Dickersons Pit

Location: Milton Pits, Milton Road, Cambridge
Type and Size: Large matured gravel pit
Carp Stock: Well stocked with carp to over 20lbs
Category: Mixed Fishery
Other Species: Pike, tench and rudd
Permits: Try Cooper Brothers Tackle Shop, Milton Road, Cambridge for permits and information
Cost: About £10 per person
Control: Histon AC
Restrictions: Most of this pit has recently been designated a 'Nature Reserve', and, as so often in these cases, has been closed to anglers, most of whom are true nature lovers! However, the small pit attached to the main one by a narrow stretch of water, remains open, and other pits on the site, including Todds Pit, which also contains carp, are still in the control of Histon AC - Secretary: R Cooper, 236 Histon Road, Cottenham, Cambridge (members only).

Earith Lakes

Location: Holme Fen Drove, Earith, near St. Ives
Type and Size: Originally an 18 acre matured gravel pit, now divided into two parts
Carp Stock: Larger lake (11 acres) - several hundred to 31lbs; smaller lake (7 acres) - heavily stocked with smaller carp to low twenties.
Category: Carp Water (both lakes)
Other Species: Perch, rudd, roach, chub, tench and pike
Permits: From the owner, Ken McLennan, on site. Tel: 0487 740301.
Cost: Both lakes - syndicate at £120 per year
BK Rating: Moderate for both waters
Control: Private
Restrictions: No sacks. No tiger nuts or peanuts.
W/A: Anglian
Comments: This is a very pleasant carp fishery, very well stocked with large numbers of good carp. There is also an 18 acre coarse fishery and a 36 acre trout lake on the site - details from the owner.

Eaton Socon Lake

Location: Eaton Socon, near St. Neots
Carp Stock: Well stocked with carp to 20lbs
Category: Mixed Fishery
Other Species: Tench, rudd and bream
Permits: Hitchin and District AC, L G Day, 14 Thatchers End, Hitchin, Herts or from local tackle shops.
Cost: Members only - season ticket at £17.50
Control: Club
BK Rating: Moderate
W/A: Anglian

Fen Drayton Complex

Location: Fen Drayton, between Cambridge and Huntingdon
Type and Size: Gravel pits - Drayton Fen quite large
How to Find: Off the A604 Cambridge - Huntingdon road
Carp Stock: Some large carp
Category: Few Carp
Other Species: General coarse fish including zander
Permits: Head Bailiff: Neil Prior. Tel: 0954 303345 (evenings).
Cost: On application
BK Rating: Moderate
Control: Private
Restrictions: None
W/A: Anglian
Comments: Also board sailing on this lake.

Fen Drayton Lake

Location: Fen Drayton, near Fenstanton
Type and Size: 30 acre gravel pit
How to Find: Fen Drayton between Huntingdon and Cambridge
Carp Stock: Very few fish to 30lbs plus
Category: Few Carp
Other Species: Mixed coarse fish
Permits: Enquire locally
BK Rating: Very Difficult
Restrictions: None
W/A: Anglian
Comments: Sailing and windsurfing also take place on this pit.

Gerrards Carp Lake

Location: Woodgate Lane, Maxey, Peterborough. Tel: 0945 780309
Type and Size: 10 acre pit
Carp Stock: Well stocked with carp to 20lbs
Category: Carp Water
Other Species: Some coarse fish
Permits: In advance only, telephone as above.
Control: Private
BK Rating: Easy
W/A: Anglian

Hatton Park Pool

Location: Longstanton, near Cambridge
Type and Size: Gravel pit of 1½ acres
How to Find: In the middle of a field on the east side of Station Road, 300 yards outside Longstanton
Carp Stock: Stocked in 1982 with 15 carp to 10lbs that have since bred
Category: Carp Water
Other Species: Tench to 6lbs, plus rudd
Permits: Free
BK Rating: Moderate
W/A: Anglian

Little Paxton Fishery

Location: Near St. Neots
Type and Size: Gravel pits, 4 lakes, total about 30 acres
How to Find: Take the A1 north from London. After the A45 turn off, take the left turn marked 'St. Neots – Little Paxton', B1041. Turn left at the signpost marked 'Paxton Quarry' and continue for 600 yards to car park
Carp Stock: All lakes have some large carp to 20lbs. The car park lake has been stocked with carp to 20lbs.
Category: Mixed Fishery
Other Species: Bream, tench, roach, rudd, perch, pike
Permits: Day tickets from site office near car park. Must be obtained before fishing. At weekends ONLY anglers may fish from 8am before obtaining tickets and the bailiff will sell them later on the bank. Season tickets from Fishery Manager, Ian May, 8 Davis Close, Little Paxton. Tel: Huntingdon 212059.
Cost: Day tickets: £2 (juniors/OAP/evenings £1). Season tickets: £25. Limited night fishing at £25 extra.
BK Rating: Moderate
Restrictions: No night fishing. Open daily 7.30am until sunset. Season and advance day ticket holders may fish from sunrise till dark. No sacking.
Baits/Methods: Normal modern carp methods and baits
Control: Redland Angling Scheme
W/A: Anglian
Comments: Commercial fishery. Season ticket holders may night fish for carp by arrangement with the fishery manager. Do not go to the works area. Park only in the car park.

Long Reach

Location: Off St. Ives by-pass
Type and Size: 20 acre gravel pit
How to Find: Take A604 towards Cambridge, St. Ives turning (B1040); St. Ives by-pass, lake on right by third roundabout
Carp Stock: Sparsely stocked to 35lbs plus
Category: Few Carp
Other Species: General coarse fish
Permits: Enquire locally
BK Rating: Difficult
Control: Private
Restrictions: None
W/A: Anglian
Comments: Water ski-ing on this lake during the day. A good venue for the pioneering type angler – full potential unknown

Milton Lake

Location: Near Cambridge
Type and Size: Large lake
Carp Stock: Stocked with carp to over 20lbs
Category: Mixed Fishery
Other Species: Most coarse fish
Permits: Try local tackle shops
Control: Club – possibly Cambridge AS

Cost: 65p per day
BK Rating: Difficult
W/A: Anglian

Milton Pits

Location: Old School Lane, Milton, Cambridge
Type and Size: 4 acre gravel pit
How to Find: Take the A45 north to Cambridge to Milton village. Take the High Street, turn into Coles Road and Old School Lane
Carp Stock: Well stocked with carp to 20lbs
Category: Mixed Fishery
Other Species: General coarse fish
Permits: Cooper Brothers Tackle Shop, Milton Road, Cambridge, in advance only.
Cost: Approximately £10 per season, no day tickets
BK Rating: Moderate
Control: Histon Angling Club
Restrictions: None
W/A: Anglian
Comments: Pleasant lake run by club.

North House Lake

Location: The North House, Great North Road, Wyboston, near St. Neots
Type and Size: Gravel pit of 5 acres
How to Find: Can be seen from the A1 at Wyboston

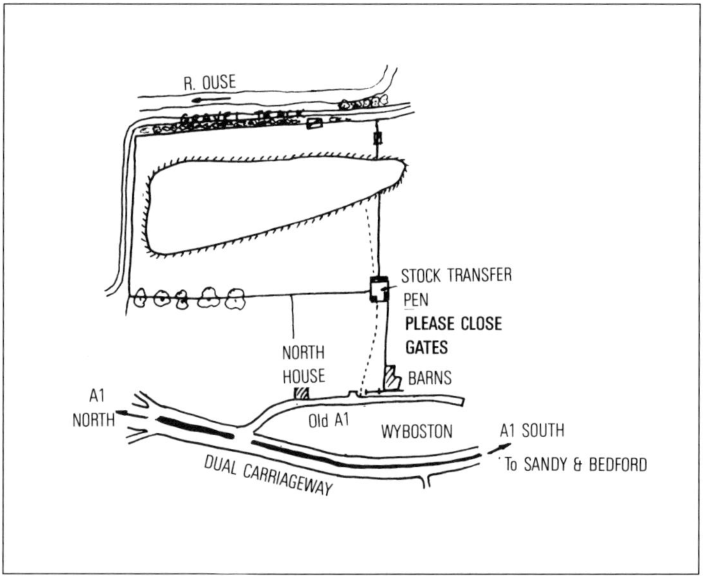

Carp Stock: Quite well stocked - 40-60 fish to 23lbs. Average 14lbs
Category: Mixed Fishery
Other Species: Crucians, tench and rudd

Permits: Luton AC or Leslie's of Luton, 89 Park Street, Luton, Beds.
Cost: Approximately £7.50 per season
BK Rating: Moderate
Control: Club
W/A: Anglian
Comments: Pear-shaped open gravel pit. Luton Angling Club, D Bacon, 18 The Hedgerows, Parkside, Furzton, Milton Keynes, MK14 1BP. No night fishing.

Paxton Lake

Location: Great Paxton, near St. Neots
Type and Size: Medium sized lake
Carp Stock: Well stocked with carp, said to go to 30lbs
Category: Mixed Fishery
Other Species: Tench, chub, bream and roach
Permits: Day tickets on bank from bailiffs, or the Secretary, St. Neots and District, Watling, 43 Shakespeare Road, Eaton Socon, Cambs PE19 3HG.
Cost: About £1 per day; £4 per week; £9.40 per season - includes fishing on the Great Ouse.
Control: Club
BK Rating: Not known
W/A: Anglian

Pisces Caravan Park and Fishery A

Location: Bedford Bank, Welney, Wisbech, PE14 9TB. Tel: 035471 (Welney) 257
Type and Size: Lakes of 4 acres and 2 acres
Carp Stock: Larger lake well stocked with carp to about 15lbs. Smaller lake contains crucian carp
Category: Mixed Fishery
Other Species: Bream, roach, rudd, perch, pike; some tench in smaller lake
Permits: No day tickets. Fishing is free, and is for residents only.
Control: Pisces Caravan Park - private
BK Rating: Not known
Restrictions: Barbless hooks only. No keepnets. No groundbait. No boilies to be thrown in the lake.
W/A: Anglian
Comments: Catches listed includes pike to over 30lbs, bream to 11lbs 6ozs, tench to over 8lbs, perch to 2lbs, rudd to 3lbs 11ozs, roach to 2½lbs and an eel of 6½lbs.
There are 16 letting caravans round the lake, and the rivers Bedford and Delph run alongside the Park - fishing free in the River Bedford, local tickets for the Delph. There is also a new trout lake on the site, with a small charge for the fishing. Rod licences and bait on site. Costs for caravans and bungalow from £100 to £205 per week according to time of year.

St. Ives Complex

Location: Fen Drayton, near St. Ives
Type and Size: Several gravel pits
How to Find: Near St. Ives
Carp Stock: Trior Lake contains some carp; St. Ives Lagoon - a few large carp; Anderson's Lake - good carp

Category: Mixed Fisheries
Other Species: General coarse fish
Permits: Site Warden: Bernard Hunt. Tel: 0480 86444 (day); 0480 212815 (evenings).
Cost: Day tickets on application
BK Rating: Not known
Control: Private
W/A: Anglian
Comments: Lowry's also contains some carp. Little known about this fishery.

The Stew Pond

Location: St. Neots
Type and Size: Pit of about 1½ acres
How to Find: The pit is in the Wyboston Complex just off the A1
Carp Stock: Many carp up to 2lbs, with some bigger ones up to 18lbs
Category: Carp Water
Other Species: General coarse fish
Permits: Day tickets from the Club House on the golf course next to the pit.
Cost: Approximately £1 per day
Control: Private
BK Rating: Moderate
W/A: Anglian
Comments: Night fishing allowed.

Werrington Lake

Location: Werrington, near Peterborough
Type and Size: Medium sized pits
Carp Stock: Very well stocked with carp to over 20lbs
Category: Carp Water
Other Species: Some tench, roach and catfish
Permits: Seasonal - information and details on 0733 70226
Cost: On application
Control: Private
BK Rating: Moderate
W/A: Anglian

Wimblington Mere

Location: Wimblington, near Wisbech
Type and Size: Small gravel pit
How to Find: Just off the B1098 between Chatteris and Wisbech
Carp Stock: Some carp, numbers and sizes unknown, but a schoolboy had a 21¼lb here in 1987, reported in Angling Times
Category: Mixed Fishery
Other Species: Crucians, rudd, roach, tench, bream
Permits: Head Bailiff Keith Bradshaw. Tel: 0354 740350 (evenings).
Cost: On application - about £12 per season.
BK Rating: Moderate
Control: Private
Restrictions: No cereal groundbaits; no keepnets.
W/A: Anglian
Comments: On the same site as Browns Water, containing carp, and Honey Pond with some carp and tench. The 21¼ was caught on slow sinking flake.

Woburn Close Lake A

Location: Hemingford Grey, St. Ives
Type and Size: Gravel pit of 3 acres
Carp Stock: Very heavily stocked with about 2,000 carp. Average size is about 8lbs and the best fish is about 17lbs
Category: Carp Water
Permits: Fishing can only be obtained by renting a holiday on the property. All information and bookings from: Jim Eggett, Woburn Close, Meadow Lane, Hemingford Grey, St. Ives, Cambridgeshire.
Cost: On application
Control: Private
Restrictions: No night fishing
BK Rating: Very Easy
W/A: Anglian

Woolpack Fishery

Location: On the main road north of Hilton, near St. Ives
Type and Size: 4 acre gravel pit
Carp Stock: Quite well stocked with carp which range from 12lbs to 27lbs, and which average 20lbs in weight
Category: Carp Only
Permits: At the time of going to press the control of this water was changing - visit lake for further details.
Cost: About £125 a year
Control: Private syndicate
Restrictions: No peanuts to be used
BK Rating: Moderate
W/A: Anglian

CHESHIRE

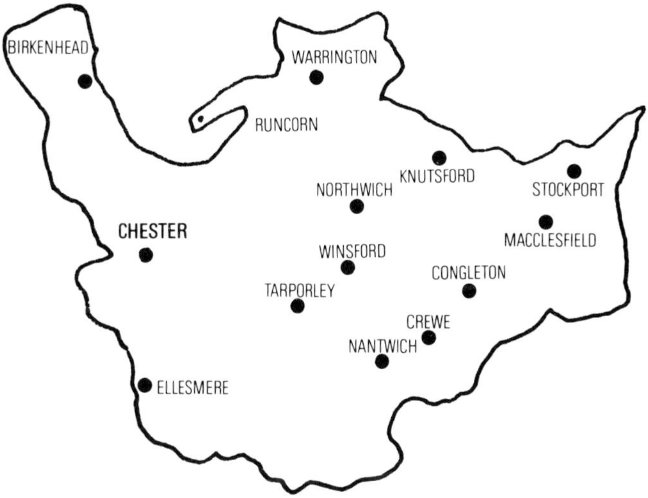

Ashenhurst Lakes

Location: Blackely, Manchester
Type and Size: Two lakes of about three-quarters of an acre each
Carp Stock: Very heavily stocked with carp to about 16lbs, though most are singles
Category: Carp Water
Other Species: Roach and a few grass carp
Permits: Club season tickets, very hard to obtain – try local tackle shops.
Control: Broughton Angling Club. G Guy, 27 Geralds Road, Salford M6 6DW, who may be able to help with membership.
Baits/Methods: Floaters and all other methods successful
BK Rating: Very Easy
W/A: North West
Comments: A very pleasant and attractive venue, which explains why it is so hard to obtain membership.
Restrictions: No night fishing; members only. Advertised for sale in 1990.

Billinge Green

Location: Off the A556, south of Northwich, near Davenham
Type and Size: Small pool
Carp Stock: Well stocked with carp to doubles
Category: Mixed Fishery
Other Species: Roach, bream, perch and tench
Permits: Northwich AA, PO Box 18, Northwich CW9 5SE.
Control: Club
BK Rating: Moderate
Restrictions: Members only
W/A: North West

Blakemere

Location: Off the junction of the Shrewsbury/Whitchurch roads, about one mile from town centre of Ellesmere; park the car at the junction and walk 200 yards along canal towpath to lake
Type and Size: Lake of about 7 acres
Carp Stock: Carp to doubles
Category: Mixed Fishery
Other Species: Roach, bream, tench, perch and pike
Permits: Ellesmere AC
Control: Club
BK Rating: Not known
W/A: North West

Bosley Reservoir

Location: Bosley, near Macclesfield
Type and Size: Huge reservoir of 90 acres
Carp Stock: Carp were stocked in 1964. There are not many, but one thirty has been reported
Category: Few Carp
Other Species: General coarse fish
Permits: Prince Albert AS, season tickets only. Secretary: C Clarke, 2 Avon Close, Upton, Macclesfield, Cheshire.
Cost: Around £35 entry fee and £35 per season
Control: Club. Members only
BK Rating: Very Difficult
W/A: North West

Bridgewater Canal

Location: Broadheath Bridge to Preston Brook
Type and Size: Canal some miles in length
Carp Stock: Well stocked with carp to 17lbs
Category: Mixed Fishery
Other Species: General coarse fish
Permits: Warrington Anglers. Secretary: Mr J S Jackson, 23 Nora Street, Warrington.
Control: Club
BK Rating: Moderate
W/A: North West
Comments: Carp have been growing well in this part of the canal and many are now caught in matches. There is some good carp fishing here as a change from lakes, and it should be noted that Warrington Anglers have several carp waters mentioned in this book, all on the same ticket.

Budworth Mere

Location: Near Great Budworth, off the B5075, north of Northwich
Type and Size: Large lake
Carp Stock: Well stocked with carp to about 20lbs
Category: Mixed Fishery
Other Species: Tench, roach, rudd, bream, perch and pike
Permits: Northwich AA, PO Box 18, Northwich ,CW9 5SE.

Control: Club
Restrictions: Members only
BK Rating: Not known
W/A: North West

Burton Mere A

Location: Burton, off the A540 Chester to Hoylake road - in Burton, turn right into Puddington Lane, then take the first right to the lakes
Type and Size: Two small man-made lakes
Category: Mixed Fishery
Other Species: Roach, rudd, perch, bream, crucians, tench, chub, catfish and trout
Permits: Day tickets from the lodge on site. Tel: 051-253 0115.
Cost: £4 per day; £2.50 per evening, from 5pm.
Control: Private
Baits/Methods: Float fishing works well, with standard baits
BK Rating: Moderate
Restrictions: No keepnets; no groundbaiting
W/A: Welsh
Comments: The larger lake is day ticket, and the smaller one is a members only carp fishery. No close season on the day ticket water, as rainbow trout are stocked in March, but worm fishing only is allowed in the coarse fish close season.

Canal Pit

Location: Whatcroft, off the A530 south of Northwich
Type and Size: Small pit
Carp Stock: Some carp to doubles
Category: Mixed Fishery
Other Species: Usual coarse fish
Permits: Northwich AA, PO Box 18, Northwich CW9 5SE; Scotts Tackle, Northwich. Tel: 0606 46543.
Control: Club
Restrictions: Members only
BK Rating: Not known
W/A: North West

Capesthorne Hall Garden Pool

Location: Capesthorne Estate, Siddington, near Macclesfield
Type and Size: Estate lake of 7 acres
How to Find: The estate is just off the A34, 3 miles from Macclesfield, and 6 miles from Knutsford and Wilmslow
Carp Stock: The lake is well stocked with carp under 10lbs, and there are about 60 doubles, of which 6 are twenties - best 28lbs
Category: Mixed Fishery
Other Species: Tench, crucians, perch, roach, rudd, pike and gudgeon
Permits: Season tickets form Stoke-on-Trent AS. Secretary: Mr Broadgate, 'Lynton', 5 Kingsfield Oval, Basford, Stoke-on-Trent ST4 6HN. Members only, some guest tickets.
Baits/Methods: All methods and baits. Float fishing works well near lilies and bushes; surface fishing very successful in summer.
Control: Club. Bailiff: Mrs E Shapley. Tel: Wilmslow 520061.

BK Rating: Moderate
W/A: North West
Comments: Stocked with mirror carp in 1958 and 1963. Good spawning and carp spawned in 1976 now up to 20lbs.

Cheshire Fishing

Location: Tattenhall, near Chester
Type and Size: Three small lakes
How to Find: From Chester take the A41 Whitchurch road. The Tattenhall turn is on the left in about 8 miles. At the T-junction in Tattenhall, turn left towards Burwardsley. In 1½ miles you will see a 'Cheshire Fishing' sign on the left
Carp Stock: Lakes 1 and 2 well stocked with carp to 20lbs; Lake 3, the smallest contains many small carp
Category: Mixed Fishery
Other Species: Bream, tench, roach
Permits: On site - match bookings in advance.
Cost: £6.50 per day per rod, dawn to dusk only; £4 for a 5 hour ticket, extra rods £1 each.
Control: Private. Tel: 0829 70041
Restrictions: No night fishing; all fish over 1lb to be returned immediately; barbless hooks only.
Baits/Methods: Most baits and methods, though most carp are taken on boilies.
BK Rating: Moderate
Comments: There are also two trout lakes on the same site.

Cicely Mill Pool

Location: Knutsford
Type and Size: Small mere of about 3 acres
Carp Stock: Not many carp, but some to low doubles
Category: Few Carp
Permits: Warrington Anglers. Secretary: Mr Jackson, 23 Nora Street, Warrington.
Control: Club. Members only
BK Rating: Difficult
W/A: North West

Crabmill Flash

Location: Moston, near Sandbach
Type and Size: Estate lake of about 10 acres
Carp Stock: Plenty of doubles and about twenty 20's with the best fish over 30lbs
Category: Carp Water
Permits: Season tickets from Wheelock Angling Society, and local tackle shops.
Control: Club
BK Rating: Moderate
W/A: North West
Comments: Long, narrow canal-like lake, about ¼ mile long. Good twenties water.

Crosemere

Location: About 3 miles from Ellesmere on the main Shrewsbury road; parking down lane about half a mile past the lake
Type and Size: Large Cheshire mere
Carp Stock: Some carp to doubles
Category: Few Carp
Other Species: Roach, bream, perch, tench and pike
Permits: Ellesmere AC
Control: Club
BK Rating: Very Difficult
W/A: North West
Comments: As this area is an S.S.S.I., great care must be taken to observe rules and signs, and to keep to marked paths. No cutting of undergrowth etc.

Dovemere, Sandmere and Woodlands

Location: Allostock, near Knutsford
Type and Size: 3 lake complex, lakes dug to provide material for the motorway. Dovemere - 17 acres; Sandmere - 15 acres; Woodlands - 10 acres
How to Find: Lakes are alongside the M6 at Allostock
Carp Stock: Well stocked with mostly carp doubles
Category: Carp Water
Other Species: Mixed coarse fish
Permits: Season tickets only from Prince Albert Angling Society. Secretary: C Clarke, 2 Avon Close, Macclesfield, Cheshire.
Cost: About £35 entry fee plus £35 annual subscription
Control: Club
BK Rating: Generally Easy, waters may vary
W/A: North West

Founders Pool

Location: Near Warrington
Type and Size: Small pond of 1 acre
Carp Stock: Well stocked with carp to doubles
Category: Mixed Fishery
Other Species: Roach and perch
Permits: Members only water of Lymm AC. Secretary: S Griffiths, 18 Manor Road, Lymm WA13 OAT. Tel: 092575 2763
Cost: £23 per season, and a joining fee of £13
Restrictions: No night fishing; members only.
BK Rating: Easy
W/A: North West

Godwins Pool

Location: Near Congleton
Type and Size: Small pool
Carp Stock: Some carp to about 20lbs
Category: Mixed Fishery
Other Species: Tench and most other coarse fish
Permits: Congleton Anglers' Society. Secretary: Mr N Bours, 8 Norfolk Road, Congleton. Tel: Congleton 277284.

Cost: Membership (to include other waters) costs £20 per season plus a £5 entry fee.
Control: Club
BK Rating: Moderate
W/A: North West

Grey Mist Mere

Location: Wooston, near Warrington
Type and Size: Mere of about 10 acres
Carp Stock: Very well stocked with carp. Plenty of doubles with a few low twenties, best fish 21lbs
Category: Carp Water
Other Species: General coarse fish
Permits: Warrington Anglers, season tickets only. Secretary: Mr J S Jackson, 23 Nora Street, Warrington.
Control: Club
BK Rating: Moderate
W/A: North West
Comments: A well known carp water, very good for doubles.

Grimesditch Pool

Location: Stretton, near Warrington
Type and Size: Small pool of 2 acres
How to Find: Stretton is near junction 10 of the M56 motorway
Carp Stock: Not many carp, sizes not known
Category: Few Carp
Permits: Lymm Angling Club. Secretary: S Griffiths, 18 Manor Way, Lymm WA13 OAY.
Control: Club
BK Rating: Difficult
W/A: North West
Comments: It should be noted here that Lymm Angling Club has several carp waters on the same ticket.

Hack Green Lake

Location: Hack Green, 3 miles from Nantwich
Type and Size: Man-made lake of 2 acres
Carp Stock: Well stocked with carp (in 1986) to doubles
Category: Mixed Fishery
Other Species: Tench, roach and bream
Permits: See below
BK Rating: Moderate
W/A: North West
Comments: This water was advertised for sale, within a 4½ acre site, in March 1991 so you will need to enquire at local tackle shops to find out who controls it now. The agents were Wright-Manley. Tel: Tarporley (0829) 732151.

King George V Pool

Location: Altrincham
Type and Size: Small, shallow lake of about 3 acres
How to Find: Altrincham is near Sale on the SW outskirts of Manchester. Take the Manchester - Northwich road
Carp Stock: Well stocked mainly with small carp, but there are fish to upper double figure size with the odd 20
Category: Carp Water
Permits: Day tickets from bailiff on bank
Control: Trafford Metropolitan Council
BK Rating: Easy
W/A: North West

Little Budworth

Location: Little Budworth, near Tarporley
Type and Size: 5 acre lake
Carp Stock: Some carp to doubles
Category: Mixed Fishery
Other Species: Tench, bream, roach and small perch
Permits: Tarporley and District AC. Secretary: Mr M J Clays, 58 Churchill Drive, Tarporley CW6 OBZ; members only.
Control: Club
Restrictions: Membership is restricted to those living within a 5 mile radius of Tarporley.
BK Rating: Not known
W/A: North West

Little Mill

Location: Near Tarporley
Type and Size: Mill pool of just over 3 acres
Carp Stock: Carp to over 20lbs
Category: Mixed Fishery
Other Species: Tench, perch, bream, roach and a few crucians
Permits: Tarporley and District AC. Secretary: Mr M J Clays, 58 Churchill Drive, Tarporley CW6 OBZ; members only.
Control: Club
Restrictions: Membership is restricted to those living within a 5 miles radius of Tarporley.
BK Rating: Difficult
W/A: North West

Lymm Dam

Location: Near the village of Lymm, near Warrington, Manchester
Type and Size: 15 acre lake
How to Find: Go through Lymm onto the A56 and the lake will be seen on the right
Carp Stock: There are not thought to be many carp but there are some very big ones. Largest known caught recently was 27lbs, but we know of a least one thirty caught a long time ago, and there are rumours of even bigger fish
Category: Few Carp
Other Species: Bream, roach, pike and a few catfish

Permits: Day tickets from bailiffs on the bank.
Cost: £1.50 per day
BK Rating: Moderate
Baits/Methods: Advanced carp fishing methods needed; high protein boilies
Control: Lymm Angling Club, which has a number of other good carp waters. Secretary: S Griffiths, 18 Manor Way, Lymm WA13 OAY.
W/A: North West
Comments: This is known mainly as a match water, but there are some big fish of most species, and probably some very big carp, which are hard to find in this large water. Uncontrollable fish are occasionally hooked and lost - thought to be big catfish.

Macclesfield Canal

Location: Kidsgrove and Congleton lengths especially good
Type and Size: Some miles of a narrow canal
Carp Stock: Plenty of carp to about 5lbs, with possibly some bigger fish present
Category: Mixed Fishery
Other Species: Bream, roach, tench and pike
Permits: Local angling clubs - try tackle shops in Congleton and Kidsgrove.
Control: Club
BK Rating: Easy
W/A: North West
Comments: No close season.

Marbury Mere

Location: Marbury
Type and Size: Mere of 30 acres
Carp Stock: Only a small number of carp, but some are upper 20's
Other Species: General coarse fish
Permits: Season tickets only. Prince Albert AS. Secretary: C Clarke, 2 Avon Close, Macclesfield, Cheshire.
Cost: About £35 entry fee plus £35 per season
Control: Club
BK Rating: Very Difficult
W/A: North West
Comments: All Prince Albert club waters are members only. This is one of the largest clubs in the country with a fine selection of waters.

Mobberley Pool

Location: Small Lane, Mobberley, near Altrincham
Type and Size: Small pool of less than an acre
How to Find: Mobberley is near Knutsford on the B5085 road from Knutsford to Alderley Edge, south of Manchester
Carp Stock: Well stocked with small carp to lower double figure size
Category: Mixed Fishery
Permits: Altrincham AS. A Lea, 37 Crossgates Avenue, Sharston, Manchester.
Control: Club
BK Rating: Easy
W/A: North West

Moss and Mossbank Pools

Location: Lymm, near Manchester
Type and Size: Two small ponds
Carp Stock: Well stocked with carp to about 10lbs
Category: Carp Water
Other Species: Crucians and grass carp (these are not really carp at all - Latin name: *Ctenopharyngodon Idella*!)
Permits: Members only water of Lymm AA. Secretary: S Griffiths, 18 Manor Road, Lymm WA13 0AY. Tel: 092575 2763.
Restrictions: No day tickets; no night fishing
BK Rating: Easy
W/A: North West

Ocean Pool

Location: Winsford
Type and Size: Medium sized lake
How to Find: Winsford is south of Northwich on the A54 Chester to Congleton road
Carp Stock: Small number of carp to mid-twenties
Category: Few Carp
Other Species: General coarse fish
Permits: Winsford and District Angling Association, J Bailey, 22 Plover Road, Winsford.
Control: Club
BK Rating: Difficult
W/A: North West

Oulton Mill

Location: Near Tarporley
Type and Size: 4 acre mill lake
Carp Stock: Very well stocked with carp to 20lbs
Category: Carp Water
Other Species: A few tench and roach
Permits: Tarporley and District AC - M J Clays, 58 Churchill Drive, Tarporley.
Cost: Season tickets at £60 per season, open to all
Control: Club
BK Rating: Moderate
W/A: North West
Comments: Some waters in the NRA North West Region now have no close season.

Petty Pool

Location: Sandiway, off the A556 to the south west of Northwich
Type and Size: Medium-sized lake
Carp Stock: Some carp to doubles at least
Category: Mixed Fishery
Other Species: Usual coarse fish
Permits: Northwich AA, PO Box 18, Northwich CW9 5SE; Scotts Tackle, Northwich. Tel: 0606 46543.
Control: Club
Restrictions: Members only
BK Rating: Not known
W/A: North West

Plex Flash

Location: Oakwood Lane, Moston, Sandbach
Carp Stock: Contains about 55 doubles to 18lbs 10ozs
Category: Mixed Fishery
Other Species: General coarse fish
Permits: Wheelock Angling Club, and local tackle shops.
Control: Club
BK Rating: Moderate
W/A: North West
Comments: Little is known about this water. Further details from Club Secretary.

Redesmere

Location: Capesthorne Estate, Siddington, Macclesfield
Type and Size: Estate mere of 58 acres
How to Find: The lake is just off the A34 Alderley Edge to Congleton road
Carp Stock: There are reliably estimated to be about 150 doubles in the lake, of which 45 fish are over 20lbs. There are two thirties, a common of 33lbs 6ozs, and a mirror of 32lbs. Water was stocked with 150 fingerlings in 1958, and in 1963 a further 100 fish were stocked. Small number of carp including some doubles have been put in since
Category: Mixed Fishery
Other Species: Large bream, pike, tench, crucians, roach and perch
Permits: Season tickets from Stoke-on-Trent Angling Society. Mr S Broadgate, 'Lynton', 5 Kingsfield Oval, Basford, Stoke-on-Trent ST4 6HN. Members only, some guest tickets allowed.
Baits/Methods: Normal carp fishing baits and methods
Control: Club. Bailiff: Mrs E Shapley. Tel: Wilmslow 520061.
BK Rating: Difficult
W/A: North West
Comments: This is one of the best big fish carp waters in the north west, but due to its large size it is not an easy water to succeed on. It has the potential to produce even bigger fish than at present. A 31 pounder was reported in 1990.

Rhodes Lodges

Location: Middleton, near Manchester
Type and Size: Old mill pits - one of 5 acres and two smaller ones
Carp Stock: Very well stocked with small carp, with some double figure mirrors and commons to about 15lbs
Category: Carp Water
Other Species: Some roach and perch
Permits: Day tickets on site
Control: Private
Restrictions: No night fishing; no season tickets
BK Rating: Moderate
W/A: North West
Comments: Heavily fished, crowded water open to all.

River Weaver

Location: Rises near Macclesfield and flows through Northwich to the Mersey
Type and Size: Short river
How to Find: Northwich area
Carp Stock: 100lb catches in a day reported, of carp to 5lbs and up to 9lbs
Category: Mixed Fishery
Other Species: General coarse fish
Permits: Enquire from local tackle shops
Cost: On application
BK Rating: Easy when carp are located
Control: Club
W/A: North West
Comments: Fish caught on match tackle - waggler and double maggot. Best area described as 'the boatyard' but we can't find out where this is! Above Vale Royal locks also said to be good. For information try Northwich AA, R Hankey, PO Box 18, Northwich - tickets supplied.

Roman Lakes

Location: Near Marple
Type and Size: Six acre lake, with islands and gravel bars
Carp Stock: Well stocked with many low doubles, up to just over 20lbs
Category: Carp Water
Other Species: Roach and tench
Permits: Day tickets from bailiff at the water
Cost: About £4 per day
Control: Private
Restrictions: Barbless hooks only; no night fishing; no multiple baits; no fishing on one side
BK Rating: Difficult
W/A: North West
Comments: A hard fished carp water, which is now quite difficult because the fish are well educated.

Sale Water Park

Location: Rifle Road, Sale.
Type and Size: Lake excavated to provide material to build the motorway, 55 acres
How to Find: Come off the M63 at junction 8
Carp Stock: Stocked with mirror carp in 1978, two years after the lake was completed. Numbers not known but there are now a reasonable head of carp mostly between 4 and 12lb, with some upper doubles and one or two lower twenties
Category: Mixed Fishery
Other Species: Catfish, grass carp, pike, eels, roach, perch, bream and tench
Permits: About £1 per day from office on site, or £1.80 from bailiff on bank during the weekends; 20p extra on Bank Holidays and at weekends. Season tickets: Adults £10; Junior £4.
Control: Mersey Valley Joint Committee. Tel: 061 969 7063.
BK Rating: Easy
Restrictions: Fishing 8am till sunset only, unless special night permit obtained
Baits/Methods: Legering with boilies best method
W/A: North West
Comments: Water is 80 feet deep in places and the very deep areas would not be likely to produce carp. This water is only 4½ miles from Manchester City Centre.

Shakerley Mere

Location: Allostock, near Northwich
Type and Size: Large mere
How to Find: Just off the M6 near Northwich
Carp Stock: Some carp to over 20lbs
Category: Mixed Fishery
Other Species: Tench, roach, perch, bream
Permits: Congleton Angling Society – try local tackle shops. Secretary: N J Bours, 8 Norfolk Road, Congleton.
Cost: On application
Control: Club
BK Rating: Insufficient information
W/A: North West
Comments: Formerly Council controlled. Local tackle shops have details; water advertised for sale in 1990.

Springwood Pool

Location: Mobberley, near Knutsford
Type and Size: Small pool
Carp Stock: Well stocked with carp to doubles
Category: Mixed Fishery
Other Species: Most common coarse fish
Permits: Congleton Anglers' Society. Secretary: Mr N Bours, 8 Norfolk Road, Congleton. Tel: Congleton 277284.
Cost: Membership costs £20 per season, with a £5 entry fee.
Control: Club
BK Rating: Moderate
W/A: North West

Statham Pool

Location: Lymm, near Warrington
Type and Size: Small pond
Carp Stock: Well stocked with carp to doubles
Category: Mixed Fishery
Other Species: Roach, bream, tench and perch
Permits: Day tickets from bailiff on bank – enquire local tackle shops for details.
Control: Club – name not known – possibly Lymm AA?
Restrictions: No night fishing
BK Rating: Moderate
W/A: North West

Stock Pool

Location: Capesthorne Estate, Siddington, Macclesfield
Type and Size: Estate stock pond of ¼ acre
Carp Stock: This water is well stocked with small carp and is ideal for youngsters or beginners.
Permits: Day tickets can be booked in advance from the bailiff: Mr A Bradley. Tel: 861584.
BK Rating: Easy

Taxmere

Location: Near Sandbach
Type and Size: Medium sized lake
Carp Stock: Some carp, numbers and sizes not known
Category: Mixed Fishery
Other Species: Bream, roach, tench, perch and pike
Permits: Day tickets from I F McDonald, 49 Welles Street, Sandbach.
Control: Club
BK Rating: Moderate
W/A: Severn-Trent

Tetton Lake

Location: Near Middlewich
Type and Size: Three acre lake
Carp Stock: Well stocked with carp to doubles and possibly larger
Category: Mixed Fishery
Other Species: Tench, bream and roach
Permits: An Association of local angling clubs - try local tackle shops for details.
Control: An Association of Middlewich AS, Middlewich British Legion and Middlewich Big Lock AC. Permits also include river fishing and 8 miles of two local canals.
BK Rating: Moderate
W/A: North West

Thorneycroft Hall Lakes

Location: Henbury, near Macclesfield
Type and Size: 2 lakes; Lower - 6 acres, Top - 12 acres
Carp Stock: Lower Lake - well stocked with plenty of small carp to 20lbs.
Top Lake - not many carp but some good ones to 19lbs
Category: Lower - Carp Water. Top - Few Carp
Other Species: Mixed coarse fish
Permits: Prince Albert Angling Society, season tickets only. Secretary: C Clarke, 2 Avon Close, Macclesfield.
Cost: About £35 entry fee plus £35 per season
Control: Club
BK Rating: Lower - Easy to Moderate. Top - Difficult
W/A: North West

Town Park Lake

Location: Housing estate on the outskirts of Runcorn; take the road to Castelfields and Norton Sports Centre - the lake is near the car park
Type and Size: Man-made lake of about 3 acres with an island
Carp Stock: Some carp to doubles
Category: Mixed Fishery
Other Species: Bream, pike, roach, perch, tench and gudgeon
Permits: Day tickets on bank
Cost: 15 pence!
Control: Council
BK Rating: Moderate
W/A: North West

Village Pool

Location: Whitley, near Warrington
Type and Size: Village pond of about ½ acre
How to Find: The pond is in the centre of the village of Whitley. Come off the M56 motorway at junction 10 and from Stretton take the A559 south of Whitley
Carp Stock: Quite well stocked with carp, most of which are mid-doubles to about 21lbs
Category: Mixed Fishery
Other Species: Usual coarse fish
Permits: Lymm Angling Club. Secretary: S Griffiths, 18 Manor Way, Lymm WA13 OAY.
Control: Club
BK Rating: Moderate
Baits/Methods: Normal carp fishing methods
W/A: North West

Wetgate Pool

Location: Near Lymm, west of Manchester
Type and Size: Tiny pond
Carp Stock: Well stocked with small carp – ideal for youngsters
Category: Mixed Fishery
Other Species: Rudd and tench
Permits: Members only water of Lymm Angling Club. Secretary: S Griffiths, 18 Manor Road, Lymm. Tel: 092575 2763.
Control: Club
Restrictions: No night fishing
BK Rating: Easy
W/A: Severn-Trent

Whirley Pool

Location: Henbury, near Macclesfield
Type and Size: Small pit
Carp Stock: Said to be quite well stocked with small carp to mid-double figure size
Category: Mixed Fishery
Permits: Prince Albert Angling Society. Secretary: C Clarke, 2 Avon Close, Macclesfield.
Cost: About £35 entry fee plus £35 annual subscription. Season tickets only.
Control: Club
BK Rating: Thought to be Moderate
W/A: North West
Comments: It will be noticed that whilst the cost of joining Prince Albert Angling Society is high compared with many clubs, they have a number of very fine carp waters, all on the same ticket.

Whitemere

Location: About one mile from the town of Ellesmere, on the Shrewsbury road
Type and Size: Large lake
Carp Stock: Some carp to doubles
Category: Mixed Fishery

Other Species: Roach, bream, tench, perch and pike
Permits: Ellesmere AC
Control: Club
BK Rating: Difficult
W/A: North West
Comments: This mere is also used for sailing, and not all of the lake can be fished. It is also a Site of Special Scientific Interest (S.S.S.I.), and care must be taken only to use marked paths, and to observe all rules and notices.

Winterley Pool

Location: Winterley Farm, Wheelock, near Sandbach
Type and Size: Pleasant 8 acre lake, rather snaggy and surrounded by trees
Carp Stock: Plenty of small carp to doubles, and a few 20's to about 25lbs
Category: Mixed Fishery
Other Species: Usual coarse fish
Permits: Day tickets on bank
Cost: £3 per rod; £5 for 24 hours
Control: Private
BK Rating: Moderate
W/A: North West

Woodlands Lake

Location: Allostock, near Knutsford, just off the M6
Type and Size: 10 acre lake, with two other lakes on site
Carp Stock: Not many carp, but most are doubles to about 20lbs
Permits: Prince Albert AS, J T Lovatt, 63 Beggerman's Lane, Knutsford or Queens Hotel, Waters Green, Macclesfield.
Control: Club - season tickets only
Restrictions: No day tickets - check before night fishing.
BK Rating: Fairly Hard
W/A: North West

CLEVELAND

Ascott Ponds

Location: Cleveland, North Yorkshire border
Type and Size: Three small lakes
Carp Stock: Not known, some carp
Category: Few Carp
Other Species: Trout, tench, bream, dace, perch, gudgeon
Permits: D Speight, 10 Stainsby Gate, Thornaby, Cleveland.
Control: Club
BK Rating: Moderate
W/A: Northumbrian
Comments: Little is known about this fairly new water.

Hemlington Lake

Location: Hemlington, near Middlesbrough
Type and Size: Large lake, much used for match fishing
Carp Stock: Well stocked with small carp
Category: Mixed Fishery
Other Species: Crucians, bream and roach
Permits: Try Cleveland Angling Centre, Hemlington for permits and information.
Control: Club
BK Rating: Easy
W/A: Northumbrian
Comments: No close season – we weren't able to find out much about this water, but local enquiry may help, as there are few waters containing carp in this area.

Hutton Rudby Ponds

Location: Near Middlesbrough
Type and Size: Small ponds
Carp Stock: Some carp
Category: Mixed Fishery
Other Species: Roach, perch and bream
Permits: Members only water of Middlesbrough AC - membership open to all from Redcar Angling Centre, Cleveland Angling Centre, Thornaby, Adams Tackle, Darlington and Middlesbrough and the Tackle Box, Billingham.
Cost: £12 per season, with a £6 joining fee, to include other waters; Juniors half price
Control: Club
Restrictions: No night fishing; members only
BK Rating: Not known
W/A: Northumbrian

New Marske Reservoir

Location: Near Middlesbrough
Type and Size: 10 acre reservoir
Carp Stock: Well stocked with carp to over 20lbs
Category: Mixed Fishery
Other Species: Bream, roach, tench and perch
Permits: Redcar Angling Centre, High Street, Middlesbrough.
Cost: £2 per day
Control: Middlesbrough AC
Restrictions: No night fishing
BK Rating: Not known
W/A: Northumbrian
Comments: No close season

CLWYD (Wales)

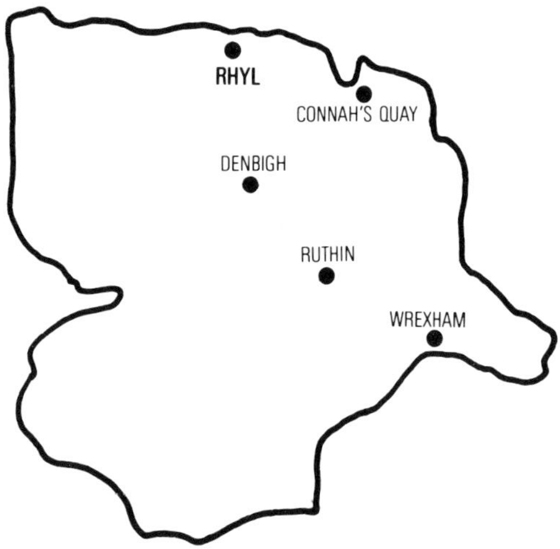

Llay Reservoir

Location: Llay, near Wrexham
Type and Size: Small reservoir
Carp Stock: Some carp, numbers and sizes not known
Category: Mixed Fishery
Other Species: Tench, rudd, perch and pike
Permits: Members only water of Llay A.A. J Henshaw, 2 Queens Terrace, Mold Road, Cefn-y-Bedd, Wrexham, Wales.
Cost: About £6 per year
BK Rating: Moderate
W/A: Welsh

Ponky Pool

Location: Johnstown, Wrexham
Type and Size: 1½ acre pond
Carp Stock: Well stocked with carp to upper doubles
Category: Mixed Fishery
Other Species: Roach, tench and bream
Permits: Day tickets at low cost from Morris Tackle, Wrexham. Tel: 0978 364450.
Control: Local club?
Restrictions: No night fishing
BK Rating: Moderate
W/A: Welsh
Comments: There might be a 20 or two in this pond.

Swan Lake

Location: Near Connah's Quay, Deeside
Type and Size: 5 acre lake
Carp Stock: Well stocked with carp to 20lbs
Category: Mixed Fishery
Other Species: Tench and roach
Permits: Connahs Quay and District AC. P Ryan, 5 New Brighton Road, Sychdyn, Mold.
Restrictions: Members only - no day tickets; no night fishing.
Control: Club
BK Rating: Moderate
W/A: Welsh
Comments: Connahs Quay AC also has Wepre Park Lake in the area, which contains good carp; on the same ticket.

The Flash

Location: Gresford, Llay, near Wrexham
Type and Size: Small lake
Carp Stock: Some carp, numbers and sizes not known
Category: Mixed Fishery
Other Species: Tench, pike and rudd
Permits: Members only water of Llay AS - J Henshaw, 2 Queens Terrace, Mold Road, Cefn-y-Bedd, Wrexham.
Cost: About £6 per year
Control: Club
BK Rating: Not known
W/A: Welsh

A mid-double common from Angler's Paradise, Devon

CORNWALL

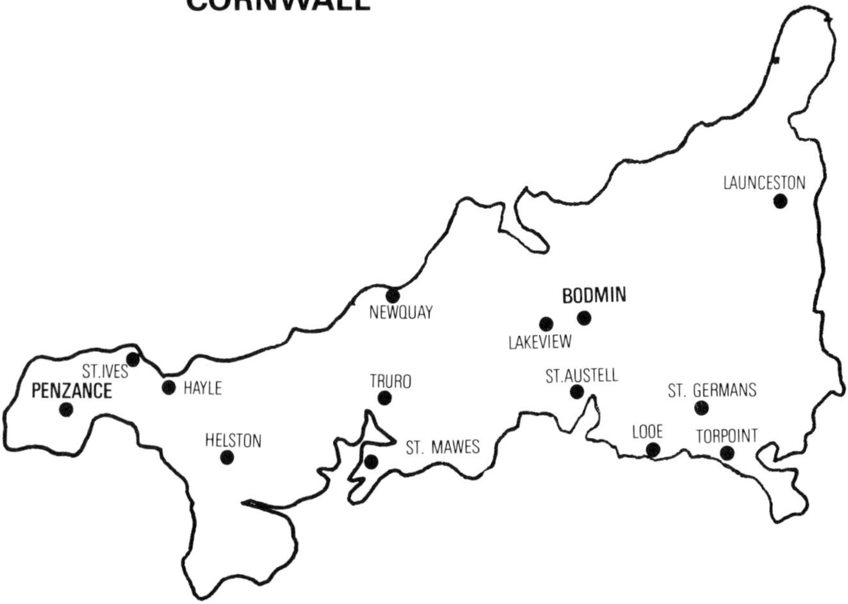

Avallon Holiday Park

A

Location:	Near Newquay
Type and Size:	Small lake on dairy farm
Carp Stock:	Well stocked with carp to doubles
Category:	Mixed Fishery
Other Species:	Bream, tench and roach
Permits:	For information and permits phone 0502 501501.
Control:	Private
BK Rating:	Not known
W/A:	South West
Comments:	This is a small site on a farm, with self-catering Norwegian Pine Lodges to rent for holidays with fishing; open all year - no close season.

Bilberry Pool

Location:	Bilberry, near Roche
Type and Size:	Old pit of about 5 acres
How to Find:	Roche is on the B3274 road between St. Austell and Newquay
Carp Stock:	Carp to mid doubles
Category:	Mixed Fishery
Other Species:	Rudd and tench
Permits:	Roche Angling Club. Membership available from D Burn, Angling Centre, 25 Penpol Terrace, Hayle. Tel: Hayle 754292.
Control:	Club
BK Rating:	Moderate
W/A:	South West
Comments:	Roche Angling Club have carp in some waters; details from the address given above. No close season.

Bolingey Lake A

Location:	Penwartha Road, Bolingey, Perranporth TR6 ODH
Type and Size:	Lake of 4 acres
How to Find:	From Perranporth take the road towards Cos Hill, and turn right at the crossroads towards Bolingey. Pass the Post Office on your right and the Bolingey Inn, and the entrance to the lake will be seen on your left
Carp Stock:	Well stocked with carp to about 22lbs. 100 doubles
Category:	Mixed Fishery
Other Species:	Tench, roach, rudd, perch and trout
Permits:	From the site lodge. Tel: Truro 572388.
Cost:	£4 per day for 2 rods
Restrictions:	No night fishing. No keepnets or sacks. April to October.
Control:	Private
BK Rating:	Very Easy
W/A:	South West
Comments:	Tackle and comprehensive range of bait and snacks and drinks on site. No close season. Carp tackle hired on site. Accommodation at an anglers pub - The Airways, St. Mawgan. Tel: 0637 860595. Voted one of Britain's top ten waters in Angling Times Yearbook!

Bude Canal A

Location:	From the sea at Bude
How to Find:	Town of Bude
Type and Size:	Shallow old canal about 2 miles long and 2ft to 8ft deep
Carp Stock:	Said to be fairly numerous, mostly to 10lbs. Commons to 20lbs caught in recent years by Gerry Savage of Lakeview Country Club, Lanivet, Bodmin.
Category:	Mixed Fishery
Other Species:	Tench, roach, perch and big eels
Cost:	£1 day tickets, £5 for week from Tourist Info Centre, Bude. Hotels - The Globe, The Strand
Permits:	On the bank, or from tackle shops in Bude
Restrictions:	No fishing from 1st April to end of May
BK Rating:	Difficult
W/A:	South West
Baits/Methods:	Normal carp tactics and baits
Control:	Club. Bude Canal Angling Association. Day tickets, P Braund, Wesley House, Leven Terrace, Bude
Comments:	Clear weedy water, like many disused canals

Bussow

Location:	Near St. Ives
Type and Size:	Reservoir of 4 acres
How to Find:	Take the B3306 from St. Ives. Turn left onto the B3311 and then right. The entrance to the reservoir is then on the left.
Carp Stock:	Moderately stocked with carp to 16lbs
Category:	Mixed Fishery
Other Species:	Eels to 10lb, tench, bream, rudd and roach
Permits:	Ken's Tackle, 9 Beachfield Court, The Promenade, Penzance. Tel: (0736) 61969; Lanxon's Sports, 18 Causewayhead, Penzance Tel: (0736) 62736; The Shirehorse Inn, Towendnack Road, Hessesveor, St. Ives. Tel: (0736) 796724; Newtown Angling Centre, Germoe. Tel: (0736) 763721.
Cost:	Day £2.50. Concession rate for OAP's SDP/MOB, students and children

	under 16 £1.50: 24 hours £5: 7 day castabout (valid at all Peninsular Coarse Fisheries, except Jennetts and Crafthole), day £15, concession day £10: Day and night £30. No season permits.
Control:	Mr Dell Mills, Manager, Peninsular Coarse Fisheries, St Cleer Depot, Liskeard, Cornwall PL14 6EQ. Tel: (0579) 43929.
W/A:	South West Water
BK Rating:	Moderate
Restrictions:	No keepnets for carp. Barbless hooks requested. Permits must be obtained before fishing.
Comments:	No closed season

Choone Farm

Location:	Choone Farm, St. Buryan, Penzance. Tel: 0736 810220
Type and Size:	Two small lakes
Carp Stock:	Well stocked with carp to at least 10lbs
Category:	Mixed Fishery
Other Species:	Tench, rudd and perch
Permits:	From Mr V B Care at the address above.
Control:	Private
Restrictions:	No night fishing - open 7am to 8pm in summer
W/A:	South West
Comments:	No close season

Chyraise Lodge Hotel A

Location:	Millpool, Goldsithney, Penzance TR20 9JD
Type and Size:	Two large lakes ½ mile from hotel
How to Find:	Just off the A394 between Helston and Marazion
Carp Stock:	Some carp, numbers not known
Category:	Mixed Fishery
Other Species:	Tench, bream, roach
Permits:	From hotel. Tel: 0736 763485.
Cost:	On application
BK Rating:	Insufficient information
Control:	Private
W/A:	Southern
Comments:	No close season. There are carp in some other waters in the Marazion area. Accommodation/holidays in hotel.

College

Location:	Near Falmouth
Type and Size:	Reservoir of 38 acres
How to Find:	Take the A38 from Falmouth to Penryn, then turn onto the B3291. A right turn will then take you into the car park
Carp Stock:	The reservoir is well stocked with carp to 32lbs, with a good number in the 20-30lbs bracket. It was restocked in 1990 with 1850 carp to 15lbs and early 1991 with commons to 22lbs
Category:	Mixed Fishery
Other Species:	Tench to 8½lbs, bream to 8lbs 6ozs, eels to 7lbs, roach, rudd and perch
Permits:	Day permits from the self service unit at Argal car park: Ken's Tackle, 9 Beachfield Court, The Promenade, Penzance. Tel: (0736) 61969: Newtown Angling Centre, Germoe. Tel: (0736) 763721. Season permits

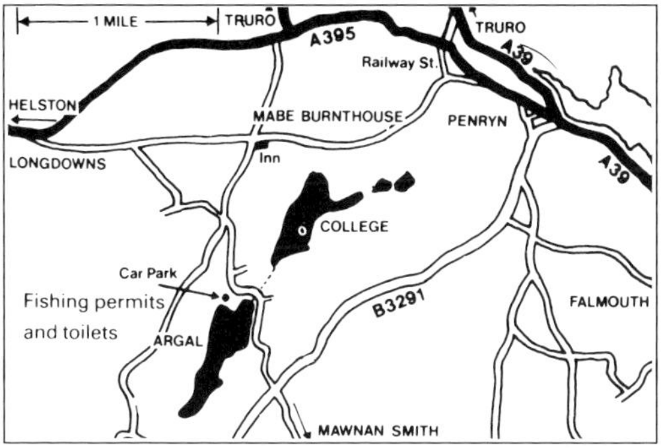

from the Ranger, Bob Evans, Little Argal Farm, Budock, Penryn, Cornwall. Tel: (0326) 72544.

Cost: Day £3. Concession rate for OAP's, SDP/MOB and students £2, children under 16 £1.50: 24 hour permits £6.00: 7 day castabout, (valid at all Peninsular Coarse Fisheries, except Jennetts and Crafthole), day £15, concession day £10: Day and night £30: Castabout season permits, (valid for College, Porth, Lower Tamar, Slade and Squabmoor), day £45, concession OAP's, SDP/MOB and students £30, children under 16 £15: Day and night £67.50.

Control: Mr Dell Mills, Manager, Peninsular Coarse Fisheries, St Cleer Depot, Liskeard, Cornwall PL14 6EQ. Tel: (0579) 43929.

W/A: South West

BK Rating: Moderate

Restrictions: No cereal based groundbaits, except swimfeeders. No keepnets for carp. Barbless hooks requested. Permits must be obtained before fishing.

Comments: Mature and picturesque water with NO CLOSED SEASON. Night fishing is now allowed. Long casting is necessary to reach deep water from some areas. Long stay carp anglers generally do well.

Crafthole

Location: Village of Crafthole, near Torpoint

Type and Size: Disused reservoir of 2 acres

How to Find: Leave the A38, Plymouth to Liskeard road at Trerulefoot roundabout onto the A374, towards Torpoint. After Sheviock turn right to Crafthole. The pathway to the reservoir is almost opposite Crafthole Post Office

Carp Stock: Very heavily stocked with carp to 22lbs

Category: Carp Water

Other Species: Tench

Permits: Day permits only, (one hour before sunrise to one hour after sunset), from Post Office Store, Crafthole, St. Germans. Tel: (0503) 30225. Limited day permits.

Cost: Day £3. Concession rate for OAP's, SDP/MOB and students £2, children under 16 £1.50. No season permits.

Control: Mr Dell Mills, Manager, Peninsular Coarse Fisheries, St Cleer Depot, Liskeard, Cornwall PL14 6EQ. Tel: (0579) 43929.

W/A: South West

BK Rating: Small carp: Very Easy. Larger carp: Easy

Restrictions: Children under 16 must be accompanied by an adult. No cereal based groundbaits. No keepnets for carp. Barbless hooks requested. Permits must be obtained before fishing.

Comments: NO CLOSED SEASON. Very popular and attractive water, deep in a valley and surrounded by mature trees and hedgerows. Limited permits, so advance booking is sensible. Due to the rather long and steep climb from the water, this venue is not recommended for the elderly or infirm.

Dutson Water A

Location: Lower Dutson farm, Launceston
Type and Size: Old clay pit, about an acre
How to Find: Take the A388 road from Launceston to Barnstable. Lower Dutson Farm is about two miles from Launceston
Carp Stock: Fairly well stocked with carp to about 15lbs
Category: Mixed Fishery
Other Species: Perch, rudd, tench, crucians
Permits: From the farmer Mr E Broad at the farm. Tel: Launceston 2607.
Control: Private
Restrictions: No groundbaiting
BK Rating: Moderate
W/A: South West
Comments: Some weed and depths to about 10ft. Float fishing or legering methods can be used and luncheon meat and bread will catch carp. Many small rudd. There are sometimes caravans at the water and there is also a cottage to rent.

Forda Holiday Lodges A

Location: Kilkhampton, near Bude
Type and Size: Small lake
How to Find: Near Bude on the north coast
Carp Stock: Some carp to double figures
Category: Mixed Fishery
Other Species: Bream, rudd, tench
Permits: On site. Tel: 028 882 413
Cost: On application
BK Rating: Not known
Control: Private
W/A: Southern
Comments: No close season. Scandinavian style self-catering lodges for 4/5 people by lake. Near Tamar Lake and Bude Canal. Sandy beaches 10 minutes. Other accommodation: Tamar Lake Farm, near Bude. Stable and barn cottages and caravan. Tel: 028 882 426 for details and brochures

Lakeview Country Club A

Location: Old Coach Road, Lanivet, Bodmin. Tel: 0208 831011
Type and Size: Three lakes, dug in 1988; carp lake 2½ acres, stream-fed with island
How to Find: Where the A391 St. Austell road joins the A30 Bodmin by-pass, take the second exit at the roundabout, keeping in the outside lane, signposted 'Truro'. After 30 yards, turn right to Wheal Prosper, and in half a mile, turn left at the crossroads. Lakeview is in half a mile, on the right hand side

Carp Stock:	Long Island, the carp lake, is heavily stocked with many doubles and about 10 twenties, most of which are commons to 25lbs plus; the Cornish record common was caught here
Category:	Carp Water
Other Species:	A few big tench only
Permits:	Day tickets from the Lodge, or on bank from Gerry Savage or Frank Barry. Free to residents in 1991, but expected to be a charge for 1992
Cost:	£4.50 per day for two rods; juniors/OAP's £2.50 per day

Gerry Savage, of Lakeview Country Club, Cornwall, with his 25¾lb Cornish record common, caught from Long Island Pool at the club

Control: David and Barbara Daw, Lakeview Country Club
Restrictions: Night fishing by arrangement with Gerry Savage, for residents only; no baiting with shelf-life boilies.
Baits/Methods: Standard methods work well, with boilies, sweetcorn and luncheon meat
BK Rating: Moderate
W/A: South West
Comments: There are two other lakes at the Club - Moorland Lake, which is small, and contains some mirrors to about 8lbs, and the 3 acre Wood Pool, which has some small carp; both contain other species. Fishery Manager is Gerry Savage, one of the most successful carp anglers of all time, and former BBC radio angling programme presenter. For up to date information on the fishing, phone Gerry Savage at his Lodge and tackle shop on 0208 831079. Although a comparatively new water, this is rapidly becoming one of the best places in the country for top class carp fishing, with luxury accommodation.

There are over 60 A-Frame Lodges (very popular with the children), and fabulous detached bungalows, each set well away from anyone else, many with dishwashers, spa baths, and en-suite shower, and all self catering, with an outside barbecue. The Country Club, close to the carp lake, has a heated indoor swimming pool, sauna, solarium, fitness room, snooker room, and a first class restaurant. There is a shop and just about every conceivable facility for a luxury holiday for the family at reasonable prices - and all within sight of the big carp being caught! Outside there are tennis courts, pitch and putt golf course, facilities for other sports, and an 18 hole golf course, an hotel, and sports centre is planned for 1993.

This is one where we have been fortunate enough to stay, and we were very impressed with the fishing, the friendly but 'up-market' atmosphere of the country club, the pleasant surroundings and the beautiful detached bungalow, well away from others, and easily good enough for a permanent home. Lakeview is very strongly recommended, both for fishing and holidays; it is situated right in the centre of Cornwall, with easy access to both coasts, and is ideal for a day's fishing or for a long, luxurious family holiday.

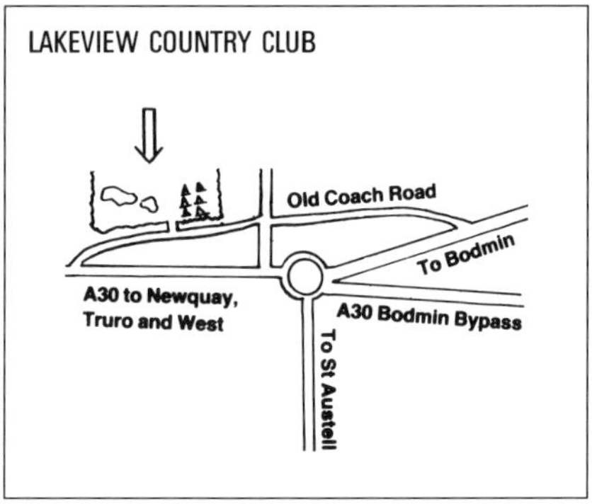

Langarth Pool

Location: 99 Polstain Road, Threemilestone, Truro. Tel: 0872 75638
Type and Size: Two three quarter acre ponds
Carp Stock: Well stocked with carp to double figures
Category: Mixed Fishery
Other Species: Tench, roach, rudd, bream and perch
Permits: From Des Hart at the address above.
Cost: £2.50 per day; £6 per week; season - £15; reduced prices for children and OAP's
Control: Private
BK Rating: Not known
W/A: South West
Comments: No close season; open 24 hours a day. Swims for the disabled.

Mellonwatts Mill Fishery

Location: Pensagillas Farm, Grampound, Truro - on the main road from Grampound to Mevagissey. Tel:087 253 232
Type and Size: 2¼ acre farm pond
Carp Stock: Well stocked with carp to doubles
Category: Mixed Fishery
Other Species: Crucians, tench, roach and rudd
Permits: From A W P Kent at the address above.
Cost: £2.50 per day; £10 per week; £35 per season. Reduced prices for children and OAP's.
Control: Private
Restrictions: No night fishing - open dawn till dusk only
BK Rating: Not known
W/A: South West
Comments: No close season. Camping, barbecues and picnic areas.

Neets Valley Park

Location: Near Bude
Type and Size: Small lake
Carp Stock: Well stocked with carp
Category: Mixed Fishery
Other Species: Tench and rudd
Permits: Full details and permits from Russell Baker, 02888 395.
Cost: £3.50 per day - half price for juniors
Control: Private
BK Rating: Not known
W/A: South West
Comments: This water was stocked in 1988, but had not been fished until 1991, so the potential is unknown. No close season.

Old St. Erth

Location: St. Erth, near Penzance
Type and Size: 2½ acre lake
Carp Stock: Well stocked with carp to 20lbs plus
Category: Mixed Fishery
Other Species: Bream, roach, and some other coarse fish

Permits:	Marazion Angling Club. W T Knott, Little Bosvenning, Newbridge, Penzance. Tel: 0736 65638; The Shop, Newtown. Tel: 0736 763721; Ken's Tackle, Penzance. Tel: 0736 61969.
Cost:	Day - £2.50; annual visitors - £10; annual - £25
Control:	Club
Restrictions:	Night fishing by arrangement only
BK Rating:	Moderate
W/A:	South West
Comments:	No close season. Permit includes several other waters.

Porth

Location:	Near St. Mawgan Airfield, Newquay
Type and Size:	Reservoir of 40 acres
How to Find:	From Bodmin, leave the A30 at Indian Queens and join the A39 towards Wadebridge. At St. Columb Major, turn left onto the A3059. Turn left at the water tower and the reservoir will be found on the left, after about three quarters of a mile
Carp Stock:	Moderately stocked with carp to 17lbs
Category:	Mixed Fishery
Other Species:	Tench to 10lbs, bream to 9lbs 2ozs, roach, perch and rudd
Permits:	Day or day and night permits from the self service unit at the car park: Ken's Tackle, 9 Beachfield Court, The Promenade, Penzance. Tel: (0736) 61969: Newtown Angling Centre, Germoe. Tel: (0736) 763721. Season permits from Mrs P Ford, The Bungalow, Porth Reservoir. Tel: (0637) 879481.
Cost:	Day £3. Concession rate for OAP's, SDP/MOB and students £2, children under 16 £1.50: 24 hours £6: 7 day castabout, (valid at all Peninsular Coarse Fisheries, except Jennetts and Crafthole), day £15, concession day £10: Day and night £30: Castabout season permits, (valid for College, Porth, Lower Tamar, Slade and Squabmoor), day £45, concession OAP's, SDP/MOB and students £30, children under 16 £15: Day and night £65.50.
Control:	Mr Dell Mills, Manager, Peninsular Coarse Fisheries, St Cleer Depot, Liskeard, Cornwall PL14 6EQ. Tel: (0579) 43929.
W/A:	South West
BK Rating:	Fairly Hard
Restrictions:	No cereal based groundbaits except swimfeeders. No keepnets for carp. Barbless hooks requested. Permits must be obtained before fishing.
Comments:	NO CLOSED SEASON. Night fishing now allowed.

Retallack Water

Location:	Frontier City Wild West Theme Park, near Newquay
Type and Size:	4 acre lake
Carp Stock:	Well stocked with carp to double figures
Category:	Mixed Fishery
Other Species:	Very large perch, and some other species
Permits:	Day tickets on site
Control:	Private
BK Rating:	Moderate
W/A:	South West
Comments:	No close season. There is a proposal at present to allow jet water ski-ing on this lake, which could ruin it for anglers.

Rosewater Lake A

Location: Hendravossan Farm, Rose, Truro. Tel: 0872 573992/572261/573040
Type and Size: 1½ acre lake, with another soon to be built
Carp Stock: Well stocked with carp, numbers and sizes not known
Category: Mixed Fishery
Other Species: Crucians, tench, roach, rudd, perch and chub
Permits: From Mike or Andy Waters at the address above
Cost: Day - £3; evening - £1.50; second rod - £1
Control: Private
Restrictions: Barbless hooks; no keepnets; no night fishing - open dawn till dusk only.
BK Rating: Not known
W/A: South West
Comments: No close season. Bed and breakfast available at certain times of the year. Caravan Club.

Sharkey's Pit

Location: Strawberry Lane, Joppa, Hayle - one mile from Hayle Town Centre
Type and Size: 2½ acre lake
Carp Stock: Some carp to double figures
Category: Mixed Fishery
Other Species: Tench, crucians, roach, rudd, gudgeon, golden orfe
Permits: Self service at fishery
Cost: On application from Dave and Jenny Burn at the above address
Control: Private
Restrictions: No night fishing
BK Rating: Moderate
W/A: South West
Comments: No close season - fishing dawn to dusk.

Shillamill Lakes A

Location: Lanreath, Looe off the B3359
Type and Size: Four small dammed lakes
Carp Stock: Heavily stocked with commons and mirrors to 10lb. Some doubles and a few 20's to 25lbs reported - record fish 33lbs 2oz
Category: Mixed Fishery
Other Species: Roach, rudd, tench, perch
Permits: John Facey, Shillamill Lakes, Lanreath, Looe, Cornwall. Tel: 0503 20271 Day and week permits.
Cost: Day tickets £3.50 for one rod. Weekly £12
Baits/Methods: Normal carp baits and methods
Control: Private commercial fishery, day and season tickets
Restrictions: Brolly camps must be booked in advance - night fishing by arrangement only.
BK Rating: Easy
W/A: South West
Comments: Commercial fishery with caravans and accommodation in flats and cottages. No close season. Meals and bar snacks. Games room and TV in the Old Mill Country Club.

St. Germans Lake

Location: St. Germans, 1½ miles off the A38 between Saltash and Liskeard
Type and Size: Two acre lake
Carp Stock: Well stocked with carp to double figures
Category: Mixed Fishery
Other Species: Roach, rudd, perch, tench and bream
Permits: Clives Bait and Tackle, Exeter Street, Plymouth.
Cost: £2 per day
Control: Plymouth and District Coarse Angling Club
BK Rating: Moderate
W/A: South West
Comments: No close season

St. Tinney Farm Holidays A

Location: Otterham, near Penzance PL32 9TA. Tel: 08406 274
Type and Size: Small farm lakes
Carp Stock: Well stocked with carp to doubles
Category: Mixed Fishery
Other Species: Tench, rudd, roach, bream, perch and trout
Permits: From St. Tinney Farm
Control: Private
BK Rating: Not known
W/A: South West
Comments: Comfortable chalets to rent for self-catering holidays with fishing. 70 acre farm off the A39 coastal road in north Cornwall. Free colour brochure. No close season.

Tindeen Fishery

Location: Bostrase, Goldsithney, Penzance. Tel: 073676 3486
Type and Size: Three small pools of about one acre each
Carp Stock: Some carp, number and sizes not known
Category: Either Few Carp or Mixed Fishery
Other Species: Tench, rudd, roach and perch
Permits: From G J Laity at the above address
Cost: £2 per day; £1.50 for under 14's
Control: Private
Restrictions: Night fishing by arrangement only
BK Rating: Not known
W/A: South West
Comments: No close season.

Tredidon Barton Lake

Location: Near Launceston
Type and Size: Small farm pond
Carp Stock: Some carp, best reported 23¾lbs
Category: Mixed Fishery
Other Species: Tench and some other coarse fish
Permits: G Jones. Tel: 056-686-288
Cost: About £2 per day
Control: Private

BK Rating: Moderate
W/A: South West
Comments: No close season - open all the year round.

Trenestrall Lake

Location: Trenestrall Farm, Ruan High Lanes, near St. Mawes. Tel: 0872 501259
Type and Size: 2 acre lake on the King Harry Ferry road
Carp Stock: Well stocked with carp to at least 10lbs
Category: Mixed Fishery
Other Species: Tench and roach
Permits: From Mr Palmer at the above address
Cost: £1.50 per day
Control: Private
BK Rating: Not known
W/A: South West
Comments: No close season

Trevella Caravan and Camping Park A

Location: Crantock, Newquay. Tel: 0637 830308
Type and Size: Two man-made lakes of about 2 acres each
How to Find: Take the A30 to Indian Queens, turn right onto the A392, and follow the Newquay signs to Quintrell Downs roundabout. Take the Crantock road to the Trevemper Bridge roundabout, then turn left onto the A3075 Redruth road. In 200 yards you will see the signpost to Crantock
Carp Stock: Both lakes well stocked with carp including some twenties - best fish a mirror of 27¾lbs, caught in 1990
Category: Mixed Fishery
Other Species: Tench to 6lbs, bream, roach and rudd
Permits: Free at reception to all residents
BK Rating: Moderate
Control: Trevella Caravan Park
Restrictions: None listed
W/A: South West
Comments: A very attractive site with many facilities, such as showers, launderette, childrens play area, heated swimming pool, restaurant, shop, games room etc. Lakes are on a Nature Reserve, with a new third lake nearby. Beautiful sandy beaches within half a mile. Featured in 'Coarse Fishing Today' (Angling Times) in February 1991, with a picture of Gerry Savage with a 23 pounder from the lake. Ideal for a family holiday with good fishing, and only an hour's drive from anywhere in Cornwall - 41 miles to Land's End. 4 to 8 berth caravans to rent from £115 per week to £429 per week, according to size of van and season. Sites to rent nightly for your own caravans, with no charge for tents, touring caravans, or motorhomes - electrical hook-up £1.75 per night. No close season.

Wheal Grey Pool

Location: Ashton, on the main Penzance-Helston road
Type and Size: Old 4 acre pit
Carp Stock: Well stocked with carp to 20lbs
Category: Mixed Fishery

Other Species: Bream, roach, rudd
Permits: Marazion Angling Club. W T Knott, Little Bosvenning, Newbridge, Penzance. Tel: 0736 65638; The Shop, Newtown. Tel: 0736 763721; Ken's Tackle, Penzance. Tel: 0736 61969.
Cost: Day - £2.50, £1.50 for juniors; annual visitor - £10; annual - £25
Control: Club
Restrictions: Night fishing by arrangement only
BK Rating: Moderate
W/A: South West
Comments: No close season. Permit includes several other waters.

Woodley Farm A

Location: Herodsfoot, Liskeard
How to Find: Near Liskeard
Type and Size: Five small farm lakes
Carp Stock: Well stocked with carp to 24lbs
Category: Mixed Fishery
Other Species: Tench, roach, rudd
Permits: A T Hawke, Woodley Farm, Herodsfoot, Liskeard. Tel: 0503 20221
Control: Private
BK Rating: Easy
W/A: South West
Comments: Holiday fishery with self catering country cottages. Picturesque surroundings. No close season.

Anna Gregorek, of Angler's Paradise, Devon with her first big carp

CUMBRIA

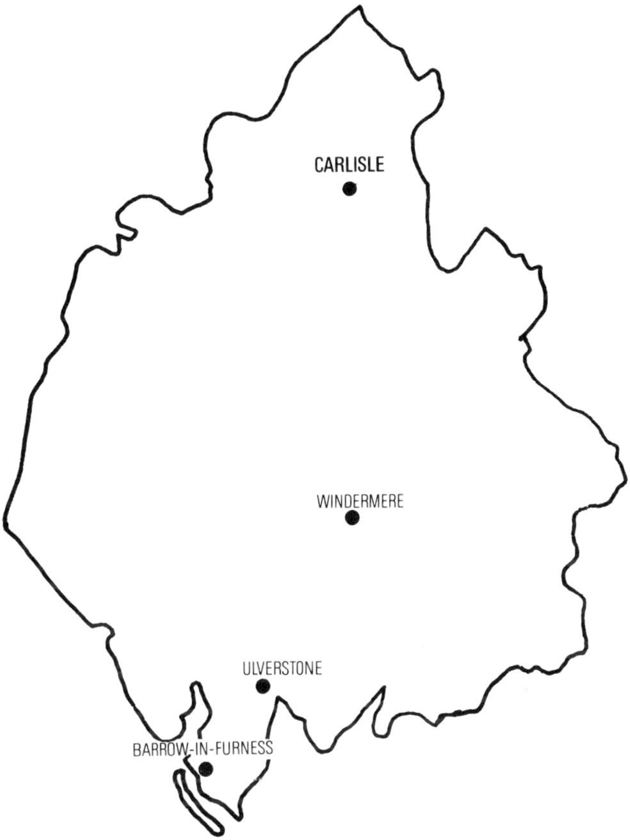

Bigland Hall Lake

Location: Ulverstone, close to the canal
Type and Size: Small lake
Carp Stock: Some small carp to about 6lbs
Category: Few Carp
Other Species: Roach and tench
Permits: Day tickets from local tackle shops
Control: Local club, name not known
Restrictions: No night fishing
BK Rating: Difficult, due to hordes of other species
W/A: North West
Comments: No close season

Brayton Pond

Location: Brayton Hall Farm, Aspatria
Type and Size: Large shallow lake of the farm type; 8 acres
How to Find: Take the A596 from Carlisle, 15 miles west to Brayton
Carp Stock: Very heavily stocked with genuine wild carp to about 8lbs. Fish up to 12lbs reported
Other Species: Crucians
Permits: Day tickets from the farm. Must be bought in advance.
Control: Private. Mr R H Ward, Home Farm, Brayton, Aspatria. Tel: Aspatria 20262.
BK Rating: Easy
Restrictions: No night fishing
W/A: North West
Comments: Heavily fished, especially at weekends. Many matches are held. Cafe.

Cleabarrow Lake

Location: Near the golf course at Windermere; take B5284 to Bowness
Type and Size: Small lake
Carp Stock: Well stocked with carp to 10lbs
Category: Carp Water
Permits: Day tickets from Smyths Record Shop, Ashe Street, Bowness-on-Windermere
Control: Private
Restrictions: No night fishing
BK Rating: Moderate
W/A: North West

Holehird Tarn

Location: Near Windermere, off the A592
Type and Size: Three acre Lake District tarn
Carp Stock: Quite well stocked with carp to 10lbs, and one or two low doubles
Category: Mixed Fishery
Other Species: Coarse fish including perch; some trout
Permits: Day tickets on site
Control: Private
BK Rating: Moderate
W/A: North West

Mockerkin Tarn

Location: Mockerkin, near Loweswater
Type and Size: Small tarn
How to Find: Just off the A5086 Cockermouth road, west of Loweswater village
Carp Stock: Well stocked with carp, sizes unknown
Category: Carp Water
Other Species: Not known
Permits: Day and week tickets from The Gun Shop, Lorton Street, Cockermouth.
Cost: On application
BK Rating: Insufficient information
Control: Cockermouth Angling Association

W/A: North West
Comments: This water has been stocked with carp by the club and we can find out little about it, but as there are so few carp in Cumbria...

Roanhead Fisheries

Location: Near Barrow-in-Furness
Type and Size: Six very deep pits of about 10 acres
Carp Stock: Quite a few carp to well over 20lbs
Category: Mixed Fishery
Other Species: Roach and rudd; big eels
Permits: Members only water of Furness AA, Hannay, 50 Crellin Street, Barrow.
Cost: About £10 per year
Control: Club
BK Rating: Difficult
W/A: North West

Ulverston Canal

Location: Ulverston, near Barrow-in-Furness, southern Lake District
Type and Size: Short, narrow canal
Carp Stock: Restocked water containing some carp, numbers and sizes not known
Category: Mixed Fishery
Other Species: Tench, roach and other coarse fish
Permits: Day and season tickets from the Canal Tavern Inn, Ulverston; Angling and Hiking Centre, 62 Forshaw Street, Barrow-in-Furness.
Cost: About £2 per day, £15 per season
Control: Ulverston Angling Association. H B Whittam, 29 Lyndhurst Road, Ulverston.
BK Rating: Difficult
W/A: North West

DERBYSHIRE

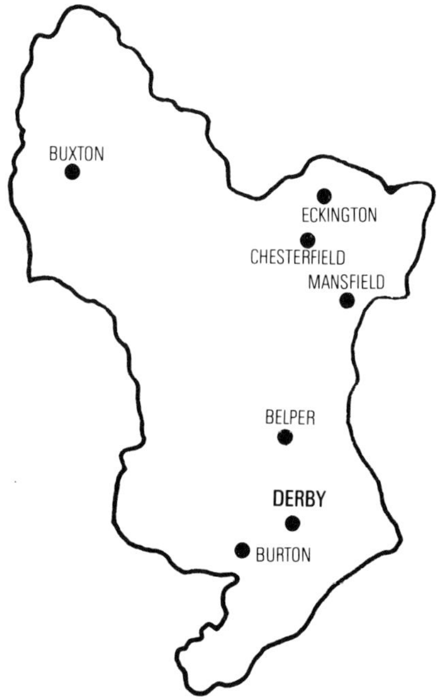

Chapel Wheel Dam

Location: Just outside Chesterfield
Type and Size: Old reservoir of about 10 acres
Carp Stock: Lake stocked long ago, but contains a few good carp
Category: Few Carp
Other Species: Mixed coarse fish
Permits: Enquire locally - no details obtainable
Control: Possibly small local angling club - name not known
Restrictions: No night fishing
BK Rating: Super-Difficult
W/A: Severn-Trent

Codnor Park Reservoir

Location: Ambergate, near Belper
Type and Size: Small reservoir
Carp Stock: Some carp, sizes not known
Category: Mixed Fishery
Other Species: Roach, bream, tench and pike
Permits: From tackle shops and on bank
Cost: About £1 per day; £6 per season
Control: Club - Ripley and District AC. R Turner, 2a Argyll Road, Ripley
BK Rating: Not known
W/A: Severn-Trent

Foxton Dam

Location: Eckington, just off the A616 between Sheffield and Bolsover
Type and Size: Small lake
Carp Stock: Probably only one or two to 20lbs - stocked many years ago
Category: Few Carp
Other Species: Roach, perch, tench and pike
Permits: Day ticket on bank
Control: Private - enquire locally
BK Rating: Super-Difficult
W/A: Severn-Trent

Harwick Hall Lakes

Location: Between Mansfield and Chesterfield, close to the M1 at junction 29
Type and Size: Two estate lakes of 3 and 7 acres
Carp Stock: Very well stocked with small carp, and a few doubles and 20's to about 27lbs
Category: Mixed Fishery
Other Species: Roach, tench, perch and bream
Permits: Day tickets from bailiff on bank at low cost. Season tickets also available at about £25.
Control: Private
Restrictions: No night fishing
BK Rating: Moderate
W/A: Yorkshire
Comments: This is a beautiful venue in the grounds of a National Trust property. Most of the bigger fish have come from the small lake. The water is shallow and weedy, but very attractive.

Higham Farm

Location: Higham Farm, near Alfreton
Type and Size: 4 farm lakes, about 3 acres each
How to Find: Take the A61 road from Alfreton to Higham
Carp Stock: Fairly well stocked with carp to 20lbs plus
Category: Mixed Fishery
Other Species: Tench, chub, roach and bream
Permits: Higham Farm Hotel, Old Higham, Alfreton. Tel: Alfreton 833812.
Baits/Methods: Normal carp methods and baits. Boilies are good
BK Rating: Moderate

W/A: Severn–Trent
Comments: Pleasant surroundings. Lakes contain little weed and are quite deep, up to 12ft in places.

High Farm

Location: Near Derby (or perhaps Higham – we think!)
Type and Size: Small lake
How to Find: Consult local tackle dealers
Carp Stock: Well stocked – plenty of doubles
Category: Carp Water
Other Species: Not known
Permits: Try local tackle dealers
Cost: Not known
Control: Private
BK Rating: Not known
W/A: Severn–Trent
Comments: Yes, we know, we shouldn't really have put this in, as we can find out so little about it; can you do better? After all, we can find so few carp waters in Derbyshire that we couldn't resist it.

Mapperley Reservoir

Location: Near Ilkeston
Type and Size: Big reservoir
How to Find: North west of Ilkeston off the A609
Carp Stock: Some large carp
Category: Few Carp
Other Species: General coarse fish
Permits: On site. Ranger post, Tel: 07737 5480
Cost: On application
Control: Derbyshire County Council
Restrictions: Much of the lake cannot be fished
BK Rating: Very Difficult
W/A: Severn–Trent
Comments: Once a famous carp water, where the 26lb record was caught in 1930. Part now a Nature Reserve, with no fishing (in spite of protests by the Carp Anglers' Association, which were ignored).

Ringwood Lake

Location: In the town of Chesterfield
Type and Size: Attractive, 4 acre town lake, very busy and open to the public
Carp Stock: Heavily stocked with many doubles to over 15lbs
Category: Carp Water
Permits: Day tickets from bailiff on bank
Cost: About £2 per day
Control: Council
BK Rating: Easy
W/A: Severn–Trent

Swarkestone Gravel Pits

Location: Swarkestone
Type and Size: Large gravel pits
How to Find: South west of Derby on the A5132
Carp Stock: Few Carp
Other Species: Roach, bream, tench, perch, pike
Permits: Day tickets from the Rising Sun Public House, Willington
Cost: About £1
Control: Derby Angling Association, J Callaghan, 3 Calvin Close, Alvaston, Derby DE20 OHS.
BK Rating: Insufficient information
W/A: Severn-Trent

The Coppice Water

Location: Heanor/Ilkeston
Type and Size: 5 acre lake
How to Find: Near the American Adventure Theme Park, off the A6007 between Ilkeston and Heanor
Carp Stock: Stocked with carp to 25lbs
Category: Mixed Fishery
Other Species: Tench, roach, perch, pike
Permits: The Coppice Inn and Restaurant, Shipley Park, Shipley. Tel: 0773 712606.
Cost: Day tickets about £5; Season about £25.
BK Rating: Insufficient information
Control: Private
W/A: Severn-Trent

Trent and Mersey Canal

Location: Egginton, on the A38 between Derby and Burton-on-Trent. Park by the road, walk over the bridge, and the canal is to your right towards the trees
Type and Size: Attractive, narrow canal
Carp Stock: Some carp to doubles
Category: Few Carp
Other Species: Roach, perch, gudgeon, and a few chub
Permits: Season tickets from Derby AA - send an SAE to the Membership Secretary, Derby AA, PO Box 167, Derby DE3 7UE. Information from Mrs D Taft, Tel: 0332 766866.
Control: Derby AA
BK Rating: Difficult
W/A: Severn-Trent

DEVON

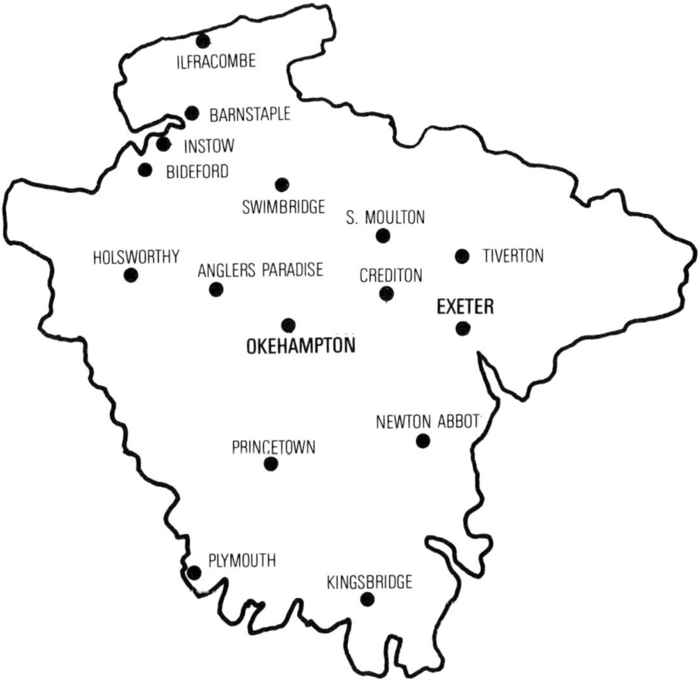

Abbrook Pond

Location: Abbrook, near Kingsteighton, Newton Abbot
Type and Size: Old matured pit of about 3 acres
Carp Stock: Well stocked with carp to double figures; in the past this lake contain carp to over 30lbs, some probable 20's spotted recently
Category: Mixed Fishery
Other Species: Tench, roach and bream
Permits: Exeter and District AA; Hon Sec, D Cornish, 9 Denmark Road, Exeter. Tel: 0392 56770; also from tackle shops in Exeter, such as Exeter Angling Centre, Smythen Street, Torquay and Newton Abbot.
Cost: Day visitors: £2; week - £6. Club membership £14 per season, open to all
Control: Club
BK Rating: Moderate
Comments: There is a normal close season on this water. Could contain some very big carp, though those of the original stocking are almost certainly all dead.

Alder Farm Quarry A

Location: On the left hand side of the A30 Okehampton–Launceston road, just before crossing into Cornwall
Type and Size: Large, very old quarry, said by local people to be bottomless
Carp Stock: Some carp, sizes not known, but probably to 10lbs or so
Category: Mixed Fishery
Other Species: Trout, roach, rudd, bream and tench
Permits: Call at Alder Farm for day tickets and accommodation
Control: Private
BK Rating: Not known
W/A: South West
Comments: There are self-catering chalets close to the lake, which can be rented from the farm. A very deep quarry.

Allerton Ponds

Location: Allerton, Loddiswell, near Kingsbridge. Tel: 550306
Type and Size: Two small man-made ponds on private land – ½ acre and ¼ acre
Carp Stock: About 30 carp in each pond, from 7lbs to 15lbs – best reported 24lb mirror
Category: Carp Only
Permits: From owner on bank
Cost: £3 per day
Control: Private
Restrictions: Barbless hooks; no night fishing; no fixed leads. Minimum breaking strain – 6lbs. Two rods only. No dogs or radios.
BK Rating: Easy
W/A: South West

Zyg Gregorek, of Anglers' Paradise, with 'Neptune', at 30¼lbs – the first ever 30 from his lakes, which he caught on New Year's Day, 1991

Anglers Eldorado

Location: Chilla Road, opposite the entrance to Anglers' Paradise, Halwill Junction, Beaworthy

Type and Size: 4 man-made lakes from one to 3 acres, with many more lakes soon to be opened on the same site

How to Find: Take the old A30 from Okehampton, and at the top of the hill turn right on the B3218 to Halwill Junction (10 miles). At Halwill Junction, turn right by the new houses, pass the pub on your right, and the entrance to Eldorado is 400 yards on the left hand side

Carp Stock: The two acre lake is very heavily stocked with high singles and some doubles; the 3 acre lake has many good doubles, including commons, and more good carp are being stocked regularly in both waters

Category: Mixed Fishery (Carp Only lake now being made)

Other Species: Big koi and other coarse fish, including golden carp, golden tench, golden rudd, and koi

Permits: Day tickets from Zyg at Anglers Paradise, The Gables, Winford, Halwill Junction. Tel: 0409 221559 (down track opposite lakes); from the Newsagents in the village, from the bailiff's house in Chilla Road, close to the lakes; and from selected tackle dealers in the towns.

Cost: About £3.50 per rod per day

Control: Private; Zyg Gregorek

Restrictions: No night fishing; barbless hooks; fixed leads only if back-stops used; min. line b/s - 3lbs; no keepnets or carp sacks.

BK Rating: Easy for all lakes

W/A: South West

Comments: No close season. A brand new day ticket water in a holiday area where there are very few fisheries of this kind. Pleasant, quiet fishing, which, we are sure will soon become as famous as Zyg's other fishery, Anglers' Paradise. Easy fishing for plenty of carp of all sizes, which will soon go to over 20lbs.

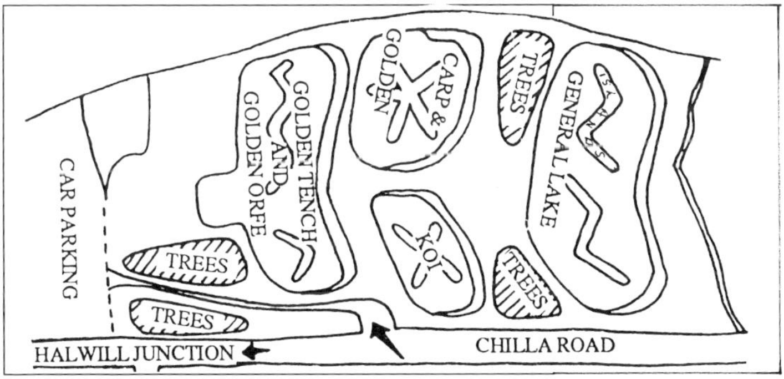

Anglers' Paradise Holidays A

Location: The Gables, Winsford, Halwill Junction, Beaworthy. Tel: 0409 221559

Type and Size: Main lake: 4½ acres, stream fed with 5 islands and a boathouse; 4 other carp lakes close to each other, of about 1½ acres each

How to Find: Call first at Zyg's house, The Gables. To get there take the B3218 Holsworthy road, turning right off the A30 a mile west of Okehampton. At Halwill Junction, turn right, pass the pub and take the right turn signposted 'Winsford' in 400 yards, opposite the entrance to Zyg's day ticket water Anglers' Eldorado. Continue down the rough track until you reach Anglers' Paradise on your left

Zyg and friends with some of the 20's and 30's from the Specimen Lake at Anglers' Paradise, Devon

Carp Stock: Main Lake - very heavily stocked with carp to 30lbs, 20-30 twenties, and about 165 doubles, average size 16lbs; Spessy Lake - 18 carp, most of which are twenties! The first 30 was caught in January 1991 by the owner Zyg, and there have been several thirties caught since to about 32lbs. There are 5 thirties in this small lake and about 20 young fish of around 10lbs growing quickly for the future. Octopussy Lake - 40 doubles, many of which are over 15lbs. Beginners Lake - heavily stocked with small carp.

Category: All 4 lakes are Carp Only

Permits: Fishing only for those who book accommodation, except for occasional syndicate vacancies for the famous 'Five C's Carp Syndicate'. No day tickets.

Control: Zyg and Rose Gregorek. Tel: 0409 221559

Baits/Methods: All normal carp fishing methods and rigs, and float fishing with sweetcorn often succeeds when boilies fail

Restrictions: Night fishing by arrangement only, barbless hooks; no bent hook rigs; minimum 8lb b/s line and size 10 hook

BK Rating: Main Lake - Moderate. Spessy - Difficult. Octopussy - Easy. Beginners - Very Easy.

W/A: South West

Comments: Beautiful 128 acre estate, with 5 other lakes full of koi, crucians, golden tench, golden rudd, golden and blue orfe, and even a tench-shaped lake! Plenty of easy float fishing for beginners and youngsters. Fish farm - quality fish for sale including golden tench and rudd, and blue orfe. Woodland sculpture walk.

Luxury up-market self catering accommodation, with 25 villas and cottages, some with whirlpool baths, ornate four posters, leather Chesterfields, and decorated with antique fishing rods and other valuable tackle. Anglers Paradise is justly rated as the best place in the country for an angling holiday, either for dedicated carp anglers, or for the family. There is clay pigeon shooting, a games room, a table tennis room, a tackle shop, and many attractions for the children, including donkey rides. The large, fabulously decorated African bar is the social centre of the complex, where you can drink Zyg's homemade wine and look at the many pictures of big carp caught in the lakes - some of which are soon expected to reach 40lbs, and all of which were 'grown on' from small fish by Zyg himself - no big imports here to create an instant fishery.

Anglers' Paradise has appeared on a number of TV programmes, and in 1990 was given the gold award by the English Tourist Board - a paradise indeed! PM stays there twice a year - and there is nowhere in the country where you can have a better angling holiday, with a most pleasant and friendly atmosphere. Telephone Zyg for his first class colour brochure, and book well in advance, as those who holiday there once, usually keep going back. Zyg and Rose have three young daughters, Wanda, Anna, and Zenia, all of whom are very beautiful (they made me put that!), so Anglers' Paradise is understandably a family centre - but it's a serious carp fishery too: some of the leading carp anglers in the country have stayed and fished there, and more will do so now the fish are into the thirties - and the central location in Devon makes it ideal for all types of holidays.

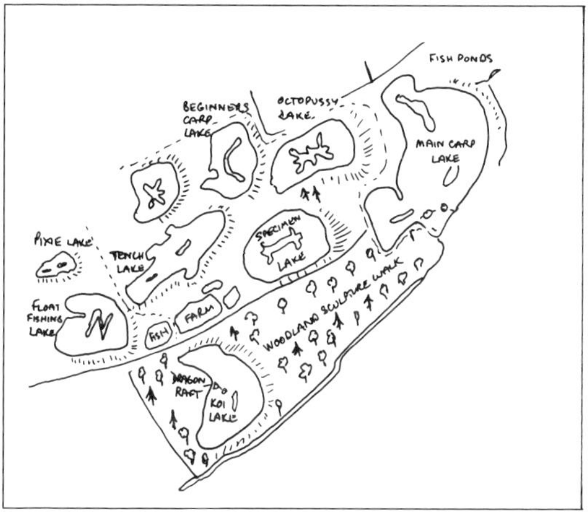

Berrynarbor Mill Pond A

Location: Mill Park Caravan and Camping Site, Berrynarbor, Combe Martin
Type and Size: 3 acre lake
How to Find: The camping and caravan site is near the village of Berrynarbor in North Devon. Take the A399 from Combe Martin towards Ilfracombe, and turn south to the village
Carp Stock: A reasonable number of mirrors to about 15lbs. One fish of 24lbs reported, but this could be the only 20
Category: Mixed Fishery
Other Species: Roach, perch and bream
Permits: Mr Brain, Mill Park Caravan Site, Berrynarbor, Combe Martin. Tel: 027188 2647.
Cost: About £1 per day, day tickets
Control: Private
BK Rating: Moderate
W/A: South West
Comments: No close season

Clifford Farm Holidays A

Location: Woolsery, near Clovelly
Type and Size: Small farm pool
How to Find: Woolsery is a village near Clovelly on the North Devon coast
Carp Stock: Well stocked with carp of good size
Category: Carp Water
Other Species: Trout
Permits: On site
Cost: On application
BK Rating: Moderate
W/A: South West
Comments: No close season. Luxury self catering cottages in beautiful countryside near coast. Brochure and information from: Tel: 02373 319. Also game and clay pigeon shooting.

Cofton Park Farm A

Location: Cofton Park Farm, Starcross, Dawlish
Type and Size: Small lake
How to Find: Between Starcross and Dawlish in South Devon
Carp Stock: Well stocked
Category: Mixed Fishery
Other Species: Tench, roach, skimmer bream
Permits: On site
Cost: On application
BK Rating: Moderate
Control: Private
W/A: South West
Comments: Holiday caravans, tourers, camping. Heated swimming pool, shopping and all amenities. Free brochure and details from Mrs T Jeffery. Tel: 0626 890358. No close season.

Coombe Water Fishery

Location: Near Kingsbridge, South Devon
Type and Size: One acre lake
How to Find: Enquire from owner
Carp Stock: Well stocked with carp to 18lbs
Category: Mixed Fishery
Other Species: Bream and tench
Permits: Jonathan Robinson. Tel: 0548 852038
Cost: £3 per day
BK Rating: Moderate
Control: Private
W/A: South West
Comments: This lake is in the beautiful South Hams area of Devon where there is little carp fishing. All details from the owner

Creedy Carp Lake

Location: Off the A3072 Tiverton road; turn left one mile from Crediton, and then first right, and right again; the lake is opposite a farm
Type and Size: 18th century lake of about 5 acres
Carp Stock: Heavily stocked with carp to over 20lbs, most of which are commons, though small mirrors have been stocked, and some have now reached 15lb
Category: Mixed Fishery
Other Species: Tench and eels
Permits: Day tickets from machine on bank
Cost: £4 for 5.30am to 11pm, and an evening ticket from 5pm to 11pm costs £2.50
Control: Private
Restrictions: No season tickets; no night fishing; no keepnets; 3 rods allowed
Baits/Methods: Floaters, boilies, luncheon meat and sweetcorn
BK Rating: Moderate, though an angler has taken more than 100lbs of carp in a day
W/A: South West

Darracott

Location: Off the Bideford to Barnstaple road, near Torrington
Type and Size: Reservoir of 2.6 acres

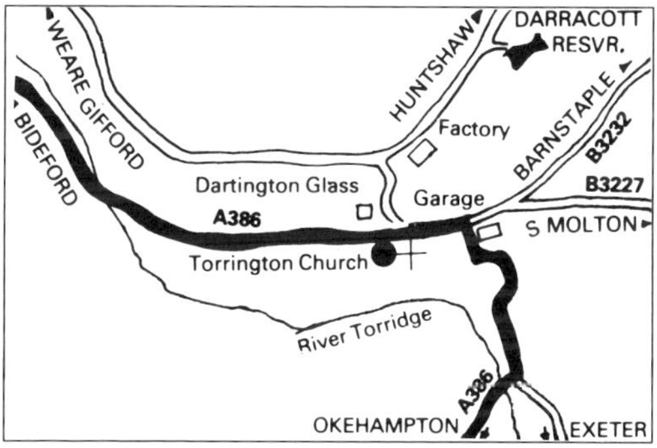

How to Find: Turn off the A386 Okehampton to Bideford road opposite Torrington Church, and then turn right towards Huntshaw. The entrance to Darracott is past the factory on the right
Carp Stock: Well stocked with carp to 14lbs
Category: Mixed Fishery
Other Species: Bream, perch, roach and rudd
Permits: Sports, 9 High Street, The Square, Torrington: The Kingfisher, 22 Castle Street, Barnstaple. Tel: (0271) 44919: The Tackle Box, Kings Shopping Centre, Cooper Street, Bideford. Tel: (0237) 470043: Summerlands Tackle, 3 Golflinks Road, Westward Ho. Tel: (0237) 471291.
Cost: Day £2.50. Concession rate for OAP's, SDP/MOB, students and children under 16 £1.50: 24 hours £5: 7 day castabout, (valid at all Peninsular Coarse Fisheries, except Jennetts and Crafthole), day £15, concession day £10: Day and night £30. No season permits.
Control: Mr Dell Mills, Manager, Peninsular Coarse Fisheries, St Cleer Depot, Liskeard, Cornwall PL14 6EQ. Tel: (0579) 43929.
W/A: South West

BK Rating: Moderate
Restrictions: No keepnets for carp. Barbless hooks requested. Permits must be obtained before fishing.
Comments: NO CLOSED SEASON. Night fishing is now allowed.

Dunsley Farm A

Location: West Anstey, South Molton. Tel: 03984 246
Type and Size: Half acre farm pond
Carp Stock: Well stocked with small carp
Category: Mixed Fishery
Other Species: Tench, roach and rudd
Permits: On site
Control: Mrs M Robins, at the above address
BK Rating: Moderate
W/A: South West
Comments: Self-catering cottage, overlooking a valley, and the woodland pond. Cost from £100 per week, to include fishing.

East Devon Pond A

Location: Near Honiton
Type and Size: Small farm pond - about half an acre
Carp Stock: Well stocked with carp to about 15lbs
Category: Carp Water
Other Species: Some coarse fish
Permits: Tel: 0404891 244 for information and details
Control: Private
BK Rating: Not known, as the water was not fished until 1991
W/A: South West
Comments: Country bungalow to let for self catering holidays with fishing on own pond. Six acres of land - cottage sleeps six. Open during the winter for the week or weekend booking. No close season. Cost from £200 per week, to include fishing.

Exeter Canal

Location: Exeter
Type and Size: 6 mile canal from Basin to Turf
Carp Stock: Some carp to doubles
Category: Few Carp
Other Species: Dace, roach, rudd, perch, tench, bream, pike and eels
Permits: Exeter and District AA. Hon Sec D Cornish, 9 Denmark Road, Exeter. Tel: 0392 56770. Tickets from tackle shops in Exeter, such as Exeter Angling Centre, Smythen Street; Bennett's, Crediton; Drum Sports, Newton Abbot; Plainmoor Angling Centre, Torquay.
Cost: Visitor's day ticket at £2; weekly - £6. Season £14. Reductions for juniors and OAP's
Control: Club
Restrictions: Limited access points - details from Agents and Secretary
BK Rating: Very Difficult
W/A: South West
Comments: No close season

Fishponds House

Location: Fishponds House, Dunkeswell, Honiton. Tel: 0404 891287
Type and Size: 3 acre lake
Carp Stock: Carp to double figures
Category: Mixed Fishery
Other Species: Tench and rudd
Permits: Mr and Mrs K Farmer at the address above
Cost: Day tickets at £1.75
Control: Private
Restrictions: No night fishing - open 8am till sunset only
BK Rating: Not known
W/A: South West
Comments: No close season

Grand Western Canal

Location: Tiverton Basin to Burlescombe
Type and Size: Narrow, weedy disused canal
Carp Stock: Said to be some carp to double figures
Category: Few Carp?
Other Species: Big pike and tench; perch, roach, rudd, bream and eels
Permits: Local tackle shops, in Tiverton
Cost: £17 per season (£12 associate member); £6 per week; £2.50 per day. Reduced prices for juniors and OAP's
Control: Malcolm Trump, Canal Liaison Officer, 5 Middle Lane, Cullompton. Tel: 0884 34448 (home), or 0884 32059 (work)
Restrictions: Dawn to dusk fishing only. Open from June 1st to last day in February
BK Rating: Difficult
W/A: South West

Hogsbrook Lake

Location: Greensdale Barton, Woodbury Salterton, Exeter
Type and Size: Two lakes of 2½ acres and 1½ acres
Carp Stock: Well stocked with carp to doubles
Category: Mixed Fishery
Other Species: Tench, roach and bream
Permits: Miss M McDowell, FWS Carter and Sons Ltd, Greensdale Barton, Woodbury Salterton. Tel: 0395 32855 (day); 0395 68183 (evening)
Cost: £2.50 per day; £1.25 evening after 6pm. Reduced prices for children under 8. Season ticket at £50 annually (no close season)
Control: Private
BK Rating: Not known
W/A: South West
Comments: No close season; night fishing allowed. No fish under 1lb in keepnets (!); children under 14 must be accompanied by adults. Touring caravan and camping site.

Hollies Trout Farm

Location: Sheldon, near Honiton. Tel: 040484 428
Type and Size: Half acre lake
Carp Stock: Well stocked with carp, numbers and sizes unknown

Category:	Mixed Fishery
Other Species:	Roach, bream, tench, dace and rudd
Permits:	From J Roles at the address above
Cost:	Day tickets at £2.50
Control:	Private
Restrictions:	No night fishing; open sunrise to sunset
BK Rating:	Not known
W/A:	South West
Comments:	No close season

Indio Pond A

Location:	Greywalls Lodge, Newton Road, Bovey Tracey, near Newton Abbot
Type and Size:	Estate lake of 2 acres - now for sale
How to Find:	Take the M5 to Exeter, then the A38 towards Plymouth. After 8 miles at the big roundabout turn right onto the road to Bovey Tracey; this is the Newton Road. After 1½ miles the entrance to Greywalls Lodge will be seen on the right, 200 yards after crossing the old railway bridge
Carp Stock:	Well stocked with carp to 27lbs
Category:	Mixed Fishery
Other Species:	Tench, trout, rudd, eels, perch
Permits:	Day tickets are limited, and are sold in advance only by the resident owner, Mr M Charlier, at the house on the property. Fishing is from 6am till dusk; night fishing is by arrangement with the owners. Fishing is available at a reduced price for those staying at the Lodge. There are plans for a unique free exclusive membership scheme - details from Mr Charlier.
Cost:	On application
Restrictions:	No bolt rigs. Barbless hooks only. No keepnets.
Category:	Carp up to 10lbs - Easy; 10-15lbs - Moderate; 20lbs plus - Difficult (April till June). Carp to 20lbs - Moderate; over 20lbs - Difficult (June till October). Winter - Easy if you find the fish. (Categories provided by the proprietor in this instance).
Control:	Private
W/A:	South West
Baits/Methods:	Normal carp fishing baits and methods. Hard boilies needed to defeat the numerous tench
Comments:	First class accommodation is available at the Lodge which is only a few yards from the lake. Bed and breakfast and evening meal. Rooms have wash basins and tea-making facilities, and there is a guest lounge with colour TV. The house is a beautiful 100-year old stone built property in 10 acres of private grounds situated between Torquay and Dartmoor - ideal for a family fishing holiday. No close season. Brochure from Mr Charlier, Greywalls, Newton Road, Bovey Tracey, Devon TQ13 9DY. Tel: 0626 832508. Record fish a mirror of 27lbs 3ozs. The owner has planning permission for 12 holiday lodges, but wants to SELL this beautiful estate; if you're interested, try making an offer.

Jennetts A

Location:	Near Bideford, North Devon
Type and Size:	Reservoir of 8 acres
How to Find:	Signposted from the Torrington to Bideford road
Carp Stock:	Heavily stocked with carp to 27½lbs

Category: Carp Water
Other Species: Tench, roach and bream
Permits: The Tackle Box, Kings Shopping Centre, Cooper Street, Bideford. Tel: (0237) 470043.
Cost: Day (6.30am to 10.00pm only) £3. Concession rate for OAP's, SDP/MOB and students £2. Children under 16 £1.50. No season permits.
Control: Mr Dell Mills, Manager, Peninsular Coarse Fisheries, St Cleer Depot, Liskeard, Cornwall PL14 6EQ. Tel: (0579) 43929.
W/A: South West
BK Rating: Moderate
Restrictions: No night fishing. No cereal based groundbaits, except swimfeeders. No keepnets for carp. Barbless hooks requested. Permits must be obtained before fishing.
Comments: NO CLOSED SEASON. Attractive enclosed water. Accommodation at the Beaufort Hotel, Torrs Park, Ilfracombe. Tel: 0271 865483

Little Comfort Farm A

Location: Little Comfort Farm, West Down, Braunton, North Devon. Tel: 0271 812414
Type and Size: One acre farm pond
Carp Stock: Well stocked with carp to double figures
Category: Mixed Fishery
Other Species: Rudd, bream and trout
Permits: From Rolf Alvsaker at the address above
Cost: £5 per day; £4 half day; £3 evening
Control: Private
Restrictions: No night fishing - daylight till dark only
BK Rating: Moderate
W/A: South West
Comments: No close season. Self-catering cottages available

Longlands Farm A

Location: Near Coombe Martin, Ilfracombe, North Devon EX34 OPD. Tel: 0271 883522
Type and Size: Small farm pond
How to Find: Off the A399 Ilfracombe–Lynmouth road; turn left by RAC box going south
Carp Stock: Some carp, numbers and sizes not known
Category: Mixed Fishery
Other Species: General coarse fish
Permits: Fishing free to residents, details from Mary Peacock at the address above
BK Rating: Not known
W/A: South West
Comments: Little is known, as the brochure only mentions a private fishing lake, but gives no details. Bed and breakfast, evening meal if required, on working farm near Exmoor and the sea. B and B £12.50 per person per night, £87 a week.

Lower Tamar

Location: Between Holsworthy and Bideford, North Devon
Type and Size: Reservoir of 40 acres

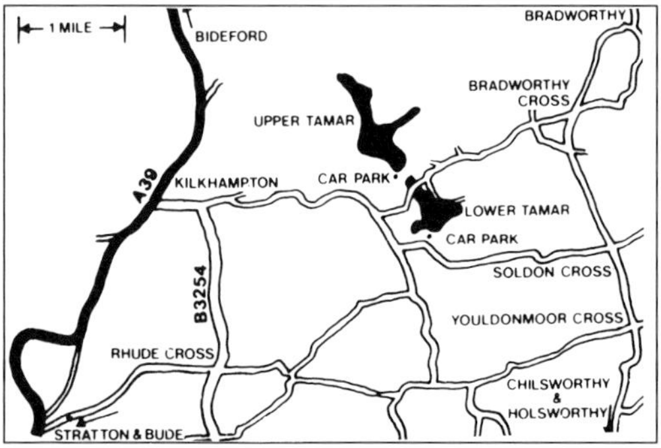

How to Find: Turn off the A39 Bideford to Bude road at Kirkhampton and proceed towards Bradworthy Cross. The water will be seen on the right. The car park is to the south of the lake
Carp Stock: Well stocked with carp to 28lbs. Restocked in early 1991 with commons to 26½lbs
Category: Mixed Fishery
Other Species: Tench, bream, roach and rudd
Permits: Day or day and night permits from the self service unit on the car park: The Tackle Box, Kings Shopping Centre, Cooper Street, Bideford. Tel: (0237) 470043: Summerlands Tackle, Golflinks Road, Westward Ho. Tel: (0237) 471291. Clive's Tackle and Bait, 182 Exeter Street, Plymouth. Tel: (0752) 228940. Season permits from the ranger at Upper Tamar Lake. Tel: (028882) 262.
Control: Mr Dell Mills, Manager, Peninsular Coarse Fisheries, St Cleer Depot, Liskeard, Cornwall PL14 6EQ. Tel: (0579) 43929.
W/A: South West
BK Rating: Moderate
Restrictions: No cereal based groundbaits except swimfeeders. No keepnets for carp. Barbless hooks requested. Permits must be obtained before fishing.
Comments: NO CLOSED SEASON. Night fishing is now allowed. Long casting is necessary to reach deep water in some areas. Long stay carp anglers generally do well.

Melbury

Location: Parkham, near Bideford, North Devon
Type and Size: Reservoir of 12 acres
How to Find: From the Bradworthy to Bideford road, the fishery is 1 mile from Powlers Piece Garage
Carp Stock: Moderately stocked with carp to 22lbs. Restocked early 1991 with commons to over 20lbs - a 27 pounder was caught in 1990, hooked on a boilie
Category: Mixed Fishery
Other Species: Rudd, tench, bream and roach
Permits: The Tackle Box, Kings Shopping Centre, Cooper Street, Bideford. Tel: (0237) 470043: Powlers Piece Garage, Powlers Piece, East Putford. Tel:

(02375) 282: Summerlands Tackle, Golflinks Road, Westward Ho. Tel: (0237) 471291.

Cost: Day £2.50. Concession rate for OAP's, SDP/MOB, students and children under 16 £1.50: 24 hours £5: 7 day castabout, (valid at all Peninsular Coarse Fisheries, except Jennetts and Crafthole), day £15, concession day £10: Day and night £30. No season permits.

Control: Mr Dell Mills, Peninsular Coarse Fisheries, St Cleer Depot, Liskead, Cornwall PL14 6EQ. Tel: (0579) 43929.

W/A: South West

BK Rating: Moderate

Restrictions: Fishing is allowed from 6.30am to 10.00pm only. No cereal based groundbaits, except swimfeeders. No keepnets for carp. Barbless hooks requested. Permits must be obtained before fishing.

Comments: No closed season

Old Mill

Location: Near Dartmouth in South Devon

Type and Size: Reservoir of 4.7 acres

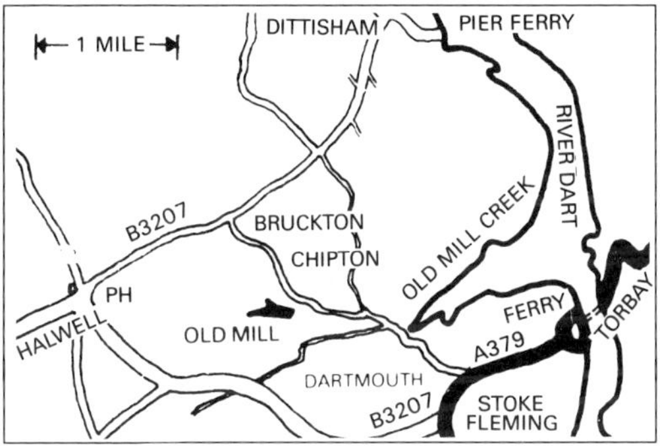

How to Find: The reservoir is off the B3207 Halwell to Dittisham road, near Old Mill Creek on the River Dart

Carp Stock: Well stocked with carp to 21lbs. Restocked early in 1991 with commons to 20½lbs

Category: Mixed Fishery

Other Species: Roach, bream and tench

Permits: The Sport 'n' Fish, 16 Fairfax Place, Dartmouth. Tel: (0803) 833509. No season permits.

Cost: Day £2.50. Concession rate for OAP's SDP/MOB, students and children under 16 £1.50: 24 hours £5: 7 day castabout, (valid at all Peninsular Coarse Fisheries, except Jennetts and Crafthole), day £15, concession day £10: Day and night £30. No season permits.

Control: Mr Dell Mills, Manager, Peninsular Coarse Fisheries, St Cleer Depot, Liskeard, Cornwall PL14 6EQ. Tel: (0579) 43929.

W/A: South West

BK Rating: Moderate

Restrictions: No cereal based groundbaits except swimfeeders. No keepnets for carp. Barbless hooks requested. Permits must be obtained before fishing.

Comments: NO CLOSED SEASON. Night fishing is now allowed. Very mature and attractive water

Pyewell Farm A

Location: Pyewell Farm, Holmacott, near Instow, North Devon. Tel: 0271 830357
Type and Size: Two small farm ponds
Carp Stock: Well stocked with carp to doubles
Category: Mixed Fishery
Other Species: Tench
Permits: From Mrs Steer at the address above
Control: Private
BK Rating: Not known
W/A: South West
Comments: Dinner, bed and breakfast in 16th century farmhouse with fishing from £16 per day, which includes food and overnight accommodation. Three miles from sandy beach and only 4 miles from the North Devon link road. No close season.

Rackerhayes

Location: Newton Abbot
Type and Size: Island Pond is about 5 acres - old pit
How to Find: Take the Exeter road from Newton Abbot, and the lakes are down a track opposite the Racecourse
Carp Stock: Quite well stocked with small carp to 10lbs, small number of doubles including some twenties and one fish of about 30bs
Category: Mixed Fishery
Other Species: General coarse fish
Permits: For Rackerhayes you must live within a 25 mile radius of Newton Abbot. The Newton Abbot FA has other waters with carp in the area, for which day and season tickets are issued. Details and tickets from Percy Hodge (Sports), 104 Queen Street, Newton Abbot; Drum Sports, 48a Courtenay Street, Newton Abbot.
Control: Newton Abbot Fishing Association. Secretary: D Hooder, 22 Mount Pleasant Road, Newton Abbot, Totnes.
BK Rating: Rackerhayes - Difficult. Other waters - Moderate to Easy
W/A: South West

Riverton Fishery

Location: Off the A361 at Swimbridge. Tel: 0271 830009
Type and Size: Two lakes of 4 acres and 3 acres
Carp Stock: Well stocked with carp to at least 10lbs
Category: Mixed Fishery
Other Species: Tench, bream, roach, rudd and perch
Permits: Martin or Brian Corke on the number above
Cost: £2.50 per day; £1.75 for the evening; reduced price for juniors
Control: Private
Restrictions: No night fishing - open dawn till dusk only
BK Rating: Not known
W/A: South West
Comments: No close season

Salmonhutch Fishery A

Location: Upton, near Crediton
Type and Size: Three small spring fed lakes
Carp Stock: Well stocked with commons and mirrors to doubles
Category: Carp Water
Other Species: Tench
Permits: From the fishery. Tel: 03632 3570/2615
Control: Private
BK Rating: Moderate
W/A: South West
Comments: Camping and caravan site; facilities for disabled anglers

Sampford Peverell Ponds

Location: Just off the M5, where the A373 Tiverton road crosses the railway near the village of Sampford Peverell
Type and Size: Two little pits of about half an acre and ¼ acre
Carp Stock: Some good carp to upper doubles
Category: Mixed Fishery
Other Species: Tench, bream, pike and roach
Permits: Members only water of Exeter and District AA (no day tickets). Permits from tackle shops in Exeter. Secretary: D Cornish, 9 Denmark Road, Exeter. Tel: 0392 567700. Includes a number of other good waters.
Restrictions: Normal close season
BK Rating: Difficult
W/A: South West
Comments: We have personal experience of this one. The pond on the Tiverton side of the railway line is known as The Clear Pond. This used to contain only a dozen or so carp, most of which were doubles to about 20lbs, which could be seen but were very hard to catch, (a friend had an 18 on a floating Osborne biscuit many years ago, believe it or not); we are not sure if these big fish still survive. The other pond, part of which was taken for road construction, was always so heavily weeded that it was almost impossible to get the fish out, even on very heavy line, though this may have changed now. PM once tried to go in for a hooked double, and sank in mud almost to chest level, managed to scramble out... and never did get the fish out!

Shobrooke Park

Location: Off the A3072 between Crediton and Tiverton, on the Shobrooke Estate
Type and Size: Attractive 20 acre estate lake
Carp Stock: Quite well stocked with carp of over 20lbs
Category: Mixed Fishery
Other Species: Roach and tench
Permits: Day tickets from Ladds Sports, High Street, Crediton
Cost: £2 per day; £5 per week - half price for juniors, OAP's and the disabled
Control: Shobrooke Park Estate, 27 South Street, Molton, North Devon EX36 4AA
Restrictions: No night fishing; no fishing allowed on about half of the bank - the other side is private
BK Rating: Moderate
W/A: South West

Simpson Valley Fishery

Location: One and a half miles from Holsworthy on the A3072 Holsworthy to Hatherleigh road. Tel: 0409 253593
Type and Size: 4 small farm pools in valley
Carp Stock: Carp Pool - heavily stocked with carp to upper doubles; other pools - some carp
Category: Carp Pool - Carp Only; other pools - Mixed Fisheries
Other Species: Tench, roach and rudd
Permits: Day tickets from the farm - there is a sign on the main road
Cost: Carp Pool - £3 per day; other pools - £2 per day; half price for children and pensioners on all pools
Control: Private
BK Rating: Easy
Restrictions: Barbless hooks only; no boilies; no cereal groundbait
W/A: South West
Comments: Two further ponds will probably be open by the time this book appears. Pleasant farm fishery with good fishing in the carp pool

Slade

Location: Near Ilfracombe, North Devon
Type and Size: Two reservoirs. Upper Slade 4 acres. Lower Slade 6 acres
How to Find: From Ilfracombe, pick up the B3231, and the entrance to the reservoirs is on the left

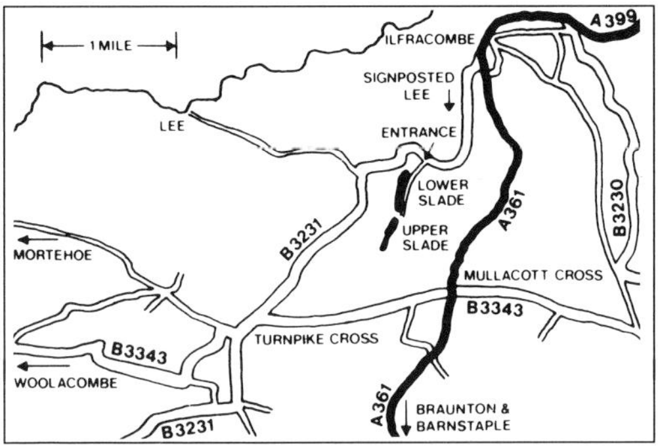

Carp Stock: Well stocked with carp to 20lbs
Category: Mixed Fisheries
Other Species: Tench to 7lbs, roach to 3lbs 7ozs, bream and perch
Permits: The Tackle Box, 2b Portland Street, Ilfracombe. Tel: (0271) 862570: The Kingfisher, 22 Castle Street, Barnstaple. Tel: (0271) 44919: Summerlands Tackle, 3 Golflinks Road, Westward Ho. Tel: (0237) 471291. Season and day permits from The Post Office, Slade. Tel: (0271) 862257.
Cost: Day £2.50. Concession rate for OAP's, SDP/MOB, students and children under 16 £1.50: 24 hours £5: 7 day castabout, (valid at all Peninsular Coarse Fisheries, except Jennetts and Crafthole),. day £15, concession £10: Day and night £30. Season permits day £37, concession OAP's SDP/MOB and students £20, children under 16 £12.50: Day and night £56.
Control: Mr Dell Mills, Manager, Peninsular Coarse Fisheries, St Cleer Depot, Liskeard, Cornwall PL14 6EQ. Tel: (0579) 43929.

W/A: South West
BK Rating: Moderate
Restrictions: No cereal based groundbait except swimfeeders. No keepnets for carp. Barbless hooks requested. Permits must be obtained before fishing.
Comments: Attractive water with NO CLOSED SEASON. Night fishing is now allowed

South Farm Ponds A

Location: Blackborough, Cullompton
Type and Size: Two small farm ponds
How to Find: South Farm, Blackborough, Cullompton, near Exeter EX15 2SE
Carp Stock: Well stocked with carp
Category: Mixed Fishery
Other Species: Tench and roach
Permits: From A B Donnithorne, South Farm. Tel: 0823 680483
Cost: On application
BK Rating: Moderate
Control: Private
Restrictions: Not known
W/A: Southern
Comments: No close season. Holidays in four holiday homes. Health spa, games room, swimming pool. Colour brochure on application.

South Hay Farm A

Location: South Hay Farm, Shebbear, Beaworthy. Tel: 40928 614
Type and Size: Two acre lake
Carp Stock: Said to be some carp, numbers and sizes not known
Category: Mixed Fishery
Other Species: Some coarse fish
Permits: Mr Nigel Brown or Miss Penelope Douglas, at the above address
Cost: £5 per day
Control: Private
Restrictions: No night fishing - open 7.30am till sunset. Barbless hooks
BK Rating: Not known
W/A: South West
Comments: No close season. Accommodation on site. Children's fishing pond

South Reed Fisheries Carp Lake

Location: Boasley Cross, Bratton Clovelly, near Okehampton EX20 4JJ. Tel: 083787 295
Type and Size: 3 acre man-made lake
How to Find: The fishery is signposted from the B3218 road between Okehampton and Halwill, about 4 miles from Okehampton, on the left hand side of the road
Carp Stock: 30 doubles, including several 20's
Category: Carp Only
Permits: In advance only - phone or call for bookings. Only 3 anglers per day from June till October
Cost: £10 per day

Control: Private
Restrictions: Barbless hooks, not smaller than size 8; nets to be knotless and not smaller than 30 inches; 8lb minimum line strength; no dogs
BK Rating: Easy to Moderate
W/A: South West
Comments: This lake has been specially stocked for specialist carp anglers - each fish is marked for identification purposes. Pleasant nature conservation area - other lakes on site (see separate entry). Quiet, peaceful site well away from main roads.

South Reed Fisheries Coarse Lake

Location: Boasley Cross, Bratton Clovelly, near Okehampton EX20 4JJ. Tel: 083787 295
Type and Size: 3½ acre man-made lake
How to Find: Take the old A30 from Okehampton towards Launceston, and turn right onto the B3218 Holsworthy road at the top of Okehampton Hill. You will see a sign to the fishery on the left about 4 miles from Okehampton
Carp Stock: Well stocked with carp to 23lbs
Category: Mixed Fishery
Permits: On bank
Cost: £4 per day
Control: Private
Baits/Methods: All normal methods, including float fishing, with maggots, sweetcorn, luncheon meat and boilies
Restrictions: Barbless hooks; no keepnets for carp; all fish to be returned; no dogs
BK Rating: Easy
W/A: South West
Comments: Tackle hire is available for £1 per day; angling tuition if required, by appointment only. Coarse fish, koi and ornamental fish for sale from fish farm on site, also water lilies and other aquatic plants. Some non-fishing ponds available for bird watching by special arrangement on this nature conservation area. Very quiet and peaceful site well away from main roads

Squabmoor

Location: Near Budleigh Salterton
Type and Size: Reservoir of 4.3 acres
How to Find: Turn off the A377 Exeter to Exmouth road at Clyst St. George into the B3179, and the reservoir is on the left, just before Knowle and Budleigh Salterton
Carp Stock: Well stocked with carp to over 20lbs
Category: Mixed Fishery
Other Species: Roach to over 3lbs, tench to 5½lbs, bream and rudd
Permits: The Tackle Shop, 20 The Strand, Exmouth; Exeter Angling Centre, Smythen Street, Exeter. Day and season permits from Knowle Post Office.
Cost: Day £2.50. Concession rate for OAP's, SDP/MOB, students and children under 16 £1.50: 24 hours £5: 7 day castabout, (valid at all Peninsular Coarse Fisheries, except Jennetts and Crafthole),. day £15, concession £10: Day and night £30. Season permits day £37, concession OAP's SDP/MOB and students £20, children under 16 £12.50: Day and night £56.

Control:	Mr Dell Mills, Manager, Peninsular Coarse Fisheries, St Cleer Depot, Liskeard, Cornwall PL14 6EQ. Tel: (0579) 43929.
W/A:	South West
BK Rating:	Moderate
Restrictions:	No cereal based groundbaits except swimfeeders. No keepnets for carp. Barbless hooks requested. Permits must be obtained before fishing.
Comments:	Attractive water with NO CLOSED SEASON. Night fishing is now allowed

Star Barton Ponds

Location:	Cowley, near Exeter
Type and Size:	Two small farm ponds
Carp Stock:	Well stocked with carp to doubles
Category:	Carp Water
Other Species:	Tench
Permits:	Exeter and District AA. Secretary: D Cornish, 9 Denmark Road, Exeter. Tel: 0392 56770. Tickets from tackle shops such as Angling Centre, Smythen Street, Exeter; Bennets, Crediton; Drum Sport, Newton Abbot; Plainmoor Angling Centre, Torquay
Cost:	Day visitors - £2; weekly - £6; season - £14
Control:	Club
BK Rating:	Easy
W/A:	South West
Comments:	No close season. Exeter and District AA is an excellent club with many other waters on the same ticket.

Stone Farm Quarry

Location:	Stone Farm, near Bridestow, just to the right hand side of the old A30, about 7 miles from Okehampton
Type and Size:	Large and remarkably deep quarry, with very steep sides at one end, but easy access and fishing from the farm end
Carp Stock:	Some carp, thought to go to about 10lbs
Category:	Mixed Fishery
Other Species:	Rudd, roach, tench and bream; possibly a few trout
Permits:	From Stone Farm
Control:	Private
BK Rating:	Difficult
W/A:	South West
Comments:	PM has known this one for 50 years, although it probably only had a few trout in it from the nearby river then. Dangerous, almost vertical sides at the end away from the farm. Last time he put out an Arlesey Bomb from the 'easy' bank, it just kept going straight down, perhaps to 60 feet or more!

Stour Farm Fishery

Location:	Billingsmoor Farm, Butterleigh, Cullompton
Type and Size:	Small farm pond
How to Find:	Come off the motorway at junction 28, and take various lanes to the west. Butterleigh is south of Tiverton and west of Cullompton
Carp Stock:	The pond mentioned has been well stocked with carp to double figure size

Category: Carp Water
Permits: Day tickets from E Berry, Billingsmoor Farm, Butterleigh. Tel: 08845 248
Cost: About £2 per day
Control: Private
BK Rating: Thought to be Fairly Easy
W/A: South West
Comments: No close season. Two other ponds contain mixed coarse fish, on same ticket.

Swimbridge Pool

Location: Swimbridge, near Barnstaple
Type and Size: Small quarry
Carp Stock: Quite well stocked with carp to doubles
Category: Mixed Fishery
Other Species: Tench, bream, rudd and perch
Permits: Barnstaple and District AA. Visitors tickets from local tackle shops, who give details of membership
Control: Club
Restrictions: Members only weekends and Bank Holidays; visitors' tickets weekdays only
BK Rating: Moderate
W/A: South West

Trago Mills

Location: On the Newton Abbot - Bovey Tracey road
Type and Size: Small lake
Carp Stock: Well stocked with carp to double figures
Category: Mixed Fishery
Other Species: Rudd, roach, bream and tench
Permits: The Warden on site; Geoff Mole. Tel: 0626 821111
Cost: £3 per day; children and OAP's £2
Control: Trago Mills
Restrictions: Open March 1st to November 30th only, from 8.30am to 5pm
BK Rating: Not known
W/A: South West
Comments: Trago Mills is a large supermarket (see local papers for publicity)

Upham Farm

Location: Upham Farm, Farringdon, Exeter
Type and Size: 4 small farm ponds
How to Find: Farringdon is 6 miles east of Exeter on the A3052 Exeter–Sidmouth road
Carp Stock: Plenty of carp - many doubles to 24lbs
Category: Carp Water
Other Species: Tench
Permits: W J Willocks, Upham Farm, Farringdon, Exeter. Tel: 0395 32247
Cost: Day tickets £2.50. £3.50 two rods
Control: Private
BK Rating: Moderate
W/A: South West
Restrictions: Night fishing must be booked in advance, no keepnets
Comments: No close season. Parties of 20 or more must book in advance

Venn Pool

Location: Near Barnstaple, North Devon
Type and Size: Small and very deep quarry
Carp Stock: Well stocked with carp to upper doubles
Category: Mixed Fishery
Other Species: Tench, bream, rudd, perch
Permits: Barnstaple and District AA. Martin Turner, 67 Taw View, Freminton, Barnstaple. Visitors' tickets from local tackle shops
Control: Club
Restrictions: Visitors' tickets weekdays only; members only on weekends and Bank Holidays
BK Rating: Moderate
W/A: South West

West Pitt Farm Pool A

Location: Uplowman, Tiverton, North Devon EX16 7DU
Type and Size: Three farm ponds, the biggest 1¼ acres
How to Find: Village near Tiverton, 2½ miles from the M5
Carp Stock: Well stocked with carp to 21½lbs
Category: Mixed Fishery
Other Species: Tench, rudd, roach, koi
Permits: From farm - Mrs G Brent. Tel: 0884 820296
Cost: £3.50 per day - night by arrangement
BK Rating: Fairly Hard
Control: Private
Baits/Methods: Normal carp methods
W/A: South West
Comments: Farmhouse accommodation available. 21½lb mirror caught in 1987. Also self catering accommodation in cottages and lodge. Indoor heated swimming pool and sauna; tennis and games room. Groundbaiting limited. No close season.

West View Pond

Location: Ottery St. Mary, near Exeter
Type and Size: 5 acre lake
Carp Stock: Plenty of small carp
Category: Mixed Fishery
Other Species: Rudd and roach
Permits: Members only water of Exeter and District AA. Secretary: D Cornish, 9 Denmark Road, Exeter. Tel: 0392 56770; also from tackle shops in Exeter, Newton Abbot and Torquay
Cost: £14 a year, open to all
Control: Club
BK Rating: Easy
W/A: South West
Comments: Membership includes a number of other carp waters. Normal close season.

DORSET

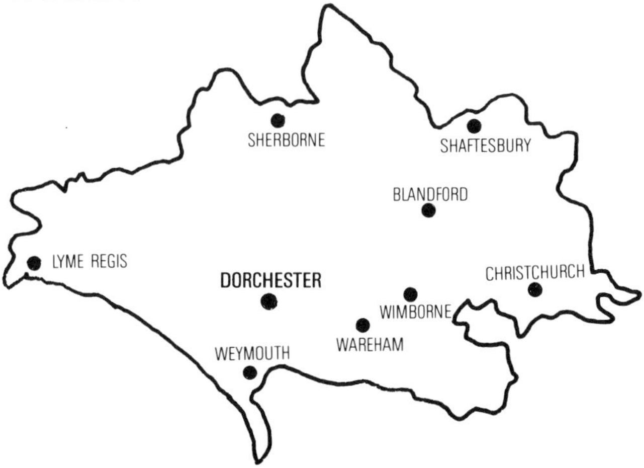

Blashford Lakes

Location: Off the A338 near Christchurch
Type and Size: Two lakes, one large, and one small, which contain carp
Carp Stock: Spinnaker Lake (large) - well stocked with carp, average low doubles. Roach Pit - few carp to 29lbs
Category: Spinnaker - Carp Water; Roach Pit - Few Carp
Other Species: Roach Pit - Roach, pike, tench, chub and bream
Permits: Members only water of Christchurch AC; C Bungay, 8 Purewell, Christchurch or P Reading, 17 Mayford Road, Poole.
Cost: £54 per season, to include many other waters
Control: Club
Restrictions: No night fishing; some parts of the bank are out of bounds; locked gate open with club key for members only; no day tickets; fishing allowed to 11pm on Roach Pit
BK Rating: Moderate
W/A: Wessex

Butterwick Farm A

Location: Butterwick Farm, Holnest, near Sherborne
Type and Size: Half acre farm pond
How to Find: Near Sherborne
Carp Stock: Up to 6lbs, well stocked
Category: Mixed Fishery
Other Species: Tench, rudd, eels
Permits: From Mrs Vickery. No day tickets.
Cost: Price on application
BK Rating: Easy/Moderate
Control: Private
Baits/Methods: General angling baits and methods
W/A: Wessex
Comments: This lake can only be fished by those who book mobile homes - no other permits available. Some accommodation in the farmhouse.

Crow Pool

Location: Ibsley Pools, near Christchurch, just off the A38
Type and Size: Small, irregularly shaped pool alongside the Ibsley Trout Stream off the Avon
Carp Stock: Well stocked with carp from 10-18lbs - about 20-30 doubles
Category: Mixed Fishery
Other Species: Chub, dace, perch, pike, roach, rudd and tench
Control: Members only water of Christchurch AC; C Bungay, 8 Purewell, Christchurch or P Reading, 17 Mayford Road, Poole, Dorset; details and some tickets from Ringwood Tackle, Ringwood. No day tickets.
Cost: £54 per season, to include many other waters
Control: Club
Restrictions: No night fishing; no cars before 9am; lakeside car park for disabled anglers only
BK Rating: Moderate
W/A: Wessex

Dorset Springs Fishery

Location: Sturminster Marshall
Type and Size: Small lake
Carp Stock: Well stocked with carp from 7lbs to 25lbs
Category: Mixed Fishery
Other Species: Big pike and crucians
Permits: Day tickets on site
Control: Private
BK Rating: Moderate
W/A: Wessex

Harrow Pond

Location: Harrow Lodge, Holmesley, near Christchurch
Type and Size: Small forest pool
Carp Stock: A few carp to 22lbs
Category: Few Carp
Other Species: Pike, roach and tench
How to Find: Take the Lyndhurst road from Christchurch (A35), and turn left just after the Cat and Fiddle pub, then turn first right up Harrow Hill. A white house - Beech House Lodge - is on the right, and the entrance to the pond is 100yds further on left
Permits: Members only water of Christchurch AC; C Bungay, 8 Purewell, Christchurch or P Reading, 17 Mayford Road, Poole.
Cost: £54 per season, to include many other waters
Restrictions: No night fishing; members only; locked gate with key; no litter; carp must not be retained in keepnets or sacks; no access in close season.
BK Rating: Difficult
W/A: Wessex

Hillview Farm Lake

Location: Hillview Farm, Corfe Mullen
Type and Size: Sheltered farm lake of 2 acres
Carp Stock: Heavily stocked with carp from 4lbs to 20lbs
Category: Carp Water
Other Species: Crucians
Permits: Day tickets from farmhouse
Cost: £4 per day
Control: Private
BK Rating: Easy
W/A: Wessex

Holtwood Ponds

Location: Holtwood, Horton, near Wimborne
Type and Size: Three small forest-type ponds
How to Find: Take the B3078 from Wimborne towards Cranborne
Carp Stock: All three ponds are well stocked with small carp, mostly 5-9lbs and possibly commons
Category: Upper Pond - Carp Only; Middle Pond - Carp Water; Lower Pond -Mixed Fishery
Other Species: Middle Pond - tench; Lower Pond - crucians, rudd and tench
Permits: Members only water of Christchurch AC; C Bungay, 8 Purewell, Christchurch or P Reading, 17 Mayford Road, Poole.
Cost: £54 per season, to include many other waters
Restrictions: Members only; barbless hooks only; no night fishing - open 6am to 11pm only; carp must not be put in sacks or keepnets; no picnics; no groundbait; entrance gate must be kept locked at all times; arrive and depart quietly.
BK Rating: Easy
W/A: Wessex

Hyde Lake

Location: Hyde, near Wareham
Type and Size: 1½ acre lake
How to Find: 5 miles from Wareham, just off the Bovington to Wareham road
Carp Stock: Stocked with mirrors and commons to 20lbs. Good head of carp
Category: Mixed Fishery
Other Species: Tench, roach, rudd and crucians
Permits: Hyde AC. Secretary: Jim Bagley, Heather Lodge, Hyde, near Wareham. Tel: Bere Regis 471402 or Bindon Abbey 463127.
Cost: About £20 per season
BK Rating: Moderate
Control: Club/syndicate
Restrictions: None
W/A: Wessex
Comments: Night fishing allowed. 3 rods also allowed. Quiet countryside lake, very peaceful surroundings.

Kingsbridge Lakes

Location: Near Wareham, on a complex of trout waters
Type and Size: Old pit of about 6 acres
Carp Stock: Well stocked with carp to over 15lbs with quite a few doubles
Category: Mixed Fishery
Other Species: Roach and bream
Permits: Members only water of Dumbourne and District AC. Season tickets only from local tackle shops.
Control: Club
BK Rating: Easy
W/A: Wessex

Luckfield Lake

Location: Broadmayne, near Dorchester
Type and Size: Clay pit of about 1¼ acres
How to Find: On the B352 Dorchester to Wareham road, about 3 miles from Dorchester
Carp Stock: Good head of mirrors to about 18lbs. Two fish of 20lbs+. Recent stocking of commons to 9lbs
Category: Carp Water
Other Species: Tench and roach to over 2lbs
Permits: Only from John Aplin Specialist Angling Supplies, 1 Athelstan Road, Dorchester. Tel: 0305 66500; in advance only.
Cost: £3.50 per day; £5 per night
BK Rating: Moderate
Control: Private
Baits/Methods: Bottom baits at night; floaters during the day
W/A: Wessex
Comments: A peaceful, attractive water in natural surroundings with overhanging trees.

New Meadows Lake

Location: Off the Christchurch to Lymington road (A337), turning right up New Road and Smugglers Copse Way, close to the bowling green
Type and Size: 3 acre lake
Carp Stock: Well stocked with carp to 15lbs
Category: Mixed Fishery
Other Species: Roach, perch and bream
Permits: Members only water of Christchurch AC; C Bungay, 8 Purewell, Christchurch or P Reading, 17 Mayford Road, Poole
Cost: £54 per season, to include many other waters
Restrictions: Members only; no night fishing
BK Rating: Not known
W/A: Wessex

Osmington Mills Lake A

Location: Osmington Mills is by the sea, just off the A353 between Weymouth and Wareham. Turn off the main road at Osmington about 4 miles from Weymouth
Type and Size: 2 acre gravel pit
Carp Stock: Many carp, average 10–13lbs, quite a few doubles to 19lbs and said to be two thirties
Category: Mixed Fishery
Other Species: Tench, roach, rudd, perch and crucians
Control: Private
Permits: Tackle dealer L Rathbone, The Tackle Shop, West Bay, Bridport. Tel: 0308 23475. Also on bank and The Ranch House, Caravan Park, Osmington Mills.
Cost: £4 per day
BK Rating: Easy
W/A: Wessex
Comments: Busy in summer, fishes well in winter. Accommodation. Fishing for residents only.

Pallington Lakes

Location: Tincleton, near Dorchester
Type and Size: Lake of about 7 acres
How to Find: Off the B3390 at Waddock Cross, 7 miles east of Dorchester
Carp Stock: Many small mirrors and commons. A few low doubles. Lake record is a common of 19lbs 4ozs
Category: Mixed Fishery
Other Species: Tench to over 7lbs; roach, chub, perch and bream
Permits: On site to be purchased before fishing. Tel: 0305 848141
Cost: £4.50 per day
BK Rating: Moderate
Control: Private
W/A: Wessex
Comments: Fishing 8am to dusk only - open all year

Radipole Lake

Location: In the town of Weymouth
Type and Size: Very large lake close to the sea (70 acres plus)
How to Find: Weymouth
Carp Stock: Some commons to about 10lbs. Bigger fish rumoured but hard to find possibly up to 26lbs, but we are told this was 60 years ago! A 33lb mirror was caught in 1990
Category: Few Carp
Other Species: Eels, roach, dace and mullet
Permits: Day tickets from tackle shops in Weymouth
Control: Local council
BK Rating: Difficult
W/A: Wessex
Comments: Not seriously fished for carp, but might contain a few good fish. Boats, amusements, people, refreshments, etc especially at south end nearest town. No fishing in bird sanctuary.

Revells Farm A

Location: Buckland Newton, near Dorchester
Type and Size: 5 small lakes - about an acre each
How to Find: On the old Sherborne road about 8 miles from Dorchester
Carp Stock: All varieties to 26lb in top pond. Small carp in other ponds; one lake doubles only
Category: Mixed Fishery
Other Species: Bream, tench, chub, perch, rudd and roach
Permits: Obtainable from shop on site, or on bank. Tel: 03805 301
Cost: On application
BK Rating: Easy
Control: Private
W/A: Wessex
Comments: A recently set up coarse fishery in pleasant surroundings. Accommodation available.

River Stour

Location: Different sections of the lower Stour
Type and Size: Famous river where most fish grow very big
Carp Stock: Not known, but big carp reported from time to time - a 16¾ was caught on luncheon meat in 1990, and the same angler had caught other Stour carp to 15lbs
Other Species: Most of them, including big barbel and chub
Permits: Local angling clubs - enquire in tackle shops for information and permits, especially in Christchurch
BK Rating: Difficult, though once the carp are located, they can be quite easy to catch, as few have been taken before
W/A: Wessex

Throop Fisheries

Location: 2½ miles from Christchurch Station
Type and Size: Dorset Stour and a mill pool
Carp Stock: Well stocked with carp to 25lbs
Category: Mixed Fishery
Other Species: Pike to nearly 30lb, barbel to 13½lb, chub to over 7lbs, and roach to 3¾lb; some bream in mill pool
Permits: Glen Sutcliffe, Manager, South Lodge, Holdenhurst Village, Bournemouth. Tel: 0202 35532
Cost: Day tickets - £4; weekly tickets - £16; season - £54
Control: Private
BK Rating: Moderate
W/A: Southern
Comments: Throop is a famous fishery, with 5½ miles of the River Stour and the mill pool. All species run to a very big size. Reduced rate for juniors and OAP's and special rates for clubs - booking essential.

Wedgehill Ponds

Location: Verwood, near Ringwood

Type and Size: Three small forest ponds close to disused railway line - possibly old ballast pits

How to Find: From Christchurch take the B3081 to Verwood, and turn left down Manor Road, then right into Church Hill and Margards Lane. Then turn left into Horton Way, and after going under the railway bridge turn right at the T-junction, and the ponds are at the end of the lane - 10mph speed limit

Carp Stock: Well stocked with carp of from 4-6lbs

Category: Mixed Fishery

Other Species: Goldfish, golden rudd, crucians and tench

Permits: Members only water of Christchurch AC; C Bungay, 8 Purewell, Christchurch or P Reading, 17 Mayford Road, Poole

Cost: £54 per season, to include many other waters

Restrictions: Members only; barbless hooks; no carp to be put in sacks or keepnets; no night fishing - fishing is 6am to 11pm only; one rod only; gate must be locked at all times; quiet arrival and leaving essential

BK Rating: Easy

W/A: Wessex

DURHAM

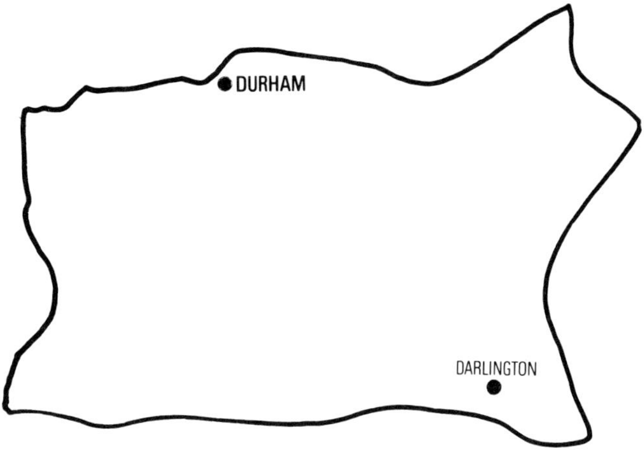

Brasside Pool

Location: Newton Hall, Brasside, near Durham
Type and Size: Five acre, weedy lake, with depths up to 10 feet, and gravel bars in one area
Carp Stock: Well stocked with smallish carp, mostly 4 to 9lbs, a few low doubles, including some commons
Category: Mixed Fishery
Other Species: Roach, bream, tench and pike
Permits: Members only water of Durham City AC – try local tackle shops
Cost: About £35 per year
Control: Durham City AC. Open to all – Secretary: G Hedley, 3 Hawthorn Crescent, Durham
Restrictions: Members only
BK Rating: Moderate
Comments: There is no close season on this water, and it fishes well all the year.

Fighting Cocks Reservoir

Location: Middleton St. George, Darlington
Type and Size: 10 acre reservoir
Carp Stock: A few carp
Category: Few Carp
Other Species: Perch, roach, bream
Permits: J and M Allenden's shop, Middleton St. George, near fishery entrance; Mr Race, 3 Palm Tree Villas or Miss Willans, 3 Waterview, Middleton St. George
Cost: Day tickets – about £1. Annual permits about £10 adults, £6 juniors
BK Rating: Moderate
W/A: Northumbrian

Middleton Water Park

Location: Middleton St. George, Darlington
Type and Size: Small park lake
Carp Stock: Some carp, numbers and sizes not revealed by the Parish Clerk who replied to our questionnaire, but didn't divulge this information, nor the names of the other species which he said were present!
Category: Mixed Fishery
Permits: From the bailiff on site, or from the Parish Clerk, 8 Grendon Gardens, Middleton St. George, Darlington. Tel: 0325 332917
Cost: £2 per rod per day (£1.50 for children). Annual permits also available
Control: Council
BK Rating: Not known
W/A: Northumbrian

Turnside Pool

Location: Ferryhill, near Durham
Type and Size: Attractive one acre pool, very weedy and heavily fished
Carp Stock: There are only a small number of carp, but they go to over 20lbs
Category: Few Carp
Other Species: Roach, tench and perch
Permits: Try local tackle shops for club membership - no day tickets
Control: Ferryhill and District AC. Secretary: A Roxley, 60 Linden Road, West Cornforth, County Durham
Restrictions: Members only; one rod only; no multiple baits; no night fishing
BK Rating: Very Difficult
W/A: Northumbrian

EAST SUSSEX

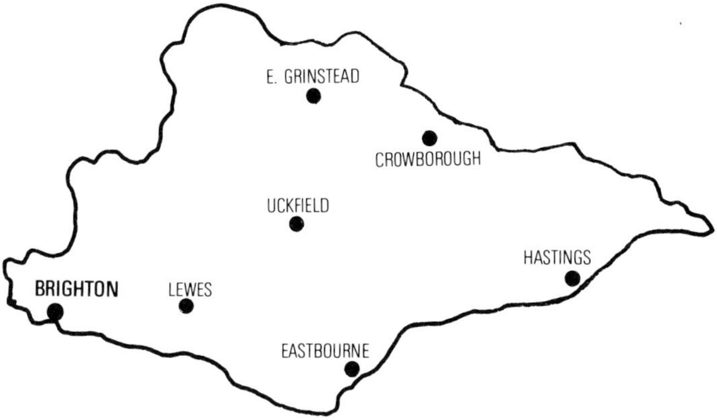

Buckshole Reservoir

Location: Hastings
Type and Size: 10 acre town reservoir
Carp Stock: Well stocked with carp to over 20lbs - a thirty was reported in 1991
Category: Mixed Fishery
Other Species: Roach, bream, tench and pike
Permits: Possibly Clive Vale AC - try local tackle shops
Control: Club
Restrictions: No night fishing; no day tickets
BK Rating: Moderate
W/A: Southern

Clive Vale and Ecclesbourne Reservoirs

Location: Hastings
Type and Size: Small reservoirs
How to Find: In Hastings
Carp Stock: Well stocked with carp to 30lbs
Category: Mixed Fishery
Other Species: General coarse fish, including large pike
Permits: Hastings Clive Vale Angling Club. J Greenhalf, 33 Hollington Park Road, St. Leonards-on-Sea, TN38 OSE. Try local tackle shops
Cost: About £2 per day. £11 per season
BK Rating: Moderate
Control: Club
Restrictions: No juveniles
W/A: Southern
Comments: Enquire locally for more information

Farthings Lake

Location: Near Battle, Hastings
Type and Size: Estate lake of 3 acres
How to Find: Take the B2095 west from Battle towards Catsfield and Bexhill. After about 1½ miles you will see a track on the right marked 'Millers Farm'. The footpath to the lake is opposite this. The car park is a further 100 yards on the right
Carp Stock: Some carp, sizes not known
Category: Mixed Fishery
Other Species: Tench, bream, roach and rudd
Permits: Day tickets (limited) from local tackle shops in advance, or from Stiles Garage and Surridge Newsagents, both in Battle High Street, after 9am. Tickets must be obtained before fishing. Season tickets from 6 Warwick Road, Bexhill-on-Sea, East Sussex. Tel: 0424 224908
Cost: Day tickets £2 (juniors/OAPs/evening fishing £1.25). Season tickets £20 (juniors/OAPs/evening £11.50)
Restrictions: No night fishing. Lake is open 8am till sunset. Season ticket holders may start at sunrise
BK Rating: Moderate
Control: Redland Angling Scheme
W/A: Southern
Comments: Attractive lake in beautiful wooded valley. If you want to start before 9am you will need to get a ticket the previous day or hold a season ticket

Furnace Pond

Location: Near East Grinstead
Type and Size: 7 acre estate lake
How to Find: Ordnance Survey Sheet No. 187; Ref. 348391
Carp Stock: Overstocked with small carp mainly to 10lbs, many of which are said to be in poor condition
Category: Carp Water
Other Species: Some coarse fish
Permits: Wallington Specimen Group. No day tickets but season tickets at about £60. Contact: Mrs A Yexley, 25 Oakley Road, South Norwood, London SE25
Control: Private
BK Rating: Easy
W/A: Southern

Hastings Lake

Location: In the town of Hastings
Type and Size: 10 acre lake
Carp Stock: Heavily stocked with carp to 10lbs
Category: Mixed Fishery
Other Species: Tench and pike
Permits: Local tackle shops, or the Secretary, Hastings, Bexhill and District FA, P K Jury, 5 Old Church Road, St. Leonards, East Sussex
Cost: Day tickets at £1.25
Control: Club; season tickets £12–£13 only for those living within 25 miles of Hastings
BK Rating: Easy
W/A: Southern

Michelham Priory Moat

Location: Michelham Priory, Upper Dicker, Hailsham, near Eastbourne (off the A22 Eastbourne-East Grinstead road)
Type and Size: Possibly the largest moat in England, with several acres of water
Carp Stock: Carp to 10lbs, probably commons and possibly wildies
Category: Mixed Fishery
Other Species: Tench, roach and bream
Permits: Day tickets from the 14th century gatehouse
Cost: £1.50 per day
Control: Private
Restrictions: Thought to be no night fishing; no dogs
BK Rating: Not known
W/A: Southern
Comments: One of the most beautiful buildings and grounds in the country - an Augustinian Priory which dates from the 13th century, but which became a farmhouse at the Dissolution of the Monasteries. There is an Elizabethan wing, and lovely gardens. There is a restaurant and halls for conferences and dinners, the specialities being home-made bread and cakes from their own bakery, using flour ground in the Priory Water Mill, fed from the moat, and local ale, apple juice and Sussex wines. Art exhibitions etc are held in the house, which is open from 25th March until 31st October from 11am to 5.30pm, and on Sundays in February, March and November. Information at the address above. Tel: 0323 440161 or 0323 844224

Piltdown Pond

Location: Piltdown Common, near Newick, between Haywards Heath and Uckfield
Type and Size: Small common land pond
How to Find: Take the A272 from Maresfield towards Newick. Turn left at Piltdown Common. The pond is 100 yards further on the left
Carp Stock: Some carp to 10lbs
Category: Mixed Fishery
Other Species: General coarse fish
Permits: Free fishing
Cost: None
BK Rating: Difficult
W/A: Southern
Comments: Very heavily weeded pond - but worth a try, as there's not much free fishing these days!

Pippingford Park Estate Lakes

Location: Pippingford Corner, Nutley, Near East Grinstead
Type and Size: 5 man-made lakes of ¾ acre to 5 acres
How to Find: Take the A22 from East Grinstead towards Eastbourne. Estate is one mile before Nutley and Pippingford Corner. Entrance on left. Pathfinder OS Map Ref. TQ43/53
Carp Stock: Army Lake (¾ acre) - 20 carp to 15lbs; Lake 1 (4 acres) - 40 carp to 18lbs (average 8lbs); Lake 2 - as for Lake 1; Lake 3 (5 acres) - many small commons to 15lbs; Lake 4 (¾ acre) - very few small fish
Category: Carp Waters
Other Species: Many good chub to 5lbs; bream, tench, orfe

Permits: Richard Morris, Home Farm, Pippingford Park, Nutley TN22 3NW. Tel: 082571 2205 (estate office)
Cost: Senior - £100 per season. Junior - £30 per season
BK Rating: Army - Easy to Moderate. Others - Easy for small fish
Control: Pippingford Estate Co. Ltd.
Restrictions: No carp sacks or keepnets
W/A: Southern
Comments: No day tickets. Half season tickets available. Camouflage clothing not advised as this is an army training area. A truly beautiful lake to fish, situated in Ashdown Forest in a peaceful wooded valley full of wild animals and rare plants. Weedy waters, excellent for stalking, 3 fish per day common, 7 to 8 a day possible. Army often on night manoeuvres - beware!

Searles Lake

Location: Near Nutley, off the A22 just south of Ashdown Forest (home of Winnie the Pooh)
Type and Size: Large estate lake, much used for match fishing
Carp Stock: Some carp, numbers and sizes not known
Category: Mixed Fishery
Other Species: Roach, rudd, tench, pike and bream
Permits: Tanyard Fisheries, Tanyard Lane, Furners Green, Danehill. Tel: 082571 2070 (evenings)
Cost: £5 per day, in advance only
Control: Private, although a club fishes one bank
Restrictions: Barbless hooks; no keepnets; no night fishing - open 8am till 9pm; no pike fishing until October 1st; 20 anglers only per day
BK Rating: Not known
W/A: Southern

Withyham Mill Carp Lake

Location: Near Crowborough
Type and Size: 6½ acre lake on private estate, 10 to 25 ft deep
Carp Stock: Well stocked with carp to 32lbs
Category: Mixed Fishery
Other Species: Tench, bream, roach and rudd
Permits: Cornell Fishery Developments, Charter House, 29a London Road, Croydon CR0 2RB - syndicate only, to include other carp waters
Cost: About £30 per season
Control: Cornell Fishery Developments
BK Rating: Moderate
Restrictions: No night fishing at present - open from 5am to 7pm only
W/A: Southern

Wyland Lakes A

Location: Powdermill Lane, Catsfield, Battle
Type and Size: Six farm lakes
How to Find: Take the A2100 Hastings–Battle road and turn left on the B2095 just before Battle. Wyland Farm is on the left
Carp Stock: All the lakes contain some carp. One is designated as a specimen carp lake and the record fish for the water is said to be 28lbs. Best common in 1985 was 20lbs 1oz; best mirror 15¼lbs
Category: Mixed Fishery
Other Species: Rudd, tench, perch, bream and roach
Permits: From Wyland Farm, Powdermill Lane, Battle. Tel: Ninfield (0424) 892963. Day tickets. Chalet tariffs include 24 hours a day fishing
Cost: Specimen Carp Lake - about £5 per day, other lakes about £3 per day
Control: Private
BK Rating: Moderate
W/A: Southern
Comments: This is a working farm, mainly sheep, where you can go for a holiday. There are chalets with various tariffs, for example £100 a week for two adults including fishing. One day costs £20, with £15 for each subesquent day. Touring caravans pay £3 per day (fishing extra). Tents are £1–£3 per day; £5 to £15 per week, fishing extra. Bivvies allowed at lakeside at no extra charge - fishing rates only. Near Hastings, Eastbourne and Rye. Three 20's to 25lbs caught in October 1989. Please note prices are approximate

ESSEX

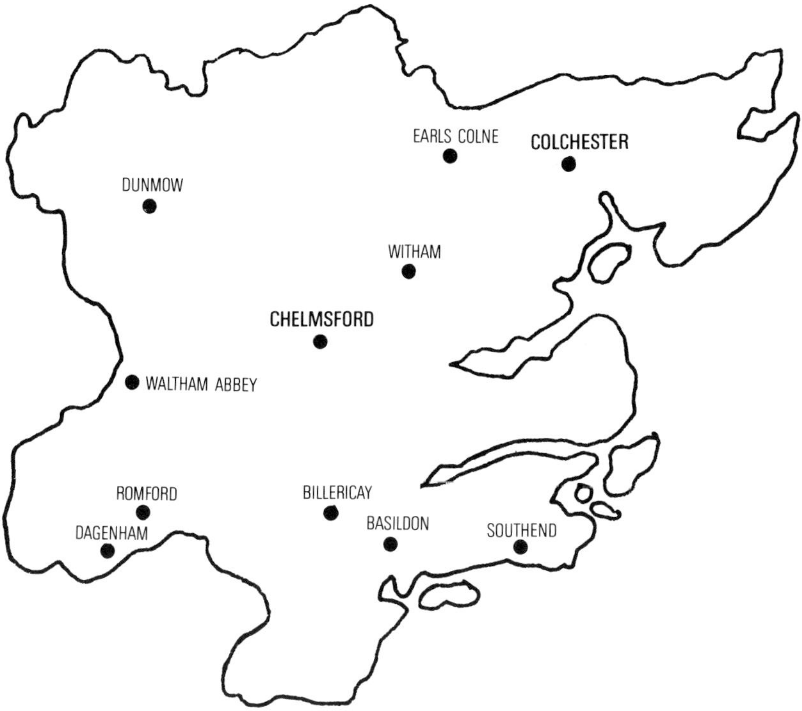

Ardleigh Reservoir

Location: Near Colchester
How to Find: On the road to Manningtree, about 4 miles out of Colchester
Type and Size: 440 acre reservoir
Carp Stock: Few carp, but very large
Category: Mixed Fishery
Other Species: Most species to specimen sizes. Pike to 44¾lbs
Permits: From the lodge at fishery entrance
BK Rating: Super-Difficult
W/A: Anglian
Comments: Location of carp very difficult. Depths to 60 feet. Upper 30's caught every year by the specialist – larger fish present

Arena Lake

Location: Near Thurrock – off the old A13 and not far from the M25/Dartford Tunnel
Type and Size: Open pit of about 10 acres; very weedy
Carp Stock: Well stocked with carp to mid-doubles, and a few 20's
Category: Carp Water
Permits: Day tickets on bank
BK Rating: Moderate
W/A: Thames

Aveley Lakes

Location: Romford Road, Aveley, near Romford
Carp Stock: Well stocked with carp to over 20lbs
Category: Mixed Fishery
Other Species: Tench and rudd
Permits: Aveley Lakes, Romford Road, Aveley, near Romford... waiting list, season tickets only
Control: Private
BK Rating: Moderate
W/A: Thames

Boreham

Location: Wallace's Farm, Russell Green, Little Waltham, near Chelmsford

Type and Size: Gravel pit of 1¼ acres

How to Find: Take the A12 towards Chelmsford, then the B1137 towards Boreham. Keep to the right of the slip road and turn right at the traffic lights along 300 yards of dual carriageway under the main A12 to the roundabout. Take the Boreham exit and go through the village to the Cock Inn. Turn left over the A12 bridge and follow the road for about 1½ miles to the Anglia Building Supplies Yard on the left. Wallace's Farm is opposite this. Car park is opposite the RMC Plant area

Carp Stock: About 40, mainly doubles

Category: Mixed Fishery

Other Species: Pike, bream, tench and roach

Permits: This is a Leisure Sport Angling Special Venue. Limited tickets for the season from LSA, Thorpe Park, Staines Road, Chertsey, Surrey. Tel: Chertsey 64872

Cost: £16 for the season, juniors/OAP/disabled £8

Restrictions: No night fishing, dawn to dusk only

BK Rating: Easy

Control: Leisure Sport Angling

W/A: Anglian

Comments: This is another of those waters which we have put in for those carp anglers who might want to fish a water where there is not much carp fishing, and few carp, but where they might just get a reasonable sized fish. Waters of this kind should not be regarded as carp waters; only as waters which are said to contain a few good carp

Bournebridge Lakes

Location: Bournebridge Lane, Stapleford Abbotts, Romford. Tel: 04028 279
Type and Size: Three small lakes
Carp Stock: All well stocked with carp to about 12lbs
Category: Mixed Fishery
Other Species: Tench and rudd
Permits: Day tickets in advance, from the above address - phone for details
Control: Private
BK Rating: Easy
W/A: Anglian
Comments: Refreshments and toilets on site; good family water

Braxted Park Lake

Location: Braxted Park, Braxted, near Witham
Type and Size: 11 acre estate lake
Carp Stock: About 200 carp, of which most are over 10lbs, a number of 20's, including two commons, and at least one 30 pounder
Category: Carp Water
Other Species: Some coarse fish
Permits: We think this water is now controlled by a syndicate; you might be able to get information from Mr M Clark, Braxted Park Estate Office, Braxted, near Witham
Control: Private syndicate
Restrictions: Syndicate membership only - no other permits
BK Rating: Moderate
W/A: Anglian

Braxted Park Reservoir

Location: Braxted Park, Braxted, near Witham
Type and Size: 7 acre estate reservoir
Carp Stock: Stocked in 1987 with about 50 carp from 8-14lbs. As this has been a trout fishery several carp have been caught on the fly, the best weighing 24lbs
Category: Mixed Fishery
Other Species: Trout and possibly some other coarse fish apart from the carp
Permits: Probably now controlled by a syndicate. For information try Mr M Clark, Braxted Park Estate Office, Braxted, near Witham
Control: Private syndicate
Restrictions: No permits - syndicate members only
BK Rating: Moderate
W/A: Anglian

Bulphan Park

Location: Off the A128 near Brentwood
Type and Size: Tiny park lake
Carp Stock: Well stocked with carp to 20lbs
Category: Carp Water
Permits: Day tickets on bank
BK Rating: Fairly Easy
W/A: Thames

Central Park Lake

Location: Chelmsford
Type and Size: Good sized town park lake
Carp Stock: Well stocked with carp - a 19 pounder was reported in 1990
Category: Mixed Fishery
Other Species: Tench, roach and rudd
Permits: From tackle dealers in Essex
Cost: Season £12.50 per rod; day tickets £1
Control: RHP Angling Club - try tackle shops, or Chelmsford Borough Council for details
Restrictions: No barbless hooks, boilies, particle baits or floating baits (sounds as if they don't want the carp caught, doesn't it?)
BK Rating: Moderate
W/A: Anglian
Comments: The draconian restrictions are apparently because the Council was under pressure by the Royal Society for the Prevention of Cruelty to Birds to close the lake to anglers (I hope no angler supports the RSPB in any way, as we have come across many 'anti-angling' instances by this organisation, which we understand often catches birds in fine nets in which they become trapped, so that they can examine and 'ring' them!)

Chigborough Lakes

Location: Maldon, not far from Southend
Type and Size: Several large, matured gravel pits with island and bars
Carp Stock: Heavily stocked with carp to upper doubles

Category: Mixed Fishery
Other Species: Roach, bream, tench, perch and pike
Permits: Day tickets from bailiffs on bank - season tickets also available
Control: Private
BK Rating: Easy
W/A: Thames

Churchwood Fisheries

Location: Doddington Place, Blackmore Road, Brentwood CM15 0HX. Tel: Brentwood 200985 or Coxtie Green 372948
Type and Size: Two estate lakes of 3 acres and 1 acre
Carp Stock: Jenkinsons - carp between 12lbs and 24lbs. Bottom Lake (3 acres) - some small carp
Category: Mixed Fisheries
Other Species: Tench (Jenkinsons); tench, bream, roach, rudd and perch (Bottom)
Permits: Day tickets in advance only, by post, telephone or in person at the address above. No fishing without a ticket in advance
Cost: £10 per day; £5 per half day; £15 for 24 hours
Restrictions: No animals; no carp sacks; no keepnets; barbless hooks recommended
BK Rating: Moderate
W/A: Anglian
Comments: Private nature reserve - over 400 species of wild flowers. 20 anglers per day only. Club bookings allowed. Tackle and bait to order when booking ticket - all bookings on 0277 200985

Claverhambury Lake

Location: Claverhambury Road, Waltham Abbey
Type and Size: Dammed estate lake, a bit less than 2 acres
How to Find: Find Galley Hill Road, Waltham Abbey and follow this to Claverhambury Road
Carp Stock: Well stocked with carp to double figure size
Category: Carp Only
Permits: P and B Hill, 44 Highbridge Street, Waltham Abbey. Tel: Waltham Cross 711932
Baits/Methods: Normal carp methods with boilies and multiples as baits
Control: Private, day ticket
Restrictions: 10 anglers a day only
BK Rating: Moderate
W/A: Thames
Comments: A pleasant little fishery, stream-fed with trees on one side. Depths from 2ft to just over 8ft

Cobblers Mead Lake

Location: Herd Lane, Corringham
Type and Size: 5 acre gravel pit
How to Find: In Corringham
Carp Stock: Some big carp to 24lbs
Category: Mixed Fishery
Other Species: Bream, tench, roach and crucians
Permits: M.G.H. Properties, Box 18, Canvey Island, Essex. Tel: 0268 683946
Restrictions: Members only
BK Rating: Moderate
Control: Private
Comments: Information and permits also from Basildon Angling Centre, Whitemore Way

Dedham Mill

Location: Clovers Mill Ltd, Gunhill, Dedham, Colchester
Type and Size: Mill Pool and River Stour
Carp Stock: Well stocked with carp to at least double figure size
Category: Mixed Fishery
Other Species: Bream, pike and dace
Permits: Day and season tickets from the mill, or from K D Radcliffe Fishing Tackle, High Street, Colchester
Cost: £1 per day - £6 per season
Control: Private
BK Rating: Moderate
W/A: Anglian

Dunmow Lake

Location: Near Dunmow in north Essex, just off the M11
Type and Size: 9 acre lake
Carp Stock: Well stocked with carp to 20lbs plus
Category: Carp Only
Permits: Season (syndicate) only; for details tel: 0376 20662

Control: Private
Restrictions: No day tickets
BK Rating: Moderate
W/A: Anglian

Epping Forest Ponds

Location: Epping Forest
Type and Size: Small ponds
How to Find: Chingford, Loughton area off the A11
Carp Stock: Most have small carp, but fish to over 30lbs have been taken
Category: Mixed Fisheries
Other Species: General coarse fish
Permits: Many are free: Warren Pond; Perch Pond; Hollow Pond; Eagle Pond; Highams Park Lake; Connaught Water; Ornamental Water
Cost: Day tickets about £1 per day on bank
BK Rating: Moderate, some are Easy
Control: Superintendent of Epping Forest, The Warren, Loughton
Restrictions: On application
W/A: Thames
Comments: Busy forest ponds, some of which contain more and bigger fish than might be expected - never despise 'public' waters

Gosfield Lake

Location: Halstead
Type and Size: Big 45 acre gravel pit
How to Find: Gosfield, near Halstead, off the A1017 north of Braintree
Carp Stock: Well stocked with carp
Category: Mixed Fishery
Other Species: Perch, roach, tench, pike
Permits: C W Turp, Gosfield Lake, Church Road, Gosfield
Cost: Season ticket - about £66. 12 hour - about £2.75 (1 rod); 24 hours - about £5.50
BK Rating: Difficult
Control: Private
Restrictions: 75% of the bank, fishing not allowed
W/A: Thames
Comments: Details and permits from shop on site. Boats for hire

Hainault Park

Location: Hainault, off the Romford-Chigwell road
Type and Size: 5 acre lake
Carp Stock: Heavily stocked with small carp, doubles, several twenties and two 30's, the best about 35lbs
Category: Mixed Fishery
Other Species: Roach, perch and pike
Permits: Day tickets on site. Night syndicate - enquire at lake
Restrictions: No night fishing except for syndicate members
BK Rating: Moderate
W/A: Thames
Comments: A well known water, heavily fished - danger of cars being broken into

Hatfield Forest Lake

Location: Near Bishops Stortford
Type and Size: Large lake
How to Find: Information from the Lake Warden
Carp Stock: Some carp
Category: Mixed Fishery
Other Species: Pike, tench, roach, rudd
Permits: In advance only from: The Warden, The Shell House, Takeley, Bishops Stortford. Tel: 0279 870477
Cost: Season tickets about £40; day tickets - £2
BK Rating: Easy
Control: National Trust
Restrictions: No groundbait
W/A: Thames
Comments: Little known - might be worth investigating

Holy Field Carp Fishery

Location: Fishers Green Lane, Crooked Mile, Waltham Abbey. Tel: 0992 768012
Type and Size: Large lake near London
Carp Stock: Heavily stocked with carp, many doubles and several twenties to 23lb 14oz (a common)
Category: Carp Water
Permits: Don Spinks on the phone number above
Cost: Season tickets at £115
Control: Private
Restrictions: Season tickets only
BK Rating: Moderate
W/A: Thames
Comments: Clubhouse, cafeteria, full licensed bar, toilets, showers and colour TV

Lake Meadows

Location: Billericay
Carp Stock: Well stocked with many carp of all sizes
Category: Carp Water
BK Rating: Easy
W/A: Anglian
Comments: We have not been able to find out much about this water, so those wishing to fish there will have to enquire locally about permits etc

Layer Pits

Location: Colchester
Carp Stock: Very heavily stocked with many small carp, but plenty of doubles and 20's, and one or two thirties up to 35lbs
Category: Mixed Fishery
Control: Colchester Angling Preservation Society. Secretary: D. Upsher, 36 Winsley Road, Colchester
Restrictions: No night fishing
BK Rating: Easy
W/A: Anglian
Comments: A very easy water where you can catch many carp in a day. An ideal place for one to practice methods and tactics

Lyatts Lake

Location: Just off main A120 between Dunmow and Braintree at Rayne in Essex
Type and Size: Approx 10 acres - gravel pit, spring fed, very clear water
Carp Stock: Recently stocked with 350 mirror, leather and common carp up to 20lbs. Most fish between 7lbs - 14lbs
Category: Carp Water
Restrictions: No night fishing, no sacking. See season ticket for all club rules
Control: Privately owned. For season tickets, contact the owner, John Harvey, on (0376) 20662, numbers restricted
W/A: Anglian
Comments: Attractive lake with excellent water quality, car parking available

Nazeing Lake

Location: Nazeing, near Dagenham, London
Type and Size: 6 acre lake
Carp Stock: Very well stocked with carp to over 20lbs
Category: Mixed Fishery
Other Species: Tench and bream
Permits: Lee Valley Regional Park Authority, Myddelton House, Bulls Cross, Enfield. Tel: 0992 717711
Cost: Weekly permits, cost on application
Control: Lee Valley RPA
BK Rating: Moderate
W/A: Thames
Comments: Known in the past as an excellent winter water, with some big commons present

Newland Hall Carp Fishery

Location: Near Colchester
Type and Size: Lake of two acres
How to Find: The lake is on the A1060, 4 miles from Chelmsford
Carp Stock: Well stocked with carp to 25lbs
Category: Carp Water
Permits: Tel: 0245 31463 for details
Cost: Day tickets about £4. Season tickets about £30
BK Rating: Not known
Control: Private
W/A: Anglian
Comments: Small spring-fed lake in pleasant surroundings

Old Heath Lake (Snake Pit)

Location: Colchester
How to Find: In the town of Old Heath, 5 miles from Colchester
Type and Size: Sand pit of about 8 acres
Carp Stock: Three fish! A 45lb common, a 35lb common and a 20+ mirror
Category: Mixed Fishery
Other Species: Roach, rudd, bream, tench and pike
Permits: Maulden AC. Available from local tackle shops
Cost: Approx £20 a season

BK Rating: Super-Difficult
W/A: Anglian
Comments: A very difficult water producing only two or three carp each year including Britain's biggest ever common carp. About 30% of the lake has hawthorn bushes and trees in the water. There is a severe litter problem in and out of the water and the lake is slowly being filled in

Pipps Hill Fisheries A

Location: Basildon
Type and Size: 25 acre lake, with big hotel by the lake
How to Find: Cranes Farm Road, Basildon
Carp Stock: Some large carp, doubles and twenties
Category: Mixed Fishery
Other Species: General coarse fish
Permits: Day tickets on bank
Cost: £2 per rod for 12 hours; £3.50 per rod for 24 hours; weekend - £7.50 (two rods)
BK Rating: Very Difficult
Restrictions: No sacking
Control: Pipps Hill Country Club, Cranes Farm Road, Basildon. Tel: Basildon 23456
W/A: Thames
Comments: Formerly known as Aquatels. Carp caught to 25¾lbs in 1990

Priory Park Lakes

Location: Priory Park, Southend
Type and Size: Park lake
How to Find: In Southend
Carp Stock: Well stocked with carp to over 20lbs
Category: Carp Water
Other Species: Mixed coarse fish
Permits: Day tickets on site
Cost: On application
BK Rating: Moderate
Control: Council
W/A: Thames
Comments: Busy park lake, heavily fished by carp anglers. Plenty of doubles

River Roding

Location: Passingford Bridge, near Romford
Type and Size: 30 miles long river, tributary of the Thames
Carp Stock: Some carp in the Passingford Bridge area, sizes not known
Category: Few Carp
Other Species: Roach, chub, pike, bream and tench
Permits: From bailiff on bank upstream of bridge
Control: Woodford AS, north of bridge, members only, details from Secretary, 22 Evanrigg Terrace, Woodford Green, Essex (no day tickets). Barkingside and District AS has 1½ miles downstream of bridge, Secretary: D J French, 64 Khartoum Road, Ilford. Other information from Edko Sports, 136 North Street, Romford
BK Rating: Difficult
W/A: Thames

Rockells Farm

Location: Duddenhoe End, Saffron Walden
Type and Size: 34 acre lake, with fishing platforms
Carp Stock: Heavily stocked with many small carp, and plenty of doubles to 18lbs
Category: Mixed Fishery
Other Species: Tench, roach and chub
Permits: Day tickets on bank during the week; booking in advance only at weekends from the owner, E Westerhuis, at the above address. Tel: 0763 838053
Cost: £4 per day
Control: Private
Restrictions: Weekend fishing must be booked in advance - no tickets on bank. Barbless or semi-barbed hooks only; no groundbait or boilies(!)
BK Rating: Easy
W/A: Anglian
Comments: Some good doubles, but 50-100lb 'bags' of fish using match tactics are common which is perhaps why they ban boilies... about the best food a carp could get!

Shoebury Park

Location: Elm Road, Shoeburyness
Type and Size: Small park lake of about 2 acres
Carp Stock: Well stocked with small carp and several 20lb commons
Category: Mixed Fishery
Other Species: Tench and roach

Permits: Day tickets on bank
BK Rating: Moderate for small fish. Difficult for the big ones
W/A: Anglian

Southminster Pits

Location: Southminster, near Maldon
Type and Size: Several small pits
Carp Stock: Well stocked with carp to 20lbs
Category: Mixed Fishery
Other Species: Pike, roach and bream
Permits: Members only water of Billericay AC – membership from local tackle shops, open to all
BK Rating: Easy
W/A: Anglian
Comments: Trout lake also on site. Billericay AC have other good carp waters on the same ticket, including Straight Mill

South Weald

Location: South Weald Park, near Brentwood
Carp Stock: Well stocked with carp, including a number of 20's to 28lbs
Category: Carp Water
Permits: Day tickets on bank for one lake; other lake, members only
Baits/Methods: Advanced carp fishing baits and methods
Control: Elm Park, Hornchurch and District Angling Society. Secretary: W Holton, 4 Fairford Way, Harold Hill, Romford, Essex
BK Rating: Difficult
W/A: Thames
Comments: We have not been able to find out much about this fishery, so those wishing to fish there will have to enquire locally about permits

Stanford-le-Hope

Location: Wharfe Road, Stanford-le-Hope
Type and Size: Two open gravel pits of 6 and 7 acres. Few carp, but fish to 18½lbs reported
How to Find: Take the A13 from the Dartford Tunnel towards Southend. After 6½ miles take the A1014 Stanford-le-Hope/Crayton turn off. Follow the Stanford signs to Southend Road, fork left at the Burmah Garage, and take Wharfe Road under the railway bridge onto the unmade road and the entrance is on the left. Park cars in either car park but not on the causeway between the lakes
Carp Stock: Not known; thought to be not many
Category: Few Carp
Other Species: Pike, perch, roach, bream, tench, rudd, eels, crucian carp, all of which grow to large sizes
Permits: Season tickets only from Leisure Sport, Thorpe Park, Staines Road, Chertsey, Surrey. Tel: Chertsey 64872
Cost: £22 per season. Juniors/OAP/disabled £11
Restrictions: No restrictions – night fishing allowed
BK Rating: Probably Difficult as there are not many carp, but many fish of other species

Control: Leisure Sport Angling
W/A: Anglian
Comments: Like a number of gravel pit fisheries we have included this water because control (Leisure Sport) has reported carp from the water, but they are often few and far between on such waters, some of which may well not be worth serious carp fishing

Starlane

Location: Wakering, near Southend
Type and Size: Two small lakes, and a larger water
Carp Stock: Small lakes - well stocked with carp to just under 20lbs; large lake - plenty of carp to 35lbs
Category: Mixed Fishery
Other Species: Pike, tench and roach
Permits: Small lakes - day ticket on bank; larger lake - syndicate (enquire at small lakes)
BK Rating: Moderate
W/A: Anglian

Swanscombe Farm Fishery

Location: Lamberts Lane, off Tey Road, Earls Colne. Tel: 0787 223562
Type and Size: Lake of about 3 acres
Carp Stock: Well stocked with carp, best reported was 22lbs
Category: Carp Water
Other Species: Tench
Permits: Day tickets on site
Cost: £5 per day
Control: Private
BK Rating: Moderate
W/A: Anglian
Comments: Reduced rates for OAP's and children. Lodge, toilets and tackle hire. Facilities for the disabled. There is also a 4½ acre trout lake stocked with rainbow and brown trout to 10lbs. The fishery is open all the year

The Chase

Location: Dagenham
Type and Size: Large gravel pit
How to Find: Near Dagenham East Underground Station
Carp Stock: Good carp
Category: Mixed Fishery
Other Species: Roach, bream, tench, pike, perch, crucians
Permits: Day tickets from bailiff on bank
Cost: On application
BK Rating: Moderate
Control: White Hart Anglers' Club
Restrictions: No night fishing
W/A: Thames
Comments: Information from Edko Sports, 136 North Street, Romford

Thorndon Park

Location: Halway Lane, off the A127 near Brentwood
Type and Size: Park lake of 2-3 acres
Carp Stock: Only about twenty, from 20-25lbs
Category: Mixed Fishery
Other Species: Pike, tench, bream, roach
Permits: Day tickets on bank
Restrictions: No night fishing
BK Rating: Difficult
W/A: Anglian

Wanstead and Woodford Ponds

Location: Woodford and Snaresbrook areas
Type and Size: Small ponds
How to Find: Near Wanstead
Carp Stock: Some carp, sizes not known
Category: Eagle Pond, Hollow Pond, Whipps Cross Pond, Knighton Wood Pond - Mixed Fisheries
Other Species: General coarse fish
Permits: None required
Cost: Free
BK Rating: Insufficient information
Control: Public
W/A: Thames
Comments: Some free fishing near London! Make sure that you have Water Authority Licences

Warren Pond

Location: Near Chingford
Type and Size: Medium sized gravel pit
Carp Stock: Sizes and numbers not known, but some carp to double figures
Category: Mixed Fishery
Other Species: Bream and roach
Permits: From bailiff on bank
Control: Private, but we have not been able to find out much about this water, so we suggest you enquire about the location and other details from local tackle shops
BK Rating: Not known
W/A: Thames

GLOUCESTERSHIRE

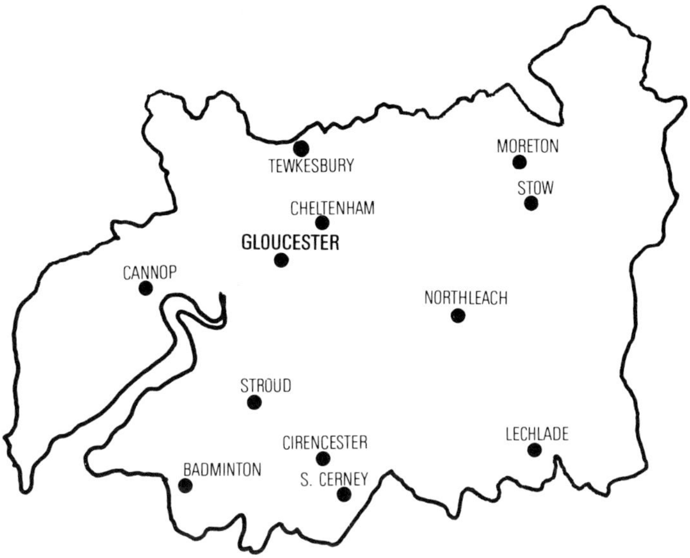

Adlestrop Lake

Location: Near Adlestrop Station, Stow-on-the-Wold

How to Find: Take the A436 road from Stow-on-the-Wold towards Chipping Norton. After about 2 miles and immediately after a railway bridge, turn left towards Evenlode. The lake is on the right

Type and Size: Stream-fed dammed estate lake, long and narrow, 2½ acres

Carp Stock: Probably only 20–30 mirrors, mostly doubles to about 18lbs. Now restocked with smaller carp

Category: Few Carp

Other Species: Tench, roach

Permits: Moreton-in-Marsh Angling Club. Enquire locally

Control: Moreton-in-Marsh Angling Club

BK Rating: Difficult

W/A: Severn Trent

Comments: Weedy water, quite shallow, with a big bed of broad-leaved pondweed at the dam end. Most carp caught after dark, but can be stalked in weed at shallow end in daytime in warm weather. This is the only water we know of on which a sheep has been hooked and played! Whilst Roger Emmet was fishing there several sheep jumped into the water and swam across the lake. One of these swam through Roger's line before he could remove it and was hooked. He was unable to control the sheep, which swam across the lake, climbed the further bank and went through a barbed wire fence, breaking the line!

Apperley Pools

Location: Apperley, near Tewkesbury
Type and Size: Two pools, about 4 acres in all
How to Find: Take the A38 Gloucester road from Tewkesbury, turn right at the sign for Apperley. Continue from village on Gabbs Lane to where road bears left. Pools are on your left
Carp Stock: A few small carp to 3 or 4lbs
Category: Few Carp
Other Species: Bream, roach, chub, perch
Permits: Birmingham Anglers Association (members only), 100 Icknield Port Road, Rotton Park, Birmingham B16 OAP. Tel: 021-451 9111 (9.30am to 1.30pm, and 7pm to 9pm)
Cost: About £13 per year (includes all BAA waters)
BK Rating: Difficult, as there are few carp
Control: Birmingham AA
Restrictions: No groundbait of any kind
W/A: Severn-Trent
Comments: Not worth considering for serious carp fishing, unless you just want a day's fishing, with the chance of an occasional carp

Badminton Lake

Location: On Duke of Beaufort's Badminton Estate, Badminton village
Type and Size: Estate lake, 1½ acres
How to Find: Turn off A46 Bath to Stroud road at traffic lights by Cross Hands Hotel. Right turn is signposted Badminton. In village, turn right and take left turn at end into the Badminton estate. Lake on right in front of house
Carp Stock: Numerous small commons; a few mirrors to 19lbs recently introduced
Category: Carp Water
Other Species: Roach
Permits: Badminton Estate Office, Badminton, Glos. Season only, limited
Cost: About £25 per season
Baits/Methods: Normal carp methods, some surface fishing. Usual baits
Control: Season ticket, Badminton Estate
Restrictions: No night fishing
W/A: Wessex
BK Rating: Easy
Comments: Muddy type water, very open with no cover and little weed

Bradley's Pit

Location: On the edge of the village of South Cerney, near Cirencester
Type and Size: Huge gravel pit of 115 acres
How to Find: Take the Cerney Wick road from South Cerney and Bradley's will be seen on the right just outside the village
Carp Stock: Few carp, but said to be some very big fish. Commons to about 15lbs and every year there are rumours of 30's and 40's being caught, none of which are authenticated. Authenticated 26¼lb common caught in July 1985. The lake almost certainly contains some thirties
Category: Few Carp
Other Species: Tench, pike, roach, bream, perch, chub
Permits: South Cerney Angling Club. Secretary: D Savage, 35 Alexandra Drive, Cirencester, Glos, and from tackle shops in Swindon and Cirencester
Cost: About £10 a season

Control: Club
BK Rating: Very Difficult
W/A: Thames
Comments: South Cerney AC have a club house here and the club has most of the best fishing in this area, which contains thousands of acres of flooded gravel pits. Ignore the stories of huge carp caught from this lake and only believe what you see

Bredons Hardwick

Location: Tewkesbury to Bredon road, about two miles from Tewkesbury
Type and Size: 10 acre gravel pit
Carp Stock: Heavily stocked with small carp and doubles, and said to be fish to 30lbs
Category: Mixed Fishery
Other Species: Roach, bream tench, perch and rudd
Permits: Tredworth Tackle, High Street, Gloucester. Tel: Gloucester 23009
Cost: Season tickets only at £30 - syndicate
Restrictions: No fishing allowed in the shallows(!)
BK Rating: Fairly Hard
W/A: Severn Trent
Comments: Very clear, weedy water; fish location very important

Peter Mohan with a 20 caught from a Gloucestershire water on a KM Maestro Cream RM30 boilie in September 1990

Burley Fields Lake

Location: Crippetts Lane, Leckhampton, Cheltenham. Tel: Cheltenham 862905
Type and Size: 2½ acre man-made, spring-fed lake
Carp Stock: Heavily stocked with carp to 20lbs
Category: Mixed Fishery
Other Species: Perch, roach, bream, rudd and tench
Permits: In advance only from the address above - open to all
Cost: £5 per season, then £3 per day, or £5 per day for non-members
Restrictions: No keepnets
BK Rating: Easy
W/A: Severn Trent
Comments: Weed-free fishery with easily accessible pitches for disabled anglers

Peter Mohan with a typical Crooked Withies 10 pounder

Cannop Ponds

Location: Cannop Valley, Parkend, between Coleford and Lydney
Type and Size: Two very beautiful forest lakes, in the Forest of Dean - 4½ and 5½ acres. Most of the carp are in the lower lake
Carp Stock: Not a large number, and hard to locate, but they do go to over 20lbs, with some good commons
Category: Few Carp
Other Species: Bream, roach, tench and pike
Permits: Bailiff on bank
Control: Yorkley and District AC. Permits and details from Sport and Leisure, Market Place, Coleford; Robert Sports, 31 Market Street, Cinderford; Peter James Sports, 17 Newerne Street, Lydney. Tel: Dean 842515
BK Rating: Very Difficult
W/A: Severn Trent
Comments: Ranges from 2 feet deep at the top end, where a stream comes in from the upper lake, to 18 feet at the big dam. There are said to be a few big carp in the upper lake

Chad Lakes

Location: Near Stow-on-the-Wold, off the B4450 near Bledington
Type and Size: 2 acre lake
Carp Stock: Well stocked with carp to about 14lbs
Category: Mixed Fishery
Permits: Day tickets. Information on 0608 74252
Control: Private
BK Rating: Moderate
W/A: Thames
Comments: There is another lake on the site, a syndicate carp water; attractive Cotswold location, with toilet and car park

Cokes Pit

Location: On the road from South Cerney to Ashton Keynes
Type and Size: Gravel pit of about 12 acres
Carp Stock: Some carp to 18lbs; bigger fish have been seen and a fish of well over 30lbs was caught several years ago, although this fish is now dead
Category: Mixed Fishery
Other Species: Tench, roach, rudd, bream and pike
Permits: Ashton Keynes AC - tickets from local tackle shops in Cirencester and Swindon at £10 per season, to include other waters
Control: Club
BK Rating: Difficult
W/A: Thames
Comments: This lake is little fished by carp anglers, though it is a good tench water. Since it is a Nature Reserve quite a large part of the bank cannot be fished. Very weedy with lots of shallow bars and islands

Cotswold Hoburne A

Location: Cotswold Water Park, near Cirencester
Type and Size: Two quite large gravel pits
Carp Stock: Said to be some carp - numbers and sizes not known
Category: Few Carp?

Other Species: Roach, bream, tench, rudd and perch
Permits: Residents only - at reception
Control: Private
BK Rating: Difficult
W/A: Thames
Comments: 70 acre site with timber built lodges to let. Swimming pool, licensed lakeside club, boating, shop etc - holiday camp type atmosphere. Open Easter to end of October. Bookings from Hoseasons Holidays, Sunway House, Lowestoft NR32 3LT. Tel: 0502 500 500. Dozens of other lakes in the area, a number of which hold carp to over 20lbs

Court Farm

Location: Court Farm, Lemington, near Moreton-in-Marsh
Type and Size: 2½ acre man-made lake
Carp Stock: About 150 fish to 16lbs, best to date is 20lbs, but the average is about 4lb
Category: Carp Water
Other Species: Rudd and roach
Permits: Bill Gadsby, Court Farm
Cost: Day tickets at £5 per day
Control: Private
BK Rating: Moderate
W/A: Severn Trent
Comments: Night fishing is allowed, and another pond for carp is being constructed. There is also a one acre trout lake on the farm

Crooked Withies Lake

Location: Near Tewkesbury
Type and Size: 2½ acre lake
Carp Stock: Heavily stocked with carp only to about 14lbs
Category: Carp Only
Permits: Syndicate season tickets only from: The Fishery Controller, 15 Stafford Court, Riverside Close, Bedford MK42 9DE. Tel: 0234 212066. Some vacancies in April each year, and occasionally throughout the season
Cost: About £95 per season
Control: Private
BK Rating: Easy
Restrictions: No long stay fishing or camping (maximum 24 hours). Alternate Saturday and Sunday rota
W/A: Severn Trent
Comments: A very attractive lake with an island, and surrounded by mature flowering bushes and trees. Very quiet and peaceful. Plenty of mirrors and commons from 4 to 10lbs, and a good number of lower doubles. Small exclusive syndicate, with vacancies every year. Guest tickets for friends of members. Night fishing allowed, though the water fishes best in the daytime. Good winter water. Warning - private property; do not visit without permission. Season and day tickets available on other carp only waters, on application to the above address

Gardners Pool

Location: Village of Saul, 8 miles south of Gloucester
Type and Size: Mature gravel pit - 5 acres
How to Find: On the Gloucester-Bristol road (A38), turn right for Frampton-on-Severn just after roundabout. Cross Gloucester-Sharpness canal, water is on the right just before the village of Saul. Ordnance Survey Sheet 163
Carp Stock: Number not known, but not very heavily stocked. A number of doubles and perhaps two or three 20's to about 21lbs. Bigger fish are mirrors - some commons to about 13lbs
Category: Mixed Fishery
Other Species: Roach, tench, many eels
Permits: Gloucester United Anglers' Association, from tackle shops in Gloucester. Secretary: J Gibby, 70 Robert Raikes Avenue, Tuffley, Gloucester. Tel: 413972
Cost: £10.50 per season, limited in number
Baits/Methods: Normal, fairly advanced carp rigs and methods with boilies or some multiple baits
Control: Club
W/A: Severn Trent
BK Rating: Difficult
Comments: Shallow, weedy water. Very patchy - long spells with no takes

Ham Pool

Location: Near South Cerney, Cirencester
Type and Size: Gravel pit of 11 acres
How to Find: Ham Pool is the smaller water next to Bradley's on the edge of South Cerney village
Carp Stock: Some carp, sizes and numbers unknown
Category: Few Carp
Other Species: General coarse fish
Permits: South Cerney Angling Club. Membership Secretary: D Savage, 35 Alexandra Drive, Cirencester, Glos, and also from tackle shops in Swindon and Cirencester
Cost: About £10 per season
Control: Club
BK Rating: Very Difficult
W/A: Thames

Heron-Lily Pool

Location: Stroud area
Type and Size: Estate lake, 2½ acres
Carp Stock: 100+, mostly mirrors. Good average size, plenty of doubles
Category: Carp Only
Permits: Fishery Controller, 15 Stafford Court, Riverside Close, Bedford MK42 9DE. Tel: 0234 212066
Cost: About £110 per season
Baits/Methods: Normal fairly advanced carp fishing methods and baits
Restrictions: No bread, as water birds must not be hooked. No long stay fishing or camping
Control: Syndicate
BK Rating: Moderate
Comments: Very beautiful location; small exclusive syndicate with occasional vacancies. Fishes better in winter than summer. Never freezes!

Horseshoe Lake

Location: Just north of the village of Lechlade
Type and Size: Very large gravel pit of about 80 acres
How to Find: From Lechlade take the A361 road towards Burford. The entrance to the lake is about a mile from Lechlade on the right hand side going north
Carp Stock: Well stocked with carp, most of which are about 10lbs, but twenties are now being caught on a fairly regular basis. Fish over 30lbs are rumoured
Category: Mixed Fishery
Other Species: Bream, rudd, perch, tench
Permits: Season and day tickets from: Arthur Chase, The Paper Shop, Burford Road, Lechlade. Tel: Lechlade 52323. Tickets must be obtained before fishing
Cost: About £2 per day, season - about £17 (sunrise to sunset); around £35 - night season
Control: Private
Restrictions: Carp must not be retained
BK Rating: Easy
Baits/Methods: Normal carp fishing baits and methods
W/A: Thames
Comments: A huge lake, also used for sailing. Good catches possible, fish at present average about 12lbs

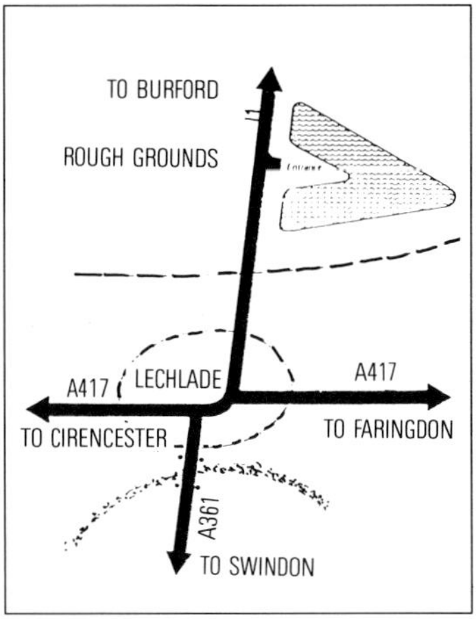

Lake 19

Location: South Cerney, near Cirencester
Type and Size: 8 acre gravel pit
Carp Stock: Well stocked with carp to 15½lbs, mostly commons from 8-10lbs, but growing well
Category: Carp Water
Other Species: Some other coarse fish
Permits: Club membership of Isis Angling Club from local tackle shops in Cirencester and Swindon
Cost: £15.50 per season
Control: Isis Angling Club - P Gilbert, Havelock Street, Swindon, Wilts
BK Rating: Easy
W/A: Thames

Lydney Boating Lake

Location: On the edge of the town of Lydney, between Gloucester and Chepstow
Type and Size: Town boating lake, 5 acres
How to Find: Take the A40 from Gloucester towards Ross, then the A48 towards Chepstow. At Lydney, turn left opposite Woolworths, and then right again past the houses
Carp Stock: Heavily stocked with commons to about 8lbs. Two or three mirrors to 19lbs
Category: Mixed Fishery
Other Species: Roach, tench, bream, rudd, eels, barbel
Permits: Sports shop in Lydney High Street on left going towards Chepstow
Cost: About £8 per season
Baits/Methods: Fairly unsophisticated carp methods and baits. Float fishing
Control: Lydney Angling Club. Secretary: M G Nash, 42 Templeway West, Lydney, Glos
BK Rating: Easy
W/A: Severn Trent
Comments: Busy town water, walkers, children and boats which are restricted to one end only. Very large island. Fishes best at night

Norton Fruit Farm

Location: Tewkesbury Road, Norton, Gloucester GL2 9LH. Tel: Gloucester 731203
Type and Size: One acre irrigation reservoir
How to Find: Norton Fruit Farm is on the A38 between Coombe Hill and Twigworth
Carp Stock: Heavily stocked with 40 doubles to about 20lbs
Category: Mixed Fishery
Other Species: Roach, rudd, tench, bream and perch
Permits: Mr Feakins, Norton Fruit Farm - day tickets
BK Rating: Very Easy
W/A: Severn Trent
Comments: Open banks with room for about 20 anglers; night fishing allowed

Roughgrounds Farm Lake

Location: Just north of Lechlade
Type and Size: Gravel pit of about 3 acres
How to Find: Take the A361 Lechlade to Burford road, and the entrance to the lake will be seen on the left hand side after about a mile, and just beyond the entrance to Horseshoe
Carp Stock: Well stocked with carp including a number of doubles
Category: Carp Water
Other Species: Some small mixed coarse fish
Permits: Day tickets from the Paper Shop, Burford Road, Lechlade. Tel: Lechlade 52323. Limited to 15 anglers per day
Cost: About £3 per day
Control: Private
BK Rating: Easy to Moderate
Restrictions: No keepnets
W/A: Thames

Staunton Court

Location: A417 from Gloucester 8 miles. From M50 (junction 2) 3 miles A417 by church at Staunton
Type and Size: Lake ¾ acre and small deep lake
Carp Stock: Stocked well with mirrors, commons and crucians up to 20lbs
Category: Mixed Fishery
Other Species: Tench, rudd, roach and bream
Permits: On bank - £4 per day; or night
Control: Private
Restrictions: Night arrival before 10.30pm. Barbless hooks. No keepnets or weigh sacks
BK Rating: Easy - Moderate
W/A: Severn Trent
Comments: Must dip nets on arrival in tanks provided

Watersmeet A

Location: Hartpury, near Gloucester. Tel: 0452 70358
Type and Size: Two mature pits of about 2 acres and a quarter of an acre
How to Find: Take the A40 Gloucester to Ross-on-Wye road and after about a mile turn right on the A417 towards Ledbury. The ponds will be seen on the left hand side just after the village of Hartpury and next to a white-painted guest house called 'Watersmeet'
Carp Stock: Numbers not known, although there are enough to be worth fishing for. Some commons to about 9lbs, and mirrors to around 15lbs. A few larger fish have been reported
Category: Mixed Fishery
Other Species: Tench, roach, rudd, bream
Permits: From Mr and Mrs Ring at the guest house. Some day tickets are issued and you can fish if you stay at the guest house, which is right on the edge of the lake. There is a bar and you can have meals etc - quite a pleasant spot for a fishing holiday, though quite busy in the summer
Cost: On application to Watersmeet, Hartpury, Gloucester
BK Rating: Difficult
Control: Private
Baits/Methods: This is not an easy water and there are not great numbers of carp, so fairly advanced baits and methods would be needed
W/A: Severn Trent
Comments: Quite a pleasant place to stay and the fishing is very close to the accommodation. Most carp caught after dark

GREATER LONDON

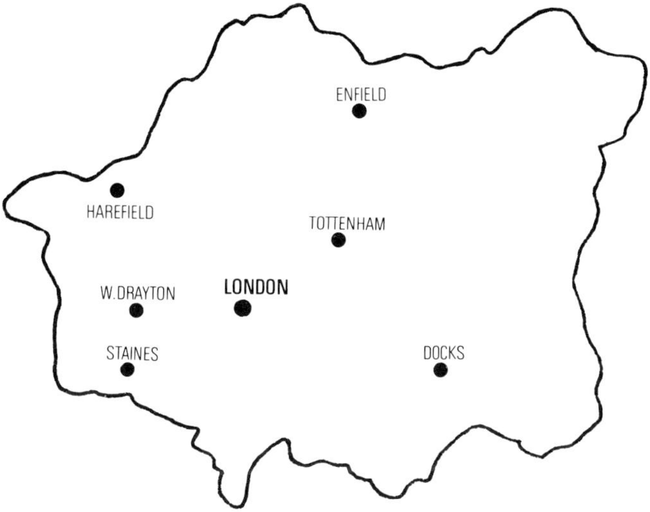

Bedfont Lake

Location: Off the B137 between Ashford and Feltham
Type and Size: Small lake
Carp Stock: Well stocked with carp to 20lbs; stocked 3 times recently with big fish
Category: Mixed Fishery
Other Species: Crucians, tench, perch, roach and pike
Permits: Boyer Leisure, Farlows Lake, Ford Lane, Iver SLO 9LL. Tel: 0753 655909
Cost: £25 per season; junior - £15; OAP's/disbled - £12. Day tickets (June 16th to March 14th) - 1 rod, 12 hours = £2.50; 2 rods, 12 hours = £4. Reductions for juniors, OAP's and the disabled. Also open, like Farlows, during the close season (see below)
Control: Boyer Leisure
Restrictions: No keepnets or carp sacks; no groundbaits
BK Rating: Moderate
W/A: Thames
Comments: After Farlows, this is the best known of the Boyer lakes, and is a first class carp fishery. Night fishing on a day ticket is permitted. Any method trout fishing is allowed during the close season for coarse fish. Costs: 1 rod - £5.50 (limit 2 trout); 2 rods - £7.50 (limit 4 trout). Reduced prices for juniors, OAP's and the disabled. Open all the year

Clapham Common Pond

Location: Clapham Common, SE London
Type and Size: 2 acre park lake
How to Find: Clapham
Carp Stock: Well stocked with carp to over 20lbs. Mirrors and commons
Category: Mixed Fishery
Other Species: General coarse fish
Permits: Free fishing
Cost: No cost
BK Rating: Moderate
Control: Council
W/A: Thames
Comments: Crowded park lake. Anglers have reported up to 12 carp in a night's fishing, mostly of 8-10lbs, with the best at 20lbs

Colnbrook West

Location: Between Langley and West Drayton
Type and Size: Small lake
How to Find: Off the A4 going towards London - turn left to lake
Carp Stock: Well stocked with carp to over 20lbs
Category: Mixed Fishery
Other Species: Tench, perch, roach and pike
Permits: Boyer Leisure, Farlows Lake, Ford Lane, Iver SL0 9LL. Tel: 0753 655909. Season tickets to include 4 other venues - single water permits possibly available on application
Cost: £35 per season for the 5 venues; £20 junior; £17.50 OAP's and disabled
Control: Boyer Leisure
Restrictions: Season tickets only; no keepnets or carp sacks. Locked gate
BK Rating: Moderate
W/A: Thames
Comments: Regular catches of double figure carp reported in 1990

Coppermill Stream

Location: Ferry Lane, Tottenham
Type and Size: One mile of river
How to Find: Near Tottenham Hale Underground Station, Ferry Lane
Carp Stock: Some carp to about 16lbs
Category: Mixed Fishery
Other Species: Barbel, bream, roach, chub, dace, pike and grayling
Permits: From machine. £1, 50p and 20p coins required. Day or season
Cost: About £1.80 per day; £30 per season
Control: Thames Water
Restrictions: No night fishing. Fishing is from 7.30am to half an hour after sunset. No groundbaiting
BK Rating: Moderate
W/A: Thames
Comments: The only 'stream' in our Guide!

East Warwick

Location: Ferry Lane, Tottenham N17 (opposite Ferry Boat Inn)
Type and Size: Reservoir of 43 acres
How to Find: Find the Ferry Boat Inn in Ferry Lane, Tottenham; Underground Station – Tottenham Hale
Carp Stock: Some carp present, sizes not known
Category: Few Carp
Other Species: Tench, roach, bream, perch
Permits: From machines at reservoir. £1, 50p and 20p coins needed
Cost: £2.50 per day, £35 per season
Control: Thames Water
Restrictions: No night fishing; fishing 7.30am to half an hour after sunset. Closed Christmas Day
BK Rating: Very Difficult
W/A: Thames
Comments: Not a carp water, but it does contain a few. Suitable for ambulatory and some wheelchair anglers, although they may need help to net fish. Additional swims for anglers have been provided on steep banks

Farlows Lake

Location: Ford Lane, off Iver Lane, Iver, Bucks SLO 9LL – can be seen from M25
Type and Size: Large old gravel pit
Carp Stock: Heavily stocked with carp to 35lb, two other 30's, about 60 twenties and many doubles
Carp Stock: Carp Water
Other Species: Bream, perch, roach, tench, pike and trout – stocked initially with 3,000 trout, and thereafter stocked annually
Permits: Boyer Leisure, at the above address
Cost: Season – £45 (£30 junior; £22.50 OAP's and disabled). Day tickets (June 16th to March 14th) – 1 rod, 12 hours for £2.50 (24 hours £4.50); 2 rods – £4 for 12 hours; £7 for 24 hours. Reductions for juniors, OAP's and the disabled
Control: Boyer Leisure
Restrictions: No keepnets; no groundbait; carp sacks for members only and not for day ticket anglers
BK Rating: Moderate, although Difficult for the very big fish
W/A: Thames
Comments: Farlows is the 'flagship', and headquarters, for Boyer Leisure, who have a number of well run waters with big fish and excellent facilities. The water is open all year round and during the coarse fish close season (March 14th to June 15th), any method trout fishing is allowed, from 6am till dusk. Cost during this period is £5.50 for one rod (two fish trout limit), and £7.50 per day for two rods, with a 4 fish limit – reductions for juniors and OAP's. Carp are caught on all methods and baits, from maggots to boilies. The prices quoted above also include some stretches of the Rivers Colne and Colnbrook

On site at Farlows Lake is a cafeteria, open all day, 7 days a week. Hot meals, sandwiches and drinks supplied all the year round. There is also a bar. When these facilities are closed there is a hot drinks machine.

The Heron Point Bar is on the same site, and is open for normal pub hours, and is pleasantly situated on the water's edge. Drinks till midnight for sit-down meals at the cafeteria on Friday and Saturday nights. Low price drinks, pool table, juke box, fruit machine and darts – shall we have time for fishing, you may ask!? Boyer Leisure is an excellent organisation and Farlows is one of the best big carp waters in the country. Tackle and bait shop on site - Tel: 0753 630302.

For full details of all the Boyers Fisheries apply to the office for their excellent and well illustrated brochure and application form, which gives details and maps of all their waters

Hampstead Heath Pond

Location: Hampstead Heath
Type and Size: Small commons pond, very weedy and shallow
Carp Stock: A few carp to about 15lbs
Category: Few Carp
Other Species: Roach, rudd, bream and perch
Permits: None necessary - free fishing
BK Rating: Difficult
W/A: Thames

'Big Carp' magazine editor, Rob Maylin with the Harefield Lake record of over 38 pounds caught in June 1991

Harefield Carp Lake

Location: Moorhall Road, Harefield, opposite the Horse and Barge pub and one mile from Denham station

Type and Size: Huge gravel pit of more than 50 acres

Carp Stock: One of the best big fish carp waters in the country, with at least 15 thirties, and over 100 twenties

Category: Carp Water

Other Species: Large bream and large roach

Permits: Boyer Leisure, Ford Lane, Iver, Bucks SLO 9LL. Tel: 0753 655909

Cost: £165 per season - waiting list. Apply to Boyer Leisure to be put on waiting list

Control: Boyer Leisure

Restrictions: Long waiting list. 90 places only. Peanuts and tiger nuts banned. Unhooking mats advised. Carp sacks with names affixed for members only

BK Rating: Difficult

W/A: Thames

Comments: Harefield is one of the best known and most famous carp waters in the country, and is fished by many of the leading carp anglers. Advanced methods and baits needed. The water is very hard to get into, due to the long waiting list, but occasional places are available. Members are allowed to take guests, by arrangement in advance only. Two guests only allowed per season, at £15 for the weekend, and £25 for the week. No fishing allowed at the gravel works. More big carp stocked in 1990.

From the 1991-92 season, 4 permits for the famous Harefield Carp Lake will be available to Boyer season ticket holders from other waters. Tickets run from midday Sunday to midday the following Sunday at £30 per week; no juniors

Tim Hodges with a 34.6 from Harefield Lake

Heath Vale Pond

Location: Hampstead Heath, London
Type and Size: Small, weedy lake, one of several ponds containing carp on the Heath
Carp Stock: Quite well stocked with carp to just over 20lbs
Category: Mixed Fishery
Other Species: Roach, rudd, bream and pike
Permits: None necessary - free fishing. Rod licences essential
Restrictions: No fishing on one bank
BK Rating: Moderate
W/A: Thames
Comments: Like most of the free London waters, this pond is heavily fished, and the carp are caught quite often

High Maynard

Location: Blackhorse Lane, Walthamstow. Car park Ferry Lane, Tottenham, N17 (opposite Ferry Boat Inn)
Type and Size: Reservoir of 38 acres
How to Find: Blackhorse Lane, near Blackhorse Lane Underground Station or Tottenham Hale Underground Station (nearest)
Carp Stock: Some carp to over 20lbs
Category: Mixed Fishery
Other Species: Mixed coarse fish, including tench and perch
Permits: Day and season tickets available on site from ticket machine
Cost: £2.50 per day; £35 season

Control: Thames Water. Send for leaflet to Amenity and Recreation Officer, Thames Water, Nugent House, Vastern Road, Reading, Berks. Tel: Reading 593391. Thames Area Angling Guide also published at £1.95 from tackle dealers and bookshops
Restrictions: No night fishing; fishing is from 7.30am to half an hour after sunset. No groundbait
Baits/Methods: Boilies best at present
BK Rating: Difficult
W/A: Thames
Comments: It is said that this reservoir could produce a surprise in the form of a big carp; its potential is not really known

Hollow Pond

Location: Whipps Cross Road (A114), north west of Wanstead, NE London
Type and Size: Large, shallow and weedy forest/commons-type lake
Carp Stock: Small number of carp to about 10lbs
Category: Few Carp
Other Species: Roach, bream, rudd, perch, pike and tench
Permits: None necessary - free fishing. Rod licence essential
BK Rating: Very Difficult
W/A: Thames

Kingfisher Lake (Pit 4)

Location: Pass the entrance to Savay on your right, coming from Denham. Cross the canal bridge and the entrance is on the right, just before the houses. Very long rough track
Type and Size: Mature gravel pit of 19 acres
How to Find: With difficulty. The lake is down a very long track of about a mile between Savay Lake and Harefield. There is a locked gate at the beginning of the track so it is better not to visit until you have a permit
Carp Stock: Most of the carp are doubles with a good number of twenties and one or two thirties. Probably not heavily stocked for its size. Carp occasionally escape upstream to next lake!
Category: Carp Water
Other Species: Tench, pike, roach, bream
Permits: Formerly controlled by the Greater London Council, now Hillingdon Borough Council: M Francis, Civic Centre, Uxbridge UB8 1UW. Tel: Uxbridge 50111 ext 2352
Cost: £50 season ticket
Control: Council
Restrictions: No night fishing. Rules against long stay fishing
BK Rating: Difficult
Baits/Methods: You will need the most advanced baits and methods at this water. Peanuts did well in the past but most now seem to use boilies
Comments: A well-known carp water hard fished by leading carp specialists. Chance of some very good twenties, but you can go very long periods without a take. An attractive lake, L-shaped and surrounded by trees and bushes. Very tranquil and pleasant to fish

Lea Valley Leisure Park A

Location: Enfield area
Type and Size: A number of lakes and gravel pits
How to Find: In the Lea Valley near Enfield
Carp Stock: Some carp lakes - details from Fisheries Manager
Category: Mixed Fisheries
Other Species: General coarse fish
Permits: Fisheries Manager, Lea Valley Park, PO Box 88, Enfield EN2 9HG. Tel: 0992 717711
Cost: On application
BK Rating: Insufficient information
Control: Lea Valley Leisure Park
W/A: Thames
Comments: Details of fishing holidays can also be obtained from the Fisheries Manager. Includes Northmet Pit, Cheshunt, with pike to 35lbs

Lockwood Reservoir

Location: Lea Bridge Road, Walthamstow
Type and Size: Reservoir of 80 acres
How to Find: Lea Bridge Road, in Walthamstow. Underground Station - Blackhorse Road, 1 mile
Carp Stock: 300-500 carp to over 30lbs; average size about 18lbs
Category: Carp Water
Other Species: Bream, pike, chub, roach
Permits: Not easy to obtain membership - mainly for employees
Cost: £5 a season
Control: Private - EMWA Employees Sports Club
Restrictions: No night fishing - 7am till dusk only. No groundbaiting, no wading
BK Rating: Difficult
Comments: A huge London reservoir, sometimes with waves on it almost like the sea. Concrete bank. Very hard to find the fish. Leading carp angler Kevin Maddocks says that if this lake was drained he wouldn't be surprised to find a carp of over 40lbs

London Docks

Location: East End of London
Type and Size: Very large freshwater Docks; big areas of very deep water
Carp Stock: Said to be some very big carp, but they are hard to find because of the huge areas of these disused docks. One or two twenties have been reported caught
Category: Few Carp
Other Species: Most coarse fish
Permits: Try the Isle of Dogs AC, which is open to all; Jim's Tackle, Bethnal Green. tel: 071-791 2961
Control: Club
BK Rating: Super-Difficult
W/A: Thames

Low Maynard: Walthamstow Nos 2 and 3

Location: Ferry Lane, Tottenham N17
Type and Size: Reservoirs: Low Maynard - 25 acres; No 2 - 13 acres; No 3 - 12 acres
How to Find: Take the A10 from London and at Tottenham turn right along High Cross Road to Ferry Lane. Tottenham Hale tube station on left
Carp Stock: All well stocked with carp, with plenty of doubles. There was a 28 pounder from Low Maynard in 1985
Category: Mixed Fishery
Other Species: Tench, bream and roach
Permits: Day and season permits from machines at the reservoir
Cost: £2.50 per day; £35 per season. £1, 50p and 20p coins needed for machines
Control: Thames Water
Restrictions: No night fishing. Fishing is from 7.30am until half an hour after sunset. Closed Christmas Day
BK Rating: Moderate
W/A: Thames
Comments: Car park and toilets. Fishes quite well in winter

New Cut

Location: Ferry Lane, Tottenham
Type and Size: River Cut about ¾ mile long
How to Find: Near Tottenham Hale Underground Station, Ferry Lane, Tottenham
Carp Stock: Occasional carp only, but we hear some large carp have been sighted
Category: Few Carp
Other Species: Roach, chub, bream
Permits: Day and season from machines. £1, 50p and 20p coins required
Cost: £2.50 per day; £35 season
Control: Thames Water
Restrictions: No night fishing. Open from 7.30am to half an hour after sunset
BK Rating: We cannot assess this, as we do not know of anyone who has taken carp from the water, so we should have to enter an estimated rating of Very Difficult
W/A: Thames
Comments: Not suitable for disabled anglers

Old Slade Lake

Location: Old Slade Lane, North Park, Thorney Mill Road, West Drayton (close to M4)
Type and Size: Large old pit
Carp Stock: Some carp to double figures - being restocked
Category: Few Carp
Other Species: Roach, bream and tench
Permits: Boyer Leisure, Farlows Lake, Ford Lane, Iver, Bucks SLO 9LL. Tel: 0753 655909. Season tickets
Cost: £35, to include 4 other venues - single lake tickets sometimes available
Cost: Boyer Leisure
Restrictions: No fishing on northern or western banks, as this is a bird sanctuary
BK Rating: Not known
W/A: Thames

Orlitts Lake

Location: Alongside the River Colnbrook, Lakeside Road, off the M4 between Langley and West Drayton
Type and Size: Large old pit, now being divided into two by the management
Carp Stock: About 100 carp recently stocked - sizes not known, but thought to be small at present
Category: Few Carp
Other Species: Perch, bream and pike
Permits: Boyer Leisure, Farlows Lakes, Ford Lane, off Iver Lane, Iver SLO 9LL. Tel: 0753 655909
Cost: Season tickets at £35, which includes Colnbrook West, the River Colnbrook, River Colne, Bedfont Lake and two stretches of the Thames
Control: Boyer Leisure
BK Rating: Not known
W/A: Thames

Osterley Park

Location: Osterley Park, near Twickenham
Type and Size: Park lake of about 7 acres
Permits: Day tickets on bank
Cost: About £1 per day
BK Rating: Easy
W/A: Thames
Comments: We could not find out much about this water, but it certainly contains carp

Potomac Pond

Location: Gunnersbury Park, Brentford, West London
Type and Size: Small pond
Carp Stock: Well stocked with small commons to about 5lbs
Category: Mixed Fishery
Other Species: Roach, rudd and perch
Permits: Day tickets from bailiff on bank
Control: Council
Restrictions: No night fishing
BK Rating: Easy
W/A: Thames
Comments: A good town water for beginners and float anglers

River Thames

Location: Best areas for big carp are said to be at Twickenham, Canbury Gardens, Walton-on-Thames and Shepperton
Type and Size: Wide river
Carp Stock: Few fish, and hard to find, but carp to well over 20lbs have been caught
Category: Mixed Fishery
Other Species: Nearly all of them!
Permits: Most of the Thames in these areas is free fishing
W/A: Thames
BK Rating: Very Difficult
Comments: Carp to about 30lbs have been caught from the Thames, but there are not many of them, they are notoriously hard to find and to catch intentionally, although every now and then they are caught whilst fishing for other species

Savay Lake

Location: Moorhall Road, Harefield, Denham. Ordnance Survey Map Sheet No. 160. Ref. 048 885

Type and Size: Mature gravel pit of 60 acres

How to Find: Take the A40 from London and at Denham turn right onto the A412 towards Watford. After half a mile go under the railway bridge and leaving Denham station on your right turn right into Moorfield Road towards Harefield. The Savay lake entrance is about half a mile on the right

Carp Stock: Whilst this lake does not contain a huge number of carp there are plenty of very big fish, enough for it to be regarded as a specialist carp water although it is really a mixed fishery. There are many twenties and possibly more thirty pound carp than any other water in the country. Carp to 45lbs have been caught and this is almost certainly now the 'top' carp fishery in the country as far as very big carp are concerned

Category: Carp Water/Mixed Fishery

Other Species: Bream, tench, pike, roach and perch. The bream, tench and pike all grow very large

Permits: Day tickets from Peverills Newsagents, 3 Moorhall Road, Harefield (out of fishery and half a mile to the right) or Balfours Newsagents, 12 Station Parade, Denham (near Denham station). Permits MUST be obtained before fishing. Season tickets from Fishery Manager, Peter Broxup, 309 Shirland Road, London W9. Tel: 081-969 6980 by written application only, enclosing an SAE or from Harefield Tackle Shop

Cost: Day ticket £2 (juniors/OAP/evening fishing £1). Season tickets £25 (juniors/OAP £12.50)

Restrictions: No night fishing. Fishery open daily 8am until sunset. Season ticket holders with a gate key may fish from 6am till 9pm. About half the lake is not open to the public and is fished by a club, but there are 100 swims on the open part. Unaccompanied juniors not allowed on the fishery unless they hold a season ticket

BK Rating: Very Difficult

Baits/Methods: You will need all the latest rigs, methods and baits to stand much chance of catching any of the big carp from this famous water. Many are caught at ranges of 100 yards plus, although in some swims they are taken close in

Control: Redland Angling Scheme

W/A: Thames

Comments: There is a night fishing syndicate on this huge water, but membership is expensive and very hard to obtain. Contact the Fishery Manager for details. Some of the leading carp anglers in the country fish here, and long-stay fishing is common and is often needed to catch the very big fish; you can go for weeks without a run. There are islands and sharp gravel bars, and most of the carp are caught from certain well-known areas. You do have some chance in the daytime but many big carp are caught at night. You will normally need the most sophisticated rigs and baits as the fish are wary and most have been caught a number of times. Not the sort of water to fish unless you are a very experienced carp angler, but you are always in with the chance of catching some of the biggest carp in the country - many of which, as you can see from this book are not in private and secret syndicate waters

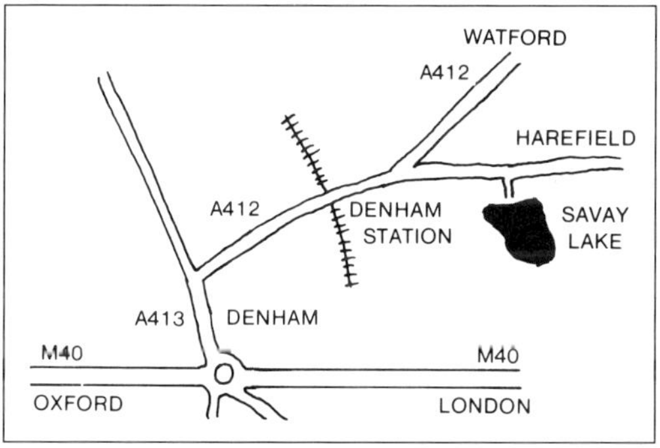

South Norwood Lake

Location: Woodvale, South Norwood

Type and Size: 2 acre park lake, very shallow

Carp Stock: The occasional carp is reported

Category: Few Carp

Other Species: Pike, roach, rudd, tench and perch

Permits: Day tickets on bank at low cost

Restrictions: No sacks; no night fishing

BK Rating: Very Difficult

W/A: Thames

Stockley Road Lakes

Location: Stockley Road, Hillingdon, Hayes
Type and Size: Two old pits, of 3 acres and half an acre - heavily weeded
How to Find: Turn off the M4 at junction 4, go straight across the 2 roundabouts, and the lake is on the right
Carp Stock: Well stocked with carp to 20lbs
Category: Mixed Fishery
Other Species: Tench, rudd, roach, perch and pike
Permits: Boyer Leisure, Farlows Lake, Ford Lane, Iver, Bucks SLO 9LL. Tel: 0753 655909
Cost: £35 per season, to include 4 other venues. You may be able to get a permit for this water alone on application. Reductions for juniors, OAP's and the disabled
Control: Boyer Leisure
Restrictions: Entry gate must be locked at all times
BK Rating: Difficult
W/A: Thames
Comments: A former carp syndicate, and a very pleasant water, with high and dangerous banks on the large lake

Swimming Lake

Location: Parliament Hill, Hampstead Heath
Type and Size: Small commons pond with concrete banks, much used by year round swimmers
Carp Stock: A few carp to over 20lbs
Category: Few Carp
Other Species: Roach, rudd, perch and pike
Permits: None necessary - free fishing
BK Rating: Very Difficult
W/A: Thames

Thorney Pool

Location: Thorney Road, West Drayton, just off junction 15 of the M25
Type and Size: Small pool of about an acre
Carp Stock: Well stocked with carp to 20lbs
Category: Mixed Fishery
Other Species: Pike, tench, roach, crucian carp and bream
Permits: Boyer Leisure, Farlows Lake, Ford Lane, Iver, Bucks. Tel: 0753 655909
Cost: £35 per season, to include 5 other venues. Apply to Boyer's office if you want a permit to fish Thorney Pool only. Reduced prices for juniors, OAPs and the disabled
Restrictions: No keepnets or carp sacks; no groundbait
Control: Boyer Leisure
W/A: Thames

Walthamstow No. 1

Location: Ferry Lane, Tottenham N17
Type and Size: Reservoir of 19 acres
How to Find: Near Tottenham Hale Underground Station, Ferry Lane, Tottenham
Carp Stock: Quite well stocked with carp, most of which are 6-12lbs. Record said to be 29lbs
Category: Carp Water

Other Species: Tench, roach and bream
Permits: Day and season from machines at the reservoir. £1, 50p and 20p coins needed
Cost: £2.50 per day; £35 season
Control: Thames Water
Restrictions: No night fishing. Fishing from 7.30am till half an hour after sunset
BK Rating: Moderate
W/A: Thames
Comments: A platform has been built out into the lake suitable for wheelchair-bound anglers. Reservoir rim suitable for some ambulatory disabled

Wandsworth Common Pond

Location: Wandsworth Common, London SW18
Type and Size: Small, public 'commons' pond
Carp Stock: Some fish to about 15lbs, numbers unknown
Category: Few Carp
Other Species: Roach, rudd, bream and pike
Permits: Wandsworth Borough Council, Town Hall, Wandsworth
Control: Council
BK Rating: Difficult
W/A: Thames

West Warwick

Location: Ferry Lane, Tottenham
Type and Size: Reservoir of 34 acres
How to Find: Car park near Tottenhale Hale Underground Station, Ferry Lane, Tottenham
Carp Stock: Well stocked with carp to mid-twenties. Average size 10½lbs. Growth rates of 4lbs a year recorded by Thames Water. More carp stocking in 1985
Category: Carp Only
Permits: From machines at reservoir. £1, 50p and 20p coins needed
Cost: £2.50 per day; £35 season
Control: Thames Water
Restrictions: No night fishing. Fishing is from 7.30am to half an hour after sunset. No groundbait
BK Rating: Moderate
W/A: Thames
Comments: Suitable for ambulatory handicapped able to cover long distance. Toilets. On all Walthamstow reservoirs wardens will give help and advice on request

Wraysbury

Location: Lake 1 - Douglas Lane, Wraysbury; Lake 2 - High Street, Wraysbury, near Staines
Type and Size: Gravel pits; Lake 1 - 61½ acres, Lake 2 - 76½ acres ·
How to Find: Take the A30 from Staines to the Staines by-pass. Take the B376 towards Wraysbury at the roundabout. Go through the village on Station Road, turn left onto Douglas Lane where there is a car park (Lake 1). For Lake 2: where the B276 turns left at Wraysbury village centre the

entrance is on the right by the school

Carp Stock: Not known, but probably few. However, some of these are thought by carp specialists to be very large and a 45 is reported from Lake 1. Carp are not listed in the Guide Book for Lake 2 but there are a few big ones to over 30lbs

Category: Few Carp

Permits: Season tickets only from Leisure Sport. Day tickets in advance from: Wraysbury Newsagents in Wraysbury High Street; Davies Angling, 47 Church Street, Staines, or from Leisure Sport

Cost: £22 per season. Juniors/OAP/disabled £11

Restrictions: Night fishing allowed. No fishing within casting distance of trout pens

Baits/Methods: Sophisticated baits and methods possibly needed and probably long casting techniques

Control: Leisure Sport Angling

BK Rating: Super-Difficult

W/A: Thames

Comments: Some of the top anglers in the country have tried these huge waters for the very big carp they are said to contain. Some of these anglers have reported losing big fish at extreme range, and it is thought there could be fish of up to 50lbs present, although we understand you could do a whole season of several thousand hours there and never contact a carp! Peter Springate caught a 45 pounder here in 1991

GREATER MANCHESTER

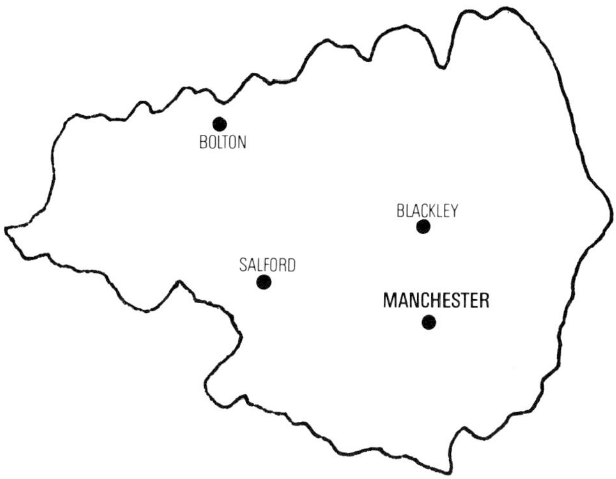

Bowker Lakes

Location: Crumpsall, North Manchester, just off the A665
Type and Size: Two small, attractive lakes
Carp Stock: Well stocked with carp to upper doubles, and one possible 20
Category: Mixed Fishery
Other Species: Roach, tench and perch
Permits: Season tickets – try local tackle shops, or enquire on bank
Control: Bowker Vale Angling Club
Restrictions: Members only; night fishing by syndicate
W/A: North West

Chorlton Water Park

Location: Maitland Avenue, Chorlton, Manchester 21
Type and Size: Water park lake of 19 acres
How to Find: Come off the M63 motorway at junction 9 and find Maitland Avenue. Water is 5 miles from Manchester centre and five miles from Stockport
Carp Stock: Quite well stocked from 1977 onwards with carp to upper doubles, the majority of which are commons
Category: Mixed Fishery
Other Species: Usual coarse fish
Permits: About £1 per day from office on site or £1.80 from bailiffs on the bank, 20p extra on Bank Holidays and weekends. Juniors about 40p and 80p. Season tickets: adults £10; juniors £4
Control: Mersey Valley Joint Committee. Water Parks Manager Tel: 061-881 5639
BK Rating: Moderate
Restrictions: Fishing 8am till sunset only, unless special night permit obtained
Baits/Methods: Normal carp fishing tactics and baits
W/A: North West
Comments: Lake is up to 18 feet deep in parts

Debdale Lakes

Location: Gorton, near Manchester
Type and Size: Three reservoirs of about 6 acres each
Carp Stock: Some carp to over 20lbs
Category: Few Carp
Other Species: General coarse fish, including some pike
Permits: Day tickets on bank. Season tickets from Manchester City Council
Control: Council
Restrictions: No night fishing
BK Rating: Very Difficult
W/A: North West
Comments: Uninteresting, like most reservoirs, but could produce a very big fish

Heaton Park Lake

Location: Bury Old Road, Manchester
Type and Size: 3 acre park lake with islands, and used by boats
Carp Stock: Well stocked with small carp, but some doubles
Category: Mixed Fishery
Other Species: General coarse fish
Permits: Day and season tickets from office on site; low cost
Control: Council
BK Rating: Easy
W/A: North West
Comments: Typical park lake, but quite pleasant and easy fishing

Lankys Mill Pond

Location: Blackley, north Manchester
Type and Size: Very clear, weedy pond of about 1½ acres
Carp Stock: Just half a dozen or so, but possibly a couple of 20's
Category: Few Carp
Other Species: Roach and bream
Permits: None necessary - free fishing
BK Rating: Very Difficult
W/A: North West
Comments: No close season; little more than a rubbish dump, but a few good fish. Usual town water problems

Melches

Location: Farnworth, near Bolton
Type and Size: Tiny, half acre pond
Carp Stock: Over 100 carp, with plenty of doubles to 22½lbs
Category: Carp Water
Permits: Season tickets only from Greater Manchester Transport Angling Club and Farnworth Cricket and Angling Club
Control: Club
BK Rating: Easy
W/A: North West

Platt Fields

Location: Fallowfield, on the edge of Manchester
Type and Size: Small, shallow lake of about three acres
Carp Stock: Quite well stocked with plenty of doubles up to about 15lbs
Category: Mixed Fishery
Other Species: Roach, tench and perch
Permits: Day tickets on bank. Day and season tickets from Manchester City Council
Control: Council
Restrictions: No night fishing
BK Rating: Moderate
W/A: North West
Comments: Used for boating, and often very busy; good fishing throughout the season

River Irwell

Location: Salford area of Manchester
Type and Size: Small river
Carp Stock: Stocked with small carp in 1990 by the Mayor of Salford
Category: Mixed Fishery
Other Species: Roach, bream and perch
Permits: Jubilee Disabled Angling Club
Control: Salford City Council
Restrictions: No night fishing
BK Rating: Not known
W/A: North West
Comments: 30 wooden platforms installed with ideal facilities for the disabled

GWENT (Wales)

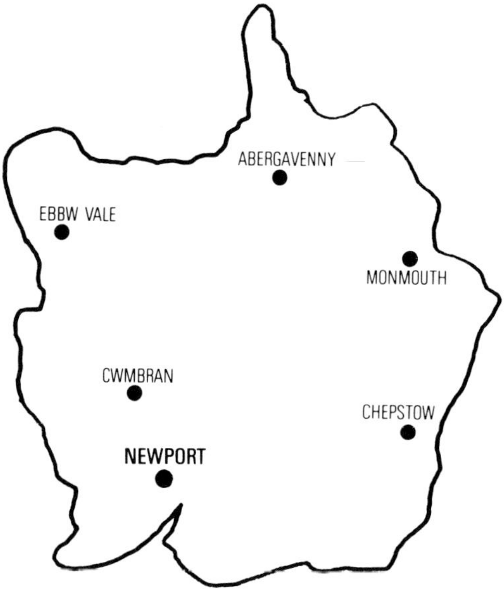

Blue Lake

Location: Waun-y-Pound Industrial Estate, Ebbw Vale
Type and Size: 4 acre reservoir
How to Find: Find the Waun-y-Pound Industrial Estate in Ebbw Vale, which is on the road from Newport
Carp Stock: Quite well stocked with smallish carp, average 4–5lbs. There are some bigger fish, with some 20's reported
Category: Mixed Fishery
Other Species: Perch, roach, chub, tench and gudgeon
Permits: Season tickets only by club membership. Ebbw Vale Welfare Angling Club Membership (no day tickets) from: 52 Bethcar Street, Ebbw Vale. Tel: 301392; or E Bynon Tackle Shop, King Street, Brynmawr; R Satterley, 8 Pen-y-Lan, Ebbw Vale. Tel: 308457
Cost: About £7 per season
Control: Club
BK Rating: Moderate
Baits/Methods: Modern carp fishing baits and methods needed
W/A: Welsh
Comments: This lake goes down to a depth of 35 feet in places and has concrete and shale banks and no features

Boat Pond, Beaufort

Location: Highlands Road, Beaufort Hill, Ebbw Vale
Type and Size: Reservoir of 3½ acres
How to Find: Address as above. Beaufort is north of Ebbw Vale just off the A465, 8 miles east of Abergavenny
Carp Stock: Well stocked with mirrors and commons to a good size
Category: Mixed Fishery
Other Species: Dace, roach, perch, crucians
Permits: Season tickets only by membership of Ebbw Vale Welfare Angling Club. Membership from 52 Bethcar Street, Ebbw Vale. Tel: 301392; or Pen-y-Lan, Ebbw Vale. Tel: 308547
Cost: About £7 per season
Control: Club
BK Rating: Difficult
Baits/Methods: Standard carp fishing baits and methods
W/A: Welsh
Comments: Fish location is easy in this very clear and very heavily weeded water, but the fish are not easy to tempt

Cwmbran Boating Lake

Location: Cwmbran, between Malpas and Pontypool
Type and Size: Man-made boating lake of 1½ acres
How to Find: The lake is near the Police HQ, just off the A4042, at Cwmbran between Malpas and Pontypool
Carp Stock: Quite well stocked with commons and mirrors to 18lbs
Category: Mixed Fishery
Other Species: Tench, bream, roach, perch
Permits: Day tickets available on the bank, but best to phone the day before to book a ticket. Torfaen Borough Council. Tel: Cwmbran 67642
Cost: About £1 per day
BK Rating: Easy
Baits/Methods: Standard carp fishing methods with boilies and floaters
W/A: Welsh, Wye Division
Comments: 'Public' water, boats etc

Cwmcelyn Club Water

Location: Blaina, near Ebbw Vale
Type and Size: Man-made lake of 1½ acres
How to Find: Take the A467 from Abertillery north, through Blaina and at the second roundabout take the third exit. Turn left at the next junction
Carp Stock: Well stocked with commons and mirrors to 17lbs
Category: Mixed Fishery
Other Species: Crucian carp, tench, trout, chub, roach, dace, perch, gudgeon and goldfish
Permits: Day tickets from Granville Derrick. Tel: Blaina 291110; or Des Hillman, 99 Roundhouse Close, Nantyglo. Tel: Nantyglo 311977
Cost: On application
Control: Club
BK Rating: Easy
W/A: Welsh

Liswerry Pond

Location: Three miles north of Newport
Type and Size: Narrow, canal-like lake, very weedy and on housing estate
Carp Stock: Well stocked with doubles to about 19lbs
Category: Mixed Fishery
Other Species: General coarse fish
Permits: Day tickets on bank
Cost: £2.50 per day
Control: Newport AA, L Currie, 14 Brynglas Road, Newport - night fishing for members only, not on day ticket
BK Rating: Moderate
W/A: Welsh

Machine Pond

Location: Warwick Road, Brynmawr, between Abergavenny and Merthyr Tydfil
Carp Stock: Well stocked with commons and mirrors to about 12lbs, average size about 7lbs
Category: Mixed Fishery
Other Species: Pike, perch, roach, chub, tench and gudgeon
Permits: Season ticket only by club membership. No day tickets. Ebbw Vale Welfare Club Angling Club. Club membership from Petsville, 52 Bethcar Street, Ebbw Vale. Tel: Ebbw Vale 301292; E Bynon Tackle Shop, King Street, Brynmawr; Ray Satterley, 8 Pen-Y-Lan, Ebbw Vale. Tel: Ebbw Vale 308547
Cost: About £7 per season
Control: Club
BK Rating: Easy
Baits/Methods: Traditional baits and methods, and also boilies and multiple baits
W/A: Welsh

Monmouthshire and Brecon Canal

Location: The canal runs between Newport and Brecon, about 40 miles
Type and Size: Narrow, shallow canal
Carp Stock: Some carp to 20lbs, mostly in concentrated areas, and hard to locate
Category: Few Carp, except in some areas which would qualify as Mixed Fishery
Other Species: Most coarse fish
Permits: Newport AA, L Currie, 14 Brynglas Road, Newport, Gwent
Control: Club
BK Rating: Very Difficult
W/A: Welsh
Comments: A 16 pounder was caught on floating crust in 1990

Morgans Pool

Location: Close to the M5, junction 26 to Cymbran
Type and Size: Lake of about 4 acres
Carp Stock: Well stocked with small carp to lower doubles
Category: Carp Water
Permits: Day tickets on bank
Cost: £2.50 per day

Control:	Newport AA. Secretary: P Climo, 2 Darwin Drive, Newport. Club membership open to all at about £20; night fishing for members only
BK Rating:	Easy
W/A:	Welsh

Tredegar House Lake

Location:	Tredegar House, Newport
Type and Size:	Estate lake
How to Find:	Tredegar is 2 miles west of Newport, turn off the M4 at junction 29. You can catch a bus there from the centre of Newport
Carp Stock:	Well stocked with carp to over 20lbs
Category:	Mixed Fishery
Other Species:	Tench and other coarse fish
Permits:	On the bank. Details from Peter Cole, Tel: Newport (0633) 62275 (daytime)
Cost:	About £1 per day
BK Rating:	Fairly Easy
Control:	Council
W/A:	Welsh
Comments:	Lake is in the grounds of a big house, now restored by Newport Council. Children's playground, orangery, bird gardens, craft workshop, and many other 'attractions'. (Details courtesy of Angling Times). NOTE: There are rumours that this water has been closed, but enquire as above

Woodstock Pool

Location:	Cymbran, near Newport
Type and Size:	2½ acre lake with island
Carp Stock:	Quite well stocked with carp, mostly doubles, to about 20lbs
Category:	Mixed Fishery
Other Species:	Roach and tench
Permits:	Day tickets on bank
Cost:	£2.50 per day
Control:	Newport AA. Secretary: P Climo, 2 Darwin Drive, Newport. Membership open to all at about £20 per season; night fishing for members only
BK Rating:	Moderate
W/A:	Welsh

GWYNEDD (Wales)

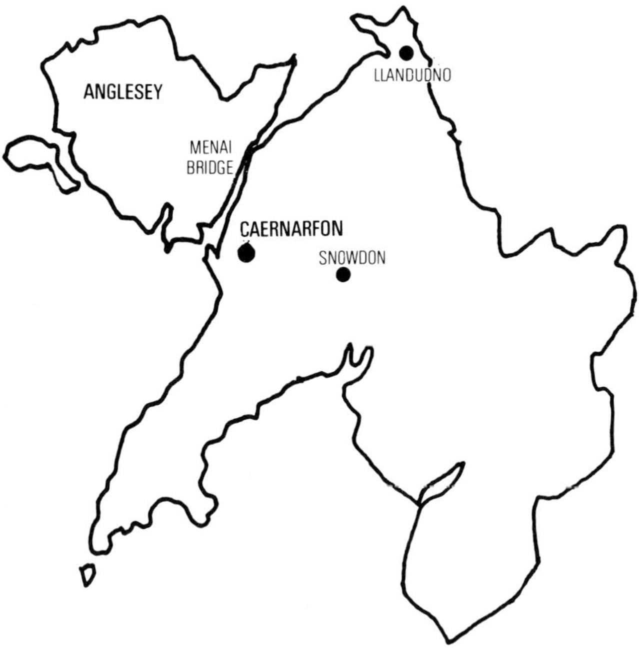

Llyn Euronwy

Location: Rhosneigr, Anglesey
Type and Size: 1½ acre farm pond
How to Find: Ty-Len Farm, Rhosneigr
Carp Stock: Some carp – sizes not known
Category: Mixed Fishery
Other Species: Tench, rudd, roach
Permits: Mr Summerfield, Ty-Len Farm, Rhosneigr. Tel: 0407 810331
Cost: Approx £2 per day
BK Rating: Insufficient information
Control: Private
W/A: Welsh

Llyn-y-Gors Lakes A

Location: Llyn-y-Gors, Llandegfan, Menai Bridge, Anglesey, Gwynedd, Wales LL59 5APN

Type and Size: Two man-made lakes; carp lake - 3½ acres; other lake - 2¾ acres

How to Find: Follow the A5 towards Holyhead. Cross the Britannia Bridge to Anglesey and take the left hand spur (A5025) to Amlwych. Follow signs to Llandegfan. Turn left at church to Llyn-y-Gors

Carp Stock: 300 fish to 24lbs, average 10–15lbs in carp lake

Category: Carp Only

Permits: On site. Tel: 0248 713410 (Roger Thompson)

Cost: £3 per day; £5 per night, bookable in advance. Prices approximate

BK Rating: Easy

Restrictions: No peanuts. Limited numbers

Control: Private - the owner is an experienced carp angler

W/A: Welsh

Comments: No close season. Attractive lakes. Regularly stocked. Other lake - mixed coarse fish - 20lb bags common. Four holiday cottages to let; send for brochure. 38 twenties reported from carp lake in summer 1991. This is a place we can both strongly recommend, as we have stayed there. There couldn't be anywhere pleasanter for a relaxed holiday of any kind, with the bonus of big carp only 75 yards from your cottage door, and a fabulous view of the Snowdon mountain range from your window...

A typical twenty pound common from Llyn-y-Gors

HAMPSHIRE

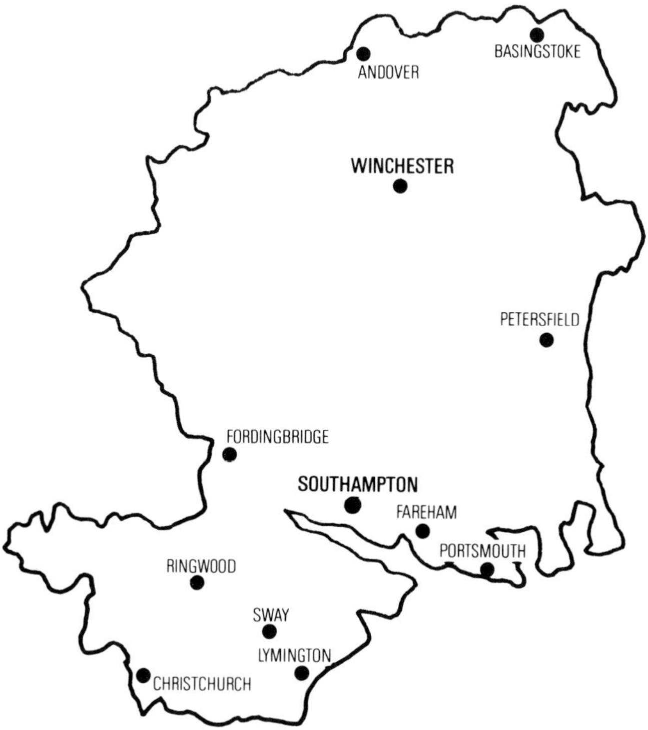

Avon Tyrell A

Location: Bransgore, near Christchurch
Type and Size: Two attractive lakes of 5 acres and one acre, close to each other
Carp Stock: Well stocked with carp to at least doubles
Category: Mixed Fishery
Other Species: Tench and roach
Permits: Group bookings only, minimum 6 persons; fishing free with full board and accommodation from Guest Services Co-ordinator, Avon Tyrell Residential Centre, Bransgore BH23 8EE. Tel: 0425 72347
Cost: £41 each per weekend, and £85 per week
Control: Private
BK Rating: Moderate
Restrictions: No day tickets
W/A: Wessex
Comments: This Centre used to belong to the National Association of Youth Clubs, and when PM was working for some years for the Avon and Bristol Federation of Boys' Clubs, he was instrumental in having the lakes partially drained, the little fish taken out, and the water stocked with carp. This was at least 10 years ago, and he has heard nothing of the

place since, so there should be some good fish in there. The many acres of grounds are very beautiful, and the huge mansion is one of the finest in the country. There is a bar, pool table, heated swimming pool, tennis courts and mountain bikes; and, I am sure, still the lovely walks in the grounds close to the famous Severals Fishery on the Hampshire Avon

Baffins Pond

Location: Portsmouth
Type and Size: Five acre lake
How to Find: Details from Portsmouth and District Angling Society
Carp Stock: Well stocked with carp to double figures
Category: Carp Water
Other Species: Bream, rudd and tench
Permits: Portsmouth and District AS: Mr R Snook, 86 Carnarvon Road, Copnor, Portsmouth PO2 7NL. Tel: Portsmouth 662986
Cost: Club membership costs £45 including entrance fee, with reductions for OAP's and youngsters. The club is a member of the Hants and Sussex Anglers Alliance
Control: Club
BK Rating: Moderate
W/A: Southern
Comments: Some of the waters mentioned as controlled by the Portsmouth club may be controlled by other clubs belonging to the Hants and Sussex Anglers Alliance; Crawley AS; Michelmarsh and Timsbury Angling Club; Salisbury and District AS; Eastleigh and District AS; Goring Fire Services AC; Shiplake and Binfield AC; Farnham AS; Guildford AS; Pulborough AC..... Members have exchange ticket facilities with the clubs mentioned above. All details, including information on waters from Mr Snook

Basingstoke Canal

Location: Aldershot - Basingstoke
Type and Size: Narrow restored canal, about 15 miles long
How to Find: Try Claycart Bridge, off the A323 between Aldershot and Fleet
Carp Stock: Plenty of carp especially at Claycart, with fish to 20lbs
Category: Mixed Fishery
Other Species: General coarse fish
Permits: Day and monthly tickets from local tackle shops and on the bank
Cost: Day tickets in advance about £1; on bank £1.50
Control: Basingstoke Canal Anglers Association
BK Rating: Moderate
W/A: Thames
Comments: Claycart area produced 14 doubles to two carp anglers on the first day of the 1988 season. This canal could produce some very big fish in the future

Broadlands Lake

Location: Ower, between Romsey and Totton, Southampton
Type and Size: Large lake formed in 1977 by the construction of the M27 motorway
Carp Stock: Well stocked with carp to about 20lbs
Category: Mixed Fishery

Other Species: The lake is noted for its pike to over 30lbs, best 39¼, and perch, roach, tench, bream and rudd
Permits: Day and season tickets from Fishery Manager, Mark Simmonds. Tel: Southampton 733167 or 869881
Cost: About £3 per day, £40 per season
BK Rating: Moderate to Difficult
Baits/Methods: Carp can be caught on luncheon meat and sweetcorn, but better methods are the use of boilies on bolt or hair rigs
Control: Private
W/A: Wessex
Comments: A new lake which has produced huge pike and may well contain some big carp in the future. All information from the Fishery Manager. 35 pounder stocked in 1988 and caught twice already

Broadleafe Lake

Location: Broadleafe Estate, Lymington
Type and Size: 15 acre, very attractive estate lake, and heavily weeded
Carp Stock: Well stocked with carp to over 20lbs; many of the smaller fish are commons
Category: Mixed Fishery
Other Species: Rudd and pike
Permits: Syndicate only - M Barry, 19 Saxon Way, Alder Holt, Hants
Control: Private
BK Rating: Moderate
W/A: Southern
Comments: A beautiful place, with lovely gardens. Water is shallow, and not far from the sea

Brockhurst Moat

Location: Between Fareham and Gosport
Type and Size: Large moat
Carp Stock: Well stocked with carp, sizes not known
Category: Mixed Fishery
Other Species: Tench, bream, perch, roach and pike
Permits: Portsmouth and District AS. Mr R Snook, 86 Carnarvon Road, Copnor, Portsmouth PO2 7NL. Tel: Portsmouth 662986, including all information about water location etc
Control: Club
BK Rating: Moderate
W/A: Southern

Brownwich Pond

Location: Titchfield, near Portsmouth
Type and Size: 4 acre lake
How to Find: Enquire from Portsmouth and District AS
Carp Stock: A specimen carp fishery, well stocked with large carp
Category: Carp Only
Permits: Portsmouth and District AS. Mr R Snook, 86 Carnarvon Road, Copnor, Portsmouth PO2 7NL. Tel: Portsmouth 662986
Control: Club
BK Rating: Moderate
W/A: Southern

Charlton Pits

Location: Charlton, near Andover
Type and Size: Matured gravel pit of about 10 acres
Carp Stock: Well stocked with carp to 20lbs, including some good commons
Category: Mixed Fishery
Other Species: Perch, roach, rudd, tench and dace
Permits: Andover AC, day tickets from local tackle shops or from the Secretary, R L Adcock, Flat 2, Bridge House, 154 Junction Road, Andover
Cost: Day tickets - £2.50; season - £18
Control: Club
BK Rating: Difficult
W/A: Southern
Comments: Back in the seventies, this was a well known (and rather secret) big carp water, but later the lake was partially drained, and most of the big fish netted and sold. The pits are flooded by the River Anton, and are said now to contain grayling as well as other species

Fishers Pond A

Location: Colden Common, near Winchester
Type and Size: 10 acre estate lake, part of an ancient fish pond
How to Find: Take the A33 from Winchester and the fishery will be found just to the south of Colden Common where the B3051 joins the main road
Carp Stock: Well stocked with carp to 20lbs - many doubles
Category: Mixed Fishery
Other Species: Tench, roach and bream
Permits: From Mr Paton, Fishers Pond Secretary. Tel: Southampton 694412. Mr Paton lives at the fishery and details of costs and permits can be otained from him at the house
Baits/Methods: The carp are caught by specialist carp methods and boilies. Floating crust may work at times
BK Rating: Moderate
W/A: Southern
Comments: This attractive lake was connected with the local monastery and carp are still reared here. It would almost qualify under our 'Carp Water' category as there are plenty of good carp present. Wildflowers and much bird life. Self-catering accommodation - cottage and houseboat with free fishing and boating

Frimley

Location: Frimley High Street, Frimley, Farnborough
Type and Size: 10 gravel pits, most of which are small, but one is 11 acres and one about 6 acres
How to Find: Find the A325 and go through Farnborough to Farnborough Green roundabout. Continue on the A325, and cross the railway bridge, to park in Frimley High Street car park. No car parking elsewhere - access to lakes by foot only
Carp Stock: Not known; Leisure Sport say 'carp to 25lbs plus'
Category: Few Carp
Other Species: Bream, tench, roach, perch, pike, crucian carp
Permits: Season tickets only from Leisure Sport, Thorpe Park, Staines Road, Chertsey, Surrey. Tel: Chertsey 64872
Cost: £21 per season. Juniors/OAP/disabled £10.50

Restrictions: No night fishing. Access not available to some parts of area which are a Nature Reserve - details from Leisure Sport Guide Book
BK Rating: Difficult
W/A: Thames
Comments: We have only included this and some other venues of this kind because the Leisure Sport Guide Book reports large carp. They are possibly very few as these waters are not recognised carp waters

Golden Springs Lakes

Location: Near Christchurch
Type and Size: 12 small pools
Carp Stock: Most of the pools contain carp to about 10lbs
Category: Mixed Fishery
Other Species: Tench, roach and trout
Permits: Christchurch AC - tickets from local tackle shops or C Bungay, 8 Purewell, Christchurch
Control: Club
Restrictions: No night fishing - 6am to 30 minutes after sunset only - do not go onto the banks of the River Frome
BK Rating: Moderate
W/A: Wessex

Hatchett Pond and Cadmans Pool

Location: Near Cadnam, New Forest
Type and Size: Medium sized forest pools
How to Find: Enquire from Forestry Commission
Carp Stock: Some carp
Other Species: General coarse fish
Permits: Forestry Commission, Queens House, Lyndhurst, on site and local tackle shops
Carp Stock: Season about £38, weekly about £3.50; day about £2.30
BK Rating: Difficult
Control: Forestry Commission
Comments: Licences not required for New Forest ponds

Hightown Lake

Location: Near Ringwood
Type and Size: 20 acre gravel pit
Carp Stock: Quite well stocked with carp to 20lbs
Category: Mixed Fishery
Other Species: Tench, roach and eels
Permits: Members only water of Ringwood and District AA. Secretary: R Smith, 1 Avon Castle Drive, Matchams Lane, Ringwood
Restrictions: No day tickets; no night fishing except for members
BK Rating: Moderate
W/A: Wessex

Hilsea Moat, Eastern

Location: Hilsea, Portsmouth
Type and Size: Large moat of about 4 acres
Carp Stock: Well stocked with carp to a good size
Category: Mixed Fishery
Other Species: Tench, crucians, roach and rudd
Permits: Portsmouth and District AS. Mr R Snook, 86 Carnarvon Road, Copnor, Portsmouth PO2 7NL. Tel: Portsmouth 662986
Cost: About £45 for new members, which includes many other local ponds and many miles of river fishing on the Rivers Arun, Rother, River Stour in Dorset, and the Chichester Canal
Control: Club
BK Rating: Not known
W/A: Southern
Comments: Like the other Portsmouth AS waters mentioned in this book, details can be obtained from the Secretary

Hilsea Moat, Western

Location: Hilsea, Portsmouth
Type and Size: Smaller part of the moat, about one acre in size, and separate from the Eastern part mentioned above
Carp Stock: Plenty of carp, sizes not known
Other Species: Tench, crucians, rudd and roach
Permits: Portsmouth and District AS, Mr R Snook, 86 Carnarvon Road, Copnor, Portsmouth PO2 7NL. Tel: Portsmouth 662986
Cost: About £45 per year for new members, to include many other club waters
Control: Club
BK Rating: Moderate
W/A: Southern

H.M.S. Dryad Lake

Location: Portsmouth
Type and Size: 4 acre lake
Carp Stock: Well stocked, mostly small carp
Category: Mixed Fishery
Other Species: Mixed coarse fish
Permits: Controlled by the Royal Navy
Carp Stock: On application
BK Rating: Easy
Control: Royal Navy
W/A: Southern
Comments: You could try the Admiralty, but more seriously, local tackle shops would be able to tell you how to go about getting permission - a Naval uniform might help!

Hollybush Lane Lakes

Location: Farnborough
Type and Size: 3 lakes totalling 20 acres. Mature gravel pits
How to Find: From London take the M3 motorway and leave at junction 4. Take the A325 towards Farnborough for 3 miles and at the Queens Hotel roundabout turn left onto the A3011. The fishery entrance is one mile along this road opposite the Fir Tree public house. Car park is 300 yards down the lane on the left
Carp Stock: Middle lake mainly carp with several 20's. Others contain some carp. Main lake suffered a fish kill in 1991
Category: Mixed Fishery
Other Species: Bream, tench, roach, perch, pike
Permits: Day tickets £3 (juniors/OAP/ £1.50) from J and A Newsagents, 201 Lynchford Road, or Raison Bros Tackle Shop, Farnborough. Tel: 0252 543470. Tickets must be obtained before fishing. Season tickets: £30 adults, £15 juniors
Restrictions: No night fishing. No sacking
Baits/Methods: Normal carp rigs and baits
Control: Redland Angling Scheme
BK Rating: Moderate
W/A: Thames
Comments: Commercial fishery, Redland. Carp to 20lbs reported. Number 44 bus from Aldershot to Woking passes fishery entrance. Ash Vale railway station 10 minutes from fishery. We are reliably informed that the lake itself is just in Surrey!

Huckelsbrook Lake

Location: Off the A338, Christchurch to Fordingbridge road, near Huckelsbrook Garage. Lake entrance on the left hand side going north, past Ibsley and over Huckelsbrook Stream
Type and Size: Unfished 12 acre matured gravel pit, with large island
Carp Stock: Sizes not known, as the water has not been fished until recently, but thought to be only about 30 fish
Category: Mixed Fishery
Other Species: Roach, rudd, perch and tench
Permits: Members only water of Christchurch AC. C Bungay, 8 Purewell, Christchurch or P Reading, 17 Mayford Road, Poole
Cost: £54 per season, to include many other waters
Restrictions: Barbless hooks; members only; no guest tickets; carp must not be put into sacks; some areas out of bounds, as this is an S.S.S.I. Car parking inside and outside gate only; no carp in nets; open for night fishing
BK Rating: Not known
W/A: Wessex

Kingfisher Lake (a)

Location: Teswood Lane, near Southampton
Type and Size: Gravel pit of 3 acres
How to Find: From Southampton take the Bournemouth road (A35) and at the roundabout take the Totton road (A36). At the Salmon Leap pub, take a track on the right to Kingfisher Lake. Ordnance Survey Sheet No 196. Grid Reference 358146
Carp Stock: Well stocked with carp doubles; a 31 has been reported which was probably genuine, but spawn bound. Many commons of 6-12lbs. We are reliably informed that the best 'normal' fish is a common of 14lbs 6ozs
Category: Mixed Fishery
Other Species: Tench, roach, perch, pike and chub
Permits: Day tickets from Mr Hoskins, 40 Aldermoor Aven, Aldermoor, Southampton. Tel: Southampton 780105, who will also give information on costs etc
BK Rating: Moderate
Control: Private
W/A: Southern

Kingfisher Lake (b)

Location: Near Ringwood
Type and Size: Matured gravel pit of 40 acres
Carp Stock: Very well stocked with good carp, many of which are 20's, up to just over 30lbs. Some big commons to 28lbs
Category: Carp Water
Permits: Day tickets from owner on site. Season tickets: Mr M Clarke. Tel: 04254 4222
Cost: About £8 per day
BK Rating: Moderate
Control: Private
W/A: Wessex
Comments: Water is hard fished by good carp anglers, although numbers are limited. Caravans, cafe and other facilities

Lake Farm

Location: Near Fordingbridge - to the west, off the road which joins the A354
Type and Size: Small farm pond
Carp Stock: Hundreds of small carp, with some to 18lbs
Category: Carp Water
Other Species: Some good tench
Permits: Members only water of Ringwood and District AC. Mr K Grozier, 15 Greenfinch Walk, Hightown, Ringwood BH24 3RJ
Cost: £40 per year, to include many other waters
Control: Club
Restrictions: Members only
BK Rating: Very Easy for the little fish
W/A: Wessex

Mopley Farm Fishery A

Location: Mopley Farm, Mopley Road, Blackfield, Southampton. Tel: 0260 224231
Type and Size: Three acre farm lake
How to Find: At Blackfield, 15 miles from Southampton on the edge of the New Forest
Carp Stock: Well stocked with carp to double figures
Category: Mixed Fishery
Other Species: Trout, grayling and some other fish
Permits: From Brian at farm - phone first
Cost: From about £4 per day
Control: Private
BK Rating: Moderate
W/A: Southern
Comments: Accommodation nearby. Any method trout fishery with some good carp

Northfield Lakes

Location: Just north of Ringwood, off the A31 - take the Fordingbridge road, and the lakes are on the left
Type and Size: Three small pits
Carp Stock: Well stocked with carp to 27lbs
Category: Mixed Fishery
Other Species: Big tench, bream and roach; pike and big eels
Control: Ringwood and District AC
Permits: A members only fishery of Ringwood AC; Mr K Grozier, 15 Greenfinch Walk, Hightown, Ringwood BH24 3RJ
Cost: £40 per season, to include many other waters
Control: Club
Restrictions: Members only
BK Rating: Moderate
W/A: Wessex

Petersfield Heath Lake

Location: On the edge of town of Petersfield
Type and Size: 8 acre park lake
How to Find: Just off the A3 at Petersfield
Carp Stock: Good carp to 27lbs
Category: Mixed Fishery
Other Species: General coarse fish
Permits: Day tickets from local tackle shop. Enquiries to Petersfield AC. Tel: 0730 66793
Cost: About £2 per day
BK Rating: Moderate
Control: Club
Restrictions: Not known
W/A: Southern
Comments: Petersfield AC has a large number of other lakes, some of which contain carp

Rotherwick Lakes

Location: Hook, near Basingstoke
Type and Size: We don't know - try local tackle shops
Carp Stock: Carp to 20lbs+
Category: Mixed Fishery
Other Species: General coarse fish and trout
Permits: Try local tackle shops
Cost: Not known
BK Rating: Insufficient information
Control: Private
W/A: Thames
Comments: No close season. In advertising the owners of this lake didn't say where they are or how permits can be obtained so we put it in, in case some of our readers might like to do some detective work! We'd be interested in further information

Sinah Warren Lake

Location: Hayling Island, near Havant and Portsmouth, and adjoining the Golf Course
Type and Size: Huge 35 acre lake
Carp Stock: Said to be well stocked with carp to well over 20lbs, with possibly some 30's
Category: Mixed Fishery
Other Species: Tench, perch, bream and roach
Permits: Portsmouth and District AS. Mr R Snook, 86 Carnarvon Road, Copnor, Portsmouth PO2 7NL. Tel: Portsmouth 662986
Cost: Club membership costs about £45 for new members, but includes many other lakes and ponds, and river and canal fishing
Control: Club
BK Rating: Difficult
W/A: Southern

Somerly Lakes

Location: Near Ringwood
Type and Size: Gravel pit of about 17 acres
Carp Stock: Well stocked with carp to upper 20's, best 27lbs
Category: Carp Water
Permits: Must be obtained in advance from Ringwood Tackle. Tel: 0425 475155
Cost: About £4 per day; £40 per season and £10 entry fee
Control: Ringwood AC
BK Rating: Fairly Hard
W/A: Southern
Comments: A well-known water, very popular and hard fished. Night fishing by prior arrangement only

Sway Lakes

Location: Barrow Lane, Sway, near Brockenhurst
Type and Size: Two lakes, about an acre and 1½ acres
How to Find: From Brockenhurst take the Sway road and turn left into Barrow Lane

Carp Stock:	Smaller lake has some carp. Larger lake contains carp to 27lbs - 6 twenties and about 10 doubles, average size 6-8lbs
Category:	Larger lake - Carp Water
Other Species:	General coarse fish
Permits:	From owner on bank
Cost:	About £2.50 per day, £3 per night
Control:	Private
BK Rating:	Moderate
W/A:	Wessex
Comments:	For information - Mr T Clarke. Tel: 0590 682010

Topacre Lake

Location:	Alresford, near Winchester
Type and Size:	Very small estate pond
Carp Stock:	Small number of carp to about 30lbs
Category:	Carp Water
Permits:	Syndicate only; details from K Cayzer, Keepers Cottage, New England Estate, Alresford. Tel: 096273 2837
Control:	Private
BK Rating:	Difficult

Waggoner's Wells

Location:	Near Hindhead (which is Surrey, but lakes are in Hampshire)
Type and Size:	3 lakes, one of which is a trout lake
How to Find:	Hindhead area
Carp Stock:	Some carp in the two coarse fishing lakes
Category:	Mixed Fisheries
Other Species:	Perch, tench, roach
Permits:	On site - The Ranger, Summerden North, Waggoner's Wells, Grayshott, Hindhead, Surrey. Tel: Liphook 723722
Cost:	About £10 - season; £1.50 - day; 50p extra for a second rod
BK Rating:	Insufficient information
Control:	National Trust
Restrictions:	Not known
W/A:	Southern
Comments:	National Trust property, so likely to be busy

Willow Park Lakes

Location:	Willow Park, near Aldershot
Type and Size:	Large but attractive gravel pit; shallow with gravel bars
Carp Stock:	Heavily stocked with over 500 carp, about 150 doubles and at least 10 twenties to about 28lbs
Category:	Mixed Fishery
Other Species:	Roach, tench, rudd, bream, perch and pike
Permits:	In advance only; day tickets from John Raison on 0252 543470
Control:	Private
Restrictions:	No boilies until after November; unhooking mats must be used
BK Rating:	Moderate
W/A:	Thames
Comments:	A well known and pleasant water often featured in the angling press. Fishes well all the year, and is run by a fishing tackle shop owner. Also used for windsurfing, unfortunately

HEREFORD & WORCESTER

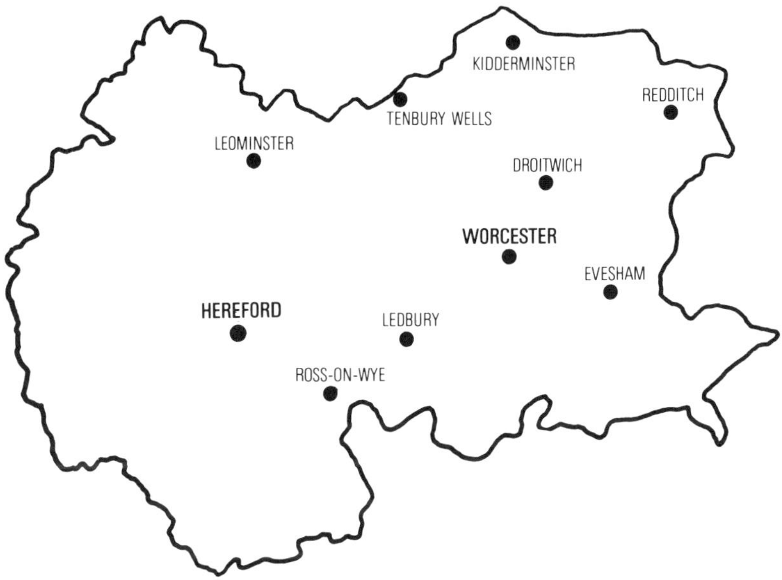

Abbots Salford Park

Location: Abbots Salford, Evesham
Type and Size: Small pool
How to Find: Off the A439 near Evesham
Carp Stock: Not known
Category: Unknown
Other Species: Tench
Permits: On site
Cost: On application. Tel: 0386 870244
BK Rating: Insufficient information
Control: Private
W/A: Severn Trent
Comments: A country park on the banks of the River Avon, which advertises 'a carp and tench pool'. Self-service shop, licensed club, bowling green and 'all pursuits enjoyed by country lovers'

A.C.R. Fisheries

Location: Evesbatch, near Worcester
Type and Size: Two small pools
How to Find: Take the A4103 from Worcester to Evesbatch - 11 miles
Carp Stock: Heavily stocked with carp to 20lbs; especially the big lake
Category: Big lake - Carp Water, small lake - Mixed Fishery
Other Species: General coarse fish
Permits: Day tickets in advance only, from Alans Fishing Tackle, St Johns, Worcester
Cost: On application
Control: Private
BK Rating: Easy
W/A: Severn Trent
Comments: Popular, heavily stocked lakes

Arrow Valley Lake

Location: Batten Drive, off Holloway Drive, Redditch
Type and Size: Large excavated lake
Carp Stock: Well stocked with carp to 25lbs
Category: Mixed Fishery
Other Species: Roach, rudd, perch, bream and tench, many very large
Permits: Day tickets from the Warden's hut by the side of the lake. Tel: Redditch 68337
Cost: About £2 per day; reductions for juniors and OAP's
Control: Redditch Borough Council, Amenities Dept, Town Hall, Redditch B98 8HA
BK Rating: Moderate
W/A: Severn Trent
Comments: Said to be one of the best waters in the area, with bream to 11lbs, and roach to 3lbs. Next to the lake is Redditch Angling Centre, with all the tackle, baits and information you need

Bankes Pool

Location: Great Witley, near Stourport
Type and Size: Small pool
How to Find: On the A451, 5 miles south-west of Stourport
Carp Stock: Well stocked with carp to doubles
Category: Mixed Fishery
Other Species: General coarse fish
Permits: Day tickets from the farm near the pool
Cost: On application
BK Rating: Easy
Control: Private
W/A: Severn Trent
Comments: Very small, overstocked water. Enquire from the farm or local tackle shops

Betula Water

Location: South Herefordshire
Type and Size: Small private fishery
Carp Stock: Well stocked with commons and mirrors to double figure size, with a couple of 20's caught
Category: Carp Only
Other Species: None except for a few golden orfe
Permits: Occasional vacancies for the season only (no day tickets) from Roger Emmet, 10 Digby Drive, Mitton, Tewkesbury, Glos. Tel: Tewkesbury 292533
Cost: On application
Control: Syndicate
BK Rating: Fairly Easy to Moderate
W/A: Severn Trent
Comments: Private property - do not visit without permission for any reason

Bewdley Pool A

Location: Bewdley, near Kidderminster
Type and Size: Small pools
How to Find: In Severn Valley near Bewdley
Carp Stock: Well stocked with carp
Category: Mixed Fishery
Other Species: General coarse fish
Permits: Severn Valley Guest House, Westbourne Street. Tel: 0299 402192
Cost: On application
BK Rating: Moderate
Control: Private
Restrictions: Not known
W/A: Severn Trent
Comments: Accommodation available in guest house. Licences, tackle and bait. Licensed bar. Also famous for its barbel fishing in the River Severn

Birmingham-Worcester Canal

Location: Best area is said to be Hanbury Wharf, Shernal Green, near Droitwich
Type and Size: Narrow canal
How to Find: Hanbury and the canal are a few miles west of Droitwich
Carp Stock: Said to be plenty of carp to 20lbs
Category: Mixed Fishery
Other Species: Usual coarse fish
Permits: Birmingham Anglers Association (members only), 100 Icknield Port Road, Rotton Park, Birmingham B16 OAP. Tel: 021-454 9111, 9.30am to 1.30pm and 7pm to 9pm, weekdays
Cost: About £13 a season, which includes all other BAA waters
BK Rating: Insufficient information, but good carp are notoriously hard to find on canals
Control: BAA
Restrictions: No groundbait of any kind
W/A: Severn Trent

Church Pool

Location: Opposite the church in the village of Clehonger, near Hereford
Type and Size: Farm pool of approximately one acre
How to Find: Take the A465 from Hereford to Abergavenney. After two miles turn right past Belmont Abbey and then right again after one mile (signed Clehonger). Park on verge, without obstructing access to the church. The pool is opposite the church
Carp Stock: Well stocked with small carp. Possibly a few doubles present
Category: Carp Water
Other Species: Two or three terrapins, very fond of maggots!!
Permits: Perkins of Hereford, Commercial Road, Hereford. Permits must be obtained before commencing fishing
Cost: £2 per day
Baits/Methods: Any bait and method will score here
Control: Private, day ticket
Restrictions: No keepnets, barbed hooks, groundbait, unsupervised children or litter
W/A: Welsh
BK Rating: Very Easy
Comments: A small water, set in a field by a quiet village. Picturesque surroundings. Source of the terrapins – unknown

Court Farm

Location: Bottom of farm track, Court Farm, Tillington, near Hereford
Type and Size: Irrigation reservoir, approx 1½ acres

How to Find: Head north from Hereford on A4110. Turn left at the Three Elms public house and follow signs for Tillington. In Tillington, turn right and follow signs for Court Farm
Carp Stock: Stocked with small mirrors and commons to 8lb
Category: Carp Only
Permits: On site from farmhouse
Cost: £1.50 per day
Baits/Methods: Standard baits and methods work well here
Control: Day ticket water
W/A: Welsh
BK Rating: Easy

Docklow Pools A

Location: West End Farm, Docklow, Leominster
Type and Size: 5 estate lakes, 2-3 acres each
How to Find: From Leominster take the A44 Worcester road. Docklow is about 3 miles from Leominster
Carp Stock: All the lakes are well stocked with carp although one is mainly a trout pool. Two of the lakes contain carp to 34½lbs, although most of the fish are mirrors of under 10lbs
Category: Carp Water
Permits: Day tickets from Mrs J Bozward, West End Farm
Cost: £3 per day
BK Rating: Easy for the smaller carp; Difficult for the bigger fish
Restrictions: No groundbait; no peanuts; no hemp; barbless hooks
Baits/Methods: Normal carp methods; maggots, luncheon meat and boilies
Control: Private
W/A: Welsh (Wye Division)
Comments: 305lbs of carp was once caught in a day on one of these pools. Most carp are small. Accommodation in the farmhouse (bed and breakfast). There are also 6 attractive self-catering cottages of high standard, some very near the lakes. Brochure from Mrs Bozward at West End Farm. Tel: 056-882256. Ideal for the family or fishing holiday. No close season; excellent fishing in the spring

Eastnor Castle

Location: Eastnor, near Ledbury
Type and Size: Estate lake about 5 acres
How to Find: Take the A449 towards Malvern and then about half a mile outside the town fork right on the A438 towards Tewkesbury. You will pass entrance to the water on the right about 3 miles further on
Carp Stock: Quite well stocked with mirrors and commons to about 15lbs
Carp Stock: Mixed Fishery
Other Species: Roach, rudd, bream, tench
Permits: From bailiffs on bank, about £3 per day
Control: Private
BK Rating: Moderate
W/A: Severn Trent
Comments: A beautiful lake surrounded by trees. A big area is thickly covered by lilies which make much of this area almost impossible to fish. Most of the carp are caught from the dam end or near the lilies

Eric's Pool

Location: Shatterford, Kidderminster
Type and Size: Small lake
Carp Stock: Sparsely stocked with carp to about 16lbs
Category: Few Carp
Other Species: Roach, bream and pike
Permits: Day tickets at the lake
Control: Private
BK Rating: Difficult
W/A: Severn Trent

Golden Valley

Location: Golden Valley Common, near Castlemorton, Ledbury
Type and Size: Dammed estate-type lake, stream fed, but on very open common land
How to Find: From Tewkesbury take the A438 Ledbury road and turn right on the B4208 after about 6 miles. After about a mile, a lane leads onto the common on the left, and the lake will be seen on the right
Carp Stock: Numbers not known but quite well stocked with commons to about 6lbs
Category: Mixed Fishery
Other Species: Crucians, roach, perch and bream
Permits: This used to be a free fishery but recently someone, presumably the local Council, has been charging 50p a day from bailiffs on the bank
BK Rating: Moderate
W/A: Severn Trent
Comments: A high and open water with some quite good fun fishing for small commons. Most fish caught at night

Haye Farm Fishery

Location: Bewdley, near Snuff Mill
Type and Size: Small farm pond
Carp Stock: Well stocked with carp to 15lbs
Category: Carp Water
Other Species: Few coarse fish
Permits: Day tickets on bank
Cost: Low
Control: Private
BK Rating: Moderate
W/A: Severn Trent
Comments: Man-made pond on farm. In same lane as Snuff Mill Pool

Herriots Pool

Location: Near Droitwich
Carp Stock: Said to contain large carp. Nothing else known
Permits: Talbot Hotel, High Street, Droitwich
Control: Droitwich and District AS. Secretary, Talbot Hotel, Droitwich
Cost: On application. Day tickets open to all
BK Rating: Fairly Hard
W/A: Severn Trent
Comments: We can find out little about this water, except that it is there! Further details from the Talbot Hotel

Lodge Park Lake

Location: Redditch
Type and Size: Small estate lake
How to Find: In the town of Redditch
Carp Stock: Very heavily stocked with small carp
Category: Carp Water
Other Species: Few
Permits: R Mayall, 19 Chaddesley Close, Lodge Park, Redditch. Apply in writing only - with an SAE
Cost: On application
Control: Private
BK Rating: Very Easy
W/A: Severn Trent
Comments: Many thousands of little carp

M50 Pond

Location: Just off junction 2 of the M50, between Tewkesbury and Ross-on-Wye, near Russells End Touring Caravan Park
Type and Size: 4 acre lake
Carp Stock: Well stocked with carp to doubles
Category: Carp Water
Permits: Tel: 0531 650687
Control: Private
BK Rating: Not known
W/A: Severn Trent

Moorland Farm

Location: Hartlebury, near Kidderminster
Type and Size: Eight small pools, two of which are for youngsters
How to Find: From Kidderminster take the A449 Worcester road, turn left where the dual carriageway starts, and turn left again on a farm track signposted to the fishery
Carp Stock: Meadow Pool and Bank Pool contain carp to doubles
Permits: Day tickets from the snack bar on the site
Cost: £3 per day; £2 after 2pm
Restrictions: Fishing is from constructed platforms, and cars can be driven to swims; keepnets banned; barbless hooks recommended
BK Rating: Moderate
W/A: Severn Trent

Moors Pool

Location: Hartlebury, Kidderminster
Type and Size: Small pool
Carp Stock: Heavily stocked with small carp, much used for match fishing; said to contain carp to about 10lbs
Category: Mixed Fishery
Other Species: Roach, bream and perch
Permits: Try local tackle shops
Control: Club
Restrictions: No night fishing
BK Rating: Easy
W/A: Severn Trent

Pixley Pool

Location: Just off A4172 Leominster to Gloucester road
Type and Size: Irrigation reservoir of approx two acres
How to Find: Go south east on A4172. Cross junction with A438 Hereford to Ledbury road. The pool is 500 yards past on the right at the top of an embankment
Carp Stock: Heavily stocked with carp up to mid doubles
Category: Carp Only
Permits: £2.50 per day, available from bailiffs on the bank
Baits/Methods: Boilies tend to work for the better fish. Floaters go very well in summer
Control: Private, day ticket
Restrictions: Night fishing by prior arrangement only - not for the heavy sleepers
W/A: Severn Trent
BK Rating: Moderate
Comments: Some matches take place here. There are other waters run by the owners, enquire locally

Ann Pillinger, of Brigstock, Northants, with a nice fish from Red Beck Lake - one of 17 fish she caught in 8 hours on freelined floating crust

Red Beck Lake

Location: Near Evesham
Type and Size: 4 acre lake
Carp Stock: 200+ of 2lbs to 10lbs, mostly mirrors. Thousands up to 2lbs, best 15¼lbs
Category: Carp Only
Other Species: None
Permits: Season tickets only, limited membership, from Fishery Controller, 15 Stafford Court, Riverside Close, Bedford MK42 9DE. Tel: 0234 212066
Cost: About £50 per season
Baits/Methods: All known methods including legering with all baits, surface fishing, float fishing with maggots and sweetcorn
Control: Season ticket only; private
Restrictions: No long-stay fishing or camping. No hair rigs; no pulses (beans and peas) as bait; barbless hooks

BK Rating: Very Easy
W/A: Severn Trent
Comments: Possibly the easiest water we know. Catches of 40 carp a day quite common. Ideal for beginners and non-carp specialists. Private estate water - do not visit for any reason without permission. Frequent vacancies throughout the season. Guest day tickets for members' friends. Other carp waters available. Warning: private property - do not visit without permission

River Severn

Location: Holt Fleet, between Ombersley and Tenbury Wells - turn right off the A443, where there is an island and a lock
Type and Size: Attractive, medium-sized river, deep above the weir, and shallow below
Carp Stock: Some carp to 17lbs
Category: Few Carp
Other Species: Barbel, chub, roach, pike, bream and perch
Permits: Day tickets from lock keeper
Cost: £3 per day - £35 per season (no day tickets on Sundays - season ticket holders only)
Restrictions: No night fishing - 5am to 10pm only; fishing on main river side only
BK Rating: Difficult
W/A: Severn Trent

River Wye

Location: Upstream of A49 road bridge in Hereford
Type and Size: Slow reach of large, normally rapid running river
How to Find: Go to A49 road bridge and look down
Carp Stock: Few commons, possibly up to 20lbs
Category: Mixed Fishery
Other Species: Chub, roach, perch, bream, tench, barbel, pike, gudgeon, salmon, trout, dace, bleak, eels, grayling, shad during May, and the occasional sturgeon has been seen!
Permits: Hattons of Hereford, St Owens Street, or Perkins of Hereford, Commercial Road
Cost: £2 daily
Baits/Methods: Most baits and methods will work here, but unless cast to specific fish, bait could be taken by the hordes of other fish present
Control: Club - day ticket
Restrictions: No night fishing
W/A: Welsh
BK Rating: Difficult
Comments: Location is *the* key to avoid problems with other fish. The water is heavily matched fished during summer

Rotherwas Long Pool

Location: Industrial Estate, south east of Hereford
Type and Size: Small, rectangular pool of about 1⅓ acres
How to Find: Take B4399 from Hereford. Turn left signed Rotherwas Chapel. The pool is on the left
Carp Stock: Very heavily stocked with small carp up to 5lbs
Category: Carp Only

Permits: On bank
Cost: £2.50 daily
Baits/Methods: Anything works on this easy water
Control: Private, day tickets
Restrictions: No keepnets
W/A: Welsh
BK Rating: Very Easy
Comments: This water is unusual in that many of the fish are fully scaled mirrors

Royal Oak Pool

Location: Village of Portway, five miles north of Hereford on A4110
Type and Size: Farm pond of approx one acre
How to Find: Leave Hereford on A4110. Royal Oak public house is on the left in village of Portway. The pool is behind the public house
Carp Stock: Well stocked with commons and mirrors up to low doubles
Category: Carp Water
Other Species: Roach
Permits: Royal Oak public house
Baits/Methods: Any standard baits and methods
Control: Private, day ticket
W/A: Welsh
BK Rating: Easy
Comments: Some match fishing takes place. Ideally positioned for those days when it gets too hot and dry to fish!

Snuff Mill

Location: Bewdley
Type and Size: Small old pool
How to Find: Near the River Severn at Bewdley
Carp Stock: Carp to 15lbs
Category: Mixed Fishery
Other Species: Tench, roach, bream
Permits: S Lewis Tackle, Severnside South, Bewdley
Cost: On application
Control: Private
BK Rating: Moderate

Stanklin Pool

Location: Just to the south of Kidderminster
Type and Size: 6 acre lake, shallow and heavily reeded, with very boggy surrounds and smelly, silty mud
Carp Stock: Very heavily stocked with small carp to about 8lbs, many of which are commons
Category: Carp Water
Other Species: Some tench, roach and eels
Permits: Phoenix AC - small local club with limited membership - enquire locally or in tackle shops
Baits/Methods: Very good floating crust water
BK Rating: Very Easy
W/A: Severn Trent

Uckinghall Pool

Location: Ripple, Uckinghall, between Worcester and Tewkesbury
Type and Size: Small pit alongside River Severn
How to Find: South from Worcester on A38 towards Tewkesbury, and then to Uckinghall
Carp Stock: Fairly well stocked with carp to about 10lbs
Category: Mixed Fishery
Other Species: Pike, roach, perch, a few rudd
Permits: Birmingham Anglers Association (members only), 100 Icknield Park Road, Rotton Park, Birmingham B16 OAP. Tel: 021-454 9111, 9.30am to 1.30pm, and 7pm to 9pm, Monday to Friday
Cost: About £13 a season, which includes all other BAA waters
BK Rating: Not known
Control: BAA
Restrictions: No groundbait of any kind
W/A: Severn Trent

Upton Warren Lake

Location: Between the M5, junction 5, and Droitwich, about a mile from the town
Type and Size: Lake of nearly 20 acres
Carp Stock: Quite well stocked with carp to 20lbs
Category: Mixed Fishery
Other Species: Bream, roach, rudd, perch, dace and eels
Permits: Day tickets from the office on the site
Cost: £1.50 per day; £1 for the unemployed, under 21's and OAP's
Control: Council
Restrictions: No night fishing - 8am till dusk only; 8am till 5pm on Tuesdays
BK Rating: Moderate
W/A: Severn Trent
Comments: Stands for disabled anglers; some match pegs often booked; no fishing on one bank, which is a Nature Reserve; sailing takes place on this lake, as well as many matches

Wellfield Pool

Location: Highley, Kidderminster
Type and Size: Small pool
Carp Stock: Some carp, mostly small
Category: Mixed Fishery
Other Species: Tench, bream, roach
Permits: Day tickets on bank
Cost: On application
BK Rating: Insufficient information
Control: Private
W/A: Severn Trent
Comments: Try local tackle shops for information

Wilden Pool

Location: Wilden, Stourport-on-Severn
Type and Size: Medium-sized pool
How to Find: Near the River Stour at Wilden, just south of Kidderminster
Carp Stock: Heavily stocked with small carp to 3lbs. A few doubles
Category: Carp Water
Other Species: Some coarse fish
Permits: Day tickets on the bank. Night fishing extra
Cost: On application
BK Rating: Easy
Control: Private - Ron Russell
W/A: Severn Trent
Comments: Standard float fishing methods and baits, as well as legering, will catch these small carp, especially near the island. Try local tackle shops for information

HERTFORDSHIRE

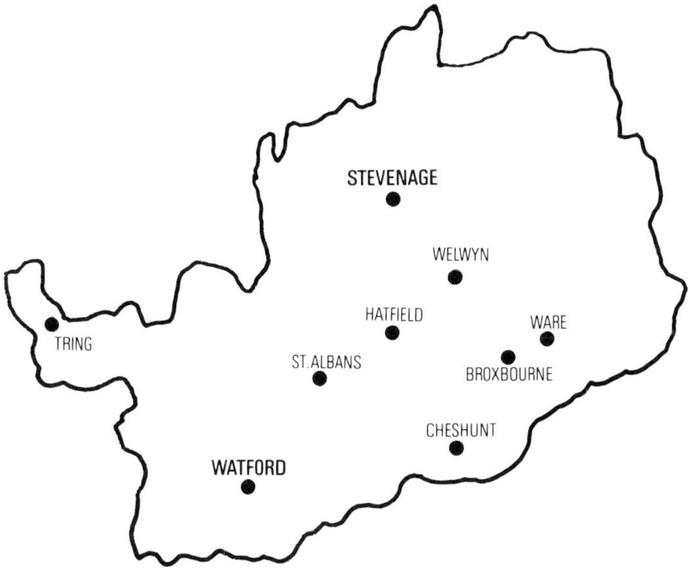

Aldenham Country Park Reservoir

Location: Aldenham, near Elstree
Type and Size: Large estate lake/reservoir
Carp Stock: Some carp, numbers and sizes not known
Category: Mixed Fishery
Other Species: Tench, roach and pike
Permits: From bailiff on site
Cost: £2 per day, juniors £1
Control: Herts County Council; tickets and information from Park Manager, Park Office, Dagger Lane, Elstree. Tel: 081-953 1259
BK Rating: Not known
W/A: Thames
Comments: Fishing is also alllowed from punts which can be hired at about £5 per day

Bowyers Water

Location: Cheshunt, on the outskirts of North London
Type and Size: 27 acre gravel pit
Carp Stock: Well stocked with carp to over 30 lbs
Category: Carp Water
Permits: Season tickets only from Lee Valley Regional Park Authority, Craig Baldwin, Myddelton House, Bulls Cross, Enfield. Tel: 0992 717711
Cost: On application
Control: Lee Valley RPA
BK Rating: Difficult
Comments: There was an authenticated carp from this water of 32lbs 3ozs in 1986

SIMPSONS

OF TURNFORD

EUROPE'S NO. 1 SPECIALIST TACKLE SHOP

FOR PROMPT EFFICENT SERVICE TELEPHONE 0992 468799 USE YOUR ACCESS OR VISA CARD. JUST QUOTE YOUR CARD NUMBER STATING YOUR REQUIREMENTS

Whether you're a novice or experienced carp angler you'll find our Turnford Tackle Superstore is stocked with everything you'll need for modern carp and specialist angling. We've been established for 20 years and all members of our staff are capable carp anglers who can answer all your questions on choice of suitable tackle and bait making problems. Mr Jack Simpson, the proprietor, has been in the tackle trade over 30 years, so you can have every confidence when dealing with us.

RODS – over 300 specialist and carp rods on display in our Turnford Tackle Superstore. Sole suppliers and manufacturers of the exclusive Simpsons/Kevin Maddocks **Dual Taper** Carbon Carp Rods. Also, Rod Hutchinson IM6 Carbons, Century Composite 'Armalite' range, Daiwa's Kevin Nash Amorphous and the superb Simpson's Multiply Ceramic Carbons including the ultimate long range carp rod the Multiply 'Magnum' 12½', 3lb test curve – a legend in its own lifetime!

SPECIALIST TACKLE – we stock the full range of specialist tackle from Kevin Nash, Drennan, Gardner, Streamside, Terry Eustace, Solar Tackle plus the full range of top quality Wychwood rucksacks luggage and holdalls. Our self-service displays contain every conceivable gadget and accessory invented to improve your chances of catching carp.

REELS – we have the full range of Shimano reels in stock including the oustanding 'Aero' Baitrunner models. Also the Daiwa Bite'n'Run reels plus selected models from ABU, Ryobi, Mitchell and DAM, plus of course, full after sales service and spare spools on all models stocked.

HOOKS – we literally have millions of hooks in stock. The full range of handmade hooks from Partridge of Redditch, including the Kevin Maddocks selection, Rod Hutchinson, Ritchie McDonald and Gardner, also Kamasan, Drennan, Mustad and Terry Eustace. If you're having problems getting particular hooks give us a try, there's every chance we stock it.

LINE – we stock Tri-lene Big Game, Sten, Maxima, Drennan, Sylcast and Simpson own Carpcatcher brands. The clear high abrasion and the ever popular 'Sorrell', all on economy bulk spools. Also hook length braids, florescent dacrons from Krystons, Cortland, Black Spider and Masterline. We also have our own line spooling service where we fill your spools with the line of your choice – this service is free you only pay for the line.

BAIT – at least ⅓ of our tackle Superstore has been set out with bait ingredients, mixes, flavours, enhancers, oils, stimulators, soluble dyes and ready-made boilies from Streamselect, KM Maestro, SBS, Rod Hutchinson Developments, Martin Locke's Seed Mixes, Zenon Bojko's mixes, oils, flavours, plus the full range of mixed and ingredients from Nutrabaits, plus over 1000 flavours plus bait guns, rollers from Gardner, KJB and Streamside. We pride ourselves in offering the best range of quality bait products available – if you have a bait problem contact us.

DOUBLE THE SIZE - From April 1992 we will have doubled our shop size, offering one of the best personalised stocks and service in Europe. We accept payment by cheque, p.o, Eurocheques, Access, MasterCard, Visa credit cards, with split payment credit facilities up to £1000 (subject to status), send 50p for our rod brochure.

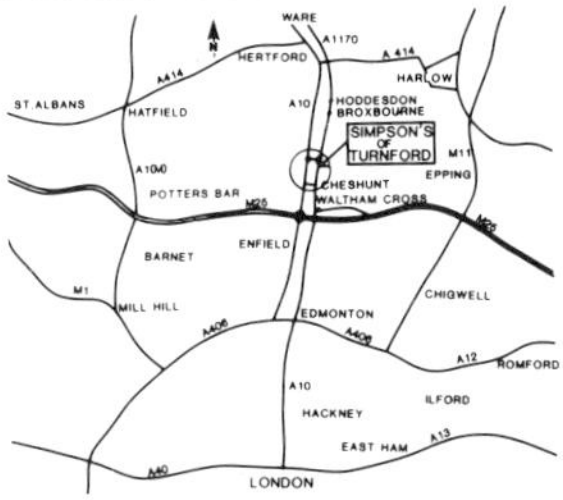

HOW TO FIND US – most major motorways now lead into the North Orbital London M25. Leave the M25 on the A10 northbound road indicating Cambridge. Travel north up the A10 for approximately 2¼ miles. You will see Tescos Brookfield Farm Superstore on your left. Leave the A10 on the next slip road indicating Broxbourne A1170 and come down to the new River Arms roundabout (Berni Inn). Go straight across on the Cheshunt B176 and we are 400 yards down the road on your left at the end of Nunsbury Road. Parking is unrestricted in our own forecourt in front of the shop.

SIMPSON S OF TURNFORD

(CRAFTSMEN RODMAKERS) DEPT. A.T.H.

NUNSBURY DRIVE, TURNFORD, BROXBOURNE, HERTFORDSHIRE · TEL: HODDESDON 468799

BUSINESS HOURS Mon to Sat 9am to 6pm Closed all day Thursday Late evening Fri 9am until 8pm

THE SPECIALIST TACKLE SHOP FOR THE SPECIALIST ANGLER

Broxbourne

Location: Meadgate Lane, Broxbourne, Hoddesdon
Type and Size: Gravel pits. Lake 1 - 24 acres; lake 2 - 30 acres, lake 3 - 68 acres; lake 4 - 3½ acres
How to Find: Take the A105 to Waltham Abbey, then the B194 1½ miles to Lower Nazeing. Take Pecks Hill Road for ¾ mile. Turn left into Meadgate Road, keep left at Tile Works, and you can then see the lakes. Car parking at Meadgate Lane only
Carp Stock: Not known but carp to 28.14 reported
Category: Mixed Fishery
Other Species: Pike, tench, chub, bream, roach, crucian carp, perch, eels
Permits: Season tickets only from Leisure Sport, Thorpe Park, Chertsey, Surrey. Tel: Chertsey 64872
Cost: £22 per season. Juniors/OAP/Disabled £11
BK Rating: Difficult
Control: Leisure Sports
W/A: Thames
Comments: The large lakes are also used for sailing

Cheshunt Reservoirs

Location: Cheshunt, Herts. in the Lea Valley, North London
Type and Size: Two gravel pits of 8 and 20 acres
Carp Stock: Well stocked with carp to mid-thirties; stocked with 2000lbs of carp between 14 and 18 lbs in 1990, with 2,500 more pounds to come
Category: Carp Water
Other Species: Big pike and tench
Permits: Lee Valley Regional Park Authority, Craig Baldwin, Myddleton House, Bulls Cross, Enfield. Tel: 0992 717711
Cost: Season only, on application
Control: Lee Valley R.P.A.
BK Rating: Fairly Hard
W/A: Thames
Comments: Heavy stocking with big fish should make these lakes excellent carp waters in the near future

Fairland Park

Location: In Stevenage
Type and Size: Park lake of about 16 acres
How to Find: Enquire at Stevenage
Carp Stock: Fairly heavily stocked with carp to 20lbs+. Plenty of doubles
Category: Carp Water
Other Species: Roach, rudd, bream, tench, pike
Permits: Day tickets from bailiff on the bank
Cost: Details from bailiff
Control: Council
Restrictions: One bank only can be fished
BK Rating: Easy
W/A: Thames

Frogmore Lake

Location: Near St. Albans
Type and Size: Small lake
Carp Stock: Said to contain some carp to a good size, but numbers and sizes not known
Category: Mixed Fishery
Other Species: Usual coarse fish
Permits: Members only water of the London Anglers Association, Forest Road Hall, Hervey Park Road, Walthamstow, London E17 6LJ. Tel: 081-520 7477
Cost: About £20 per season, to include many other waters, including rivers and canal fishing
Control: LAA
BK Rating: Not known
Restrictions: No night fishing
W/A: Thames

Grand Union Canal

Location: Watford to Milton Keynes (Herts/Beds/Bucks)
Type and Size: Canal of several miles in length
Carp Stock: Well stocked in certain area along this stretch with many carp up to 30lbs - a fish of 30lbs was reported from the Kings Langley area in 1990
Category: Mixed Fishery
Other Species: General coarse fish
Permits: Day tickets from various clubs in the area - you will need to enquire locally
Control: Mainly clubs
BK Rating: Easy to difficult depending on area
W/A: Thames/Anglian depending on area

Grand Union Canal

Location: Marsworth Basin, Tring
How to Find: Take the A489 road from Tring to Marsworth
Carp Stock: Heavily stocked with commons and mirrors mainly to 5lbs, with occasional bigger fish
Category: Mixed Fishery
Other Species: Perch, roach, bream and catfish
Permits: Permits are obtainable on the bank
Baits/Methods: Float fishing and legering with maggots, bread or sweetcorn. Specialist carp tactics not needed
Control: Tring Angling Club. Secretary: B Boucher. Tel: Chesham 782713
BK Rating: Easy
W/A: Thames
Comments: Good water for fun fishing and as a change from lakes

Hatfield Broadwater

Location: Essendon, near Hatfield, on River Lea
Type and Size: 7 acre lake
Carp Stock: Carp to over 20lbs

Category: Mixed Fishery
Other Species: Bream
Permits: Members only water of Hatfield and District AS, E F Denchfield, 44 Stockbreach Road, Hatfield, Herts
Control: Club
Restrictions: No day tickets, club members only
BK Rating: Moderate
W/A: Thames

Henlow Grange

Location: Between the villages of Henlow and Arlesey, both of which are in Bedfordshire!
Type and Size: Gravel pits of 9, 5 and 3 acres
Carp Stock: Large lake fairly well stocked with carp to 44lbs (although this was a spawnbound fish which is thought to be dead). In 1991 a 31½lb common and a mirror of over 30lbs were caught. Other two lakes well stocked with carp to low twenties
Category: Mixed Fishery
Permits: Letchworth Angling Club - season tickets from local tackle shops, in Letchworth and Hitchin
Cost: About £25 per season - no day tickets
BK Rating: Large lake - Difficult; other lakes - Moderate
W/A: Anglian
Comments: Good club waters, with a few very large fish

Holwell Hyde Lake

Location: Cole Green near Welwyn Garden City
Type and Size: 2 acre lake
How to Find: Find Hatfield and take the A405 to the left, turn onto the A414 Hertford road. After 3 miles turn left onto the B195 and continue for 1½ miles. Turn left into Holwell Hyde Lane. The lake is half a mile down the lane on the left
Carp Stock: Well stocked with carp which are thought to be small, but some upper doubles and two 20's
Category: Mixed Fishery
Other Species: Tench, roach and rudd
Permits: Day tickets from bailiffs on the bank or in advance from Fishery Manager, V Bamford Esq., Holwell Hyde Cottage, Holwell Hyde Lane, Welwyn Garden City. Season tickets about £15 (£10 for Juniors/OAP's/ evening fishing from Fishery Manager
Cost: Day tickets about £2.50 (£1.25 Juniors/OAP's). Season tickets £25
Restrictions: No night fishing. Sunrise to sunset for season ticket and advance day ticket holders. Those without tickets must not be on the fishery before 8.30am. No unaccompanied juniors unless they hold season tickets. No sacking. One rod only till October
Control: Redland Angling Scheme
BK Rating: Easy
W/A: Anglian
Comments: Little is known about this water which has been little fished previously. Do not park anywhere other than in the car park. Bus No. 324 from Welwyn Garden City to Hertford passes the end of Holwell Hyde Lane. Car parking close to water

Hook Lake

Location: Northaw, near Potters Bar
Type and Size: 1½ acre pool
How to Find: Enquire from Fourways Fisheries
Carp Stock: Well stocked with carp to 20 lbs, mostly doubles
Category: Mixed Fishery
Other Species: Tench, catfish, zander, pike
Permits: Fourways Fisheries, Poplars Nursery, Harlington Road, Toddington, Dunstable, Beds. Tel: 0525 55584
Cost: About £80
BK Rating: Not known
Control: Fourways Fisheries
W/A: Severn Trent
Comments: Details supplied on receipt of an SAE

Redlands Crown Fishery

Location: Broxbourne
Type and Size: 3 lakes totalling about 40 acres
How to Find: Take the A10 from London and turn off at Hoddesdon. At the roundabout after 400 yards take first exit sign marked 'Dobbs Weir Industrial Estate'. Pass the Fish and Eels public house and after another 600 yards enter the fishery through gates on the left near Richard White Sluices
Carp Stock: Not many carp but some are large
Category: Few Carp
Other Species: Tench, bream, roach, perch, pike
Permits: No day tickets. Season tickets only from Fishery Manager. Peter Brill, Carthagena Lock, Broxbourne, Herts. Tel: Hoddesdon 463656
Cost: About £12 a season. Juniors/OAP £6
BK Rating: Difficult, as there are few carp
Control: Redland Angling Scheme
W/A: Thames

Springwell Lake

Location: Rickmansworth, near Watford
Type and Size: Medium sized matured gravel pit
Carp Stock: Well stocked with carp to 20lbs
Category: Mixed Fishery
Other Species: Tench, roach and perch
Permits: Members only water of London Anglers Association, Forest Road Hall, Hervey Park Road, Walthamstow, London E17. Tel: 081-520 7477
Cost: About £20 per season, to include a number of other waters - 100 miles of fishing in rivers, canals, lakes and reservoirs
Control: LAA
Restrictions: No night fishing
BK Rating: Not known
W/A: Thames

Stanborough Lake

Location: Welwyn Garden City
Type and Size: Gravel pit of about 20 acres
How to Find: Edge of A1M near Welwyn Garden City
Carp Stock: Very heavily stocked with many doubles to 20lbs. Few twenties to 27lbs
Category: Carp Water
Other Species: Roach, rudd, tench and catfish
Permits: Day tickets and club membership available on bank
Control: Club
BK Rating: Very Easy
Restrictions: One rod only - you won't need more on this easy water. Two rods after 1st November - no groundbaiting and no boilies
W/A: Thames
Comments: Sailing boats and many people

Stanstead Abbots

Location: High Street, Stanstead Abbot, Ware, Herts
Type and Size: Two gravel pits of 3 acres and 7½ acres
How to Find: From London take the A10 Cambridge road and then the A414 to Stanstead Abbots. Park cars in the public car park in the High Street and walk down the path at the rear of the car park to the lakes
Carp Stock: Stocked with 1,500 carp in 1983, sizes not known, and also a few bigger carp to 31lbs, were stocked in 1984. Mixed fishery although if enough of these carp survived there should be enough to take this into our Carp Water category in the future. Many 20's and 30's caught. Fish up to 42lbs in the bigger lake
Category: Mixed Fishery
Other Species: Tench, bream, roach and chub
Permits: This is a Leisure Sport Angling Special Venue. Season tickets from LSA, Thorpe Park, Staines Road, Chertsey, Surrey. Tel: Chertsey 64872
Cost: £33 per season; Juniors/OAP/Disabled £11.50. Limited tickets on a first come, first served basis
Restrictions: Usual LSA rules but night fishing is allowed
BK Rating: Moderate
Control: Leisure Sport Angling
W/A: Thames

Startops, Tring Reservoirs

Location: Near Tring
Type and Size: Reservoir of 30 acres
Carp Stock: Not many carp, but there are some 20's and possibly much bigger fish present
Category: Few Carp
Other Species: Bream, tench, roach, perch, pike, catfish
Permits: Day tickets from bailiff on the bank
Restrictions: No night fishing, but there is a night syndicate
Control: Private
BK Rating: Very Difficult
W/A: Thames
Comments: Night syndicate, members only

Wormleybury

Location: Wormley, near Broxbourne, Church Lane
Type and Size: Estate lake of 5 acres
Carp Stock: Not many carp, but mostly very large with about fifteen 20's including two commons of over 25lbs, some upper 20's. Lake record is 36lbs, but this fish has since died. Possibly one other low 30 in the lake
Category: Mixed Fishery
Other Species: Tench, roach, rudd, bream, perch, pike
Permits: From the owner, Graham Barnes, Wormleybury House, Church Lane, Broxbourne, Herts. At the time of going to press the owner had stopped all fishing due to bad behaviour of anglers
Cost: About £80 a season; 1 rod and 2 rod tickets
Cost: Private
Baits/Methods: You will need all the most up-to-date and advanced carp tactics and methods for this water
BK Rating: Very Difficult
W/A: Thames
Comments: A beautiful crescent shaped estate water in the grounds of a big house. Lots of reeds, lilies etc. Apply in writing to the owners as fishing might never be allowed on this water again

HUMBERSIDE

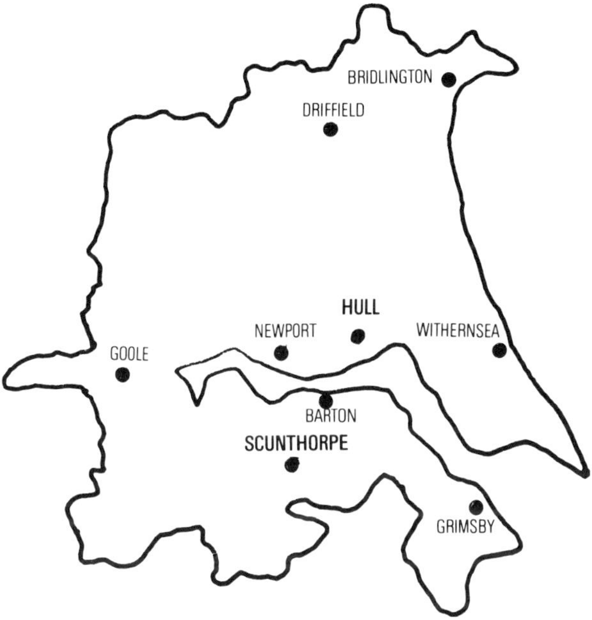

Bakers Pond

Location: Thimble Hall Lane, Newport, near Hull (white bungalow)
Type and Size: 2½ acre lake
How to Find: Newport Village is at the end of the M62
Carp Stock: Well stocked with carp to 26lbs+
Category: Carp Water
Other Species: Crucians, tench and bream
Permits: On site - Tel: Bill Baker on 0430 440350 (7am to 10.30pm)
Cost: £1 per day
BK Rating: Moderate
Control: Private
W/A: Yorkshire
Comments: Owner lives on the site. Big catches reported. 10 - 20 feet deep - snag and weed free except for central island supported by telegraph poles
Restrictions: No tic beans, no keepnets

Barton Broads A

Location: Barton-on-Humber, South Humberside
Type and Size: 11 acre clay pit
How to Find: Off the A15 just before the Humber Bridge
Carp Stock: Heavily stocked with 3,000 carp to 21.7lbs. Many doubles
Category: Mixed Fishery
Other Species: Catfish, tench, bream roach, rudd
Permits: On site or telephone 0652 32237
Cost: About £1.50 per day; £2.50 for 24 hours; syndicate £100
BK Rating: Moderate to Difficult
Restrictions: No hemp
Control: Private
W/A: Anglian
Comments: The site includes a cafe, a tackle and bait shop, and caravans for holidays - contact the resident owners for details

Big Hole Pit

Location: Rawcliffe, just west of Goole off the M62
Type and Size: 5 acre brick pit, with bars, bays and weed
Carp Stock: Well stocked with small carp to about 10lbs
Category: Mixed Fishery
Other Species: Roach, rudd, tench and bream
Permits: Members only water of Goole and Dist., AA. Secretary, L Roger, 29 Westfield Square, Goole N. Humberside DN15 6QR
Cost: About £12 per season
Restrictions: No day tickets; no night fishing; no carp sacks or weighing slings!
BK Rating: Easy
W/A: Yorkshire

Burstwick Ski Pond

Location: Burstwick, Hedon, Hull
Type and Size: Large lake
How to Find: From Hull take the A1033 to Hedon, then the B1362 to Burstwick. Go through the village towards Keyingham, and the lake is down an old railway track
Carp Stock: Quite well stocked with carp to 20lbs
Category: Mixed Fishery
Other Species: Bream, tench, roach, rudd, perch and trout
Permits: Day tickets from clubhouse on site
Cost: Tel: 0964 622674 for costs and information
Control: Private
BK Rating: Thought to be quite hard
W/A: Yorkshire
Comments: There is water skiing on this lake. Night fishing is permitted

Burton Constable Lakes

Location: Burton Constable Hall, Sproatley, near Hull
Type and Size: Several estate lakes, of about 25 acres in all
Carp Stock: Quite well stocked with carp to double figures
Category: Mixed Fishery

Other Species: Roach, bream, perch, tench and pike
Permits: The Warden, Old Lodge, Sproatley, Nr. Hull
Cost: Season - £23; month - £11; week - £5.50
Control: Private
Restrictions: Open for fishing from Ist March to 31st October only
BK Rating: Moderate
W/A: Yorkshire
Comments: Very good fishing on an attractive private estate

Fishponds Farm Fishery

Location: Bridlington
Type and Size: Three small farm ponds
How to Find: From Bridlington town centre, follow Woldgate, which becomes a narrow country lane, and the lakes are on the right
Carp Stock: Well stocked with mirrors and commons, sizes not known
Category: Mixed Fishery
Other Species: Crucians, bream, tench, roach, rudd, perch, brook trout, brown and rainbow trout
Permits: Day tickets at the office. For details, telephone the owner, Mr J Nadin, on 0262 605873
BK Rating: Insufficient information
Control: Private
W/A: Yorkshire
Restrictions: Barbless hooks only. No keepnets. No one under 18 unless accompanied by an adult angler
Comments: This is said to be the most attractive water in Yorkshire, surrounded by woodland and very peaceful

Fish Trades Pond

Location: Newport, between Hull and Goole, on B1239
Type and Size: Small pond of 1 acre
How to Find: Just off the A64 at Newport Village
Carp Stock: Well stocked with carp to upper doubles
Category: Carp Water
Other Species: Tench, bream, roach, perch, pike, trout
Permits: Day tickets
Cost: Low
Restrictions: No night fishing; no keepnets
BK Rating: Moderate
Control: Not known - enquire from local tackle shops
W/A: Yorkshire
Comments: Popular day ticket water. Try Hull and District AA, J Holdenbury, 1 Grebe Road, Thimblehall Lane, Newport, N. Humberside HU15 2PJ for information. This club has some excellent carp fisheries in Humberside. No close season

Halsham Pond

Location: Behind the New Stag public house on the B1362 at Halsham, near Withernsea
Type and Size: Small pond
Carp Stock: Quite well stocked with carp to double figures
Category: Mixed Fishery
Other Species: Bream, tench and rudd and perch
Permits: From Mr Allison, New Stag Inn, Halsham, N. Humberside. Tel: 094 670487
Cost: Low cost day tickets
Control: Private
BK Rating: Moderate
Restrictions: No night fishing - 7.30am till dusk only. Barbless hooks
W/A: Yorkshire
Comments: Park in the pub car park! Some areas suitable for disabled anglers

Holme Lake Fishery

Location: Holme Lane, Messingham, near Scunthorpe. Three miles from junction 4 off the M18
Type and Size: 20 acre sand pit
Carp Stock: Stocked in 1988 with 5,500 carp from 4oz to 8lbs and one 27 pounder
Category: Mixed Fishery
Other Species: Roach, bream, rudd and perch
Permits: Day tickets from Matt Roper, telephone 06737-453/669
Cost: £3 per day
Cost: Private
BK Rating: Moderate
W/A: Yorkshire

Langholme Hill Fishery

Location: Emmotland, North Frodingham
Type and Size: Two smallish lakes
How to Find: Take the B1249 from Driffield to North Frodingham, and after the village turn right to Emmotland. The lakes are on the left at the end of this road
Carp Stock: Well stocked carp to over 20lbs
Category: Mixed Fishery
Other Species: Big bream and tench, roach, perch, pike, trout
Permits: On bank, low cost
Control: Private
Restrictions: No night fishing. No keepnets
W/A: Yorkshire
Comments: Open for 11 months of the year. Fishing dawn till dusk

Motorway Pond

Location: Near Hull
Type and Size: Small lake
How to Find: On the edge of Hull
Carp Stock: Recently stocked with 40 big carp to 27lbs and some smaller carp
Category: Mixed Fishery
Other Species: Double figure bream and good tench

Permits: Hull and District A/C - local tackle shops
Cost: On application
BK Rating: Moderate
Control: Club
W/A: Yorkshire
Comments: Enquire for details from local tackle shops, and Hull A.C.

New Carp Fishery

Location: South Humberside
Permits: For details send SAE to 45 Wendover Road, Messingham, South Humberside DN17 3RX
W/A: Severn Trent
Comments: We didn't have time to investigate this one; give it a try! 25 places only

Rushyvars Lakes

Location: Near Preston, off the A1033 Hull road to Hedon
Type and Size: Medium-sized lake
Carp Stock: Well stocked with carp, sizes not known
Category: Mixed Fishery
Other Species: Tench, bream, rudd and roach
Permits: On site, low cost
BK Rating: Moderate
Restrictions: No night fishing - dawn to dusk only. Barbless hooks. No groundbait
Control: Private
W/A: Yorkshire
Comments: Toilet facilities, and level banks for disabled anglers. There is also a small trout lake on the site. Tel: 0482 898970 for full details of this fishery

The Billabong Caravan Park A

Location: Hempholme Bridge, Brandesburton, near Driffield. YO25 8NB. Tel: 0964 543631
Type and Size: 11 acre pit
How to Find: Off the A165
Carp Stock: Well stocked with carp to 15lbs
Category: Carp Water
Other Species: Pike, perch, roach, bream and trout
Permits: From owner on site - free at present for those staying on site, but day ticket charge being considered
BK Rating: Not known
W/A: Yorkshire
Comments: There is water skiing and other water sports on the lake, with most fishing during the mornings, evening and after dark

The Nest

Location: Wintringham, near Scunthorpe, S.Humberside
Type and Size: One acre man made pond
How to Find: Just off the A1077 between Scunthorpe and Barton-upon-Humber
Carp Stock: Well stocked, mostly 6 - 8 lbs; a few doubles to 11lbs

Category: Mixed Fishery
Other Species: Crucians, grass carp, tench, rudd, roach, perch
Permits: On bank. Tel: Wintringham 732465
Cost: About £2 per day (6am to 8pm)
BK Rating: Easy
Control: Private
Baits/Methods: Sweetcorn, maggots, luncheon meat, cheese paste
W/A: Yorkshire
Restrictions: No night fishing
Comments: Well coloured water with slippery banks when wet. Booking may be necessary in advance as only 20 anglers are allowed to fish the water. Also fished by 'small fish' anglers

Tilery Lake

Location: Broomfleet Tile Factory, near Hull
Type and Size: Clay pit, 30 acres
Carp Stock: Thought to contain about 400 carp, all of which are said to be doubles averaging 18lbs in weight. Plenty of 20's to 30lbs
Category: Carp Water/Mixed Fishery
Other Species: Pike, bream, roach
Permits: Hull and District Angling Association, Hull. Secretary: J Holdenby, 1 Grebe Road, Thimblehall Lane, Newport HU15 2PJ
Cost: Club membership about £10 a year, with an additional £20 for night fishing (locals only)
BK Rating: Difficult
Control: Club
W/A: Yorkshire
Comments: Night fishing for those living locally only. Carp said to be growing fast. Open and featureless water, 4 - 17ft deep

Winter's Pool

Location: East Halton, in S. Humberside between Grimsby and Barton-under-Humber
Type and Size: Two acre clay pit with clear banks
How to Find: Take the A180 from Grimsby, then turn onto A1173, then follow signs for East Halton
Carp Stock: Quite well stocked with carp to upper doubles, with possibly a low 20 or two
Category: Mixed Fishery
Other Species: Roach and bream
Permits: Day tickets. Tel: 0469 40238
Control: Private
BK Rating: Moderate
W/A: Yorkshire
Comments: No close season

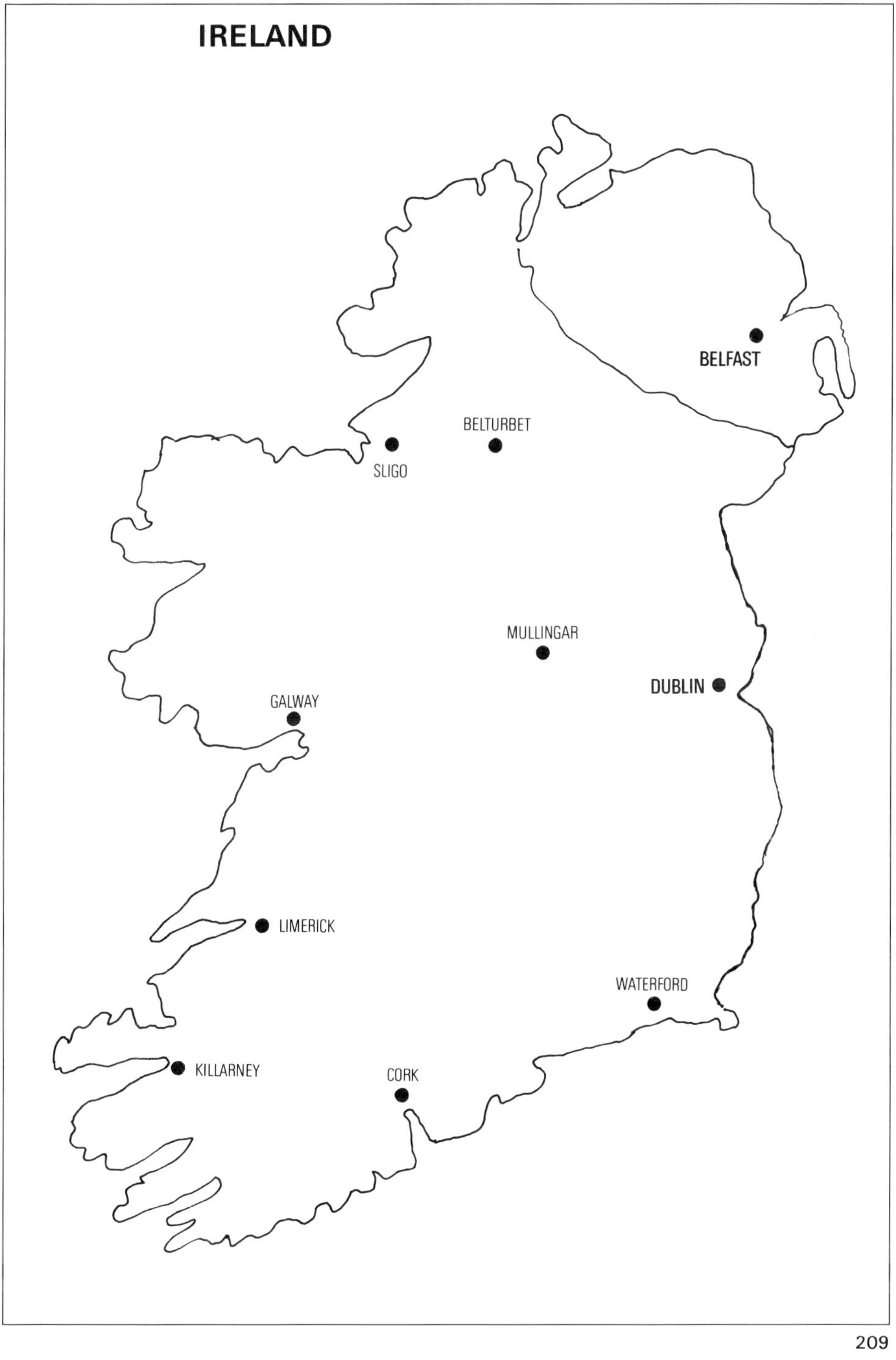
IRELAND
BELFAST
BELTURBET
SLIGO
MULLINGAR
DUBLIN
GALWAY
LIMERICK
WATERFORD
KILLARNEY
CORK

Ballinafid Lake

Location: North of Mullingar, off the N4 Mullingar–Longford road
Type and Size: Small lake
Carp Stock: Quite well stocked with carp to about 15lbs
Category: Mixed Fishery
Other Species: Bream and tench
Permits: Irish State Rod Licence, cost about £10
BK Rating: Moderate
Comments: No close season. Best fishing opposite main road. Soft banks, reeds and a platform

Bun Lough

Location: Car park on the N3 Belturbet–Cavan road, and across two fields
Type and Size: 21 acre Irish lough, very weedy, with a soft bottom
Carp Stock: Stocked with small carp about 5 years ago, present number and sizes not known
Category: Mixed Fishery
Other Species: Bream, roach and perch
Permits: Irish State Rod Licence required, cost about £10
BK Rating: Difficult - you're likely to catch lots of tench and bream!
Comments: No close season. If you do catch any carp, please report them to the Irish Fisheries Board, Mobhi Boreen, Glasnevin, Dublin 5 or local Fisheries Board offices, the address of which can be had locally. Make sure you cause no problems crossing the farmer's fields to get to the lake

Cork Lough

Location: Off the Western Road in Cork City
Type and Size: 10 acre town lake near houses, very shallow and a wildfowl sanctuary
Category: Mixed Fishery
Other Species: Tench, rudd, perch and big eels
Permits: Irish State Licence, cost about £10
Baits/Methods: Sweetcorn works well, and so do most normal carp baits and methods
BK Rating: Moderate
Comments: No close season; public water, very busy, and heavily fished, as it holds the Irish carp record of 25¾lbs, caught on sweetcorn and 3lb line. This is Ireland's best carp water. Do not leave line or tackle to damage birds

Doolin Pond

Location: Off the R400 road from Mullingar, near Gaybrook Cross
Type and Size: Small muddy, weedy lake
Carp Stock: This water was set up as an experimental carp fishery, and carp are now caught to about 10lbs
Category: Carp Water
Permits: Irish State Rod Licence, costing about £10
Baits/Methods: Standard specialist carp methods needed
BK Rating: Difficult
Comments: No close season. Easy access

Galmoylestown Lake

Location: North of Mullingar - turn left off the R394 Mullingar-Castlepollard road
Type and Size: Small lake, weedy and only about 4 feet deep
Carp Stock: Stocked with small carp by the Central Fisheries Board some years ago. These fish are now being caught up to about 10lbs
Category: Carp Water
Other Species: Some trout at this former trout fishery
Permits: State Rod Licence required, the cost which is about £10
Baits/Methods: The water is heavily fished and the carp now need sophisticated baits and methods to be caught
BK Rating: Moderate
Comments: One of Ireland's few carp waters, this pleasant little lake has good access for disabled anglers. You should not require any permits except the Irish State Licence. No close season

Paddy McNamara Lake

Location: Near O'Briens Bridge, at the junction of the R463 Limerick-Killaloe road, and the R466 O'Brien's Bridge-Broadford road, south west of Killaloe
Type and Size: 10 acre weedy lake, about 10 feet deep
Carp Stock: Stocked with carp to about 8lb by the late Paddy Mac, a well known and distinguished developer of fishing in the area
Category: Mixed Fishery
Other Species: Rudd, perch and tench
Permits: Irish State Rod Licence required, cost about £10
BK Rating: Moderate
Comments: No close season

Westmeath Farm A

Location: Co. Westmeath, near Lakes Ennel and Owel
Type and Size: Large lake
Carp Stock: Some carp to doubles
Category: Mixed Fishery
Other Species: Trout, bream and tench
Permits: Tel: 010 353 44 55292
Control: Private
BK Rating: Not known
Comments: Bed and breakfast, evening meal and packed lunch from £18, on working farm. Carp fishing nearby. No close season

ISLE OF WIGHT

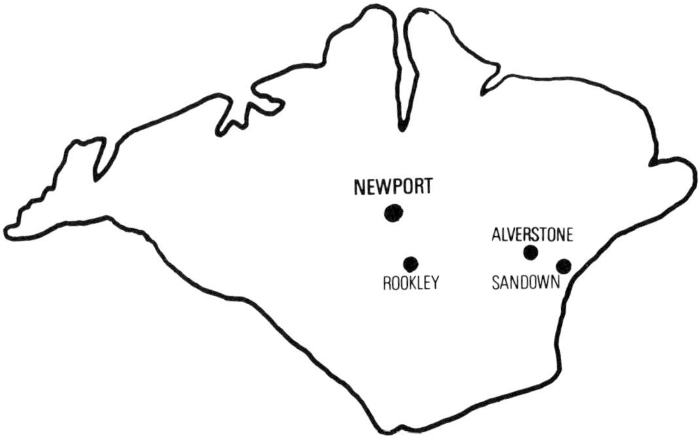

Gunville Pond

Location: Gunville Pool, Carisbrooke, near Newport
Type and Size: Lake of 3 acres
Carp Stock: Well stocked with carp to 11lbs
Category: Mixed Fishery
Other Species: Perch, tench, rudd, pike and roach
Permits: Tickets from tackle shops in most towns, such as G C Young, 74 Regent Street, Shanklin. W Bates, 5 Springhill, Ventnor. (Members only)
Cost: About £9 per season, £4 per week, £1.50 per day
Control: Isle of Wight Freshwater Angling Association. M Steed, 6 Priors Walk, Newport
Restrictions: Members only
BK Rating: Easy
W/A: Southern

River Yar (a)

Location: Alverstone
Type and Size: Small, shallow river, only about 25ft wide
Carp Stock: Some carp to 6lbs
Category: Few Carp
Other Species: Dace, roach, perch, gudgeon and eels
Permits: Day tickets from Scotties Tackle Shop, Lugley Street, Newport or Doug Stephens, Bait and Tackle, Union Street, Newport
Control: Isle of Wight Freshwater AA. Mr Mick Steed, 6 Priors Walk, Newport PO30 5RN. Tel: 0983 521267
BK Rating: Difficult
W/A: Southern

River Yar (b)

Location: Just south of the main road (A3055) between Sandown and Brading, behind the 'Anglers Inn' public house
Type and Size: Small river, only about 40ft wide
Carp Stock: Some carp to double figures
Category: Few Carp
Other Species: Dace, roach, perch, gudgeon, tench, rudd, bream and eels
Permits: Day tickets from Scotties Tackle Shop, Lugley Street, Newport or Doug Stephens, Union Street, Newport
Control: Isle of Wight Freshwater AA, Mr Mick Steed, 6 Priors Walk, Newport PO30 5RN. Tel 0983 521267
BK Rating: Difficult
W/A: Southern

Rookley Country Park A

Location: Rookley, near Godshill
Type and Size: Small lake in 20 acres of parkland
Carp Stock: Some carp
Category: Mixed Fishery
Other Species: Roach and perch
Permits: On site. Tel: 0983 70606
Cost: On application
Control: Private
BK Rating: Unknown
W/A: Southern
Comments: Luxury caravans, licensed bar, restaurant, games room, pitch and putt course, children's adventure playground, darts, pool and video games, take-away food. Prices from £80 - £200 per caravan including fishing. Rose Award caravan park 1991. Hoseasons for booking

Somerton Reservoir

Location: On the A3020 Newport to West Cowes road, about 3 miles from Newport
Type and Size: Small reservoir
Carp Stock: Well stocked with carp from 2lbs to 5lbs, best about 10lbs
Category: Mixed Fishery
Other Species: Roach, rudd and perch
Permits: Day tickets from bailiff on bank
Cost: £3; Juniors £.50
Control: Isle of Wight Freshwater AA, Secretary Mr M J Steed, 6 Priors Walk, Newport PO30 5RN. Tel: 0983 521267
Baits/Methods: Luncheon meat very good for the carp
BK Rating: Easy
W/A: Southern

KENT

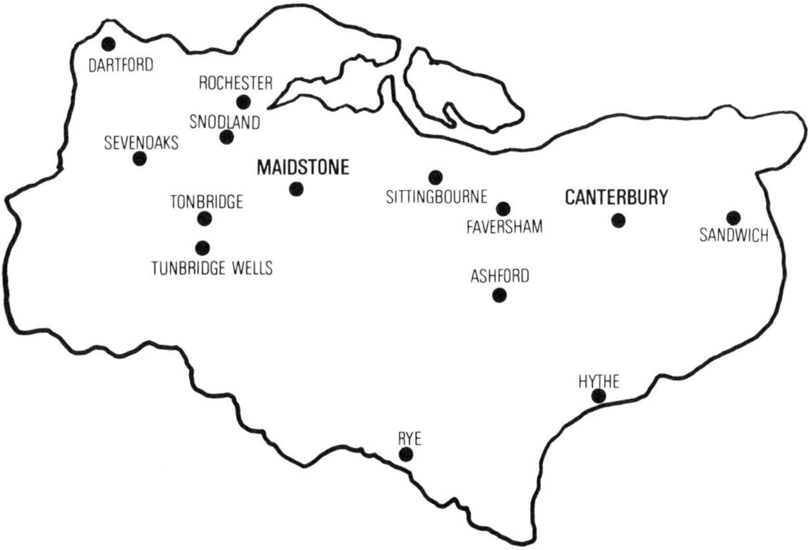

Alders Lakes

Location: Near Snodland, close to Reeds Lakes
Type and Size: Three gravel pits with island etc, the biggest of which is about 6 acres
Carp Stock: All three lakes are well stocked with carp. The biggest lake has a number of 20's to about 29lbs; the Trout Lake contains many low doubles, and the Castle Lake contains small commons
Category: Mixed Fisheries
Other Species: Roach, bream, pike, perch and big eels
Permits: Alders AC, a private club which is hard to get into - try local tackle shops for information - season tickets only
Control: Club
BK Rating: Big Lake - Moderate; others - Easy
W/A: Southern

Ashford Pit

Location: Near the town of Ashford
Type and Size: Small pit
Carp Stock: Well stocked with carp to double figures
Category: Mixed Fishery
Other Species: Big tench and rudd
Permits: Ashford Working Mens Club, members only - no day tickets. For details enquire from local tackle shops, such as M and H Angling, 1 Thirlstane Terrace, Hythe
Control: Club
BK Rating: Not known
W/A: Southern

Ashby Farm Lakes A

Location: Appledore, Ashford
Type and Size: 2 reservoirs of 2 acres each
How to Find: Near Ashford
Carp Stock: Carp to 18lbs
Category: Mixed Fishery
Other Species: General coarse fish
Permits: On site - residents only. Tel: 023-383-378
Cost: Approx £2.75 per day; group week ticket also available
BK Rating: Moderate
Control: Private
Restrictions: Not known
W/A: Southern
Comments: Holiday centre; self catering accommodation in Scandinavian style chalets at waters edge. £110 to £245 according to season. Fishing extra. No fishing unless resident. Beautiful woodland setting

Barden Park Lake

Location: Barden Park, Brook Street, Tonbridge
Type and Size: 10 acre lake
Carp Stock: Not heavily stocked for the size of water, but one or two big fish to over 30lbs. Many small commons
Category: Mixed Fishery
Other Species: Roach, bream, tench, pike, perch and eels
Permits: Enquire locally, or from local tackle shops
Restrictions: Members only; no night fishing
BK Rating: Fairly Hard
W/A: Southern

Blue Lake

Location: Near Northfleet
Type and Size: Old chalk pit of 20-30 acres
How to Find: The pit is just off the A2 road at Northfleet
Carp Stock: Quite well stocked with doubles and 20's to 30lbs
Category: Carp Water
Other Species: Tench, bream and eels
Permits: No day tickets, club membership only
Control: Thameside Working Mens Club
BK Rating: Difficult
W/A: Thames
Comments: This pit is 60-70 feet deep in places; surface fishing works well at times. Enquire locally for membership

Brooklands

Location: Dartford
Type and Size: Gravel pit of 16-20 acres
How to Find: Just off the A2 at the traffic lights where you turn towards Dartford
Carp Stock: Huge stock, many doubles and twenties, and two thirties. Said to contain more doubles and 20's for its size than any other water in England

Category: Carp Water
Other Species: Bream, tench, roach, pike, rudd
Permits: Day tickets from bailiffs on bank
Control: Club. Dartford and District APS. Hon. Secretary: D E Reeve, 29 Berkeley Crescent, Dartford, Kent. Membership very hard to obtain; mainly for locals
Restrictions: No night fishing
BK Rating: Moderate
W/A: Thames
Comments: A very well-known carp water, where some of the leading carp anglers have fished and where some of the early bait experiments with high protein baits took place. Undoubtedly one of the most heavily fished waters in the country. Here they actually queue for swims and people have been known to wait several days and nights behind someone who is fishing in order to get their place when they leave! Some of the best pitches are permanently fished, day and night for the whole season.

We have heard it said that before the start of the season carp anglers camp on the bank for a week before the season to obtain the best places

Bysingwood

Location: Bysingwood Road, Faversham
Type and Size: Mature gravel pit of about 10 acres
How to Find: Take Bysingwood Road from Faversham and the lake is on the left about 2 miles from the town centre
Carp Stock: Very heavily overstocked with doubles. Occasional 20's to 23lbs
Category: Carp Water
Other Species: Tench, bream and eels
Permits: Faversham Angling Club. Hon Secretary: A O Baldock, 5 Kennedy Close, Faversham. Tel: 533240. It is very hard to get into the club and you will almost certainly have to live in the Faversham area; worth a try for others
Cost: Approx £15 per season
Control: Club
BK Rating: Very Easy
W/A: Southern
Comments: This is most certainly one of the best known doubles carp water in the country. 10-12 doubles a day is possible and we have heard that an angler once had 25 doubles in one day. For this reason it is very hard to get into, but we have included it because it is on the same club ticket as the School Pool and you may be able to obtain membership if you live locally. For others it is unlikely, but you can apply and hope for the best. A number of well known carp anglers have fished this water

Chiddingstone Castle Lake

Location: Chiddingstone Castle, near Tonbridge
Type and Size: Estate lake of 3 acres
How to Find: Take the B2027 road from Tonbridge to Edenbridge
Carp Stock: Well stocked with commons to 10lbs. A few lower doubles
Category: Mixed Fishery
Other Species: Roach, perch, bream, gudgeon, rudd
Permits: From the bailiff on the bank. Details from the Secretary, Chiddingstone Castle, Edenbridge. Tel: Edenbridge 870347
Cost: Approx £5 per day

Baits/Methods: Normal carp fishing methods and baits. Bread will still catch the carp
Control: Private – day ticket book in advance if possible
Restrictions: No night fishing
BK Rating: Easy
W/A: Southern
Comments: Peaceful situation with tree-lined banks, weed and lilies. Grounds of ancient castle

Chilham Castle Carp Syndicate

Location: Chilham Castle grounds, Chilham
Type and Size: 5 acre estate lake
How to Find: 7 miles south west of Canterbury on the A252
Carp Stock: Very heavily stocked with thin commons to about 8lbs
Category: Carp Water
Other Species: Some coarse fish
Permits: Albert Brown, Heronsview Fisheries, Drovers End, Pudding Lane, Ash CT3 2EJ. Tel: 0304 812651 or 0843 296031
Cost: On application
Control: Private
BK Rating: Easy
Restrictions: On application; no day tickets
W/A: Southern
Comments: In the beautiful grounds of one of the finest English castles, in one of the prettiest villages in the country. Big catches in fine surroundings

Chipstead Lakes

Location: Near Sevenoaks
Type and Size: 12 acre lake
Carp Stock: Well stocked with carp to over 30lbs
Category: Mixed Fishery
Other Species: Tench, bream, roach and rudd
Permits: County Leisure Angling Association, 65 Pelham Road South, Gravesend DA11 8QS. Tel: 0474 332399
Cost: Seasonal only at £25, with reductions for those under 16. Includes other waters
Control: CLAA, but shared on weekdays with Holmesdale AC
BK Rating: Moderate
W/A: Southern
Comments: A new Association, the CLAA has a magazine, organised events and several other waters. Members may also fish CALPAC waters, some of which contain carp

Cotton Farm

Location: Near Dartford, just to the east end of the Dartford Tunnel, and almost within sight of the toll booths and the River Thames
Type and Size: Open pit of nearly 10 acres - once twice this size, but partly filled in
Carp Stock: Well stocked with low doubles, and a number of 20's to about 30lbs
Category: Carp Water
Other Species: Roach, bream and pike
Control: Private; membership and permits from The Tackle Box, Sutton-at-Hone
BK Rating: Fairly Hard
W/A: Southern
Comments: Quite a well known water, and fished by some of the top carp anglers. Fishes well in winter, with a good chance of a winter twenty

Danson Park

Location: Between Welling and Bexleyheath
Type and Size: Large shallow park lake
How to Find: Just off the A2 at Blackfen
Carp Stock: Quite heavily stocked with small carp, occasional doubles
Category: Carp Water
Other Species: Roach
Permits: Day tickets on bank
Control: Council - GLC
Restrictions: No night fishing
BK Rating: Moderate
W/A: Thames

Darenth

Location: Parsonage Lane, Darenth, near Dartford
Type and Size: 4 gravel pits: Big Lake - 13 acres; Long Lake - 4 acres; Tree Lake - 3 acres; Tip Lake - 9 acres
How to Find: Take the A2 to the traffic lights at Dartford. Turn right onto the A225, after 2 miles turn left at Parsonage Lane (signposted Darenth). Continue for half a mile and the main entrance is on right just after 2 river bridges

Carp Stock: Big Lake - well stocked with doubles and twenties to over 30 pounds. Long Lake - some doubles and 20's to about 29 pounds. Tree Lake - a few doubles and one or two twenties. Tip Lake - a few twenties and more than a dozen thirties to about 40 pounds
Category: All four lakes are Carp Waters
Other Species: Bream, tench, pike, perch, roach, rudd, chub
Permits: Leisure Sport Special Venue. Thorpe Water Park, Staines Road, Chertsey, Surrey. Tel: Chertsey 64872. Season tickets only
Cost: Approx £33 per season. Juniors/OAP/disabled - £21
Control: Leisure Sport Angling
Restrictions: See Leisure Sport Guide Book for very strict rules
BK Rating: Big Lake - Moderate; Long Lake - Fairly Hard; Tree Lake - Difficult; Tip Lake - Fairly Hard
W/A: Thames
Comments: One of the best known big carp waters in the country. Heavily fished by experienced and successful carp anglers. Modern rigs and sophisticated baits needed

Eridge Green Lake

Location: Just off the A26 at Eridge, south west of Tunbridge Wells
Type and Size: 3 acre estate lake
Carp Stock: Well stocked with carp to doubles
Category: Mixed Fishery
Other Species: Usual coarse fish
Permits: County Leisure AA, 65 Pelham Road South, Gravesend DA11 8QS. Tel: 0474 332399
Cost: £25 per season to include other carp waters
Control: CLAA
BK Rating: Not known
Comments: CLAA has a number of carp lakes, and its members can also fish all the CALPAC waters, some of which contain good carp

Fordwich Lake

Location: In the Stour valley near Fordwich
Type and Size: Large gravel pit of 33 acres, with a very irregular bottom
How to Find: Take the A28 from Canterbury to Sturry, and turn right. Follow the road past the George and Dragon Hotel, the Fordwich Arms on the left, and go down past the church on 'The Drove' a private road to the parking area
Carp Stock: Very well stocked with carp to over 20lbs
Category: Mixed Fishery
Other Species: Tench and pike
Permits: Members only water of Canterbury and District AC - Riversdale, 14 Mill Road, Sturry, Canterbury CT2 OAF. Tel: Canterbury 710830
Cost: £31 per season, with a £15.50 entry fee, which includes many other waters
Control: Club
BK Rating: Moderate
W/A: Southern
Comments: A well known big fish carp water in very attractive surroundings, well looked after by Canterbury club

Great Hollanden Farm Reservoir

Location: Near Sevenoaks, off the A25
Type and Size: Small farm irrigation reservoir, with only a few swims, very clear water
Carp Stock: Some small carp
Category: Mixed Fishery
Other Species: Tench, roach, perch, rudd and a few trout
Permits: The County Leisure Angling Association, 65 Pelham Road South, Gravesend DA11 8QS. Tel: 0474 332399 - seasonal membership only
Cost: About £25; under 16's and additional family members £15 each
Control: CLAA
BK Rating: Not known
W/A: Southern
Comments: The CLAA is a new club, with a magazine, competitions, social functions, and some other waters. Members can also fish the CALPAC waters

Horton Kirby

Location: Horton Kirby, near Dartford
Type and Size: 3 gravel pits; total area 10-14 acres
How to Find: Five minute walk from Farningham Road railway station
Carp Stock: Well stocked with many doubles and twenties to about 28lbs, and lots of small carp also
Category: Carp Water
Other Species: Tench, bream and pike
Permits: Day tickets from bailiff on banks
Control: Club; Dartford and District Angling and Preservation Society. Hon Secretary: D E Reeve, 29 Berkeley Crescent, Dartford, Kent. Membership very hard to obtain
Restrictions: No night fishing
BK Rating: Easy
Comments: A well known water, very heavily fished by day ticket anglers

Johnsons Pit

Location: Larkfield, near Maidstone
Type and Size: Two gravel pits covering about 20 acres in all
How to Find: Just off the M25 at New Hythe junction, Larkfield
Carp Stock: Doubles and 20's to about 30lbs
Category: Mixed Fishery
Other Species: Very big tench, pike, roach, bream
Permits: Day ticket from the bailiff on the bank
Control: Private
BK Rating: Fairly Hard
Comments: This water is said to be not very heavily fished and night fishing is allowed

Kentish Stour

Location: From Fordwich to Plucks Gutter and Grove Ferry, on the River Stour, a tributary of the Medway
Type and Size: Small river
Carp Stock: Some carp to 14lbs
Category: Probably Few Carp

Other Species: Famous for its big roach, and also trout, bream, rudd, tench, pike, gudgeon, dace, chub, eels and even some sea trout
Permits: Members only water of Canterbury and District AC, Riversdale, 14 Mill Road, Canterbury CT2 OAF (C Jardine, Hon Sec). Tel: Canterbury 710830
Cost: Membership, which includes other waters, costs £31 per year, with an entrance fee of £15.50
Control: Club
Restrictions: Upstream of Fordwich church is fly fishing only
BK Rating: Difficult
W/A: Southern
Comments: 3¼lb roach caught in 1985

Kingfisher Lakes

Location: Various lakes at Paddesworth and Hoo, near Rochester
Type and Size: Several small lakes, and a big chalk pit of about 30 acres known as Pollard Lake. At Hoo, three small gravel pits
Carp Stock: The three lakes at Paddesworth are all well stocked with carp up to upper 20's in size. The Hoo lakes are quite well stocked with fish to upper doubles
Category: Mixed Fisheries
Other Species: Roach, bream, perch and pike
Permits: Kingfisher Angling and Preservation Society. Mrs A Thomas, 23 Everest Drive, Hoo, Rochester ME5 9AN
Control: Club; members only, no day tickets, and membership not easy to obtain
BK Rating: Moderate
W/A: Southern
Comments: The club has a number of other waters, several of which are quite easy fishing. One or two of the lakes may produce a thirty

Longford Lake

Location: Just north of the A25 near Sevenoaks
Type and Size: 12 acre lake, 10 to 35 feet deep
Carp Stock: Well stocked with carp; plenty of doubles and six 20's reported in 1990
Category: Mixed Fishery
Other Species: Tench, bream, roach, rudd, perch and pike
Permits: Cornell Fishery Developments, Charter House, 29a London Road, Croydon CRO 2RB. Syndicate only – the water is also shared with a club
Cost: About £30, to include other carp waters
Control: Cornell Fishery Developments
Restrictions: No night fishing at weekends; no fishing on competition weekends; no stimulant baits (whatever these are!)
BK Rating: Moderate
W/A: Southern

Maidstone Lakes A

Location: Near Maidstone
Type and Size: Local lakes
How to Find: Near Maidstone town centre
Carp Stock: Well stocked with good carp

Category: Mixed Fisheries
Other Species: General coarse fish
Permits: Tel: 0622 676586
Cost: On application
BK Rating: Moderate
Control: Private
W/A: Southern
Comments: Fishing weekends and holidays offered in private hotel. Accommodation and all meals, bar, TV lounge. Fishing in nearby lakes and the River Medway (carp to 20lbs+)

Nicholls Pit

Location: Hythe
Type and Size: Large pit
How to Find: By the Army ranges on the coast road to Hythe
Carp Stock: Quite well stocked with doubles and twenties
Category: Mixed Fishery
Other Species: Tench, bream and roach
Permits: Day tickets from bailiffs on the bank
Control: Private
BK Rating: Fairly Hard
W/A: Southern

Orpington and District

Location: Near Sidcup
Type and Size: Two fair-sized lakes
How to Find: On the A20 at Klingers roundabout
Carp Stock: Quite well stocked with some doubles and some 20's
Category: Mixed Fishery
Other Species: Tench, bream, pike and roach
Permits: Day tickets from local tackle shop at St. Mary's Cray
Control: Club - Orpington and District
BK Rating: Fairly Hard
W/A: Thames

Pett Pools

Location: Between Winchelsea and Hastings
Type and Size: Small pools
How to Find: Winchelsea - 2 miles; Rye - 4 miles; off the Winchelsea-Hastings road
Carp Stock: Some carp
Category: Mixed Fishery
Other Species: General coarse fishing
Permits: M Piddington, Market Stores, Pett
Cost: Approx £2.50 per day; season tickets
BK Rating: Moderate
Restrictions: None
W/A: Southern
Comments: Local clubs have other waters containing carp on Romney Marsh; try Cinque Ports AS - R MacGregor, 31 Burmarsh Road, Hythe, Kent. Bob MacGregor is a well known local carp angler and a BCSG member

Reeds Lake

Location: Near Snodland, just on the London side of the M20 at junction 4
Type and Size: Three attractive estate-type lakes
Carp Stock: Well stocked with carp to about 20lbs, many of which are lower doubles
Category: Carp Water
Permits: N Martin, 13 Masefield Road, Larkfield, Maidstone - in advance only
Control: Private
BK Rating: Moderate
W/A: Southern

Royal Military Canal A

Location: Hythe and Ashford areas
Type and Size: Short, shallow canal
How to Find: Off the A2070 south of Ashford
Carp Stock: Some very good carp up to 30lbs
Category: Mixed Fishery
Other Species: General coarse fishing
Permits: Day tickets on the bank for some stretches; also from J B Walker Ltd, 84 Slade Street, Hythe. Tel: 0303 66228; and Ashford and District A and PS, C Hyder, 37 Northumberland Avenue, Kennington, Ashford
Cost: Approx £1.50; season £10
Control: Club
Restrictions: None
W/A: Southern
Comments: A very hard water, with some big fish if you can find them. Tickets also available from some local pubs. Ashford APS also has a lake with some big carp - enquire from Secretary. Accommodation at the Railway Hotel, Appledore. Tel: 023-383-253 for brochure. B&B from £25 per night for a double room

Scarlett's Lake

Location: Near East Grinstead
Type and Size: 3 acre lake, stream fed
How to Find: East Grinstead area, access from the A264 near church at Hammerwood
Carp Stock: Many carp, to 23lbs
Category: Mixed Fishery
Other Species: Crucians, grass carp, tench, rudd, roach and perch
Permits: On bank, or J Jackson, Furnace Lane, Cowden, Edenbridge, Kent. Tel: 0342 850414 (6.30 to 9.30pm)
Cost: Day - £3.50, season - £42 (from 8am on bank). Reduced prices for OAP's, the disabled, students and unemployed
BK Rating: Fairly Hard
Control: Private
Restrictions: No preserved boilies. No groundbait till July 16th. Season ticket holders may night fish
W/A: Southern
Comments: Picturesque lake suitable for well controlled families. Easy access for wheelchairs. 20p per ticket donated to conservation or wildlife charities. Bus passes end of road - alight Hammerwood; Tunbridge Wells - East Grinstead

School Pool

Location: In the town of Faversham
Type and Size: Old gravel pit of about 18 acres, many gravel bars
How to Find: Just off the M2 at the Faversham junction; in the town
Carp Stock: Fairly well stocked with quite a number of twenties, and at least two thirties. These include 'She', a famous mirror of about 35lbs
Category: Carp Water
Other Species: Bream, tench, pike
Permits: Day tickets from the Club Secretary in advance only – Faversham and District AC membership
Control: Faversham and District AC, 5 Kennedy Close, Faversham. Tel: Faversham 533240
Restrictions: No night fishing
BK Rating: Difficult
W/A: Southern
Comments: Another water very well known to carp anglers. Twenties including some upper 20's have been caught here, for as long as we can remember, and the water is famous for a couple of good thirties including 'She', already mentioned which has been caught by a large number of carp anglers including some of the best known names in the country. The lake is surrounded by a school, houses, a road and a factory!

Sittingbourne Lakes

Location: Murston, near Sittingbourne
Type and Size: 3 large gravel pits
How to Find: Murston is 1½ miles north of Sittingbourne
Carp Stock: Plenty of good carp to over 20lbs
Category: Mixed Fishery
Other Species: General coarse fishing
Permits: No day tickets; information from Hon Sec, Sittingbourne AC, C Brown, 5 Sunnybanks, Murston, Sittingbourne, Kent
Cost: On application
BK Rating: Difficult
Restrictions: Ask the club secretary
W/A: Southern
Comments: Try also Deans Tackle Shop, East Street, Sittingbourne, Kent

Station Pool (Rookery Lake)

Location: Near Bromley
Type and Size: Small lake of about 1¾ acres
How to Find: Enquire from owners
Carp Stock: Well stocked with carp to 25lbs
Category: Mixed Fishery
Other Species: Tench, bream, roach and pike
Permits: Fourways Fisheries, Poplars Nursery, Harlington Road, Toddington, Dunstable. Tel: 0525 55584
Control: Fourways Fisheries
W/A: Thames
Comments: Season tickets only, about £65

Stonar Lake

Location: Near Sandwich
Type and Size: Small lake
Carp Stock: Well stocked with carp to 20lbs; plenty of doubles
Category: Mixed Fishery
Other Species: Roach, bream and perch
Permits: Try local tackle shops - possibly an angling club in Sandwich?
Control: Club?
BK Rating: Easy
W/A: Southern

Sundridge Lakes

Location: Sundridge, near Sevenoaks
Type and Size: Gravel pits of about 5 and 15 acres
Carp Stock: Carp to over 20lbs
Category: Carp Water
Permits: Rod and Line Ltd, 70/72 Loampit Vale, Lewisham, London SE13. Tel: 081-852 1421
Cost: Approx £60.00
Control: Private
BK Rating: Moderate
W/A: Southern
Comments: We understand that there is a waiting list for this water. No day tickets are issued. There are rumours that the water contains some very big carp

Sutton

Location: Sutton-at-Hone, near Dartford
Type and Size: Gravel pit of about 10 acres
How to Find: On the Horley road from Farningham
Carp Stock: Heavily stocked with many doubles and plenty of 20's to 28lbs
Category: Carp Water
Other Species: Tench, pike, roach and bream
Permits: Dartford and District Angling Society. D E Reeve, 29 Berkeley Crescent, Dartford, Kent. Very long waiting list, membership difficult to obtain. No day tickets, club members only
Restrictions: No sacks
BK Rating: Easy
Comments: This club is mainly for people living in the Dartford area; it is difficult to obtain membership. We thought we would include it as it is a good water and you may obtain membership if you live locally

Vauxhall Lakes

Location: Canterbury Nature Reserve, off Broad Oak Road, on the edge of the city
Type and Size: Very large old gravel pits
Carp Stock: Stocked with carp in 1973, which are now being caught to mid-twenties; plenty of doubles
Category: Mixed Fishery
Other Species: Roach, perch, bream, rudd, tench, eels and pike
Permits: Members only water of Canterbury and District AC, Riversdale, 14 Mill Road, Sturry, Canterbury. Tel: 710830

Cost: £31 per season with an entry fee of £15.50
Control: Club
BK Rating: Moderate
W/A: Southern
Comments: A pleasant Nature Reserve on the edge of the city, with a Field Centre. No fishing from jetties or bridges. Rich waters with big fish of most species. Some restrictions on fishing hours, indicated on notice boards. Available to local members only. The Canterbury AA is an excellent club with a permanent headquarters with offices open from 9am to 4pm on weekdays

LANCASHIRE

Baubles Pools

Location: Near Pilling, Fylde – enquire locally
Type and Size: Three small pools, with the best fish in the middle one
Carp Stock: Mainly small carp to doubles
Category: Carp Waters
Permits: Day tickets on bank
Control: Private
BK Rating: Very Easy
W/A: North West
Comments: Many waters in this area now have no close season

Brinsall Lodges

Location: Brinsall, Chorley
Type and Size: Small pond of about 1½ acres
Carp Stock: Quite well stocked with carp to about 10lbs
Category: Mixed Fishery
Other Species: Roach, tench and bream
Permits: Day tickets from local tackle shops
Control: Private
BK Rating: Difficult
W/A: North West
Comments: No close season in some places in this area - check first

Cargate Farm Pool

Location: Near Oldham
Type and Size: Small farm pool, much used for match fishing
Carp Stock: Well stocked with small commons and mirrors
Category: Mixed Fishery
Other Species: Roach, tench, crucians and perch
Permits: Day tickets in advance only
Cost: £3
Control: Oldham and District AA. Secretary: B Boff, 369 Shaw Road, Oldham OL1 3JZ. Tel: 061-620 0883 - season tickets available
Restrictions: No night fishing - sunrise to sunset only
BK Rating: Easy
W/A: North West

Clevely Bridge

Location: Garstang - on the A6 between Preston and Lancaster
Type and Size: Small, pleasant fishery
Carp Stock: Well stocked with carp to about 14lbs
Category: Mixed Fishery
Other Species: Usual coarse fish
Permits: In advance only - Tel: 0524 791637
Control: Private
BK Rating: Moderate
W/A: North West

Coronation Lodge

Location: Near Oldham
Type and Size: Tiny pond, with room for 9 anglers only; very weedy
Carp Stock: Quite well stocked with carp to doubles
Category: Mixed Fishery
Other Species: Tench, roach, rudd, perch and crucians
Permits: Members only water of Oldham and District AA. Secretary: B Boff, 369 Shaw Road, Oldham. Tel: 061-620 0883 - memberships available
Cost: About £12 per season
Restrictions: No night fishing
BK Rating: Moderate
W/A: North West

Doffcocker Reservoir

Location: Manchester Road, Bolton
Type and Size: Small reservoir
Carp Stock: About 100, and stocked recently with 6-10lb fish. Quite a few doubles
Category: Mixed Fishery
Other Species: Usual coarse fish
Permits: Bolton and District AC - members only. Secretary: T McKee, 1 Lever Edge Lane, Great Lever, Bolton, Greater Manchester
Control: Club
BK Rating: Easy
W/A: North West

Farington Lodge Pools

Location: Farington, between Leyland and Preston and between the A59 and the A582, five miles south of Preston
Type and Size: Two small mill lakes
Carp Stock: Well stocked with carp to about 10lbs
Category: Carp Water
Permits: Day tickets from bailiff on bank
Control: Private
Restrictions: No night fishing except by special arrangement
BK Rating: Easy
W/A: North West
Comments: Some of the waters in this area have no close season

Heapey Lodges

Location: Chorley, near Manchester
Type and Size: 4 reservoirs, totalling about 30 acres, and up to 30 feet deep
How to Find: Off the M61 north west of Manchester
Carp Stock: Fairly well stocked
Category: Mixed Fisheries
Other Species: General coarse fish and trout
Permits: Wigan AA. W Gralton, 66 Balcarres Road, Asphull, Wigan. Day tickets on the bank
Cost: Approx £12 season ticket
BK Rating: Insufficient information
Control: Club
Restrictions: Not known
W/A: North West
Comments: Only Lodge No. 1 worth fishing for carp - contains many doubles and a few 20's. Floater fishing best. No close season

Hoddlesdon Reservoir

Location: Darwen, off the A666 north of Bolton
Type and Size: 20 acre reservoir
Carp Stock: Not many to lower doubles
Category: Few Carp
Other Species: Roach, bream, pike, some trout
Permits: Darwen AA - F W Kendall, 45 Holden Fold, Darwen; and from County Sports, Duckworth Street, Darwen

Cost: About £10 per season - no day tickets; in advance only
Restrictions: No night fishing
BK Rating: Very Difficult
W/A: North West
Comments: No close season

Leeds-Liverpool Canal

Location: Jacksons Bridge, 12 miles from Liverpool
Type and Size: Small canal with little boat traffic
How to Find: Take the M58 or M57 from Liverpool, then the B5147 north past Lydiate towards Halsall. After the church, turn right to Jacksons Bridge
Carp Stock: Recently stocked with carp, numbers and sizes not known
Category: Mixed Fishery
Other Species: Bream, tench, roach and perch
Permits: Day tickets and annual tickets on bank, or from local tackle shops
Cost: £1.75 per day; £8 per year for juniors, OAP's and the disabled
Control: Jack Johnson. Tel: 051-526 4083 (Liverpool and District AA)
BK Rating: Difficult, until the carp grow and become established
W/A: North West
Comments: No close season

Mere Brow Lakes

Location: Near Tarleton, just off the A565 between Southport and Preston
Type and Size: Four small pools on a leisure complex
Carp Stock: Some carp to about 12lbs, exact number and sizes not known
Category: Mixed Fishery
Other Species: Roach and bream
Permits: Day tickets from bailiff on bank
Cost: About £2 per day
Restrictions: No night fishing
BK Rating: Moderate
W/A: North West

Ogdens Reservoir

Location: Wickenhall, Oldham
Type and Size: Two little ponds of less than an acre each
Carp Stock: Some small carp, and a few doubles
Other Species: Roach and bream
Permits: Day tickets on bank at low cost
Control: Council
BK Rating: Fairly Hard
W/A: North West

Oldham Reservoirs

Location: Oldham
Type and Size: Two large reservoirs
How to Find: Near Oldham
Carp Stock: Some carp in Upper Strinesdale and Ogden Reservoirs
Category: Few Carp

Other Species: General coarse fish
Permits: Oldham United AC. A Dyson, 7 Raven Avenue, Chadderton, Oldham
Cost: Approx 50p per day; £5 per season
BK Rating: Not known, probably Difficult
Control: Club
W/A: North West
Comments: Tackle etc from Grundy's, 292 Manchester Street, Werneth, Oldham

Ormsgill Lower Reservoir

Location: Near Barrow-in-Furness
Type and Size: Large reservoir
Carp Stock: Some carp, numbers and sizes not known
Category: Mixed Fishery
Other Species: Trout and tench
Permits: Hannay's, 50 Crellin Street, Barrow-in-Furness
Control: Furness Fishing Association
BK Rating: Difficult
W/A: North West

Pennington Flash

Location: Leigh, near Oldham
Type and Size: Small lake
How to Find: Near Leigh, west of Manchester off the A580
Carp Stock: Some good carp
Category: Mixed Fishery
Other Species: General coarse fishing
Permits: Pennington Flash AA. G Unsworth, 142 Chestnut Drive, Leigh
Cost: Day ticket - approx 50p; season £2.50
BK Rating: Moderate
Control: Club
W/A: North West

Pilsworth Fishery

Location: Pilsworth, Heywood
Type and Size: Lake of about 9 acres
How to Find: Take the M66 towards Bury from Manchester, and come off at junction 3
Carp Stock: Well stocked including plenty of doubles
Category: Mixed Fishery
Other Species: Mostly coarse fish
Permits: Day tickets from the bank
Control: Private
BK Rating: Moderate
Baits/Methods: Normal carp fishing baits and methods
W/A: North West
Comments: This water is controlled by famous match fishermen Kevin and Benny Ashurst

Redwell Carp Fishery

Location: 7 miles north east of Lancaster - there are signs to the fishery on the B6254 Carnforth-Kirkby Lonsdale road
Type and Size: Three acre lake in attractive surroundings
Carp Stock: Well stocked with small carp, and some doubles to about 15lbs
Category: Carp Water
Permits: Day tickets from owner on bank
Cost: £3 per day
Control: Private
BK Rating: Easy to Moderate
W/A: North West

River Calder

Location: Wigan area
Type and Size: Small river
Carp Stock: Quite well stocked with small carp, and a few doubles
Category: Mixed Fishery
Other Species: Most coarse fish and some trout
Permits: From local tackle shops
Control: Wigan AA. Secretary: W Gratton, 66 Balcarres Road, Aspull, Wigan
BK Rating: Moderate
W/A: North West
Comments: Possibly no close season in some areas

Sabden Reservoir

Location: Whalley, near Accrington
Type and Size: Small reservoir
How to Find: Enquire from Secretary
Carp Stock: Some carp
Category: Few Carp
Other Species: Small trout
Permits: Accrington and District FC. A Balderstone, 42 Townley Avenue, Huncoat, Accrington. Tel: 0254 33517
Cost: Approx £4 per day
BK Rating: Moderate
Control: Club
W/A: North West

Smiths

Location: Manchester Road, Bolton
Carp Stock: Quite well stocked with good doubles and 20's to 23lbs (common) and 24lbs (mirror)
Category: Mixed Fishery
Permits: Bolton and District Angling Club - members only. Secretary: T McKee, 1 Lever Edge Lane, Great Lever, Bolton, Greater Manchester
Control: Club
BK Rating: Moderate
W/A: North West

Swantley Lake

Location: Off the B6254, about 8 miles north east of Lancaster
Type and Size: 2½ acre lake, specially dug as a fishery a few years ago
Carp Stock: Well stocked with commons and mirrors to mid-doubles
Category: Mixed Fishery
Other Species: Roach, rudd and bream
Permits: Day and season tickets - for information and permits telephone Morecambe 422146
Control: Lonsdale Angling Club - details from local tackle shops
BK Rating: Easy
W/A: North West

Worthington Lake

Location: Worthington, a suburb of Wigan
Type and Size: Two acre pond
Carp Stock: Well stocked with carp to about 15lbs
Category: Mixed Fishery
Other Species: Roach and bream
Permits: Day tickets from local tackle shops
Control: Wigan and District AA. Secretary: W Gratton, 66 Balcarres Road, Aspull, Wigan - includes other carp waters
Restrictions: No night fishing
BK Rating: Moderate
W/A: North West

Wrightington Lake

Location: Off the A5209 at Wrighton Hospital, between Ormskirk and the M6
Type and Size: 10 acre estate type lake
Carp Stock: Quite a number of carp to upper doubles
Category: Mixed Fishery
Other Species: Usual coarse fish
Permits: From local tackle shops - day and season tickets
Control: Wigan and District AA. W Gratton, 66 Balcarres Road, Aspull, Wigan
Restrictions: No night fishing
BK Rating: Difficult
W/A: North West

Wyreside Fisheries

Location: Hampton Lane, Dolphinholme, Lancaster
Type and Size: Five man-made lakes, with more than 20 acres of water
Carp Stock: All 5 lakes contain carp, many of which are small, though there are some doubles to about 20lbs
Category: Mixed Fishery
Other Species: Roach, tench, bream and pike
Permits: Day tickets on the bank
Cost: £5 per day
Control: Private
BK Rating: Easy
W/A: North West
Comments: A pleasant and attractive complex to fish, with the chance of some big fish within a few years

LEICESTERSHIRE

Barlestone Lake

Location: Village of Barlestone, near Market Bosworth
Type and Size: 1½ acre farm pond
How to Find: To centre of village, then right towards Nailstone; lake is on right behind Baxters Farm
Carp Stock: 110–130 carp to 16lb. Few doubles
Category: Mixed Fishery
BK Rating: Easy
Permits: Day tickets on the bank
Cost: £3 per day. £1.50 per half day
Restrictions: No night fishing
W/A: Severn Trent
Comments: Plenty of carp, most 6–9lb. Margin fishing (keeping well away from the bank) and surface fishing most successful

Beadles Pit

Location: Off Broome Lane, East Goscote, north of Leicester. Down long track next to railway line
Type and Size: 29 acre gravel pit
Carp Stock: 150 carp to 23lb. Average 8–14lbs
Category: Mixed Fishery
Other Species: Tench to 7lb. Pike to 25lb. Roach, bream, perch
Permits: Day tickets on bank - £2.50
Control: Private
Restrictions: No restrictions
BK Rating: Moderate
W/A: Severn Trent
Comments: Large open gravel pit with few features; fish are not at all hard to catch – once located

Belvoir Lakes

Location: Belvoir Castle, between Melton Mowbray and Grantham
Type and Size: Chain of small estate lakes
Carp Stock: Well stocked with carp to a good size
Category: Carp Waters
Other Species: Some coarse fish
Permits: Season tickets only from the Estate Office at Belvoir Castle
Control: Private
BK Rating: Easy
W/A: Severn-Trent

Birstall Carp Pool

Location: In centre of Country Park, near Birstall
Type and Size: 2½ acre pool
Carp Stock: Heavily stocked with fish to upper doubles
Category: Carp Water
Other Species: Usual coarse fish
Permits: Season tickets £25 from Alan Smith, Broome AS. Membership open to all. Occasionally a waiting list for tickets
Control: Club
BK Rating: Easy - good winter water
W/A: Severn Trent
Comments: Small pool with good head of carp, ideal for someone starting carp fishing

Bosworth Water Trust A

Location: Half a mile west of Market Bosworth on the B585. Tel: 0455 291876
Type and Size: 20 acres of lakes
Carp Stock: Some carp to doubles
Category: Mixed Fishery
Other Species: Usual coarse fish
Permits: Nigel and Jo Riley, at the site office before fishing
Cost: £1.50 per day - free to campers and members
Control: Private
BK Rating: Not known
W/A: Anglian
Comments: There is camping, and facilities for caravans near the lake, with toilets, showers and a snack bar. From the publicity, this 'leisure and water park' is more for sailing and board-sailing than for angling, but there are certainly some carp, so it might be worth a try

Grand Union Canal

Location: Near Market Harborough
Type and Size: About 5 miles of canal
Carp Stock: Quite well stocked with carp up to 10lbs, some bigger fish
Category: Mixed Fishery
Other Species: Tench, bream, roach
Permits: Market Harborough Anglers. Seasonal membership; day tickets from bailiffs on the bank, or in advance from Sports Shop, 7 St Mary Road,

	Market Harborough. Secretary: R Haycock, 16 Maurice Road, Market Harborough
Cost:	Approx £3 per season; 50p per day
Control:	Club
BK Rating:	Moderate
W/A:	Severn Trent

Groby

Location:	Off A50 at Groby - visible from the A50
Type and Size:	Small lake in centre of pick your own farm. Watering pond (for strawberries) of 1 acre
Carp Stock:	Heavily stocked with carp to 20lb - 25+ doubles, most fish 2-8lb
Category:	Carp Water
Other Species:	Tench to 6lb, crucian carp
Permits:	Day tickets on bank - £4. Juniors £3
Control:	Private
Restrictions:	No boilies, nuts, groundbaits, hemp. No line under 6lb. No hooks smaller than 14 - must be barbless. Night fishing by arrangement
BK Rating:	Moderate
W/A:	Severn Trent
Comments:	Surface fishing at start of season gives the best chance of one of the bigger fish. During the season, mass baiting with casters, tares or any other allowed tiny bait gives the best results

Hartshorne Dams Carp Fishery

Location:	Hartshorne, off the A514 near Swadlincote and Burton-upon-Trent
Type and Size:	3 acre lake
Carp Stock:	Well stocked with carp to upper doubles, and possibly larger
Category:	Carp Water
Permits:	AMR Country Clothing, Ashby de la Zouche; Melbourne Tackle and Gun, Melbourne; The Rodney Inn, Hartshorne (opening hours only); The Farmhouse, Manor Farm, Hartshorne. No tickets on bank - tickets must be purchased before fishing at £2.50 per day
Control:	Private. Tel: 0283 215769
BK Rating:	Moderate
W/A:	Severn Trent
Comments:	There is also a 2½ acre general coarse lake on the site, and a £40 a season night syndicate on the carp lake

Hermitage Leisure Centre

Location:	Hermitage, near Coalville. Signposted for Leisure Centre
Type and Size:	Old gravel pits of 10 acres
Carp Stock:	Reasonable head of carp to 19lb. 40% are doubles
Category:	General coarse fish
Permits:	Day tickets: £1.50 on bank - night fishing by arrangement with warden
Control:	Private
Restrictions:	No night fishing
BK Rating:	Moderate
W/A:	Severn Trent
Comments:	Lake contains a large island around which the fish often congregate; large numbers of water birds

Knossington Carp Lake

Location: Knossington, near Oakham
Type and Size: Small lake
How to Find: West of Oakham
Carp Stock: Well stocked with plenty of low doubles and fish of 8-9lbs
Category: Carp Water
Other Species: Crucians, bream, roach, tench
Permits: D H Preke. Tel: 066-447-305. Advanced booking only
Cost: Approx £2 per day (£1 juniors)
Control: Private
BK Rating: Easy to Moderate
Restrictions: No night fishing, no keepnets, no groundbaiting
W/A: Severn Trent

Little Pit

Location: Hinckley
Type and Size: 5 acre clay pit
How to Find: On Barwell Lane, Hinckley (opposite ASDA superstore)
Carp Stock: A few carp to a little over 20lbs
Category: Mixed Fishery
Other Species: General coarse fish
Permits: Hinckley and District AC. Secretary: Pat Donnachie. Tel: Hinckley 636121. Also available from Tony Hortons Fishing Tackle, Burbage. Tel: Hinckley 632269
Cost: £15 per year
Control: Club
BK Rating: Difficult
W/A: Severn Trent
Comments: Typical deep clay pit, most success to surface and margin fishing

Mallory Park

Location: Mallory Park Fisheries, Kirkby Mallory LE9 7QE. Tel: 0455 842931
Type and Size: Several lakes built in 1986 by Roy Marlow
Carp Stock: Well stocked with carp to 20lbs
Category: Mixed Fishery
Other Species: Most coarse fish
Permits: Marks and Marlow Ltd, 39 Tudor Road, Leicester. Tel: 0533 537714
Control: Private - two famous anglers, Ivan Marks and Roy Marlow
BK Rating: Moderate
W/A: Anglian
Comments: This is a conservation area, with ponds and Nature Reserve. Motor Sport racing, accommodation, buffet and bars nearby. Sponsors invited to help create conservation areas for wildlife

Mill Farm A

Location: Gilmorton, 10 miles south of Leicester
Type and Size: Attractive four acre lake on a farm
How to Find: Turn right onto the A427 from junction 20 of the M1 going north, then take the first left turn to Gilmorton
Carp Stock: Fairly well stocked with carp to about 19lbs, many of which are small

Category: Mixed Fishery
Other Species: Roach, rudd, bream and tench
Permits: Day tickets in advance only - Tel: 0455 52392 for details
Cost: £3 per day
Control: Private
BK Rating: Easy
W/A: Severn Trent
Comments: Some holiday accommodation at this very attractive lake - details from the phone number above

Murphys Lake

Location: Next to both the Grand Union Canal and a Walkers Crisp Factory. Either down Canal Street, Thurmaston or by the back of Wanlip Country Club
Type and Size: Large gravel pit of 30 acres
Carp Stock: Few carp - fish caught to 27.8 - good chance of a 30lb+ fish. Maybe only 25 fish
Category: Mixed Fishery
Other Species: Specimen fish of all species
Permits: Season tickets £25.00 from Alan Smith, Broome AS. Membership open to all, but occasional waiting list for permits
Control: Club
Restrictions: None
BK Rating: Very Difficult - locating fish essential for success
W/A: Severn Trent
Comments: Very large open gravel pit, very few features; once located fish are quite catchable. Also contains pike to 26lb+, bream to 10lbs+ and large tench, specimen fish of all species. Used by water skiers

Nanpantan Reservoir

Location: Nanpantan, near Loughborough
Type and Size: Reservoir about 5 acres in size
How to Find: Take the B5350 road to Loughborough to Nanpantan
Carp Stock: After draining, the lake was stocked with mirror carp many of which are now 5-9lbs, with a few lower doubles and possibly one 20
Category: Carp Water
Other Species: Bream, tench, roach and perch
Permits: W H Wortley, 45 Baxter Gate, Loughborough. Tel: Loughborough 212697
Baits/Methods: Carp tactics and baits, including sweetcorn and luncheon meat
Control: Private
Restrictions: No groundbaiting. Thirty anglers only per day. No night fishing
BK Rating: Moderate
W/A: Severn Trent
Comments: Granite block banks - unhooking mats recommended. Part of the lake is closed to anglers

Turn Grandad's old tackle into cash see page 114

Sheepy Lake

Location: Sheepy Magna
Type and Size: Lake of 7 acres
How to Find: Take the A444 between Sibson and Twycross and then the B585 to Sheepy Parva and Magna villages
Carp Stock: Well stocked with carp between 5 and 7lbs, mostly mirrors. A few doubles, and one possible 20
Category: Mixed Fishery
Other Species: Crucians, and some other coarse fish
Permits: Day tickets on the bank
Cost: Approx £1 per day
Control: Private
BK Rating: Easy
W/A: Severn Trent

Sulby Lily Pond

Location: Near Welford, on Leics./Northants border
Type and Size: 2 acre silty pool
How to Find: Sulby is signposted just north of Welford on east side of A50
Carp Stock: Well stocked, a lot of small carp, but fish go up to about 20lb
Category: Carp Water
Other Species: Tench, small pike, roach and perch
Permits: Hinckley and District AC. Secretary: Pat Donnachie. Tel: Hinckley 636121. Also available from Tony Hortons Fishing Tackle, Burbage. Tel: Hinckley 632269
Cost: £15 per year
Control: Private
Restrictions: No night fishing
BK Rating: Moderate
W/A: Severn Trent
Comments: Very weedy little water with lilies and silkweed

Wallf Gravel Pits

Location: Near Willington
Type and Size: Large gravel pits
How to Find: Willington, near Derby
Carp Stock: Not known - some carp
Category: Few Carp
Other Species: Mixed coarse fish
Permits: Rising Sun public house, Willington
Cost: Approx £1 per day
Control: Derby Angling Assocation. J Callaghan, 3 Calvin Close, Alvaston, Derby DE2 0HX
BK Rating: Insufficient information
W/A: Severn Trent

Wanlip Country Club

Location: Wanlip Road, Syston - near Leicester
Type and Size: Virtually square gravel pit of 8 acres
Carp Stock: Carp to 27lb - most fish doubles. Possibly 10 twenties

Category: Mixed Fishery
Other Species: Tench to 7lb. Roach, perch, pike etc
Permits: Season tickets £25.00 from Alan Smith. Broome AS - enquire locally for details. Membership open to all, but occasionally waiting list for tickets
Control: Club
Restrictions: No restrictions
BK Rating: Hard
W/A: Severn Trent
Comments: Long range tactics essential on this open water. Only features are gravel bars and right in the centre of the lake, the old causeway when it was dug. Water also used by water skiers. Keep rod tips low to avoid being cut off by the speed boats!

Welford Reservoir

Location: Welford, near Leicester
Type and Size: 20 acre reservoir
Carp Stock: Quite well stocked with good carp to double figures
Category: Mixed Fishery
Other Species: Bream, pike, tench, rudd and roach
Permits: British Waterways, Willow Grange, Church Road, Watford, or the bailiff, Mr W Williams, Welford Grange Farm, Welford
Cost: Season tickets only at about £13
Restrictions: No day tickets, and there may be a waiting list
BK Rating: Moderate
W/A: Severn Trent

Willersley Lake

Location: Near Measham
Type and Size: Estate lake of 14 acres, shallower at one end
Carp Stock: Large numbers of carp to 23lb, 4 twenties, 2 twenty commons, good head of doubles
Other Species: Usual coarse fish
Permits: Day tickets on bank £3.50, or season tickets £20 from local tackle shops
Control: Club
Restrictions: No night fishing
BK Rating: Easy to Moderate
W/A: Severn Trent
Comments: Very heavily fished by match anglers due to large head of bream. No day tickets at weekends. Margin fishing productive in shallows

Willow Farm Carp Pool

Location: Off Wanlip Road, Systan; through gravel working
Type and Size: ¾ acre pool
Carp Stock: Plenty of carp to 19lb+, 10–15 doubles
Category: Carp Water
Other Species: Usual coarse fish
Permits: Season tickets £25 on bank or from Michael Winterton. Tel: 600937
Control: Private
Restrictions: No restrictions
BK Rating: Moderate
W/A: Severn Trent
Comments: Season ticket covers 10 lakes and several miles of Rivers Soar and Wreake. Most of the other lakes on the complex hold few carp to 20lb+

Don't forget – discarded line kills birds and other wild animals. Take it home.

LINCOLNSHIRE

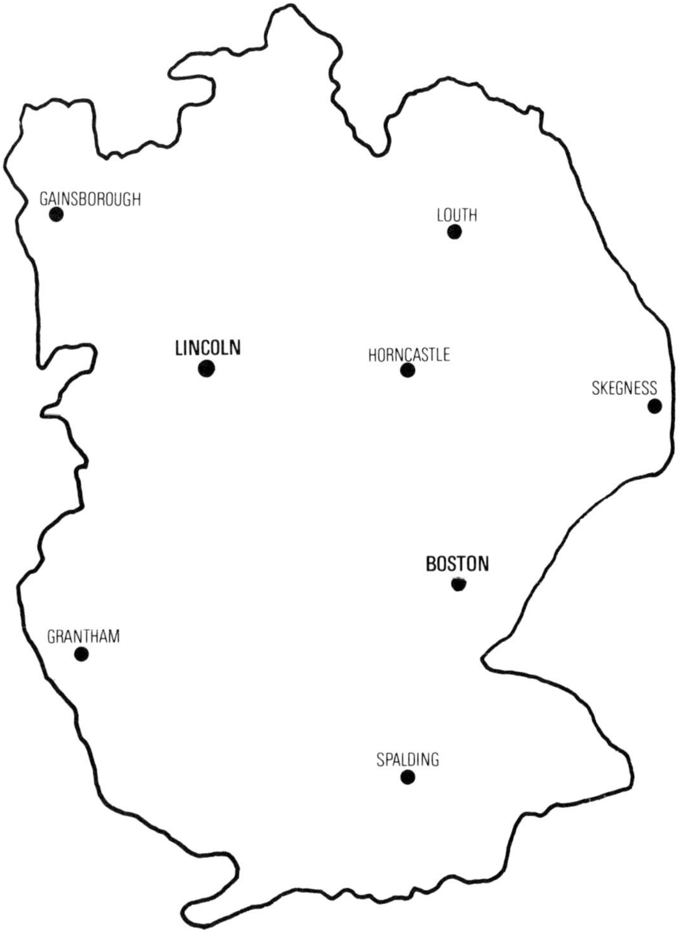

Ashby Park

Location: Ashby Park, West Ashby, near Horncastle. Tel: 06582 7966 or 0790 53321
Type and Size: 5 lakes - about 15 acres of water
Carp Stock: Well stocked with carp to doubles
Category: Mixed Fishery
Other Species: Chub, rudd, tench, bream, pike, perch, roach and eels
Permits: From Robin and Margaret Francis at the above address
Cost: Day - £2.50; one week - £15
Control: Private
BK Rating: Not known
W/A: Anglian
Comments: Touring caravan site by lake; car parking at swims, ideal for disabled anglers; no close season

Brickyard Fishery A

Location: South Somercotes, Louth
Type and Size: 4 acre brick pit
How to Find: South Somercotes road, to the east of Louth
Carp Stock: Some carp to about 20lbs
Category: Mixed Fishery
Other Species: General coarse fish
Permits: Day tickets on site
Cost: Approx £2 per day
BK Rating: Moderate
Control: Private
W/A: Yorkshire
Comments: Small quiet caravan site - static vans for hire. Toilet block. Tourers welcome

Chapel Boating Lake

Location: Near Skegness
Type and Size: Lake of 4 acres
Carp Stock: Well stocked with carp. A 32lbs common was reported in Angling Times, January 1991, on boilie
Category: Mixed Fishery
Permits: John Cook. Tel: 0754 72631
Cost: Approx £2 day ticket
Restrictions: Open March 14th to the end of October only
BK Rating: Moderate
W/A: Anglian

Denton Reservoir

Location: Denton, near Grantham
Type and Size: Large reservoir
How to Find: Off the A607, 4 miles west of Grantham
Carp Stock: Well stocked with carp to 26lbs
Category: Mixed Fishery
Other Species: General coarse fish
Permits: Enquire locally

Cost: Approx £7.50 per year
BK Rating: Moderate
Control: Not known
Restrictions: None
W/A: Severn Trent
Comments: We have been unable to find out where these permits can be obtained – try local tackle shops

Elmhurst Lake A

Location: Horncastle
How to Find: Elmhurst, near Horncastle
Carp Stock: Some carp to 15lbs
Category: Mixed Fishery
Other Species: Bream and tench
Permits: Tel: 06582 7533
Cost: On application
Control: Private
BK Rating: Insufficient information
W/A: Yorkshire
Comments: Caravan site – caravans to let. Lake described as 'picturesque'. No close season. Further information from owners on the number listed above

Hall Farm Moat

Location: Hall Farm, Harpswell, near Gainsborough. Tel: 042773 412
Type and Size: Farm moat of ¾ acre
How to Find: Off the A631 between Corringham and Harpswell
Carp Stock: Well stocked with carp of all sizes to 20lbs
Category: Mixed Fishery
Permits: Day tickets from Hall Farm
Cost: Approx £1.50 per day
BK Rating: Fairly Hard
Control: Private
Restrictions: No night fishing
W/A: Severn Trent
Comments: The carp in this water are still growing – and now we have a moat, a stream and a dock in our guide!

Hill View Lake

Location: Hogsthorpe, near Skegness
Type and Size: ¾ acre man-made lake
How to Find: Off the A52 road from Skegness to Mablethorpe, near Chapel St. Leonards
Carp Stock: Heavily stocked with carp, mainly small to 18lbs
Category: Mixed Fishery
Other Species: Tench and roach
Permits: On site. Details from owner Ken Raynor on Skegness (0754) 72979
Cost: Approx £1.50 per day for one rod; £2.50 for two rods. Juniors, pensioners and disabled £1. After 5pm 80p for all
BK Rating: Easy
Control: Private

Restrictions: Barbless hooks only; no carp to be kept in keepnets
W/A: Anglian
Comments: There is also a trout lake on the site. Tackle can be hired. Tea, coffee and snacks. No close season. Owner a National Anglers' Council qualified game fishing instructor. Ideal spot for the holidaymaker

Lincolnshire Drains

Location: Spalding area
Type and Size: A number of Fen drains, including Vernatts
Carp Stock: Some carp to about 10lbs
Other Species: Pike, perch, rudd, bream and tench
Permits: Spalding Fishing Club - try local tackle shops, such as D T Ball, 1 Hawthorne Bank, Spalding or M Tidwells, Fen Lane, Spalding
Control: Club
BK Rating: Difficult
W/A: Anglian

Lowfields Country Holiday Fishing Retreat A

Location: North Scarle
Type and Size: 3 small lakes; 2½, 1½ and ½ acres
How to Find: Off the A1133 Newark-on-Trent to Gainsborough road and south west of Lincoln
Carp Stock: Good carp to 20lbs+
Category: Mixed Fishery
Other Species: Perch, roach, bream, tench, eels, rudds and crucians
Permits: LCHFR, Lincoln. Tel: 0522 77717
Cost: On application
Control: Private
BK Rating: Moderate
W/A: Severn Trent
Comments: Formerly known as the Poplars and now surely our longest title! Self-catering accommodation in beautiful surroundings, including some caravans

Marshalls Lake

Location: Fulston, near Louth - enquire locally
Type and Size: Small farm pond
Carp Stock: Well stocked with carp to upper doubles
Category: Mixed Fishery
Other Species: Roach and rudd
Permits: Day tickets from bailiff on bank
Control: Private
BK Rating: Difficult
W/A: Anglian
Comments: There is no close season in Lincolnshire; night fishing permitted

Richmond Lake

Location: North Hykeham, near Lincoln. Tel: 0522 681329
Type and Size: Large gravel pit of 80 acres

How to Find: To west of A46 at Richmond Drive near North Hykeham
Carp Stock: Plenty of doubles to 23¼lbs
Category: Carp Water
Other Species: Double figure bream, tench and rudd
Permits: On site
Cost: £2.50 per day approx
BK Rating: Easy
Control: Private
Restrictions: No night fishing
W/A: Anglian
Comments: No close season

River Witham

Location: Bardney area
Type and Size: Large 'fen drain' type river, noted for its match fishing
Carp Stock: Not many, but a record for the river was caught on maggots and light tackle in 1990 - it was a 23½lb mirror
Category: Few Carp
Other Species: Bream and most other coarse fish, including zander
Permits: Lincoln and District AA - enquire locally or in Lincoln
Control: Club
BK Rating: Very Difficult
W/A: Anglian

Rossways Water A

Location: 189 London Road, Wyberton, Boston. Tel: 0205 361643
Type and Size: One acre clay pit
How to Find: Main A16 road Boston to Spalding, 1 mile from Boston
Carp Stock: Well stocked with carp to 25½lbs
Category: Mixed Fishery
Other Species: Perch, roach, rudd, tench, bream
Permits: On site - day tickets by prior arrangement only
Cost: Approx £2.50 per rod; £4 for 2 rods
BK Rating: Very Difficult
Control: Private
Restrictions: No nuts; no sacking, no groundbait; no particles
W/A: Anglian
Comments: Rod licences sold on premises. Night fishing by arrangement. Cafeteria, toilets, showers. Tackle and bait for sale. Attractive tree lined pond. Possibly one fish of around 30lbs. Depth of 10-14 feet. Numbers limited, swims bookable. Many carp taken on float tackle near bank. Static caravans on site for holiday stays

Swan Lake Leisure Park A

Location: Culvert Road, Thorpe Culvert, Skegness. Tel: 0754 880469
Type and Size: 2½ acre caravan park lake
How to Find: Take the A52 from Skegness to Wainfleet. At Wainfleet, turn right onto the B1195 towards Spilsby. After about 1½ miles, turn left down a lane and left again at the first crossroads
Carp Stock: Well stocked with carp, water record 26lbs

Category: Mixed Fishery
Other Species: Tench, roach and rudd
Permits: Weekly or daily, for site residents only
Cost: £2.50 per rod per day. £10 weekly per rod. £5 per week per rod for children from 12 to 16
BK Rating: Moderate
Control: Leisure Park
Restrictions: No night fishing. No groundbait. No floating baits
W/A: Anglian
Comments: The park is 7 acres in size with plenty of wildlife, and is only 5 miles from Skegness. There is a launderette and 4 caravans sleeping 7 or 8, and a four bedroomed cottage. Costs from £75 to £165 per week, according to time of year. No close season. Brochure from Mrs Caton

Sycamore Lake Carp Fishery A

Location: Willow Lodge, Willow Lakes, Newark Road, Foston, Grantham NG32 2LF. Tel: 0400 82190
Type and Size: Small and quite new, man-made lake of about three quarters of an acre and up to 7 feet deep
How to Find: Half a mile off the A1 between Newark and Grantham, and just outside the small village of Foston
Carp Stock: Well stocked with mirrors and commons between 2lbs and 12lbs
Category: Carp Only
Permits: On site
Cost: £3 per day, £2 for evening, to include two other lakes on site. Reductions for juniors and OAP's, and half price for those staying in the caravans on site
Control: Private
Restrictions: Barbless hooks; no keepnets or carp sacks. All nets to be disinfected at start
BK Rating: Easy
W/A: Anglian
Comments: Good fun fishery on pleasant site. Separate car park for day ticket anglers. 6 caravans to rent on site, with bait and tackle for sale, and usual caravan site facilities, ideal for a family holiday. Caravan prices from £65 to £113 per week, all with full mains services. No close season

West Ashby Lakes

Location: West Ashby, near Horncastle
Type and Size: Two gravel pits of 5 and 2 acres
How to Find: On A153 just north of Horncastle
Carp Stock: Many doubles up to 25lbs. Average 11lbs
Category: Carp Water
Other Species: Tench, chub, roach
Permits: On site - Tel: 0507 600473
BK Rating: Easy
Restrictions: No hair rigs; barbless hooks; no boilies; no particles (what is left?)
Control: Private
W/A: Anglian

Willow Lakes A

Location: Willow Lakes, Newark Road, Foston, Grantham NG32 2LF. Tel: 0400 82190
Type and Size: Two small lakes – Poplar is 1¼ acres; Willow is one acre
Carp Stock: Some crucians and other species in Poplar; Willow was stocked with 2,500 small mirrors and commons in 1990
Category: Mixed Fisheries
Other Species: Tench, rudd, bream, roach, chub, perch
Permits: Day tickets on site
Cost: £3 per day;,£2 for the evening. Reduced price for juniors and OAP's, and half price tickets for those renting the caravans on site
Control: Private
BK Rating: Easy
Restrictions: Barbless hooks; all nets to be disinfected at start
W/A: Anglian
Comments: There are 6 large caravans close to the lakes for rent, at prices ranging from £65 to £113 a week. They all have mains services and modern equipment, and are available from the middle of March until the end of October. The lakes are reed-fringed and attractive, and there is a further small carp fishery on the site (see separate entry). Tackle and bait available on site. No close season

MERSEYSIDE

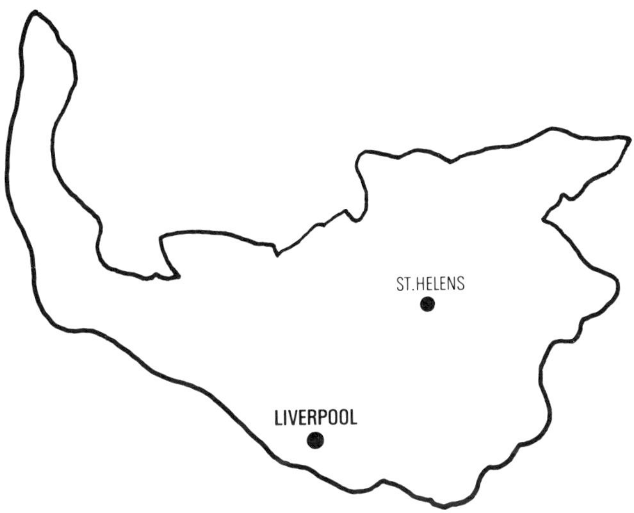

Burton Mere (b)

Location: Burton Manor, between Chester and Heswall (in the Wirral)
Type and Size: 3½ acre estate lake
How to Find: 9 miles north west of Chester off the A540 raod
Carp Stock: Heavily stocked with carp to 25lbs
Other Species: Perch, rudd, roach and tench
Permits: Tony Dean's Rod and Reel Tackle Shop, Enfield Road, Ellesmere Port. Tel: 051-356 0678
Cost: Approx £3.50 per day; £2 per half day (weekends only)
Control: Private
BK Rating: Easy
W/A: Welsh - purchase rod licence before fishing
Comments: Former home of Victorian Prime Minister Gladstone - his ghost must haunt the grounds! Mere averages 5 feet in depth. Float fishing close to the bank works well

Church Street Canal

Location: Church Street, St. Helens
Type and Size: Industrial area canal; stretch of about 400 yards
How to Find: St. Helens is north east of Liverpool
Carp Stock: Quite well stocked with carp to double figures
Category: Mixed Fishery
Other Species: Roach, bream, perch and gudgeon
Permits: St. Helens Angling Association. Details on bank or from local tackle shops. J Corkish, 65 Laffak Road, Carr Hill, St. Helens WA11 9EH
Control: Club
BK Rating: Moderate
W/A: North West
Comments: There is a warm water outlet from a factory on this stretch and it has become very popular in the winter, when the water is warm enough to paddle in and other local waters are frozen. The canal gets very busy at this time. Plenty of matches but some good carp for pleasure anglers, and well worth a try - if you can get a place to fish - in icy conditions

Figure Eight Pond

Location: Birkenhead - Hoylake road (Wirral)
Type and Size: ⅓ acre pit
How to Find: From Birkenhead take the A553. At Bidston roundabout go straight on. You will see the pit on the right in an open field
Carp Stock: Not many carp but an 18 and a 22 have been caught. No small carp
Category: Mixed Fishery
Other Species: Big tench, crucians, perch, bream, rudd
Permits: Free
Cost: None
BK Rating: Difficult
Control: Private
W/A: North West
Comments: Early season fishing and night fishing are good

Mill Dam

Location: Near Kirkby, Liverpool
Type and Size: Small lake, recently cleared out and restocked
Carp Stock: Some carp, numbers and sizes not known
Category: Mixed Fishery
Other Species: Tench, roach, perch, and (they say) one pike!
Permits: From bailiff on bank
Cost: £7 adults; £3.50 juniors
Control: Kirkby Junior AC - community hall on banks of lake
BK Rating: Not known
W/A: Severn Trent

Newsham Park Lake

Location: Newsham Park, Tuebrook, Liverpool
Type and Size: Ancient odd-shaped park lake, about 3 acres
Carp Stock: Well stocked with small carp
Category: Mixed Fishery

Other Species: Tench, roach and perch
Permits: None necessary - all fishing on the many Liverpool park lakes is free
Control: Liverpool City Council
BK Rating: Easy
W/A: North West
Comments: This lake was de-silted and restocked with over 50,000 fish in 1991. Platforms have been built for disabled anglers

Overflow

Location: Bidston Docks, Birkenhead (Wirral)
Type and Size: Formerly a 6 acre dry dock (now freshwater)
How to Find: Take the A553 from Birkenhead to St. James's Church. Turn right, then first left to Bidston Incinerator, take next entrance and follow dockside - Overflow is the furthest water
Carp Stock: Carp to 10lbs+
Other Species: Big perch (3-4lbs) and eels of 4-6lbs
Permits: Free
Cost: Nothing
BK Rating: Moderate
Control: Docks/British Rail
W/A: North West
Comments: Carp caught on snaggy tip side - beware sunken cars. Maggots and worm work well on light tackle. Dock is 30 feet deep: we now have a stream and a Dock in our guide!

Peak Forest Canal

Location: Marple area (Greater Manchester)
Type and Size: Short, narrow canal
Carp Stock: Some carp, mainly in lock pools at Marple
Category: Mixed Fishery
Other Species: Tench and general coarse fish
Permits: Try local tackle shops or County Palatine AA
Control: Club
BK Rating: Not known
W/A: North West

Sefton Park Lake

Location: A park in Liverpool
Type and Size: 4 acre park lake, very busy and public
Carp Stock: Quite well stocked with small carp
Other Species: Tench, roach, crucians and perch
Permits: None necessary - free fishing and in other park lakes containing carp in Liverpool
Control: Liverpool City Council
BK Rating: Easy
W/A: North West
Comments: No close season

NORFOLK

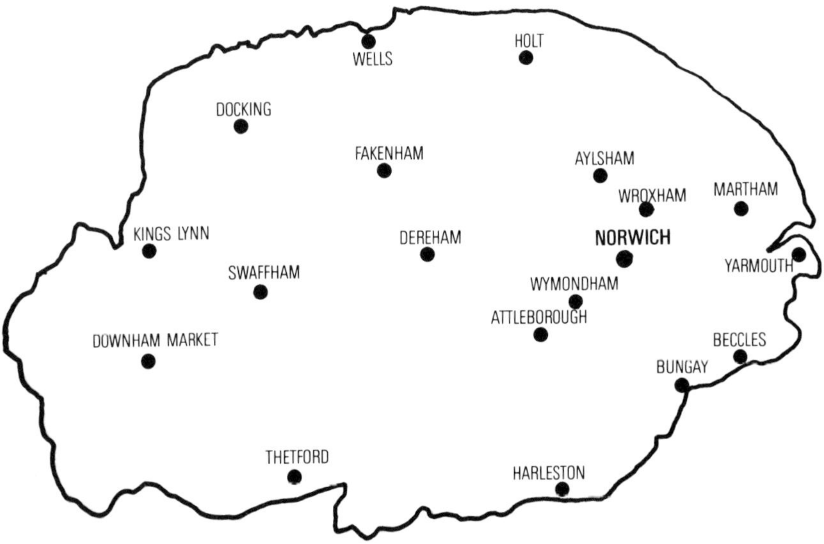

Aldeby Hall Farm Pits

Location: Aldeby Hall Farm, near Aldeby, Beccles
Type and Size: Four small pits
How to Find: Take the A146 from Norwich, and just before Beccles turn right to Aldeby. A mile after the village, find a track on the right going through a fruit farm, which is actually an old railway track; the pits are on the left in half a mile
Carp Stock: Some mirrors to 8lbs
Category: Mixed Fishery
Other Species: Crucians and bream
Permits: From bailiff on bank (day tickets)
BK Rating: Not known
Control: Private
W/A: Anglian
Comments: The two pits on the left hold the carp; the others are mainly crucians with some rudd

Bedingham Pit

Location: Woodton, just off the B1332 between Bungay and Norwich
Type and Size: 5 acre gravel pit
Carp Stock: Well stocked with quite a few doubles, and a number of 20's to nearly 30 lbs
Category: Carp Water
Permits: This is a syndicate water, with information hard to obtain, but try local tackle shops in Norwich, Beccles and Bungay
Cost: Well over £100 per season
Control: Private
BK Rating: Moderate
W/A: Anglian
Comments: It may be possible to get details of how to obtain membership in the village of Woodton. This is a very good carp water, and it would be worth some trouble to get into

Billingford Pit

Location: Billingford, near Swanton Morley
Type and Size: Three acre pit
How to Find: Take the A1067 from Norwich and turn left to Billingford at Bawdeswell. In the village, turn left towards Swanton Morley, and after 100 yards on the right there is a narrow track leading down to the pit
Carp Stock: A few big carp
Category: Few Carp
Other Species: Roach, perch and pike
Permits: Day tickets in advance only from local tackle shops, or Dereham District AS, Mr S R Allison, Pound Cottage, Cemetery Road, East Dereham. Tel: Dereham 694428. Membership is £7 for the season, to cover other pits and the river
Cost: Day tickets £1.50
BK Rating: Difficult
Restrictions: No night fishing
Control: Club
W/A: Anglian

Blickling Lake

Location: Blickling Hall, Aylsham
Type and Size: Estate lake of 20 acres
How to Find: Take the A140 from Norwich to Aylsham. Go through the town and take the Blickling road. Bear right, and this road leads to the car park at the northern end of the lake
Carp Stock: Well stocked with carp to double figures
Category: Mixed Fishery
Other Species: Famous for its big bream, also tench, roach and big pike
Permits: Day tickets from bailiff on the bank. Some season tickets from Mr B Cooper, tel: Aylsham 734181
Cost: Day tickets: £2; season: £25
BK Rating: Moderate
Control: National Trust
W/A: Anglian
Comments: In the grounds of a famous stately home, this beautiful lake holds some fine fish

Booton Clay Pit

Location: Near the village of Booton, near Norwich
Type and Size: Clay pit of about 4 acres
How to Find: Take the Reepham road from Norwich and just before Reepham turn right towards Haveringland and Buxton. After a mile and a half you will find the pit on the left behind some trees
Carp Stock: Only very few carp, but they are large. Two 30's were reported from this pit in 1984, but it is not known if these were genuine weights
Category: Few Carp
Other Species: Tench, roach, rudd, pike and bream
Permits: Day and season tickets from the bailiff on the bank
Cost: Approx. £3 per season and 50p a day
Control: Private
BK Rating: Difficult
W/A: Anglian
Comments: An attractive lake, quite deep, with reeds and sandbars

Bradmoor Lakes

Location: Narborough, near Swaffham
Type and Size: Two gravel pits, one of two acres and the other five acres
How to Find: From Norwich take the A47 to Narborough. Beyond East Dereham and Swaffham, after two bridges over the River Nar, take lane on the right. The lakes will be seen on the left
Carp Stock: Very heavily stocked with mirrors to double figures. The crucian carp record was caught here
Category: Carp Water
Other Species: Crucians, bream, tench, roach and rudd
Permits: Membership of Swaffham Angling Club is necessary to fish this water - no day tickets. The Secretary, 30 Kings Street, Swaffham
Cost: Approx. £5 per person
Control: Club
BK Rating: Easy to Moderate
W/A: Anglian
Comments: Very pleasant water, details of rules etc. from the Club Secretary

Bridge Lake

Location: Lenwade, near Norwich
Type and Size: Two gravel pits
Carp Stock: Some carp, sizes not known
Category: Probably Few Carp
Other Species: Roach, rudd, bream, tench and pike
Permits: Limited annual permits from The City of Norwich AC, Mr Tom Boulton. Tel: Norwich 426834. Waiting list
Control: Club
Restrictions: Please note that this is a syndicate water, although controlled by the Norwich Club - waiting list for syndicate membership
BK Rating: Not known
W/A: Anglian

Broadland Nurseries Lake

Location: Ormesby St. Michael, just past Ormesby Broads
Type and Size: Lake of 2 acres
How to Find: Go to Wroxham and take the A1062 to Potter Heigham. Then take the A419 to Ormesby St.Michael. The lake and cafe are on the right just past the Broads
Carp Stock: Said to contain a 'good stock' of carp to double figures
Category: Mixed Fishery
Other Species: Perch, roach, rudd, bream and tench
Permits: Day tickets in advance only from Mr Millar, Broadland Cafe, Ormesby St. Michael
Cost: About £2 per day
Control: Private
BK Rating: Moderate
W/A: Anglian

Bure Valley Fishery

Location: Bure Valley Trout Lakes, 4 miles from Aylsham off the B1354 to Saxthorpe
Type and Size: Two acre gravel pit
Carp Stock: Quite well stocked with mirrors to over 20lbs
Category: Mixed Fishery
Other Species: Roach, perch, rudd and tench
Permits: In advance only, with booking essential, from David Green on Saxthorpe 666
Cost: £5 per 12 hour day session
BK Rating: Moderate
Control: Private
W/A: Anglian

Chiswick Pit

Location: Farm near the village of Stow Bardolph
Type and Size: Small farm pond
How to Find: A47 from Norwich, then the A1122 to Stradsett. Turn right onto the A134 towards Kings Lynn. At Shouldham Thorpe turn left and a mile further on take a farm track on the left. The pond is on the left opposite the farmhouse
Carp Stock: Numbers not known but said to contain a reasonable number of mirrors and commons to double figures
Category: Mixed Fishery
Other Species: Rudd and tench
Permits: Day tickets must be obtained in advance from Stow Estates Office, Stow Bardolph. Tel: Downham Market 383194
Cost: Approx. £1 per day
Restrictions: No night fishing - dawn to dusk only. Only three permits per day are issued
BK Rating: Moderate
W/A: Anglian

Common Lakes

Location: Common Lane, Lenwade, off the A1067 Norwich - Fakenham road
Type and Size: Three gravel pits between two and five acres
Carp Stock: Some commons and mirrors, sizes not known
Category: Possibly Few Carp
Other Species: Roach, rudd, tench, perch, pike and bream
Permits: From bailiff on bank
Cost: £2 per day
BK Rating: Not known
Control: Great Witchingham Fuel Allotment Charity
W/A: North West
Restrictions: No night fishing - dawn to dusk only

Cranworth - Woodrising Carp Lake

Location: Near Jubilee Farm, Cranworth, Dereham
Type and Size: Man-made farm pond of about an acre
How to Find: From Norwich take B1108 road to Watton. After Hingham take road on the right to Shipden. Follow the signs to Cranworth, and the lake is just after Jubilee Farm in the village
Carp Stock: Well stocked with commons and mirrors, mainly small but up to double figures
Category: Carp Water
Other Species: A few tench
Permits: Day tickets from Mr Bunning at Jubilee Farm
Baits/Methods: Normal carp fishing baits and methods
Control: Private
BK Rating: Easy
W/A: Anglian
Comments: Quite shallow, coloured lake, long and narrow

Docking Village Pond

Location: Village of Docking near Fakenham
Type and Size: Clay pit of about an acre
How to Find: Take the A1067 from Norwich, and Docking is after Fakenham (A148 - B1454)
Carp Stock: Quite well stocked with small commons up to 8lbs
Category: Mixed Fishery
Other Species: Crucian carp, roach and tench
Permits: From Roys Shop, close to pond. Day tickets must be bought on the same day
Cost: Approx £1 per day
Restrictions: Fishing 8.30am to 11pm only. No Sunday fishing. Eight tickets only issued each day
Baits/Methods: Normal baits and methods
Control: Private
BK Rating: Easy
W/A: Anglian
Comments: The commons are said to be wild carp, although with crucians present hybrids must be expected

Felmingham Mill Lake

Location: Felmingham Mill, off the B1145 road, about a mile from the village
Type and Size: One acre stream-fed lake
Carp Stock: Some double figure mirrors
Category: Few Carp
Other Species: Roach, perch and crucians
Permits: Day tickets must be obtained before fishing from M Moore at the Mill House near the water. (Tel: Aylsham 735106). Tickets include fishing in the little Mill Stream for roach, trout, pike and a few grayling
Cost: £1.50 per day
BK Rating: Not known
W/A: Anglian

Fosters End Pits

Location: East Winch, near Kings Lynn - the pits are one mile down a track by the church
Type and Size: 8 acre pit and three tiny ponds
Carp Stock: Carp to double figures
Category: Few Carp
Other Species: Pike to over 20lbs, roach, rudd and crucians
Permits: Members only water of the Kings Lynn AA. Membership costs £12. Details from the Secretary, Mr George Bear. Tel: Downham Market 387114
Control: Club
Restrictions: Members only
BK Rating: Not known
W/A: Anglian

Geens Pit

Location: Shropham, near Snetterton
Type and Size: Old pit of about one acre, shallow and wooded along one bank
Carp Stock: There are said to be only a few carp, but these are very large. A 34 pounder was reported in 1984, and since this is recorded as the lake record, it could well be genuine although we cannot be sure about this
Category: Few Carp
Other Species: Roach, rudd, tench and bream
Permits: Advance booking by telephone only to the owner, Mr Geen, Tel: Caston 735. Day tickets. Cost not known.
Control: Private
BK Rating: Difficult
W/A: Anglian
Comments: We have listed a few waters of this kind, where very large carp have been reported caught. We cannot guarantee that these weights quoted are genuine, especially as all carp anglers know that the weights of many fish reported are exaggerated. If we can prove conclusively that any weights are genuine we will say so

Glen's Pit

Location: Caston, Shropham, Near Attleborough
Type and Size: One acre pit, quite deep in places
How to Find: Caston is just off the B1077 road between Attleborough and Watton. The pit is on the left hand side going into the village from the Attleborough side
Carp Stock: Quite well stocked with about 40 carp, most of which are doubles, with some bigger fish to about 34lbs
Category: Mixed Fishery
Other Species: Roach, rudd, perch, bream and eels
Permits: Syndicate - information from J Green on Caston 735
Control: Private
BK Rating: Very Difficult
W/A: Anglian

Granary Lakes A

Location: Granary Hotel, Little Dunham, near Dereham
Type and Size: 3 small interconnected long narrow lakes, plus a 1 acre lake near the hotel
How to Find: Take the A47 Norwich - Dereham road, and 8 miles from Dereham turn right towards Little Dunham. Turn left, then right in village to the Granary Hotel
Carp Stock: Carp to double figures in all lakes
Category: Mixed Fishery
Other Species: Crucians and tench
Permits: Day tickets from hotel. Tel: Fakenham 701310. In advance only
Cost: Approx £3
BK Rating: Moderate
Control: Private
W/A: Anglian
Comments: Hotel accommodation with restaurant, swimming, golf, tennis as well as fishing

Great Massingham Village Pond

Location: Great Massingham, between Norwich and Fakenham
How to Find: Take A1067 Fakenham road from Norwich and then B1145 from it at Bawdeswell. Go through Litcham and after 6 miles take the road to Great Massingham. The pond is in the middle of the village
Carp Stock: Well stocked with small commons
Category: Carp Only
Permits: Free fishing
BK Rating: Easy
W/A: Anglian
Comments: These fish are said locally to be wild carp, but readers should note that there are very few wildies left in the country. John Wilson has confirmed that these are true wildies

Great Melton Reservoir A

Location: Lombe Estate, Hall Farm, Great Melton, Norwich NR9 3BW, 6 miles from Wymondham
Type and Size: 5 acre estate lake constructed 16 years ago, alongside a Nature Reserve
Carp Stock: Well stocked with commons to about 10lbs
Category: Carp Water
Other Species: Possibly some brown trout, as it was a trout fishery until 3 years ago
Permits: David Gregory, The Estate Office, at the address above. Tel: 0603 810135. These are confined to those who book the holiday accommodation on the estate
Control: Private
Restrictions: No pets; some areas out of bounds to protect wildlife. Some fishing allowed from punts
BK Rating: Not known, but probably Easy
W/A: Anglian
Comments: Three cottages are to rent for self-catering holidays on this attractive estate, with fishing on two carp lakes, and the River Yare at Marlingford. Prices from about £200 per week, fishing included

Gunthorpe Hall Lake

Location: Gunthorpe Hall, Gunthorpe, near Melton Constable
Type and Size: 2 acre estate lake
Carp Stock: Some common carp to double figures
Category: Few Carp
Other Species: Roach, rudd, perch, pike amd tench
Permits: Day tickets by prior booking only from the Hall. Tel: 0263 861373. Only 7 tickets per day issued
Cost: £1 50 per day
BK Rating: Not known
Control: Private
Restrictions: No night fishing - dawn till dusk only. No Sunday fishing
W/A: Anglian

Hall Farm Pit

Location: Hall Farm, Burgh Castle opposite Burgh Hall on the road from Yarmouth
Type and Size: Half acre pit
Carp Stock: Well stocked with mirrors to double figures
Category: Mixed Fishery
Other Species: Crucians, roach, rudd and tench
Permits: Day tickets from the farm at the top of the field before fishing
Cost: £1 50 per day
Control: Private
BK Rating: Not known
W/A: Anglian

Haveringland Lake

Location: Haveringland, near Norwich
Type and Size: 14 acre dammed, shallow lake
Carp Stock: Carp to double figures
Category: Mixed Fishery
Other Species: Rudd, roach, bream, tench and pike
Permits: Mr K Rustige. Tel: Norwich 871302
Control: Private. Please note that you can only fish this water if you park a touring caravan on the park by the water
Restrictions: No fishing except for those with touring caravans on site
BK Rating: Not known
W/A: Anglian

Hevingham Lakes A

Location: Hevingham, 8 miles north of Norwich
Type and Size: Man-made lakes of which there are three, all quite small
How to Find: From Norwich take B1149 towards Holt. About six miles from Norwich take the second right turn marked 'Hevingham'. The fishery entrance is on the left about a mile further on
Carp Stock: Well stocked with carp, many of which are small but there are some doubles and also a few over 20lbs
Category: Mixed Fishery
Other Species: Crucians, roach, rudd, tench and bream
Permits: Day tickets in advance only from the owner who lives in the bungalow at the entrance of the fishery - Mr C J Matthewson. Tel: Hevingham 368
Cost: Free to those who stay
Baits/Methods: Normal carp fishing baits and methods
Control: Private
BK Rating: Moderate
W/A: Anglian
Comments: You can holiday here as the owner lets caravans to anglers. There are toilet and shower facilities. Touring caravans and tents are welcome and there is also a farmhouse to let. Prices approx £90 - £135 per week according to season

Holkham Hall Lake

Location: Off the A149 near Wells-next-the-Sea
Type and Size: 15 acre estate lake in the grounds of a big house which is open to the public
Carp Stock: Fairly well stocked, mainly with commons to upper doubles
Category: Mixed Fishery
Other Species: Tench, roach and perch
Permits: Day tickets from the Estate Office
Control: Private
Restrictions: No night fishing; dawn till dusk only; much of the bank cannot be fished after August 31st. No camping
BK Rating: Moderate
W/A: Anglian

Little Lake Land

Location: Wortwell, Bungay
Carp Stock: Some carp to double figures
Type and Size: Half acre lake, depths to 12ft
Category: Mixed Fishery
Other Species: Roach, perch, bream tench
Permits: Mr A Hopkins. Tel: Homersfield 646
Control: Private
Restrictions: No fishing except for those who park touring caravans at the lake
BK Rating: Moderate
W/A: Anglian

Little Melton Reservoir A

Location: Marlingford, Wymondham, near Norwich
Type and Size: Two acre estate lake
Carp Stock: Fairly well stocked with carp, sizes not known
Category: Carp Water
Other Species: Some very large brown and rainbow trout, as this was previously a trout water
Permits: David Gregory, The Estate Office, Hall Farm, Great Melton, Norwich NR9 3BW. Tel: 0603 810135 - only for those booking the self-catering cottages on the estate
Control: Private
Restrictions: No pets; some areas may be out of bounds to protect wildlife. Some boat fishing allowed
BK Rating: Easy
W/A: Anglian
Comments: There are 3 cottages as holiday rents on this attractive estate, with prices ranging from £200 per week to only about £250 in August, with fishing on three lakes and the River Yare included

Lyng Easthaugh Pits

Location: Lyng, near Norwich
Type and Size: Two acre gravel pit
How to Find: Take the A1067 Norwich-Fakenham road, and turn left for Lyng at Lenwade village. Pits on the right in 1½ miles

Carp Stock: Well stocked with carp
Category: Carp Water
Other Species: A few coarse fish
Permits: Season tickets only - Dereham and Dist. A.C. Secretary, S Allinson, Sequenta, Cemetery Road, East Dereham. Tel: Dereham 4828; the farm, Lyng, or local tackle dealers
Cost: Approx £7 per year
BK Rating: Easy
Control: Club
Restrictions: Members only
W/A: Anglian
Comments: The ticket includes other pits and river fishing. The big pit alongside may contain a few carp

Marlingford Mere A

Location: Marlingford, Wymondham, Norwich
Type and Size: 12 acre gravel pit, landscaped and now a fishery and wildlife reserve
Carp Stock: Well stocked with common carp about three years ago, numbers and sizes not known
Category: Carp Water
Other Species: Probably some
Permits: David Gregory, Estate Offfice, Hall Farm, Great Melton, Norwich NR9 3BW. Tel: 0603 810135; fishing only available to those booking the holiday cottages on the estate
Control: Private
Restrictions: No pets
BK Rating: Not known
W/A: Anglian
Comments: There are three cottages to rent for holidays on the estate, which is most attractive. Prices range from about £200 to £260 per week, with fishing on 3 carp lakes and the River Yare included. No day tickets or other permits

Martham Pits

Location: Close to the ferry on the River Thurne, near Martham village
Type and Size: A number of small, interconnected pits
Carp Stock: Some carp to double figures
Category: Mixed Fishery
Other Species: Well known as a tench fishery; also pike, bream, rudd, roach and eels
Permits: Molly's Sweet Shop, Black Lane, Martham. Tel: Great Yarmouth 740366. Only 15 issued in advance each day
Cost: £2 per day
Control: Private
BK Rating: Difficult
W/A: Anglian

Mere Farm Pond

Location: Mere Farm, Saxthorpe
Type and Size: 1 acre farm pond
How to Find: Take the B1149 Holt road from Norwich to Saxthorpe. In village, cross

the River Bure and straight across the crossroads. Mere Farm is one mile ahead on the left

Carp Stock: Well stocked with wild carp to 6lbs
Category: Mixed Fishery
Other Species: Roach and eels
Permits: From farmhouse
Cost: Approx £1 per day
BK Rating: Easy
W/A: Anglian
Comments: John Wilson tells us these carp are 'wildies' - and there are very few of those left in this country! Most fish which locals call 'wildies' are just long, thin commons

Nunnery Lakes

Location: Thetford
Type and Size: 5 gravel pits of 2-5 acres
How to Find: Enquire from local owner
Carp Stock: Well stocked with mirrors
Category: Mixed Fishery
Other Species: Tench, roach, perch, rudd
Permits: Annual syndicate only - apply in close season to Mr Lowndes, Nunnery House, Nunnery Place, Thetford with an SAE
Cost: On application
BK Rating: Moderate
Control: Private
Restrictions: No day tickets
W/A: Anglian

Railway Pit

Location: 3 miles from Attleborough
Type and Size: Tiny pit of about ¼ acre
How to Find: Take the All from Norwich and 3 miles after Attleborough turn left at Old Buckenham crossroads. Cross the railway line, and the pit is on the left, surrounded by trees
Carp Stock: Some mirror carp, sizes and numbers not known
Category: Probably Few Carp
Other Species: Small tench, roach, perch and pike
Permits: FREE fishing
BK Rating: Not known
W/A: Anglian

Reepham Fisheries

Location: Just outside the village of Reepham, on the left of the road from Norwich
Type and Size: Three acre ex-trout lake
Carp Stock: Carp to doubles
Category: Mixed Fishery
Other Species: Crucian, rudd and tench. There are also some ghost koi
Permits: From the owner, Mr Daws, at the office near the lake
Cost: £2 per day
Control: Private
Baits/Methods: Float and legering methods both work well

Restrictions: No night fishing, except by prior arrangement. Fishing from 6am until 10pm only. No keepnets, and carp to be retained for a few minutes in landing nets only for photographs
BK Rating: Moderate
W/A: Anglian

Ringland Lakes

Location: Ringland, near Norwich
Type and Size: Seven gravel pits
How to Find: From Norwich take A47 Dereham road and after two miles turn right down Longwater Lane by the Roundwell public house. Turn left at bottom of the hill, then keep left at the fork and a mile further on you will see a track on the right leading to the fishery
Carp Stock: Not a large number of carp but are said to be mostly large - from doubles to 30lbs, in the largest lake. This is called Days Waters and is the first along the track on the left
Category: Few Carp
Other Species: Perch, pike, bream, rudd, crucians and tench
Permits: Day tickets and also season tickets from the bailiff on the bank
Cost: Day tickets: approx £2
Control: Leisure Sport Angling
BK Rating: Moderate
W/A: Anglian

River Wensum

Location: Below the mill in Norwich
Type and Size: Town river
Carp Stock: Plenty of carp to well over 20lbs, and 30's - escapees from a local fish farm
Category: Mixed Fishery
Other Species: Most coarse fish, including barbel
Permits: Clubs have some water in this area, but most is free fishing
BK Rating: Difficult, as fish must first be located, usually in the deeper, slower moving parts of the river
W/A: Anglian
Comments: It was only a flood which 'stocked' this river with carp, though there is no telling how many will survive. Other fish grow to good sizes in the Wensum, so the carp should do well

Rodally Pit

Location: In the centre of the village of Old Buckenham which is on the B1077 from Attleborough
Type and Size: Half acre shallow pond
Carp Stock: Some small commons
Category: Mixed Fishery
Other Species: Rudd and tench
Permits: FREE fishing
W/A: Anglian

Scottow Pond

Location: Scottow, near Swanton Abbot, and Coltishall
Type and Size: 5 acre shallow, silty bottomed lake
Carp Stock: Well stocked with mirrors in 1983 - a rich lake so they should have grown well
Category: Mixed Fishery
Other Species: Good tench, pike and eels
Permits: Members only, no day tickets, from Mr Townsend, Hall Gardens, Scottow. Tel: Swanton Abbot 671
Cost: £6 per season
Control: Private
Restrictions: Members only
BK Rating: Not known, although it could be quite hard, as this water is very clear
W/A: Anglian
Comments: This water is just down the road from RAF Coltishall where PM was stationed during his National Service from 1949-51. He did try fishing it, and found it very difficult.... nothing but blanks!

Shallow Brook Carp Lake

Location: New Costessey, near Norwich
Type and Size: 2¼ acre lake about 12ft deep
How to Find: From Norwich take the A47 Dereham road into New Costessey. Turn right at the traffic lights into Norwich Road, and half a mile further on the lake is on the left just after the river bridge
Carp Stock: Plenty of commons and mirrors to 20lbs
Category: Mixed Fishery
Other Species: Roach, perch, tench, crucian carp and rudd
Permits: Day tickets from farm shop before fishing
Cost: £5 per day: £3 - half day: £2 - evening. Season tickets also available. For details contact Robbie Green on Norwich 742822 (daytime). Norwich 741123 (evenings)
Control: Private
Restrictions: No night fishing unless you buy a season ticket; day tickets are from dawn to dusk
BK Rating: Easy
W/A: Anglian
Comments: Car park close to lake. Facilities for wheelchair anglers. Permit includes roach, dace and chub fishing in a stretch of the little River Tub nearby

Shropham Pits

Location: Shropham, near Attleborough
Type and Size: Two pits, of from 5 to 10ft deep
How to Find: Take the A11 from Norwich to 4 miles past Attleborough, and pass the White Lodge pub on the left. After another 1½ miles, turn right at a sign marked 'By road'. At the crossroads turn right over a bridge, and take the first road on the left. The pits are 300 yds on the left
Carp Stock: Some carp to double figures
Category: Probably Few Carp
Other Species: Pike, tench, roach, rudd, eels, bream and crucians
Permits: Members only water of Wymondham and District AC. Membership from The Secretary, Mr T Binks, 25 Rosemary Road, Norwich. Tel: Norwich 405341, or from the bailiff in the house opposite the pit entrance

Cost: £12 per season
Control: Club
BK Rating: Difficult
W/A: Anglian

Stonegate Lake

Location: Off the B1145 Aylsham to Cawston road, turning left under the old railway bridge. The lake is on the right
Type and Size: Shallow three acre lake
Carp Stock: Some mirrors and commons to a good size
Category: Mixed Fishery
Other Species: Perch, rudd, crucians, bream and pike
Permits: Members only water of the Yarmouth, Gorleston and Dist.A.C. Apply to the Chairman, Tony Giacomelli. Tel: 0760 44323, or from Tom Boulton. Tel: Norwich 426834
Cost: £14 per season, to include fishing at Bawburgh Lake, Granary Lakes, and the Muckfleet Dyke
Control: Club
W/A: Anglian

Stradsett Lake

Location: Stradsett, near Kings Lynn - from Stradsett, turn right onto the A134, and the lake is also on the right, one mile further on
Type and Size: Eight acre lake, about 7ft in depth
Carp Stock: Some carp, sizes not known
Category: Mixed Fishery
Other Species: Bream, perch, pike and tench
Permits: Members only water, and a specialist syndicate, to which only members of Kings Lynn AC can apply. To join the club, apply to the Secretary, Mr George Bear. Tel: Downham Market 387114
Cost: Kings Lynn AC costs £12 to join, and then there is an extra fee to join the Stradsett Syndicate
Control: Club
BK Rating: Moderate
W/A: Anglian

Swangey Lakes

Location: Near West Carr, Attleborough
Type and Size: Two gravel pits of 4½ and 1½ acres
How to Find: Take the A11 from Norwich, and on the Attleborough by-pass turn right to West Carr. After half a mile turn left when the road forks, and then right in 100 yards, continue through a ford across the river, and the fishery entrance is on the left
Carp Stock: Well stocked with carp to 20lbs
Category: Carp Water
Other Species: Crucians, tench, rudd, roach, perch and bream
Permits: Day tickets on bank from bailiff. Further enquiries from M and M Enterprises. Tel 0953 453119
Cost: £5 per day, half price for juniors
Control: Private

Restrictions: No night fishing - fishing is from dawn to dusk only
BK Rating: Easy
W/A: Anglian
Comments: The lakes are 30ft deep in places

Swanton Morley Fisheries

Location: Swanton Morley, near East Dereham
Type and Size: Gravel pits, 3 lakes totalling 65 acres
How to Find: From East Dereham take the B1147 road, signposted Bawdeswell past the Papermakers public house and the church. Bear left at the T-junction then sharp right. Pass Waterfall Farm on your left and the entrance to the lakes is 400 yards on the right. Do NOT use the works entrance
Carp Stock: Not many carp; sizes unknown
Category: Few Carp
Other Species: Pike, perch, rudd and tench
Permits: Day tickets must be obtained in advance from; Rod and Gun, Norwich Street, Dereham; Mrs V Marsham, Waterfall Farm, Swanton Morley (Please enclose SAE). After 8am tickets can be obtained from Waterfall Farm. Season tickets from Waterfall Farm
Cost: Approx £1 per day (Juniors/OAPs/evening fishing 50p)
Restrictions: No night fishing. Fishery is open from sunrise to sunset. Do NOT go to the working site or works lake.
Control: Redland Angling Scheme
BK Rating: Difficult, as there are few carp
W/A: Anglian

Taswood Lakes

Location: Flordon, Tasburgh, Norwich
Type and Size: Four man-made lakes of from one to 3½ acres
How to Find: From Norwich take the A140 and take the right fork to Flordon in Newton Flotman. After 1½ miles turn left to Tasburgh. The lakes are on the left in 200 yards
Carp Stock: All the lakes contain some mirrors, the numbers of which are not known. The biggest lake holds some 20's, best weight recorded is 29lbs 10ozs in 1984
Category: Mixed Fishery
Other Species: Crucians, roach, rudd, bream, tench, perch, pike, some grass carp in the pond near the house
Cost: Day ticket cost approx £2
Control: Private - owner lives on property
BK Rating: Moderate
W/A: Anglian
Comments: Owner sells koi carp, goldfish and other pond fish on site

Tatts Pit

Location: The Willows, Downham Market
Type and Size: Tree-lined pit of about an acre
How to Find: Take the A47 Dereham road from Norwich, then the A1122 to Downham Market, then follow the Wisbech road and look out for Downham Tackle on your right. Just before the shop, turn left, and the pit is 100 yards on the left at 'the Willows'

Carp Stock: Some mirrors, sizes not known
Category: Possibly Few Carp
Other Species: Tench and crucians
Permits: In advance only from Downham Tackle, Railway Road, Downham Market. Tel: 0366 384338
Cost: £2 per day
Control: Private
BK Rating: Not known
W/A: Anglian

Taverham

Location: Costessey No. 2 and No. 3 pits, Taverham, near Norwich
Type and Size: Ski Pit (No. 2) - 12 acres, up to 20ft deep. The Carp Lake (No. 3) - 6 acres, and 8 to 15 feet deep
Carp Stock: No. 2 has a small number of carp to double figures. No. 3 also has very few, but mirrors between 28lbs and 30lbs are caught each season
How to Find: Take the A1067 Fakenham road from Norwich to Taverham, and turn left at the crossroads into Sandy Lane. Go straight ahead at the next crossroads, and over the River Wensum bridge. The pits are on the left, with the car park by No. 2. No parking on the roadside
Category: No. 2 - Difficult: No. 3 Very Difficult
Other Species: Tench, bream, roach, eels, perch and pike to 23lbs
Permits: Day tickets from tackle dealers, or season tickets from, The Secretary, Mr Cyril Wigg, 3 Coppice Avenue, Norwich. Tel: Norwich 423625, and *must* be purchased in advance - no tickets on the bank
Cost: Day - £1; Season - £10
Baits/Methods: Advanced carp fishing baits and techniques needed for these big hard to catch carp
Control: Club - Norfolk and Suffolk Anglers Consultative Council
Restrictions: No night fishing
BK Rating: No. 2 - Difficult; No. 3 - Very Difficult
Comments: The big carp in No. 3 are well known to carp specialists, so this is very much a specialist's water. Since there are very few of these fish they are obviously very hard to catch. There are some level swims provided near the car park for disabled anglers.

Taverham Mill Lake A

Location: Sandy Lane, Taverham, on the right just before the bridge over the River Wensum
Type and Size: 15 acre attractively matured man-made lake, dug in the '40's, with many islands, bays and peninsulas, and up to 12ft in depth. Heavily weeded in summer
Carp Stock: Plenty of carp, sizes not known
Category: Mixed Fishery
Other Species: Tench, big bream and pike, roach and rudd
Permits: Day tickets limited in advance only from Norwich Angling Centre, Sprowston Road, Norwich. Tel: 400757. Accommodation also available.
Cost: On application
Control: Private
BK Rating: Moderate
W/A: Anglian

Thompson Water

Location: Merton, near Watton, Norwich
Type and Size: Shallow lake of 30 acres
How to Find: Take the B1108 road from Norwich to Watton and then the B1110 to Merton and Thompson, Take the track straight on to Peddars Way and the huge lake is on the left
Carp Stock: There have apparently always been some commons in this big lake, although not very many. It is reported to have been 'heavily stocked' (numbers not known) with mirrors in 1984 and they are also said to be caught in double figures
Category: Mixed Fishery
Other Species: Crucians, rudd, roach, bream, tench and pike
Permits: Day tickets from bailiff on bank. Information about the water from Merton Estate Office, Watton, Thetford IP25 6QJ. Tel: Watton 883370
Cost: Approx £2 per day
Control: Private
Baits/Methods: Usual carp baits and methods, though it may be wise to select baits which are less likely to be taken by the many other fish in the water
BK Rating: Difficult
W/A: Anglian

Time-Share Lakes A

Location: Near Norwich
Type and Size: Large lakes
Carp Stock: Well stocked with carp to over 20lbs
Category: Mixed Fishery
Other Species: Tench, roach, bream and possibly others
Permits: Tel: 0603 407199 for information and details
Cost: £5,000! (This is not a misprint - this fishery has been advertised at this cost for *life membership*, which includes 4 weeks fishing and accommodation every year for life
Control: Private
BK Rating: Unknown
W/A: Anglian

University Broad

Location: Norwich University
Type and Size: Ten acre gravel pit
How to Find: In Norwich take B1108 Watton road and turn left onto Bluebell Road in Earlham. The lake will be seen on the right
Carp Stock: Good stock of mirror and koi carp to double figures
Category: Mixed Fishery
Other Species: Roach, rudd, tench, bream, and pike
Permits: Members only - University of East Anglia, Biology Department, U.E.A. Norwich. Annual permits only. Apply in writing with SAE
Cost: Approx £12 per year
BK Rating: Moderate
Control: University
Restrictions: Not known
W/A: Anglian
Comments: Only big stillwater within the city - up to 20 feet deep

Wades Pit

Location: Wymondham, near Norwich
Type and Size: Weedy pit of about an acre, up to 7 feet deep
How to Find: Take the A11 from Norwich to Wymondham, and turn left at the traffic lights into the B1135. Take the first left turn after the railway bridge, and the pit is another half mile, on the left
Carp Stock: Some mirrors to middle doubles
Category: Few Carp
Other Species: Roach, perch, tench and crucians
Permits: Day tickets from bailiff on bank, season tickets and information from:- Mr R Bartlett, 6 Vimy Ridge, Wymondham. Tel:Wymondham 605505
Cost: 70p (Juniors - 35p) for day tickets: £3 (Juniors £1.50) per season
Baits/Methods: Good float fishing water, ideal for youngsters
Control: Private
BK Rating: Easy for most fish, though we suspect harder for the carp, as there are not many of the bigger fish
W/A: Anglian

Waveney Valley Lakes A

Location: Wortwell, near Harleston, on the Suffolk border
Type and Size: Six mature gravel pits from 2 - 5 acres in size
How to Find: Take the A140 from Norwich to Pulham Market, then the B1134 to Harleston and the A143 to Wortwell. The entrance to the lakes is signposted in the middle of Wortwell
Carp Stock: All the lakes are well stocked with large carp. Plenty of doubles and 20's, and a number of very well authenticated 30's have been taken to 36lbs
Category: Carp Water
Other Species: Crucians, tench, roach, rudd, bream, perch, pike and eels
Permits: Day tickets should be puchased from the site shop if open, if not, bailiffs call around. Day tickets cover 12 hours only. Night fishing allowed but another 12 hour ticket will be needed
Cost: £3.50 for one rod for 12 hours; two rods £6. Weekly + bivvy £40 for 1 rod; £65 for 2 rods
Control: Details from shop, or Tony Knox on 0986 86676
Baits/Methods: Advanced carp fishing rigs and methods and baits are needed at this heavily fished specialist carp water. Many boilies and multiple baits go in every day. Hard boilies, such as Maestros, work best
BK Rating: Moderate though some of the lakes can be easy for the smaller fish and lower doubles; the really big fish are quite difficult
W/A: Anglian
Comments: One of the best commercial carp fisheries in the country - and for this reason very well known for its twenties and thirties, and hard fished by many expert carp anglers. Tents can be pitched for long-stay holidays at an extra charge and you can also take your touring caravan. There are luxury lakeside caravans which must be booked well in advance, and these are ideal for a family holiday. There are top class shower and toilet facilities, and the shop sells carp bait, tackle and food. G, E and D lakes are said to be the best for the really big fish, some of which are caught quite often and are well known to the regulars. No dogs. One of the comparatively few carp waters in the country which can be fished by everyone and where you are always in with a chance of a big fish. Caravans about £200 weekly. Sacking for 15 minutes only; unhooking mats compulsory. Day tickets only available on some lakes from November. Holiday cottages also to let in the area. Tel: Fressingfield 395

Wensum Fisheries

Location: Costessey, near Norwich
Type and Size: Attractive, wooded, old gravel pits of from 2 to 10 acres in size
How to Find: Take the A47 from Norwich, and after two miles turn right by the Roundwell public house down Longwater Lane. At the 'T' junction turn left, and then take a right fork in half a mile. The lakes are then 200 yards on the left, behind iron gates
Carp Stock: Clear Water Lake is well stocked with carp into double figures; Rainbow Pool contains a few carp
Category: Clear Water - Mixed Fishery; Rainbow - Few Carp
Other Species: Back Lake (the biggest) - roach, rudd and bream to over 9lbs (no carp); Roach Lake - roach, tench and bream (no carp); Clear Water Lake - tench and bream; Rainbow Pool - roach, tench and bream
Permits: Members only water of Norwich and Dist.AA. Permits from the Secretary, Mr C Wigg, 3 Coppice Avenue, Norwich. Tel: Norwich 423625 (Includes fishing on River Wensum)
Cost: On application
Control: Club
Restrictions: No night fishing
BK Rating: Clear Water - Moderate; Rainbow - Difficult
W/A: Anglian

Wereham Pit

Location: In the village of Wereham, opposite the George and Dragon pub
Type and Size: Tiny, shallow, quarter of an acre pit
How to Find: Find Wereham, near Stradsett, off the A134, and then Wereham
Carp Stock: Plenty of little carp
Category: Mixed Fishery
Other Species: Roach and pike
Permits: FREE fishing, ideal for young people
W/A: Anglian
BK Rating: Easy

West Lexham A

Location: West Lexham, near Kings Lynn
Type and Size: Beautiful moat
Carp Stock: Well stocked with carp to over 30lbs
Other Species: General coarse fish
Category: Mixed Fishery
Permits: Sue Allerton. Tel (Swaffham) 0760 755252
Control: Private
Restrictions: No fishing, except to those renting one of the self-catering holiday cottages on the site. Includes fishing on the River Nar
BK Rating: Not known
W/A: Anglian

Willsmore Water

Location: Hayes Lane near Fakenham
Type and Size: 1½ acre man-made lake
How to Find: From Fakenham cross the River Wensum at Goggs Mill, then take Sandy Lane and Hayes Lane
Carp Stock: Well stocked with carp to doubles
Category: Mixed Fishery
Permits: Fakenham A/C (members only). Membership from G Parsons, 26 St Peters Road, Fakenham. Tel: 4637
Cost: Approx £4 entry fee - £10 per season
BK Rating: Moderate
Restrictions: No keepnets, no groundbaiting
W/A: Anglian
Comments: Membership also includes some other lakes and trout and coarse fishing on the River Wensum

Wolterton Park Lake

Location: Wolterton Hall, 5 miles from Aylsham
Type and Size: Attractive estate lake, with an island and very clear water
Carp Stock: Some carp, sizes not known
Category: Few Carp
Other Species: A few big tench, eels and perch
Permits: Day tickets from the Head Gardener's Lodge, just inside the orchard which leads round the Great Hall to the lake
Cost: £2 per day
Control: Private
BK Rating: Very Difficult
W/A: Anglian
Comments: A very weedy, clear water which is very difficult to fish, as it seems to be sparsely stocked

Wood Lakes

Location: Stow, near Kings Lynn
Type and Size: Four lakes, one large and 3 small, with a total area of 20 acres
How to Find: Take the A10 from Kings Lynn and turn right at Stow Bardolph. 500 yards before the bridge carry straight on at sharp bend. The lakes will be seen on the right shortly before Stow Bridge
Carp Stock: All well stocked with carp to over 25lbs
Category: Mixed Fishery
Other Species: Roach, rudd, tench and bream
Permits: Day tickets from the reception kiosks, or on the banks from the bailiffs if the reception is closed
Cost: Approx £2 per day, £6 per 12 hours (2 rods)
Baits/Methods: Specialist carp fishing methods and baits needed for the better carp. Night fishing best, when there is less disturbance.
Restrictions: No winter fishing from November 1st onwards
Control: Private. Tel: 0533 810585
BK Rating: Moderate
W/A: Anglian
Comments: Camping is allowed at extra cost. Touring caravans are also welcomed. Family-type water during the day. Best chance for the specialist is after dark

Worthing Pits

Location: Dereham,near Norwich
Type and Size: Two pits of 8 acres and 2 acres, the larger of which is open and has depths of up to 20ft
Carp Stock: Some carp, numbers and sizes not known
Category: Few Carp
Other Species: Roach, tench, perch and pike
Permits: Day tickets, in advance only, from local tackle shops, or Mr S R Allison, Pound Cottage, Cemetery Road, East Dereham. Tel: Dereham 694828
Cost: £1.50 per day; Dereham and Dist. AC membership, which includes these waters, several other pits, and stretches of the River Wensum behind the pits; cost £7 per season, half price for juniors
Control: Club
BK Rating: Not known
W/A: Anglian

NORTHAMPTONSHIRE

Biggin Lake

Location: Biggin Estate, Oundle
Type and Size: 6 acre estate lake
How to Find: Oundle is east of Corby on the A427
Carp Stock: A few fish under 10lbs, but plenty of doubles; average about 18lbs; said to be a number of twenties, and fish of 36lbs and 34lbs have been reported, though we have no evidence of authenticity
Category: Carp Only
Other Species: None
Permits: B P Bait, Baithouse Lane, Burton Latimer (Tackle Shop). Season tickets (in advance) only
Cost: On application
BK Rating: Moderate
Control: Private
Restrictions: No sacking except for quick pics. 72 hour maximum stay
W/A: Anglian
Comments: Well established, attractive water with plenty of cover on banks. Only fished for the past 6 years so it is thought that some of the big fish have never been caught

Biggin Pit

Location: Oundle Golf Course
Type and Size: Gravel pit of 6 acres
How to Find: On the outskirts of the town of Oundle
Carp Stock: Well stocked with carp to 20lbs
Category: Carp Water
Other Species: Few other fish
Permits: Robin Sharp
Cost: Syndicate only - £100 per season
BK Rating: Easy
Control: Private
W/A: Anglian
Comments: Shallow, silty pit said to be good carp fishing. Quiet peaceful lake. Second lake about 3 acres on site also contains many small carp. Day tickets, bookable in advance - a very easy water

Billing Aquadrome

Location: Little Billing, near Northampton
Type and Size: There are a number of lakes on this holiday caravan and leisure complex, but only the Willow Pool (12 acres) is of much interest to carp anglers
How to Find: Take the A45 from Northampton and turn off to the village of Little Billing
Carp Stock: Very few, but have grown to great size in the past. The lake became famous in the 50's and 60's when a huge catch of twenties and a thirty were caught by Bob Reynolds, and in 1966 a 42 pounder was caught by Ray Clay. Still a few big fish but they are rarely caught
Category: Few Carp
Other Species: Pike, perch, roach, tench, bream
Permits: On site. Information - Tel: Northampton 45255
Restrictions: No night fishing. No fishing after mid-October
BK Rating: Super-Difficult
W/A: Anglian
Comments: Famous carp water now declined to the extent that carp are almost never caught there - although it was always very difficult. Crowds of thousands at weekends and bank hoidays - hundreds of caravans, cafes and amusements etc. There may still be a few big fish and there was a low 30 caught there fairly recently

Boddington Reservoir

Location: Byfield, 7 miles from Banbury
Type and Size: Big reservoir - 65 acres
Carp Stock: Some carp to a good size
Category: Mixed Fishery
Other Species: Pike, bream, perch, roach and tench
Permits: Season tickets from Principal Fisheries Officer, British Waterways, Willow Grange, Church Road, Watford, Herts. Tel: Watford 226422. (There may be a waiting list)
Cost: £17 per season
Control: British Waterways
BK Rating: Not known
W/A: Thames

Castle Ashby Lakes

Location: Castle Ashby, near Northampton
Type and Size: Four estate lakes of various sizes
How to Find: Take a left turn off the A248 Northampton-Bedford road about 7 miles from Northampton
Carp Stock: Two of the lakes are quite well stocked with carp to mid-doubles
Category: Mixed Fishery
Other Species: General coarse fishing
Permits: Castle Ashby Estate Office, Castle Ashby, Northampton. Tel: 0604 29223. One lake recently opened as a specimen carp water - details from the estate office
Cost: On application
Control: Castle Ashby Estate
BK Rating: Moderate. Menagerie Lake - Very Easy for carp to 18lbs
Restrictions: No night fishing. Fishing is dawn till dusk only
W/A: Anglian

Clarkes

Location: Clarkes Pick Your Own Farm, Hannington, near Kettering - off the A43
Type and Size: Small farm lake of about an acre dug for irrigation and 16 feet deep
Carp Stock: Well stocked with carp to 25lbs, although many are small
Carp Stock: Mixed Fishery
Other Species: Usual coarse fish
Permits: Day tickets on site, at £2 per day
Control: Private
BK Rating: Moderate
W/A: Anglian

Corby Boating Lake

Location: On the outskirts of Corby, Cottingham Road
Type and Size: Town lake of 3½ acres
How to Find: In Corby
Carp Stock: Stocked with carp to 20lbs; a 33lb has been reported
Category: Mixed Fishery
Other Species: Roach, bream, tench, pike, rudd and catfish
Permits: Free fishing
Control: Council
BK Rating: Moderate
Restrictions: No night fishing. barbless hooks, no groundbaiting
W/A: Anglian

Ditchford Lake

Location: Near Rushden
Type and Size: Two well matured gravel pits of about 6 and 30 acres
Carp Stock: Stocked with commons and mirrors most of which are doubles with a few twenties. Record 26lbs, from small lake; about 12 twenties in big lake with at least 4 twenty pound commons
Category: Mixed Fishery
Other Species: Most coarse fish
Permits: Rushden, High Ferrers and Irchester Angling Club. Season tickets only

	from Jack Leach Fishing Tackle, Church Street, Rushden
Cost:	Approx £10 per season with a number of other good waters on the club ticket
Control:	Club
BK Rating:	Difficult
W/A:	Anglian
Comments:	Night fishing is allowed

Ecton Lakes

Location:	Billing, near Northampton
Type and Size:	New gravel pit of 40+ acres
Carp Stock:	Low density - about 2 fish per acre, but plenty of 20's caught
Category:	Mixed Fishery
Other Species:	General coarse fish - some big pike
Permits:	Northampton Nene AC - local tackle shops
Cost:	Approx £20 per season
BK Rating:	Difficult
Control:	Club
W/A:	Anglian
Comments:	New water with few carp, but these are young, fast growing fish. Lake record about 37lbs and this fish was only seven years old. Permits from Jack Leach Fishing Tackle, Church Street, Rushden, or Northampton Nene AC, M Eaton, 12 Thorne Hill, Briar Hill, Northampton NN4 9SN

Fineshade Abbey

Location:	On the A43 between Corby and Stamford
Type and Size:	Two small lakes, recently opened
Carp Stock:	Some carp to doubles
Category:	Mixed Fishery
Other Species:	Roach, tench, perch and bream
Permits:	Day tickets on site
Cost:	Weekends 9am to 4.30pm - £5
Control:	Private. Tel: 0780 83284 for bookings and information
Restrictions:	Thought to be no night fishing; restricted fishing on weekdays
BK Rating:	Not known
W/A:	Anglian

Flecknoe Farm Fisheries

Location:	Just outside Daventry
Type and Size:	Small farm lake
Carp Stock:	Well stocked with carp to doubles
Category:	Carp Water
Permits:	Season tickets only from Flecknoe Fisheries, 4 Watts Way, Long Buckby NN6 7QX. Tel: 0327 853657
Cost:	£75 per season; numbers limited
BK Rating:	Not known
W/A:	Severn Trent

Foxholes Fisheries

Location: Crick, Northampton NN6 7US. Tel: 0788 823967. Off the A428 between West Haddon and Crick
Type and Size: Four small lakes on fish farm
Carp Stock: Day Ticket Pool - mainly carp to 8lbs; Top Lake - carp only, most from 3-8lbs in weight; Bottom Lake - carp only, all over 7lbs, including doubles and twenties; Middle Lake - some carp
Category: Day Ticket Pool - Mixed Fishery; Middle Lake - Mixed Fishery; Top Lake and Bottom lake - Carp Only
Other Species: Day Ticket - crucians and tench; Middle Lake - tench, chub, perch, roach, crucians, bream and barbel
Permits: From Roger and Joan Chaplin at the above address
Cost: Day Ticket Pool - £2.50 for one rod, £5 for two rods, issued on bank by bailiff. Season tickets for Top, Bottom and Middle Lakes £40 for one weekday; £50 for 2 weekdays; £60 for 4 weekdays; £60 for Saturday plus one weekday; £65 for Sunday plus one weekday; £80 for Saturday and Sunday; £100 for 6 days a week
Restrictions: Barbless hooks; no keepnets; season ticket waters closed on Tuesdays; day ticket pool open every day; guest tickets allowed to season ticket holders
BK Rating: Easy
W/A: Severn Trent
Comments: Shop and information office; ornamental fish for sale; conference room with seating for 50, and all conference facilities; can be booked for clubs or school trips at about £50 for an afternoon; lectures by staff at £10 per hour. Bookable on Tuesdays for business entertaining which may include fishing at £100 per day. Bookings also available on other days, with fishing for £50. Matches may be booked at £40 for Sunday mornings (15 pegs on Middle Lake). Leaflet with details on request. Demonstration nettings on some bank holidays at £1 per person. Annual open day with free fishing for tackle shop proprietors and angling correspondents. Fishery management courses... what more can you ask!? We have not been invited to visit this fishery, but after such a good write-up, perhaps we shall be...

Gayton Pool

Location: Near Northampton
Type and Size: Small pool
How to Find: Enquire from Secretary
Carp Stock: Well stocked with carp
Category: Carp Water
Other Species: Some coarse fish
Permits: Gayton AC. S Barker, 91 Battmead, Bilsworth, Northants - members only
Cost: On application
BK Rating: Moderate
W/A: Anglian

Grand Union Canal

Location: Leicester Arm, near Watford Gap
Type and Size: Narrow canal
How to Find: Near Watford Gap services on M1
Carp Stock: Plenty of carp to middle doubles

Category: Mixed Fishery
Other Species: General coarse fish
Permits: Coventry AA - try local tackle shops
Cost: On application
Control: Club
BK Rating: Moderate
W/A: Anglian
Comments: Quite easy once fish are located. Coventry AA - P O'Connor, 48 Doncaster Close, Manor Farm, Wyken, Coventry CV2 1HX

Higham Wharf Lake

Location: Off the Higham Ferrers by-pass
Type and Size: 20 year old gravel pit of about 120 acres
How to Find: The entrance is at the Ski Club roundabout on the A45, Wharf Road, in Higham Ferrers and Pine Trees Village in Irthlingborough
Carp Stock: Not known, but not many. Fish to upper doubles caught, but there are probably some bigger fish
Category: Few Carp
Other Species: Roach, tench, bream, rudd, perch and pike
Permits: Irthlingborough AC - from local tackle shops
Cost: £13 per season
BK Rating: Difficult
W/A: Anglian
Comments: A night fishing ban, and long walks, make this lake a difficult proposition to all but the most determined

Hinton Fisheries

Location: Hinton-in-the-Hedges, near Brackley
Type and Size: Lake of 1½ acres
How to Find: Take the Hinton-in-the-Hedges road from Brackley
Carp Stock: Well stocked with carp, most fish between 5 and 12lbs, although there are plenty of doubles, and several twenties
Category: Carp Water
Other Species: Tench to 7lbs, crucians, roach, rudd, chub and trout
Permits: In advance in writing only from the owner, Trevor Smith, 24 Red Poll Close, Banbury, Oxfordshire. Information on 0295 264483
Cost: On application
Control: Private
BK Rating: Moderate
W/A: Anglian
Comments: A second lake at this very pleasant fishery will be built this year. The fishery is in quiet farmland away from main roads, and is secluded by high hedges and a locked gate, to which only the members have a key. Usual rules, baits and methods. Hinton Fish and Fishing also supply a netting service, and have fish for sale, including double figure carp at very reasonable prices, with occasional twenties. Details from the owner at the number above. Hinton-in-the-Hedges has long been my favourite English place name - now I know what it looks like!

Irthlingborough Main Lake

Location: Irthingborough - off the A605 Rushden-Kettering road, then turn left on the B751. After about 1½ miles turn left into a new housing estate, and then left again along a rough track, at the end of which is a car park
Type and Size: Typical Northants matured gravel pit of about 10 acres
Carp Stock: Plenty of carp to about 20lbs
Category: Mixed Fishery
Other Species: Pike, bream, tench, roach, hybrids and perch
Permits: Irthlingborough and District AC. Secretary: Peter Pratt, 7 The Shortlands, Irthlingborough
Cost: £13 per season to include other waters; juniors and OAP's - £6
Control: Club
Restrictions: Members only
BK Rating: Moderate
W/A: Anglian
Comments: Attractive, reed-fringed lake, which is not heavily fished, and could contain some very big carp, which have been seen on the surface

Maxey No. 4 Pit

Location: Deeping St. James, Peterborough
Type and Size: Gravel pit of 8 acres
How to Find: Off the A15 north of Peterborough
Carp Stock: Well stocked with carp to upper double figures
Category: Mixed Fishery
Other Species: Bream, tench, roach, pike and catfish
Permits: Day and season tickets from N Cesare, 55 Cardinals Gate, Werrington, Peterborough. Tel: 0733 70226
Cost: On application
BK Rating: Easy
Control: Deeping St. James Angling Club
W/A: Anglian
Comments: Good club mixed fishery. An angler had 50 to 9lbs in one session in July 1988!

Mid-Northants Carp Fishery

Location: Woodford Mill, Addington Road, near Ringstead
Type and Size: 3 lakes of 10 acres, 6 acres and 1 acre; gravel pits
How to Find: Turn left at the roundabout towards Ringstead from the A605 Higham Ferrers-Thrapston road, and at Ringstead take the left turn towards Great Addington. Woodford Mill will be seen on your right just after the bridge over the River Nene
Carp Stock: 'B' Lake (6 acres) - very well stocked with carp up to 20lbs, with many doubles; 'A' Lake (10 acres) contains about 40 carp of over 20lbs, a number of thirties, and one 40, best known as 'Two-Tone', which has been caught on a number of occasions. Some doubles, but most fish over 20lbs. 'C' Lake (1 acre) is recently dug and contains a number of small carp
Carp Stock: 'B' Lake - Mixed Fishery; 'A' Lake - Carp Water; 'C' Lake - Mixed Fishery
Other Species: 'B' Lake - big tench, double figure bream, catfish to 18lbs; 'C' Lake - grass carp and other species

Kevin Maddocks with a January 40¼ from the Mid-Northants Carp Fishery

Permits: Duncan Kay, 4 Sawyers Crescent, Chelveston, Northants. Tel: 0933 460115. In advance only. No day tickets; season tickets only

Cost: 'B' and 'C' Lakes, half mile of the adjacent River Nene, including membership of Higham Ferrers AC - £107 per year, January to January. 'A' Lake - £250 per season

BK Rating: 'B' and 'C' Lakes - Easy to Moderate. 'A' Lake - Moderate

Control: Private (Duncan Kay)

Restrictions: No long stay fishing, 48 hours maximum, 24 hours at weekends

W/A: Anglian

Comments: The Mid-Northants Carp Fishery is one of the most famous big fish and carp waters in the country, with many 20's and 30's caught each season, and several 40's, which have even been caught in the winter. The fishery is in a quiet and pleasant situation alongside the River Nene, but because of the huge fish it contains, and the fact that numbers of members are strictly limited, it is very hard to get into, and there is always a waiting list. The 'B' ticket, which includes Lake 'C' and the river is used as a waiting list for Lake 'A', the big carp lake, so you will need to apply for the 'B' ticket membership first, with the idea of hoping to get into 'A', the big carp water later. Full details from Duncan Kay, who controls the fishery, and who is well known as one of the leading big fish anglers in the country. This is private property, *so do not go to the lakes* without permission - if you are caught there without first getting permission to visit from Duncan, you are not likely to be offered membership - you have been warned! Rule 13 should be carefully noted: 'No climbing the trees is allowed' (there are virtually no trees, except a few saplings to about 5 feet tall!) and also Rule 13b 'The management takes no responsibility for any injury to members from trees falling on them!' Trees and bushes are being planted, and these will soon improve this already very pleasant fishery

Naseby Reservoir

Location:	Naseby, between Kettering and Rugby, off the A50
Type and Size:	85 acre reservoir
Carp Stock:	Well stocked with carp to nearly 20lbs
Category:	Mixed Fishery
Other Species:	Tench and rudd, possibly other species
Permits:	British Waterways, Willow Grange, Church Road, Watford, Herts. Tel: Watford 226422
Cost:	£15 per season
Control:	British Waterways
Restrictions:	No juniors
BK Rating:	Moderate
W/A:	Severn Trent

Overstone Solarium

Location:	Overstone, near Northampton
Type and Size:	Two estate lakes of 4 acres and 2 acres
How to Find:	Off the A4500 between Northampton and Wellingborough
Carp Stock:	Fairly well stocked to 24lbs, mostly commons
Category:	Mixed Fishery
Other Species:	General coarse fish
Permits:	On site
Cost:	Approx £1 per day
BK Rating:	Moderate
Control:	Private
W/A:	Anglian
Comments:	Night fishing allowed. Day ticket water with caravans etc

Ransome Road Gravel Pit

Location:	Near Northampton
Type and Size:	Large gravel pit, about 30 acres plus
How to Find:	On A508 near motorway junction 15
Carp Stock:	Not many carp to 20lbs plus
Category:	Few Carp
Other Species:	General coarse fish
Permits:	Northampton Nene AC - local tackle shops

Cost: Approx £10 per season
BK Rating: Difficult
Control: Club
W/A: Anglian
Comments: Lake record 29lbs. Matured gravel pit. Details from Jack Leach Tackle, Church Street, Rushden

Red House Farm Fishery A

Location: Syresham, off the A43 between Silverstone and Brackley
Type and Size: Half acre farm pond
Carp Stock: Well stocked with carp to 18lbs
Category: Mixed Fishery
Other Species: Trout and catfish
Permits: Day tickets from bungalow on site. Tel: 0869 810306 (John Harper)
Cost: £3 per day
Control: Private
Restrictions: Fishing 5am to 11.30pm - no night fishing
BK Rating: Moderate
W/A: Severn Trent
Comments: No close season. 3 self catering cottages to rent on the farm, close to the lake

River Nene

Location: Northampton, Ditchford, Peterborough, Oundle
Type and Size: River
How to Find: The River Nene runs from Peterborough to Northampton
Carp Stock: In some areas well stocked. Average 11-12lbs. Some fish to 27lbs. Quite a few 20's. Biggest reported 27lbs from Billing stretch
Category: Mixed Fishery
Other Species: General coarse fish
Permits: Various clubs and local tackle shops. Jack Leach, Church Street, Rushden
Cost: Northampton Club - approx £10; Rushden Club £6
Control: Clubs
W/A: Anglian
Comments: Location is the problem, but simple methods and baits such as corn and luncheon meat will enable fish to be caught reasonably easily. Northampton Nene AC - M Eaton, 12 Thorne Hill, Briar Hill, Northampton NN4 9SN. Rushden AA - J Leach, Anglers Dept, Rushden, Northants. Many carp at Wellingborough, Ditchford and Higham areas, average size about 14lbs. Most fish now caught on boilies

School Water

Location: Kimbolton, near Grafham Water
Type and Size: 1½ acres
How to Find: Near Kimbolton Castle
Carp Stock: Plenty of small carp to 5lbs
Category: Mixed Fishery
Other Species: General coarse fish
Permits: On site
Cost: Approx £1 per day

BK Rating: Easy
Control: Private
W/A: Anglian

Sibson Fisheries A

Location: New Lane, Stibbington, Peterborough
Type and Size: 14 acres of lakes
How to Find: Just off the A1 between Peterborough and Stamford
Carp Stock: Well stocked with carp to a good size
Category: Mixed Fishery
Other Species: Tench, bream, rudd, roach and trout
Permits: Details from the above address. Tel: Stamford (0780) 782621. Limited day tickets. Secretary - Sharon Denny. In advance only. Cost approx £3.50 per day, same for night. Season £40, book well in advance
BK Rating: Insufficient information
Control: Private
W/A: Anglian
Comments: Also two miles of river and holiday cottages at £20 per night. Trout lake. Bailiff David Moisey also provides information. Tel: Stamford (0780) 782621 (Monday to Friday 9am to 5pm), 51 Church Lane, Stibbington. Membership limit 50 for coarse waters in advance only. Strict rules

Sulby Reservoir

Location: Welford, between Kettering and Rugby, off the A50
Type and Size: Huge reservoir of about 100 acres
Carp Stock: Well stocked with mirrors to doubles
Category: Mixed Fishery
Other Species: Roach and bream
Permits: British Waterways, Willow Grange, Church Road, Watford, Herts. Tel: Watford 26722
Cost: Season tickets only (limited) at £17
Control: British Waterways
BK Rating: Moderate
W/A: Severn Trent
Comments: These big BW reservoirs certainly contain carp, although they may be hard to find in such a huge area. There could well be some very big fish caught from them in the future

Sywell Reservoir

Location: Sywell Country Park, 6 miles from Northampton off the A45; between Earls Barton and Mears Ashby
Type and Size: 20 acre reservoir
Carp Stock: Some good carp, numbers and sizes not known
Category: Mixed Fishery
Other Species: Famous as a big tench water; also pike over 20lbs, perch and roach
Permits: Members only water of Wellingborough and District AC. Season tickets about £5 from local tackle shops, or Wellingborough and District AC, Mr H Battison, 36 Church Way, Weston Favell, Northampton
Control: Club. Tel: 0604 810970
BK Rating: Difficult

Restrictions: No day tickets - members only
W/A: Anglian
Comments: Day tickets at £2 per day, to be purchased before fishing from the Warden and local tackle shops. Very busy at weekends

Thrapston Gravel Pit

Location: Thrapston, near Kettering
Type and Size: Huge gravel pit of 300 acres - 3 miles round
How to Find: Just off the A605 at Thrapston
Carp Stock: Unknown - some small fish but a few very big carp; small head of doubles, mostly commons from the river
Category: Few Carp
Other Species: General coarse fish
Permits: Permits from Jack Leach Fishing Tackle, Church Street, Rushden
Cost: Approx £18 per season
BK Rating: Super-Difficult
Comments: Possibly the biggest gravel pit in the country - and could contain some of the biggest fish. Carp have bred and some small carp have been caught recently. Heavily match fished with many boats. Poor access and very long walks

Weedon Road Gravel Pits

Location: Weedon Road, Northampton
Type and Size: Mature lake of about 15 acres
How to Find: In Northampton
Carp Stock: Low density - lake records 24lbs, but there are said to be bigger fish
Category: Few Carp
Other Species: General coarse fish - large tench
Permits: Northampton Nene AC - local tackle shops.
Cost: Approx £10 per season
BK Rating: Difficult
Control: Club
W/A: Anglian
Comments: Northampton Nene AC. Secretary: M Eaton, 12 Thorne Hill, Briar Hill, Northampton NN4 9SN. Permits supplied

NORTH YORKSHIRE

Acaster Malbis Lake

Location: Acaster, York
Type and Size: Lake of 2 acres
How to Find: Take the A64 south from York to the village of Acaster
Carp Stock: Quite well stocked with carp to about 20lbs
Category: Mixed Fishery
Other Species: Tench, roach, perch and bream
Permits: Day tickets from the office on the site, which is also a caravan site
Cost: On application
Control: Private
BK Rating: Moderate
Restrictions: No night fishing; fish from 7am until dusk
W/A: Yorkshire

Balne Lake

Location: Off the A19 near Whitely Bridge, Selby
Type and Size: Five acre lake, quite shallow, surrounded by trees, and very weedy
Carp Stock: Very heavily stocked with mirrors between 5lbs and 10lbs
Category: Carp Water
Other Species: Roach
Permits: Season tickets only from local tackle shops - sometimes on the bank from owner
Control: Balne Moor AC
Restrictions: No night fishing; no carp sacks
BK Rating: Very Easy - multiple catches common
W/A: Yorkshire

Barlow Common Pond

Location: Barlow, near Selby
Type and Size: 4 acre lake with an irregular bottom, and quite shallow
Carp Stock: Well stocked with very small carp to about 5lbs, with the occasional double from the original stocking
Category: Mixed Fishery
Other Species: Roach, bream and tench
Permits: Day tickets on bank
Cost: £1.50 per day
Control: Private
Restrictions: No night fishing
BK Rating: Easy
W/A: Yorkshire
Comments: This is a very weedy, shallow lake, which is a Nature Reserve, so part of the bank cannot be fished

Birkdale Fishery

Location: Terrington, near York
Type and Size: Small, attractive lake in pleasant surroundings
Carp Stock: Well stocked with carp to 15lbs
Category: Mixed Fishery
Other Species: Tench, roach and bream
Permits: Day tickets on bank, or can be booked on 065 384 301
Cost: £3 per day
Control: Private
BK Rating: Moderate
Comments: Suitable for disabled anglers

Carlton Towers

Location: Off the A1041 south of Selby, and close to the M62
Type and Size: 10 acre lake in grounds of a stately home
Carp Stock: Not many, to upper doubles
Category: Few Carp
Other Species: Tench, roach, bream, perch and crucians
Permits: Carlton AC - season tickets only; enquire on 0405 860791
Restrictions: Fishing the field bank only. No night fishing
BK Rating: Very Difficult
W/A: Yorkshire
Comments: Not much fished by carp anglers - a very attractive, shallow water with much weed and lilies

Cawood Park A

Location: Cawood, near Tadcaster
Type and Size: Three acre park lake
How to Find: From Tadcaster take the A162 towards Sherburn-in-Elmet, then turn left onto the B1223 towards Selby. After the village of Ryther, the lake will be found just before Cawood, on the right
Carp Stock: Said to be well stocked with carp, sizes not known
Category: Mixed Fishery
Other Species: Large pike, roach, perch, chub, bream, pike, trout and tench

Permits: Day tickets from the site warden
Cost: Day - £2; week - £10; from 5pm onwards - £1; season - £35
Control: Private. Details of fishing and caravans and bungalows to rent from Mr W G Archer, tel: Cawood 450 or Site Warden, tel: Cawood 8865
BK Rating: Not known
Restrictions: No keepnets except in matches. All trout to be returned immediately
W/A: Yorkshire
Comments: This is a caravan site and park, with luxury caravans and bungalows to rent. Licensed bar, children's boating pond and amusements. Trout fishing from March 25th

Delves Lakes

Location: Thorne, near Selby
Type and Size: Two small lakes
How to Find: Off the A164, between Selby and Snaith
Carp Stock: Some carp to doubles
Category: Probably Few Carp
Other Species: Big bream, roach and perch
Permits: Day tickets on site - for details contact Mrs S J Bee, Ridgways, St. Nicholas Road, Thorne, Doncaster (low cost)
Control: Club - Thorne and Moorends Angling Club, membership open to all. Details from Mrs Bee
BK Rating: Difficult
W/A: Yorkshire
Comments: Pleasant surroundings, with lilies on the lakes. Clubhouse with refreshments and toilets. Good facilities for disabled anglers

Drax Lake

Location: Drax, near Selby - off the A1041 between Selby and Goole
Type and Size: Attractive, estate type lake of about 10 acres
Carp Stock: Well stocked with carp to upper 20's, heavily weeded and surrounded by trees
Permits: Season ticket only - Mr G Simms, 2 Oaklands, Camblesforth, Selby
Cost: £10 joining fee, then £8 per season - reduced prices for juniors and OAP's
Control: Private
Restrictions: No sacks, weighing slings or radio-controlled boats
BK Rating: Easy
W/A: Yorkshire
Comments: A very pleasant water, though weedy and lines of 10-12lbs BS are recommended. All methods are successful including floating baits

Dringhouses Lake

Location: Southern outskirts of York City
Type and Size: 3 acre lake
How to Find: From York take the A1036 Tadcaster road. The lake is about 3 miles from the city centre
Carp Stock: Well stocked with a number of doubles to about 20lbs
Category: Mixed Fishery
Other Species: Pike, roach, rudd, chub and perch

Permits: Day tickets from house on site, must be obtained before fishing
Cost: On application - extra cost if not bought before starting to fish
Control: Private
BK Rating: Moderate
Restrictions: Night fishing on car park bank only
W/A: Yorkshire
Comments: Pleasant water with trees, but quite heavily fished

Elvington Lake

Location: Elvington, near York
Type and Size: Lake of 3½ acres
How to Find: Take the B1228 from York towards Elvington to the south east of the city. The lake is just over 5 miles from York
Carp Stock: The lake is well stocked with carp, with plenty of small ones but some doubles to about 15lbs. Bigger fish are said to have been caught
Category: Mixed Fishery
Other Species: Trout, roach, rudd, tench, chub, perch. There are rumoured to be one or two barbel in the water
Permits: Day tickets from the house on the property - Mr T Britten, Lake Cottage, Elvington, York. Tel: Elvington 255
Control: Private
BK Rating: Easy
Restrictions: No night fishing, no groundbait
W/A: Yorkshire

Fairview Lake

Location: In Broad Lane, Cawood Common, near Selby
Type and Size: Small lake
How to Find: Take the B1233 from Selby, and the lake is near the intersection with the B1222
Carp Stock: Well stocked with carp, sizes unknown
Category: Mixed Fishery
Other Species: Tench, rudd, perch and rainbow trout
Permits: Day tickets from the cottage on the banks of the fishery
BK Rating: Moderate
Control: Private
W/A: Yorkshire
Comments: A pleasant and attractive lake

Gowdall Pond

Location: New Gowdall, Hemingbrough, near Selby
Type and Size: Small pond of just over one acre, weedy and shallow
Carp Stock: Quite well stocked with carp to middle doubles
Category: Mixed Fishery
Other Species: Roach and bream
Permits: Day tickets on site
Cost: £2 per rod per day
Control: Private
Restrictions: No night fishing, day tickets only
BK Rating: Moderate
W/A: Yorkshire

Grafton Mere A

Location: Marton-cum-Grafton, Boroughbridge
Type and Size: Man-made lake of 2½ acres, spring fed
How to Find: This village is between York and Ripon. Take the B65265 from Boroughbridge to York. After 3 miles turn right to Grafton
Carp Stock: 8 doubles to 18lbs; 80 of 5-10lbs; 200 of 2lbs+, stocked in 1987
Category: Carp Only
Other Species: None
Permits: Prospect Farm. Tel: 0423 322045 (Roger Naish)
Cost: On application
BK Rating: Easy
Control: Private
Restrictions: Barbless hooks
W/A: Yorkshire
Comments: 100 yards from good pub. Bus service to York which is 16 miles. Three holiday cottages and bed and breakfast in 18th century working farm. Ideal centre for family holiday near Yorkshire Moors, dales and coast

Hay-A-Park

Location: Knaresborough
Type and Size: Gravel pit, 60 acres
How to Find: The lake is in Chain Lane on the edge of Knaresborough
Carp Stock: Few to 25lb
Category: Few Carp
Other Species: Bream, roach, rudd, tench, pike and perch
Permits: M and C Johnson Fishing Tackle, Briggate, Knaresborough. Tel: Harrogate 863065. Permits must be obtained before fishing
Control: Private
Restrictions: Water open June 1st to end February only
Baits/Methods: Normal carp tactics and baits
BK Rating: Fairly Hard
W/A: Yorkshire
Comments: Large open clear water with much weed. Mainly big fish of most species

Knaresborough Lagoon

Location: Stockwell Lane, Knaresborough
Type and Size: 36 acre disused gravel pit
Carp Stock: Some carp to 29lbs
Category: Few Carp
Other Species: Pike, bream and tench
Permits: Day tickets from tackle shops in Knaresborough and Harrogate
Control: Knaresborough Piscatorials
BK Rating: Very Difficult
W/A: Yorkshire
Comments: A very clear water, and hard to fish. Recent restocking

Lightwater Valley Lake

Location: Lightwater Valley Theme Park, near Sheffield
Type and Size: 15 acre lake
Carp Stock: Well stocked with small carp to doubles
Category: Mixed Fishery
Other Species: Roach and bream
Permits: Day tickets on site at £1 per rod
Control: Private
Restrictions: No *day* fishing! Fishing is 6pm to 9am only
BK Rating: Easy
W/A: Yorkshire
Comments: Too many people on the park during the day, so only night fishing is allowed. Possibly no close season. Three rods allowed

Lingcroft Farm Pond

Location: One mile south off the York by-pass on the A19 towards Selby; farm is on the right
Type and Size: Small farm pond with large island
Carp Stock: Recently stocked with carp, sizes and numbers not known
Category: Mixed Fishery
Other Species: Bream, chub and roach
Permits: Day tickets from the farmhouse, cost £1.50
BK Rating: Not known
Control: Private
Restrictions: No arrivals before 8am; no night fishing. Barbless hooks and no groundbait
W/A: Yorkshire
Comments: Much wildlife on this very pleasant fishery, so no litter and no left line, which damages wildlife. All proceeds from the fishery are donated to Fulford Church - this is a new one to us; could it start a trend?

Newhay Lake

Location: Newhay Carp Farm, near Selby
Type and Size: 2½ acre lake
How to Find: Take the A63 from Selby, and at Hemingborough turn right to Newhay
Carp Stock: Well stocked with carp to upper doubles
Category: Mixed Fishery
Other Species: Bream, tench, chub, roach and perch
Permits: Day tickets on site. Details on 0756 638383
Control: Private
BK Rating: Moderate
Restrictions: No night fishing - fishing times are from 8am till dusk
W/A: Yorkshire
Comments: No close season

Northingales Fish Ponds

Location: Cawood, near York
Type and Size: Two ponds of 2 acres and 1 acre
How to Find: Take the A19 south from York towards Selby, and turn off on B1222 to Cawood

Carp Stock: Both lakes contain some carp and the bigger one has fish to about 15lbs
Category: Mixed Fishery
Carp Stock: Tench, roach, bream, perch, dace, trout and gudgeon
Permits: Day tickets from the house at the site, cost approx £1.50. Details from the owner on Cawood 414
Control: Private
BK Rating: Moderate
Restrictions: One rod only. No night fishing. No juniors (under 16) unless accompanied by an adult. No groundbait
W/A: Yorkshire

Pumping Station Lakes

Location: Angram, Barlby, near Selby
Type and Size: Two lakes of about 2 acres each, both of which are fairly deep and weedy
Carp Stock: Well stocked with carp to double figures
Category: Mixed Fishery
Other Species: Coarse fish
Permits: None necessary - free fishing
Control: Council
Restrictions: No night fishing
BK Rating: Moderate
W/A: Yorkshire

Racecourse Lake

Location: Near Ripon
Type and Size: Pit of about an acre
How to Find: The fishery is about 1½ miles south of Ripon
Carp Stock: Quite well stocked with carp which include a number of doubles. Bigger fish are rumoured
Category: Mixed Fishery
Other Species: Bream, rudd, tench, roach
Permits: Season tickets from Ripon Piscatorial Angling Association. Mainly membership only for locals but some tickets for those from outside the area. Details from the Secretary: Mr R Looney, 12 Lower Street, Agnes St Ripon, or P Godden, 3 Oak Road, Ripon. SAE required. Day tickets about £3 from Ripon Angling Centre, North Street, Ripon
Control: Club
BK Rating: Moderate
W/A: Yorkshire

Scarborough Mere

Location: In the town of Scarborough, off the Seamer Road
Type and Size: 18 acre mere
Carp Stock: Some carp to doubles
Category: Probably Few Carp
Other Species: Bream, tench, roach and pike
Permits: From bailiff on bank, or from Buckleys Tackle Shop, Leading Post Street, Scarborough. Low cost
Control: Scarborough Mere Angling Club

BK Rating: Probably Difficult for the bigger carp
W/A: Yorkshire
Comments: Refreshments on site during summer

Scrapyard Pond

Location: Drax, between Selby and Goole
Type and Size: Shallow ballast pit of about 2 acres
Carp Stock: Not very many, but some doubles to about 20lbs
Category: Few Carp
Other Species: Roach, perch and tench
Permits: British Rail Staff Association - enquire from the scrapyard or try G Harcome, 8 Upper Belmont Road, St. Andrews, Bristol - possibly day tickets
Control: British Rail
BK Rating: Very Difficult
W/A: Yorkshire

Shearons Pond

Location: Goose Hill, Carlton, near Selby
Type and Size: 2 acre lake, specially dug about 25 years ago
Carp Stock: Very heavily stocked with commons and mirrors from 5lbs to low doubles
Category: Carp Water
Other Species: Some coarse fish
Permits: Free to holders of a Yorkshire W/A licence
Restrictions: Nigh fishing is allowed
BK Rating: Very Easy
Baits/Methods: Good floater water, but any bait and method works well
Comments: Good lake all the year round, and ideal for a practice water

Staveley Lakes

Location: Staveley, between Harrogate and Ripon
Type and Size: Two lakes of three acres and two acres
How to Find: Take the A6055 from Knaresborough and turn left going north to Staveley
Carp Stock: Quite well stocked with carp to about 16lbs with a number of doubles. Fished of over 20lbs rumoured
Category: Mixed Fishery
Other Species: Tench, chub, rudd, perch and bream
Permits: Bradford City Angling Association. Season tickets from Mr H Briggs, 4 Brown Hill Close, Birkenshaw, Bradford, West Yorkshire
Control: Club
BK Rating: Moderate
W/A: Yorkshire

Angling Books and Videos: Best Sellers see page ii

Three Lakes

Location: Selby
Type and Size: Lake of about 4 acres, two other lakes, 8 acres in all
Carp Stock: Well stocked with carp to over 20lbs
Category: Mixed Fishery
Other Species: Reported are tench to 8lbs, eels to 6lbs, bream to 11lb, large perch, roach and trout
Permits: Day tickets, details from Paul Howgego. Tel: Selby 706065
Cost: Approx £2 per day for each lake
Control: Private
Baits/Methods: Normal carp fishing baits and methods. Boilies good
Restrictions: No groundbait, special permission needed for night fishing
BK Rating: Easy
W/A: Yorkshire
Comments: Catches of up to a dozen fish a day reported. many snags and sunken trees. Rumours of bigger fish. Many good 20's reported caught in 1991

Tollerton Cross Lanes Pond A

Location: Just off the A19, 10 miles from York and three miles from Tollerton
Type and Size: Three small ponds
Carp Stock: Quite a number of doubles, with the record at 28lbs
Category: Mixed Fishery
Other Species: Tench, perch, roach, chub and pike
Permits: If you arrive before 7am you can start fishing, and pay on the bank; for arrivals after 7am you can buy your day ticket from the house
Cost: £2.50 per day
Control: Private; Margaret Wackerman on 03473 336
Restrictions: No night fishing; dawn till dusk only; no groundbaiting; no keepnets for carp
BK Rating: Moderate
W/A: Yorkshire
Comments: Bed and breakfast at £10 per night, to include a day's fishing. Pleasant looking ponds, close together, with reeds etc

Welham Lake

Location: Norton Golf Club, Malton
Type and Size: 5 acre lake
How to Find: Take the Welham road from Malton, and follow the sign to Malton and Norton Golf Club. The lake is in woodland to the right after entering the golf course
Carp Stock: Stocked with carp in 1988, sizes not known
Category: Probably Few Carp, though might become a Mixed Fishery
Other Species: Tench and eels
Permits: Permits only in advance before visiting. Booking advised, from Mike O'Donnell, Moorland Trout Lake, Pickering. Tel: Pickering 73101
Cost: £5 per day
Control: Private
BK Rating: Insufficient information
Restrictions: 8 anglers only per day. No permits on bank
Comments: A famous tench water, and very picturesque

Whitfield Reservoir

Location: Barrows Lane, Steeton, off the A629 Keighley-Skipton road
Type and Size: Small reservoir
Carp Stock: Some carp, numbers and sizes not known, but thought to be at least to double figure size
Category: Few Carp or Mixed Fishery
Other Species: Pike, roach, tench and perch
Permits: Keighley Angling Club - members only but open to all - Mr D Ward, 4 Compeigne Avenue, Keighley, North Yorkshire
Control: Club
W/A: Yorkshire

Wistow Pit

Location: Broad Lane, Cawood Common, on the A1222 south of York
Type and Size: Very attractive three acre lake
Carp Stock: Well stocked with carp to low doubles, with possibly one or two just reaching 20lbs
Category: Mixed Fishery
Other Species: Tench, roach and bream
Permits: Day tickets on bank
Cost: About £1.50 per rod
Control: Private
Restrictions: No night fishing
BK Rating: Difficult
W/A: Yorkshire

Yorkshire Lakeside Lodges

Location: Outskirts of York, formerly known as 'Hoggy's Pond'
Type and Size: Small pool
How to Find: Edge of York
Carp Stock: Well stocked with carp to doubles
Category: Mixed Fishery
Other Species: Tench
Permits: Tel: York 702346
Cost: On application
BK Rating: Moderate
Control: Private
W/A: Yorkshire
Comments: Full details from the phone number above

NOTTINGHAMSHIRE

Arches Lake

Location: East Retford, off the A638
Type and Size: Small, attractive lake near town
Carp Stock: Some carp to over 20lbs
Category: Mixed Fishery
Other Species: Roach, tench and bream
Permits: Sheffield Piscatorial Association; enquire from tackle shops in Sheffield
Control: Small club, with waters not heavily fished
BK Rating: Difficult, as there are not large numbers of carp
W/A: Severn Trent

Attenborough North

Location: Long Lane, Attenborough, Beeston
Type and Size: 7 gravel pits from 13 acres to 43 acres
How to Find: Off the A6005 Beeston road through Attenborough village
Carp Stock: Not known - some carp to 13lbs
Category: Few Carp
Other Species: General coarse fish
Permits: Season tickets only
Cost: £21.00

BK Rating: Not known
Control: Leisure Sport Angling, Staines Road, Chertsey, Surrey. Tel: 0932 562633
Restrictions: No night fishing
W/A: Severn Trent
Comments: Site of Special Scientific Interest

Attenborough South (River Trent)

Location: Barton Lane, Long Eaton, Nottingham
Type and Size: Gravel pit of 114 acres; 2,500 metres of the River Trent
How to Find: Station Road, Long Eaton. Take New Hythe Street, opposite Horseshoe Sports Tackle Shop for one mile to municipal car park
Carp Stock: There may be no carp in the lake, but carp to 31lbs have been reported from the River Trent area
Category: Few Carp
Other Species: Mixed coarse fish
Permits: Frank Russel 'Wotsits' Tackle Shop, 8 Archer Road, Stapleford, Nottingham. Tel: Nottingham 396096. Day tickets
Cost: On application
BK Rating: Very Difficult
Control: Leisure Sport Angling, Staines Road, Chertsey, Surrey. Tel: 0932 562633
Restrictions: No night fishing, dawn to dusk only
W/A: Severn Trent
Comments: Main interest is in the river but it should be noted that this is regarded as a separate fishery, with fishing only allowed when no matches are taking place

Bestwood Pond

Location: Near Nottingham
Type and Size: Medium sized pool
How to Find: Enquire locally
Carp Stock: Well stocked, sizes not known
Category: Mixed Fishery
Other Species: General coarse fishing
Permits: Notts AA - local tackle shops
Cost: On application
BK Rating: Insufficient information
Control: Club
W/A: Severn Trent
Comments: Try local tackle shops for information, and also Nottingham and District Federation, W Belshaw, 17 Spring Green, Clifton Estate, Nottingham; and Notts AA, E J Collin, 224 Radford Boulevard, Nottingham NG7 5QG. Both supply tickets and information on other carp waters controlled by Nottingham clubs

Bleasby Lake

Location: Off the A38 between Mansfield and Sutton-in-Ashfield
Type and Size: 60 acre ancient lake, with much weed, and very shallow
Carp Stock: Not many carp, but they go to upper 20's

Category: Few Carp
Other Species: Most coarse fish
Permits: In advance only, low cost
Control: Members only water of Mansfield and District AA. Secretary: A Quick, 138 Huthwaite Road, Sutton-in-Ashfield NG17 2GX
BK Rating: Very Difficult
W/A: Severn Trent
Comments: This is a beautiful lake, but is very hard to fish, and very few carp are caught. In hot weather in the summer the weed makes the lake very difficult to fish, and you should only tackle this one if you are prepared for many long blanks

Butterley Reservoir

Location: Near Ripley
Type and Size: Medium sized reservoir
How to Find: No information. Try local tackle shops
Carp Stock: Well stocked, sizes not known
Category: Mixed Fishery
Other Species: General coarse fish
Permits: Ripley and District AA. From local tackle shops - day tickets
Cost: On application
BK Rating: Moderate
Control: Club
W/A: Severn Trent
Comments: Little known - try locally, Ripley and District AA - R Turner, 2a Argyll Road, Ripley - ticket supplied

Coach House Pond

Location: The Coaching House, Tickhill, Bawtry
Type and Size: Very tiny estate pond
Carp Stock: Not many carp, but a possible 20
Category: Few Carp
Other Species: Tench and roach
Permits: On application from the house on the property - enquire locally for information
Control: Private
Restrictions: No night fishing, except by arrangement
BK Rating: Difficult
W/A: Severn Trent

Daneshill Lake

Location: Daneshill Road, Torworth
Type and Size: 21 acre lake
How to Find: Just off the A1 north west of East Retford, near the main railway line
Carp Stock: Stocked in 1984 with 48 carp to 11lbs, but commons to 23lbs reported
Category: Mixed Fishery
Other Species: General coarse fish
Permits: Day tickets on site
Cost: Approx £1 per day; £10 per season - night syndicate £50
BK Rating: Moderate

Control: Rotherham Carp Bait Specialist, 28 Westgate, Rotherham, Yorks. Tel: 363085
Restrictions: Night fishing reserved for syndicate. No inflatable boats
W/A: Severn Trent

Erewash Canal

Location: Long Eaton area
Type and Size: 12 mile canal
How to Find: Close to M1 from Long Eaton northwards
Carp Stock: Some good carp
Category: Mixed Fishery
Other Species: General coarse fish
Permits: Local tackle shops
Cost: On application
Control: Long Eaton AA and Long Eaton Victoria AS
BK Rating: Moderate
W/A: Severn Trent
Comments: Once polluted, this canal is now restored and restocked, and it holds some good specimen fish. Long Eaton AA, W Parker, 75 College Street, Long Eaton, Notts; Long Eaton Victoria AS, D Kent, 18 Collingwood Road, Long Eaton, Notts. Permits available from both club secretaries

Grantham Canal

Location: Bottesford, to the west of Grantham
Type and Size: Attractive, very narrow and reeded canal stretch, with few boats
How to Find: Take the A52 Grantham to Bottesford road, then the Easthorpe road to Bottesford
Carp Stock: Some carp to over 10lbs
Category: Mixed Fishery
Other Species: Tench, bream and roach
Permits: Day and season tickets on bank, or from Matchman Supplies, Nottingham
Cost: £1.50 per day; £6 per season
Control: Bottesford DAA - Norman Chenoweth, tel: 0602 335793
Restrictions: No night fishing
BK Rating: Difficult, at least until the carp are located
W/A: Severn Trent

Hartshill Reservoir

Location: Hartshill, Worksop, off the A57
Type and Size: Two lakes of 20 acres and 5 acres, both heavily weeded
Carp Stock: Both stocked with a few big carp, most of which are doubles
Category: Few Carp
Other Species: Most coarse fish
Permits: Day tickets on bank
Control: Worksop and District AA. Secretary: R Whitehead, 72 Dryden Vale, Worksop
Restrictions: No night fishing, and sailing in daytime
BK Rating: Very Difficult
W/A: Severn Trent

Iron Mongers Pond

Location: Wilford, Nottingham
Type and Size: Small man-made pond
Carp Stock: Said to be some carp, numbers and sizes not known
Category: Mixed Fishery
Other Species: Usual coarse fish
Permits: Day tickets from bailiff on bank
Control: Nottingham AA
BK Rating: Not known
W/A: Severn Trent

Langold Lake

Location: Near Worksop
Type and Size: Big old gravel pit, very attractive, of more than 20 acres in size
Carp Stock: Not many, but most are doubles with a possible 20
Category: Few Carp
Other Species: Most coarse fish
Permits: Day tickets from bailiff on site
Cost: £3 per day
Control: Private
Restrictions: No night fishing; no season tickets; two rods only
BK Rating: Difficult
W/A: Severn Trent
Comments: A busy and heavily fished water, though as there are so few carp there are not many carp anglers

Lound Windsurf Lake

Location: Chainbridge Lane, Lound, East Retford
Type and Size: Large lake
How to Find: Off the A638, north of East Retford
Carp Stock: Some carp to over 20lbs, including commons to 27lbs
Category: Mixed Fishery
Other Species: General coarse fish
Permits: East Midlands Windsurf Centre on lake shore
Cost: About £80 per season
BK Rating: Moderate
Control: Private
Restrictions: None
W/A: Severn Trent
Comments: Obviously, there will be windsurfing on this lake! Weedy at times

Manor House Fishery

Location: North Muskham, near Newark
Type and Size: Three lakes, North Muskham, near Newark and a stretch of the River Trent (largest 12 acres)
How to Find: Find North Muskham, which is north of Newark, near the A1
Carp Stock: Some good bags of small carp of under 5lbs are taken from the Trent in this area though there is always the chance of bigger fish. No. 1 lake to 27lbs
Category: Mixed Fishery

Other Species: Roach, chub, bream, dace, tench, pike, bleak and gudgeon
Permits: Day tickets from the owner at his house on site, Walter Bower - Tel: 0636 702457
Cost: £2 per day
Restrictions: Fishing 6am to 7pm only
Control: Private
W/A: Severn Trent

Newark Dyke

Location: Just north of Newark-upon-Trent
Type and Size: Short cut off the main River Trent, much used for match fishing
Carp Stock: Not many, but fish over 20lbs have been caught
Category: Few Carp
Other Species: Chub, roach, barbel and gudgeon
Permits: Day tickets on bank
Cost: £2 per day - no season tickets
Control: Newark and District AA
BK Rating: Very Difficult
W/A: Severn Trent

Nottingham - Grantham Canal

Location: Winding canal, between both towns - Nottingham and Grantham
Type and Size: Narrow, canal many miles in length
Category: Mixed Fishery
Other Species: Most coarse fish
Permits: Different clubs - enquire from tackle shops in both towns
BK Rating: Difficult, until fish located, but in the heavily stocked areas it is quite easy
W/A: Severn Trent

River Trent

Location: Dunham Bridge
Type and Size: Large river
How to Find: West bank near Dunham Bridge, off the A57 Lincoln-Sheffield road
Carp Stock: All sizes up to 22lbs (commons)
Category: Mixed Fishery
Other Species: General coarse fish
Permits: From local tackle shops. Sheffield and District AA, PO Box 218, Sheffield S1 1BU
Cost: £5 per season
BK Rating: Difficult
Control: Club
Restrictions: Heavily match fished
W/A: Severn Trent
Comments: Tidal water

Sapphire Lake

Location: Norwell Road, Cromwell, near Newark-on-Trent
Type and Size: 12 acre lake
How to Find: On the A1 just north of Newark; the Morwell road

Carp Stock: Heavily stocked with carp to 25lbs, best 30lbs. A 35 pounder is rumoured
Category: Mixed Fishery
Other Species: Bream, perch and eels
Permits: On site. Tel: 0636 821131
Cost: £2 per day
BK Rating: Moderate
Control: Private - Ken Barker
Restrictions: Line below 10lbs BS banned in certain areas. Car keys must be left with owners when night fishing
W/A: Severn Trent
Comments: A widely publicised fishery with big catches recorded - many doubles and some twenties

Shireoaks Hall Lake

Location: Shireoaks, just of the A57 between Worksop and Sheffield
Type and Size: Four lakes of about 2½ acres on estate
Carp Stock: Very heavily stocked with small carp to low doubles
Category: Carp Water
Permits: Day tickets on bank at low cost
Control: Private
Restrictions: No night fishing
BK Rating: Very Easy
W/A: Severn Trent
Comments: Big catches common on standard baits. Bar and cafe on bank; ideal for beginners

South Muskham Fisheries (A1 Pits) A

Location: South Muskham, near Newark-on-Trent
Type and Size: 6 gravel pits, and stretch of River Trent
How to Find: Turn off the A1 at North Muskham. The entrance is by the rail crossing
Carp Stock: Very well stocked with many carp of up to 25lbs+; many commons
Category: Mixed Fishery
Other Species: General coarse fish, pike to 20lbs and big bream
Permits: On bank
Cost: £2.50 per day and £2 for night. Season - £100
BK Rating: Moderate
Control: Private
Restrictions: None
W/A: Severn Trent
Comments: These big gravel pits flood from the River Trent at times. Holiday accommodation: The Old House, North Muskham, Newark. Tel: 0636 706886. Guest house and self-catering. The 40 acre and 30 acre pits are best for carp. Cars can be driven to the swim. Can be noisy at times

Steetly Pool

Location: The village of Shireoaks, between Worksop and Sheffield
Type and Size: 4 acre quarry, quite attractive
Carp Stock: Well stocked with small carp to about 10lbs, with one or two slightly bigger fish also present

Category: Mixed Fishery
Other Species: Roach, bream and tench
Permits: In advance only from Steetly Concrete Office, Shireoaks
Control: Steetly Concrete Co
Restrictions: No day tickets on bank; no Sunday fishing; one bank private; no night fishing
BK Rating: Moderate
W/A: Severn Trent

Windmill Farm

Location: Windmill Farm, Spalford, near Newark. Tel: 0522 77305
Type and Size: Small farm lakes
Carp Stock: Well stocked with carp to doubles
Category: Carp Water
Other Species: Possibly a few
Permits: From the owner at the address above
Cost: £2 per day - £2.50 for night fishing
Control: Private
BK Rating: Not known
W/A: Severn Trent
Comments: Tents and touring caravans allowed at this fishery - good facilities provided

Windthorpe Pits

Location: Close to the A1, near Newark
Type and Size: 25 acre gravel pit, connected to the River Trent - very deep, with little cover
Carp Stock: Plenty of doubles, and possibly a few twenties
Category: Mixed Fishery
Other Species: Pike, roach, tench, bream and perch
Permits: Day tickets from the house close to the pit
Control: Sheffield Angling Club - season tickets from F Turner, 30 Mather Walk, Sheffield, or 142-144 Princes Street, Sheffield
Restrictions: Night fishing is allowed
BK Rating: Difficult
W/A: Severn Trent

Winthorpe Lake

Location: Off the Newark-Gainsborough road, near Newark
Type and Size: 20 acre gravel pit
Carp Stock: Quite well stocked with carp to 22lbs
Category: Mixed Fishery
Other Species: Usual coarse fish
Permits: Sheffield and District AA. Secretary: F E Turner, 30 Mather Walk, Sheffield S9 4GL, or 142-144 Princes Street, Sheffield S4 YUW
Control: Club
BK Rating: Moderate
W/A: Severn Trent
Comments: This water is very heavily match fished. The permit also includes some good fishing on the River Trent in the same area, with plenty of carp from 8lbs to 22lbs

Woodsetts Pond

Location: Woodsett, near Dinnington, off the A57 between Worksop and Sheffield
Type and Size: 5 acre sand pit, locally known as 'The Quarry'
Carp Stock: Quite well stocked with carp to upper doubles
Category: Mixed Fishery
Other Species: Tench and roach
Permits: Day tickets on bank
Control: Worksop and District AA. Secretary: R Whitehead, 72 Dryden Walk, Worksop
Restrictions: No night fishing
BK Rating: Very Difficult
W/A: Severn Trent
Comments: This quarry is deep and weedy, which perhaps is why it is so hard, as it is quite well stocked with good sized carp

Woodsetts Quarry Pond

Location: Off the A57 Worksop to Sheffield road, near Worksop
Type and Size: Small disused quarry
Carp Stock: Said to be some carp; numbers and sizes not known
Category: Mixed Fishery
Other Species: Roach, bream and tench
Permits: Day tickets from bailiff on bank
Control: Worksop and District AA
BK Rating: Not known
W/A: Severn Trent

OXFORDSHIRE

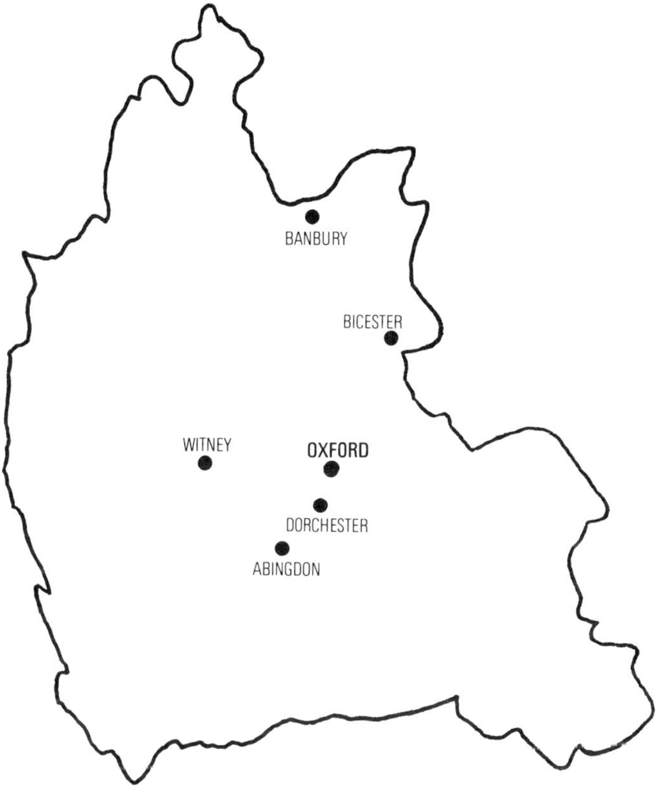

Dorchester Lagoon

Location: Dorchester Fisheries, Abingdon, Dorchester OX10 7LP. Tel: 0865 341810 (between 8am and 6pm only)
Type and Size: 40 acre gravel pit
Carp Stock: In the past there were only one or two carp, though one was probably a 30. Recent restocking included some doubles and 20's
Category: Mixed Fishery
Other Species: Tench, roach, bream and pike
Permits: Day and season tickets from Paul Bray at the address above
Control: Dorchester Fisheries, which also include Orchid Lake, Queenford Lagoon, Club Lake and several miles of the River Thames
BK Rating: Fairly Hard
W/A: Thames
Comments: Under new management - this complex was recently bought from ARC by David DeVere, owner of Old Bury Hill Lake, an excellent water containing big carp, which is near Dorking in Surrey

Dukes Lake

Location: Oxford
Type and Size: 4 acre town lake
Carp Stock: Carp to doubles
Category: Mixed Fishery
Other Species: Tench, rudd and pike
Permits: North Oxford AS - Secretary, P Jackman, 1 Churchill Road, Kidlington, Oxford. Tel: Kidlington 79582
Control: Club
BK Rating: Moderate
W/A: Thames

Horse and Groom Inn A

Location: Milcombe, near Banbury
Type and Size: Small lake
How to Find: Just off the A361 between Banbury and Chipping Norton
Carp Stock: Carp to 15lbs
Category: Mixed Fishery
Other Species: General coarse fish
Permits: Horse and Groom Inn, Milcombe. Tel: Banbury 720471
Cost: On application
Control: Private
BK Rating: No information
W/A: Thames
Comments: 16th century inn, bed and breakfast, games room, skittle alley, 220 acres of rough shooting. Edge of Cotswolds

Linch Hill Fishery A

Location: Standlake, Stanton Harcourt, near Oxford
Type and Size: Large gravel pit
How to Find: West of Oxford
Carp Stock: Some big carp to 25lbs+
Category: Mixed Fishery
Other Species: General coarse fish
Permits: S D Lawson, Linch Hill Leisure Park, Stanton Harcourt, Oxford. Tel: 882215
Cost: On application
BK Rating: Moderate
Control: Private
Restrictions: Not known
W/A: Thames
Comments: Accommodation - Hardwick Park, Downs Road, Standlake, Oxon. Tel: 0993 7752728 or 086731 501. Caravan and camping park with a few letting vans, and also 45 acre lake for fishing and sailing

Marlborough Pool

Location: On the A40 between Witney and Oxford
Type and Size: Mature gravel pit of 11 acres
Carp Stock: Well stocked with carp many years ago which have gone to over 20lbs
Category: Carp Water

Permits: Oxford Angling and Preservation Society. M Baston, 28 Mayfield Road, Farmoor, Oxford. Tel: 0865 862426
BK Rating: Moderate
Control: Club
W/A: Thames
Comments: Quite a well-known carp water, quite heavily fished and in the past some well-known anglers have fished there

Milton Common

Location: Just off junction 7 of the M40; can be seen from the motorway
Type and Size: Three lakes of 3, 2 and 1½ acres
Carp Stock: Quite well stocked with carp to 24lbs
Category: Carp Waters
Permits: From owner on site
Cost: Approximately £1.50 per rod per day
Control: Private
BK Rating: Moderate
W/A: Thames
Comments: We could find out little about this fishery, so you will need to go to the area which is near Oxford and ask locally. We have heard that this fishery may stay open during the close season

Orchid Lake

Location: Dorchester Fisheries, Abingdon Road, Dorchester OX10 7LP. Tel: 0865 341810 (between 8am and 6pm)
Type and Size: 20 acre gravel pit
Carp Stock: Stocked in 1991 with 55 carp, most of which were over 20lbs, and 4 of which were thirties. There are now said to be about forty 20's in the lake
Category: Mixed Fishery
Other Species: Tench, roach and perch
Permits: Day and season tickets from Paul Bray at the above address
Control: Dorchester Fisheries, which also includes Dorchester Lagoon, Queenford Lagoon, Club Lake and a stretch of the River Thame
BK Rating: Moderate
W/A: Thames
Comments: Under new management - David DeVere, owner of Old Bury Hill Fisheries, bought this complex recently, and the fishing is now managed by a former British Carp Study Group member, Paul Bray. A lot of very big carp have been stocked, and this is likely to be one of the top big carp waters during the next few years

Oxford Canal

Location: Banbury
Type and Size: Midlands canal, quite narrow
How to Find: On the outskirts of Banbury
Carp Stock: Plenty of carp to 15lbs+
Category: Mixed Fishery
Other Species: General coarse fish
Permits: Local tackle shops
Cost: On application

Control: Club
BK Rating: Moderate
W/A: Severn Trent
Comments: Once you can find an area containing carp, they are not hard to catch. Average 6–8lbs. Good winter fishing. Banbury and District AA, D Brewer, 42 Stanwell Lea, Middleton Cheney, Banbury, Oxon for tickets. A fish kill took place on the canal in the Banbury area in 1991

Oxford Quarry

Location: Near Stanton Harcourt, Oxford
Type and Size: Gravel pit of 16 acres
How to Find: Lake is off the B4449 road between Eynsham and Standlake
Carp Stock: Small number of carp to about 25lbs
Category: Few Carp
Other Species: Rudd, chub, tench, catfish, pike
Permits: Vauxhall Motors Angling Club, season tickets. Secretary: Mr B Matthews, 88 Langford Drive, Luton, Beds. Tel: Luton 419489
Cost: On application
Control: Club
BK Rating: Difficult
W/A: Thames
Comments: One side shallow with gravel bars. Carp baits taken mainly by chub. Best method stalking individual fish often close in

Pickford Lake

Location: Oxford
Type and Size: Small town lake
Carp Stock: Well stocked with carp to 10lbs
Category: Mixed Fishery
Other Species: Tench
Permits: North Oxford AS (members only). Secretary: P Jackman, 1 Churchill Road, Kidlington, Oxford. Tel: Kidlington 79582
Control: Club
BK Rating: Not known
W/A: Thames

POWYS (Wales)

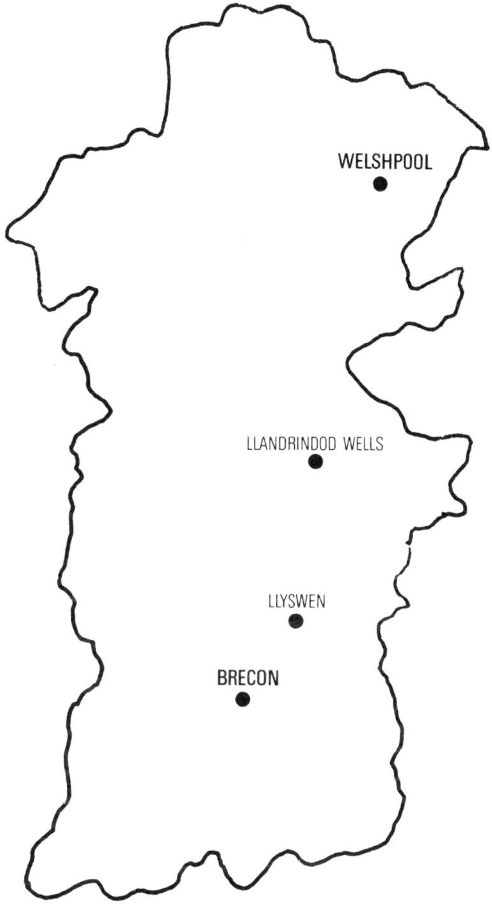

Llandrindod Wells Lake

Location: Edge of the town of Llandrindod Wells, central Wales
Type and Size: Dammed town lake with island, 16 acres
How to Find: Road leading from town centre goes round three sides of the lake
Carp Stock: Very heavily stocked, mostly mirrors. Many doubles and the occasional 20 pounder
Category: Mixed Fishery/Carp Water
Other Species: Roach, bream, pike, eels
Permits: Day and season tickets from the boathouse cafe on the lake. Night syndicate, details from the cafe

Restrictions: No night fishing unless you are a night syndicate member. No fishing on dam
Cost: On application
Baits/Methods: Fairly sophisticated carp methods and boiled baits used, but carp also caught on luncheon meat and floating baits, and on float tackle
Control: Day and season ticket, local Council
BK Rating: Moderate
W/A: Welsh
Comments: Town lake with roads and many walkers, but still attractive. Often fishes well when the boats are being used!

Llyswen Carp Pools

Location: The Dderw, Llyswen, Builth Wells
Type and Size: Two farm ponds of about an acre each
How to Find: Llyswen is on the A470 road between Brecon and Builth Wells
Carp Stock: The Orchard Pool nearest the farmhouse is quite well stocked with commons to about 10lbs and a few double figure mirrors to 20lbs. The other lake is on the other side of the road nearer the river. It is very heavily stocked with small commons to about 5lbs
Category: Carp Waters
Other Species: Tench, bream, roach, perch
Permits: Day tickets from the farm: Mr Eckley, The Dderw, Llyswen, Powys. Tel: Llyswen 224
Cost: Orchard Pool on application. Other pond about £1.50 per day
Control: Private
BK Rating: Orchard Pool - Easy. Other pond - Very Easy
Baits/Methods: Boilies and particle baits; also floaters. Rigs and methods of all types will work and on the other pond the fish will take almost any bait as it is so overstocked
W/A: Welsh, Wye Area, 4 St. John Street, Hereford. Tel: 0432 276313, or from tackle shops. Senior Coarse Licence approximately £4.10 per season, day licence £2.50
Comments: The Orchard Pool is a pleasant water surrounded by trees and reeds. The other lake is open and is near the river. Both lakes are in the Wye Valley 10 miles south east of Builth Wells

SCOTLAND

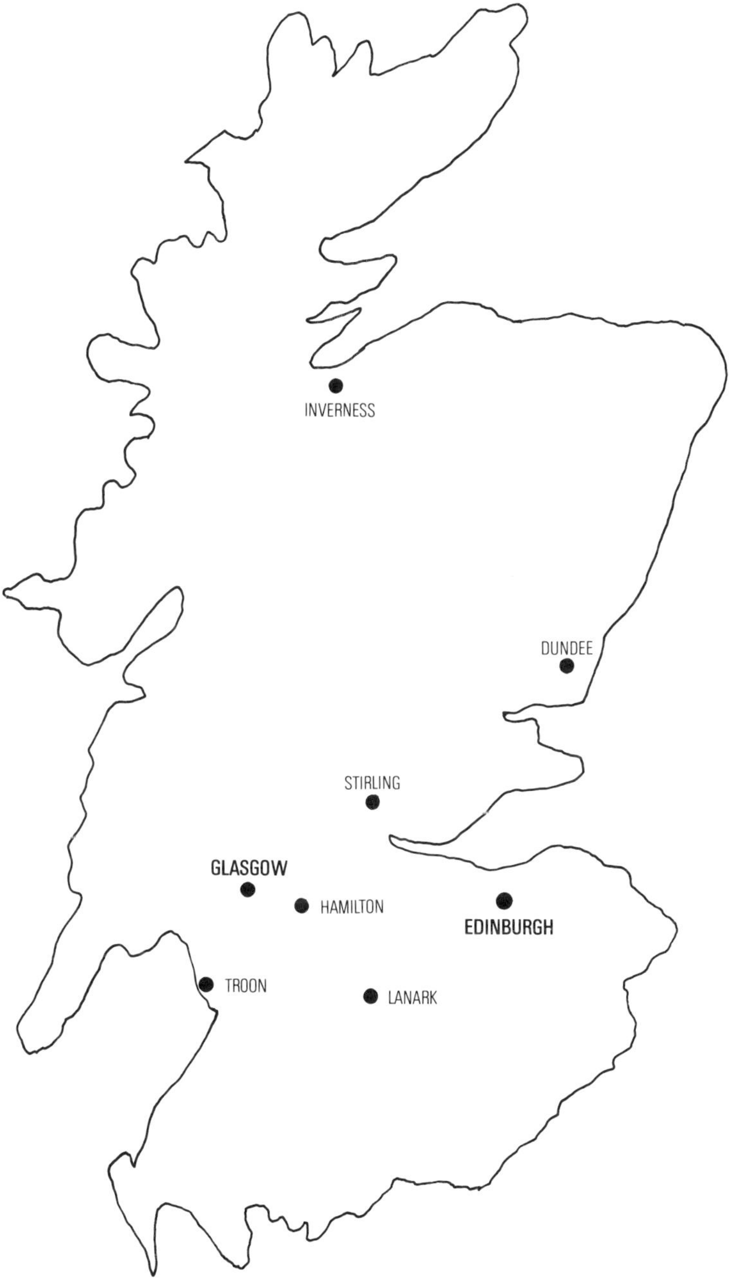
INVERNESS
DUNDEE
STIRLING
GLASGOW
HAMILTON
EDINBURGH
TROON
LANARK

Barrhead Reservoir

Location: Just off the A77 south west of Glasgow, near Newton Mearns (Strathclyde)
Type and Size: There are several lakes here, and the small one contains carp
Carp Stock: Mirrors to low doubles
Category: Mixed Fishery
Other Species: Some coarse fish and trout
Permits: None necessary - free fishing
Control: Glasgow City Council
BK Rating: Not known
W/A: Scottish
Comments: No close season; quite a pleasant water which needs investigating

Clatio Loch

Location: Centre of the town of Dundee (Tayside)
Type and Size: 10 acre town lake
Carp Stock: Stocked with small carp in about 1988, and there are now fish up to about 6lb
Category: Mixed Fishery
Other Species: Roach, bream and perch
Permits: From Dundee City Council, at no cost
Control: Council
BK Rating: Easy
W/A: Scottish
Comments: No close season; a match water

Cowans Farm and Guest House A

Location: Kirkgunzeon, Dumfries (Dumfries & Galloway)
Type and Size: 1½ acre man-made loch
How to Find: 9 miles south west of Dumfries, off the A711 Dalbeattie road
Carp Stock: Contains some carp
Category: Few Carp
Other Species: Roach, tench and rudd
Permits: Tel: 038776 284
Cost: Day permits £2.50 per rod, free fishing to residents
BK Rating: Insufficient information
Control: Private
Restrictions: No keepnets. No groundbaiting
Comments: Bed and breakfast and evening meal in licensed guest house, 200 yards from loch. Other lochs and sea close by. No close season

Craichlaw Fisheries A

Location: Near Newton Stewart (Dumfries & Galloway)
Type and Size: Lake of 6½ acres. There are 4 other lakes in the fishery, some of which also contain carp
How to Find: First ask at the owner's: Palakona Guest House, 30/32 Queen Street, Newton Stewart
Carp Stock: 150 fish to 30lbs
Category: Mixed Fishery

Other Species: Many tench and some golden orfe and bream
Permits: Day and weekly permits only from the owner, N Thornton, at Palakona Guest House. No tickets on the bank – you must obtain a permit before fishing
Cost: £4 per day
Control: Private
BK Rating: Not fished enough yet to be sure of a rating, but at present we would guess at Moderate
Comments: No close season. Comfortable accommodation in the owner's guest house. Tel: 0671 2323. There are very few carp waters in Scotland and this is one of the newest. It should have a good future, as the SW of Scotland has a very mild climate. The lake is very attractive and has a lined bottom, which was built by the monks. In fact, this was a monastery fish pond, and the monks' fish house is still there. There are trees, with an island and a boat house. Depths are from 4 to 11 feet and there is some weed. The water is unfished, as it was only stocked with carp in 1985, so the carp are uncaught

Culcreuch Castle Pool A

Location: Fintry, on the B818, 15 miles west of Stirling (Stirlingshire)
Type and Size: Two small lakes on estate
Carp Stock: Well stocked with mirrors to about 10lbs, and commons to lower doubles, which are said by locals to be wildies
Category: Carp Water
Permits: Scottish Carp Group, 57 Iona Way, Kirkintilloch, Glasgow. Tel: 041-776 7922
BK Rating: Moderate
Comments: Attractive lakes in the grounds of an hotel; members only, no day tickets

Duddingston Loch

Location: City centre of Edinburgh (Lothian)
Type and Size: 50 acre town lake, which is a bird reserve, and belongs to the Crown. Much of the bank cannot be fished
Carp Stock: Plenty of doubles to about 15lbs
Category: Mixed Fishery
Other Species: Roach, bream and perch
Permits: Available free from Edinburgh City Council, or Mikes Tackle Shop, Portobello, Edinburgh
BK Rating: Difficult
Comments: No close season – size and restrictions make it difficult to find fish

Forth and Clyde Canal

Location: Kelvindale, north west Glasgow
Type and Size: Very wide, large canal
Carp Stock: Some very big carp to well over 20lbs
Category: Few Carp
Other Species: Roach, bream, perch and pike
Permits: None necessary – free fishing
BK Rating: Super-Difficult

Comments: No close season. Fish very difficult to locate in this big canal, but they have certainly never been caught

Gooseloan Pond

Location: Kilwinning, 10 miles north of Troon, near the west coast (Ayrshire)
Type and Size: Old, deep quarry of about 4 acres
Carp Stock: Over 30 carp to about 20lbs
Category: Carp Water
Permits: Not known; enquire locally, possibly from farmers
BK Rating: Very Difficult

Hogganfield Loch

Location: City centre of Glasgow
Type and Size: 80 acre town lake, very busy and quite dangerous to fish at times!
Carp Stock: Well stocked with carp to about 20lbs
Category: Mixed Fishery
Other Species: Big bream and eels
Permits: None necessary - free fishing
Control: Council
BK Rating: Moderate
Comments: No close season, and night fishing is allowed. Thousands of water birds, and some people of dubious reputation, especially at night!

Lanark Loch

Location: Public park in Lanark, on the A73 20 miles south east of Glasgow
Type and Size: 20 acre public lake
Carp Stock: Stocked with 500 carp of about 5lbs each in 1988
Category: Mixed Fishery
Other Species: Tench and bream
Permits: About £12 per season from Clydesdale District Council and local tackle shops
Cost: About £10 per season. Possible day tickets
BK Rating: Not known, but could be quite hard, as 20 fish an acre is a low stocking density
Comments: No close season - might be a good bet if you want to catch a Scottish carp

Loch Libo

Location: Uplawmoor, Barrhead (Renfrewshire)
Type and Size: 20 acre shallow and weedy loch
Carp Stock: Well stocked with doubles to lower twenties, and a number of small commons
Category: Carp Water
Permits: Scottish Carp Group, 57 Iona Way, Kirkintilloch, Glasgow. Tel: 041-776 7922
Cost: About £30 per year
Control: Scottish Wildlife Trust

Restrictions: No fishing in some areas, which is a Nature Reserve; limited number of anglers
BK Rating: Difficult
Comments: No close season

Monkland Canal

Location: Coatbridge (Lanarkshire)
Type and Size: Narrow canal
Carp Stock: This canal area was stocked with several thousand small carp recently
Category: Mixed Fishery
Other Species: Most coarse fish
Permits: Scottish Federation of Coarse Anglers, c/o J B Angling, Townhead, Kirkintilloch, Glasgow G66
Control: Local club; details from the Scottish Federation
BK Rating: Easy
W/A: Scottish
Comments: No close season; the carp were stocked for match fishing, but eventually should grow to a good size

Strathclyde Water Park

Location: Hamilton (Lanarkshire)
Type and Size: 150 acre lake
Carp Stock: Well stocked with doubles to about 15lbs
Category: Mixed Fishery
Other Species: Roach and bream
Permits: From the Sports Centre at the lake
Cost: £4 per day
Control: Private
BK Rating: Moderate
Comments: No close season. Lots of people and match anglers

Torwood House Hotel A

Location: Glenluce, Newton Stewart, Wigtownshire (Dumfries & Galloway)
Type and Size: Two lochs
How to Find: Newton Stewart is to the west of Dumfries
Carp Stock: Little known, but does contain some carp
Category: Few Carp
Other Species: Tench, bream, roach, perch
Permits: From hotel: Tel: 05813 469
Cost: On application, day tickets
BK Rating: Insufficient information
Control: Torwood House Hotel
Comments: Accommodation in hotel, 200 yards from lochs. No close season. Pike and salmon fishing nearby. Some trout fishing – within casting distance of the hotel bar!

SHROPSHIRE

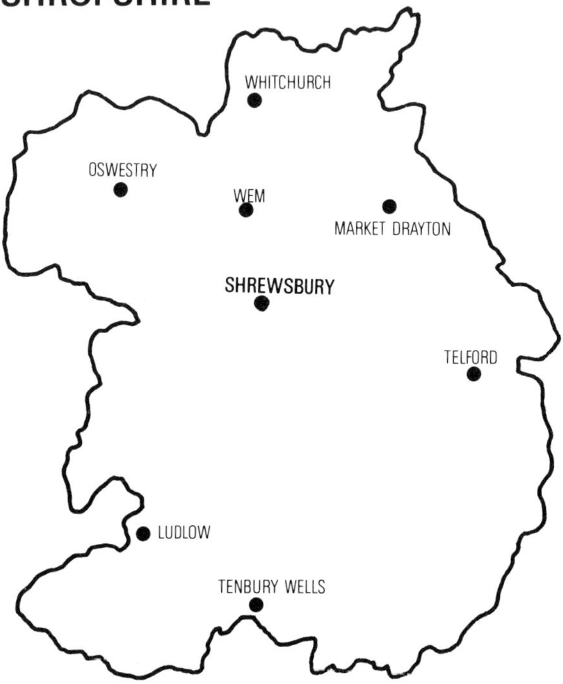

Apley Pool

Location: Near Telford at Lee Gomory
Type and Size: Small pool
Carp Stock: Heavily stocked to 10lbs
Category: Carp Only
Other Species: None
Permits: Telford Anglers Association, Malcolm Kelly, Tel: Telford 244272
Cost: On application
BK Rating: Easy
Control: Club
W/A: Severn Trent

Bache Pool

Location: Near Ludlow
Type and Size: 1½ acre farm pond
How to Find: Turn off the B4365 from Ludlow towards Craven Arms and go through some narrow winding lanes, virtually getting lost!
Carp Stock: Very heavily stocked with many small commons and a few good mirrors and commons to 25lbs
Category: Carp Water
Other Species: General coarse fish
Permits: Day tickets on bank?
Control: Club

BK Rating: Easy,though hard for the big fish
W/A: Severn Trent
Comments: Heavily fished, long narrow lake with lilies; shallow. Bigger fish very wary. Floaters good. A well known water to many Midlands carp anglers. Very opaque, 'coloured' water. Big torches, Tilley lamps and loud radios common!

Bayliss Pools

Location: Shifnal, near Telford
Type and Size: No. 1: 2 acres; No. 2: 2½ acres; No. 3: 3-6 acres
Carp Stock: No. 1: carp to 16lbs; No. 2: carp to 16lbs; No. 3: recent stocking
Category: Mixed Fishery
Other Species: Mixed coarse fish
Permits: On site. Tel: 0952 503550
Cost: £2 per day approximately. About £1 (1pm till dark)
BK Rating: No. 1 - Moderate. No. 2 - Difficult
Control: Private
W/A: Severn Trent
Comments: No. 2 pool is said to be very deep and it fishes well in the winter. Information from Rod & Gun, 3 High Street, Dawley. Tel:0952 503550

Beeches Pool

Location: Ironbridge, near Telford
Type and Size: One acre pool
Carp Stock: Doubles to 16lbs and three twenties
Category: Mixed Fishery
Other Species: General coarse fish
Permits: On site
Cost: £1.50 per day approximately
BK Rating: Moderate
Control: Private
W/A: Severn Trent
Comments: Try local tackle shops for permits and more information, such as Rod & Gun, 3 High Street, Dawley. Tel:0952 503550

Bomere

Location: In the town of Shrewsbury
Type and Size: Attractive lake of about 5 acres
Carp Stock: Probably only one or two, to upper doubles
Category: Few Carp
Other Species: Roach, tench, bream, perch and pike
Permits: Day tickets from local tackle shops
Control: Club
Restrictions: No night fishing
BK Rating: Super-Difficult
W/A: Severn Trent

Brockton Grange A

Location: Brockton, near Much Wenlock. Tel: Mrs Julia Russell on 0746 36443
Type and Size: Estate lake of about an acre
Carp Stock: Well stocked with carp to 20lbs
Category: Mixed Fishery
Other Species: Some coarse fish, trout fishing also available by arrangement
Permits: From the Grange
Control: Private
BK Rating: Moderate
W/A: Severn Trent
Comments: High class bed and breakfast accommodation in fine Victorian country house with 25 acres of its own attractive grounds and lake. Double £40 per night; single £30 per night. This property is in Corvedale, one of Shropshire's finest dales, and convenient for Ludlow, Church Stretton and Ironbridge

Brown Moss Mere

Location: Near Whitchurch off the A41
Type and Size: Lake of about 3 acres, very shallow and weedy
Carp Stock: Quite well stocked to doubles
Category: Mixed Fishery
Other Species: Roach, tench and bream
Permits: Day tickets on the bank at low cost
Control: Local club water
Restrictions: No night fishing
BK Rating: Moderate
W/A: Severn Trent

Canal Reservoirs

Location: Great Sowdley, near Market Drayton
Type and Size: Small reservoirs off the canal
Carp Stock: Some carp, most small
Category: Mixed Fishery
Other Species: Perch, pike, roach, tench
Permits: Stoke-on-Trent AS. F Broadgate, 5 Kingsford Oval, Basford, Stoke-on-Trent ST4 6HN
Control: Club
BK Rating: Difficult
W/A: Severn Trent

Castle Pool/Dandy Pool/Wide Waters

Location: LIttle Dawley, near Telford
Type and Size: 3 separate small lakes, 2 - 3 acres each
How to Find: Details from Telford Anglers Association. Tel:Telford 244272
Carp Stock: Castle and Dandy well stocked with doubles to 20lbs; Wide Waters some carp to 25lbs+
Category: Mixed Fisheries
Other Species: Mixed Coarse Fish
Permits: Telford Anglers Association
Cost: On application

BK Rating: Castle/Dandy - Moderate; Wide Waters - Difficult
Control: Club
W/A: Severn Trent
Comments: We could find out very little about these waters, but the Telford Club Secretary should be able to help

Hawkstone Park Lake

Location: Hawkstone Park, Hodnett, near Wem
Type and Size: Park Lake, very narrow and about 1½ miles long!
Carp Stock: The water is stocked with plenty of doubles and numerous twenties, both commons and mirrors to about 28lbs
Category: Carp Water
Other Species: General coarse fish
Permits: Hawk Lake Trust, Mr P Johnson, 4 Soulton Crescent, Wem SY4 5HY
Control: Hawk Lake Trust
BK Rating: Difficult
Baits/Methods: Normal carp fishing baits and methods
W/A: North West
Comments: With such an immensely long lake one of the main problems is obviously to find the fish, and it is this which makes the water hard, although it is quite well stocked with carp

Isle Estate

Location: Shrewsbury
Type and Size: Estate lake of about 5 acres
Carp Stock: One of the most heavily stocked carp waters in the country. Mostly small carp to 6lbs, but some fish present up to 20lbs
Category: Carp Water
Other Species: General coarse fish
Permits: Prince Albert AS, Secretary Mr C Clarke, 2 Avon Close, Upton, Macclesfield, Cheshire. Season tickets only
Cost: About £35 entry fee and approximately £35 per season. Members only
Control: Club
BK Rating: Very Easy
W/A: North West
Comments: One of those overstocked waters where the carp breed like rabbits. Fish can be caught by any method, and huge catches are recorded

Kyre Pool

Location: Tenbury Wells
Type and Size: Small lake
How to Find: Near Tenbury Wells
Carp Stock: Good carp to over 20llbs
Category: Mixed Fishery
Other Species: Pike and eels
Permits: S Lewis Fishing Tackle, Bewdley - day tickets
Cost: On application
Control: Private
BK Rating: Moderate
W/A: Severn Trent

Middle Pool

Location: Wombridge, near Telford
Type and Size: 2½ acre pool
Carp Stock: Carp to 20lbs, numbers not known
Category: Mixed Fishery
Other Species: Big bream
Permits: Season tickets from local tackle shops. No day tickets
Cost: On application
BK Rating: Moderate
Control: Telford Anglers Association. Tel: Telford 244272
Restrictions: No night fishing. No boilies
W/A: Severn Trent

Moss Pool

Location: Forton, near Newport, Telford
Type and Size: Pool of about 2 acres
Carp Stock: Good head of doubles to 28lbs
Category: Mixed Fishery
Other Species: Bream and tench
Permits: On bank
Cost: Approximately £2 per day
BK Rating: Very Difficult
Control: Private
W/A: Severn Trent
Comments: Try local tackle shops for permits and details. Rod & Guns, 3 High Street, Dawley. Tel: 0952 503550

Neen Sollars Bungalow A

Location: Between Cleobury Mortimer and Tenbury Wells
Type and Size: Estate lake of about an acre
Carp Stock: Some carp to about 10lbs
Category: Mixed Fishery
Permits: Fishing only available to those who rent the bungalow from the owner. Mr S R Jennings, 26 Moorpool Avenue, Harborne, Birmingham B17 9HN. Tel: 021 429 3262, weekdays after 7pm
Other Species: Roach, rudd and bream
Control: Private
Restrictions: Barbless hooks only; no keepnets
BK Rating: Not known
W/A: Severn Trent
Comments: The accommodation is a chalet type self-catering bungalow with two double bedrooms, and a pull-down bed in dining room; sitting room, small kitchen and shower room etc. Covered verandah and summer house. Large garden, aviary and swing. Electricity included in price. Some acres of beautiful private woodland and pasture with the lake and Mill Brook, with some stream fishing. 18 acre wildlife sanctuary with walks, and wildlife pool with log benches for picnics. Ideal for a holiday with children. Cost from £150 to £200 per week according to season. Only guests have access to the land and fishing, which is included in the price. Private property - do not visit without permission

Oswestry Lakes

Location: On the River Mor, near Oswestry
Type and Size: Small pools
Carp Stock: Well stocked with carp, sizes not known
Category: Mixed Fishery
Other Species: Most coarse fish
Permits: Oswestry AA, M J Shilton, 24 Windsor Close, Oswestry SY11 2UY. Tickets available for visitors. Details also from J E Ellis, Regal Stores, Oswestry; Morton Lodge Hotel, Morton
Cost: Season tickets; at £6.50 - no day tickets
Control: Club
BK Rating: Not known
W/A: Severn Trent

Rosehill Fishery

Location: Off the A41 at Rosehill, just south of Market Drayton
Type and Size: Two pools of 6 acres and two acres
Carp Stock: Some carp to middle doubles in large pool; carp to lower doubles in the newer small pool
Category: Mixed Fishery
Other Species: Crucians, roach, bream and perch in the large pool; barbel in the smaller pool
Permits: Day tickets on bank
Cost: £3.50 per day
BK Rating: Moderate
W/A: Severn Trent

Stirchley Pools

Location: Hinkshay, near Stirchley
Type and Size: Two pools of 1½ and 2½ acres
How to Find: These waters are near Dawley
Carp Stock: Small pool - carp to 10lbs: larger pool - some doubles to over 20lbs
Category: Mixed Fisheries
Other Species: Tench
Permits: Dawley Anglers Club. Tel: Telford 592899
Cost: About £1 per day
BK Rating: Moderate
Control: Club
W/A: Severn Trent
Comments: All information from Dawley Anglers. Tickets from Rod & Gun, 3 High Street, Dawley

Trench Pool

Location: Trench, near Telford
Type and Size: Large lake of 30 acres
Carp Stock: Some carp to over 20lbs
Category: Mixed Fishery
Other Species: Big pike, bream and tench
Permits: Free
Cost: None

BK Rating: Moderate
Control: Not known
W/A: Severn Trent
Comments: There are not many lakes where the fishing is free! Information from Rod & Gun, 3 High Street, Dawley. Tel: 0952 503550

Walcot East Lake

Location: Near Lydbury North, Ludlow
Type and Size: 7 acre lake
How to Find: Take the A49 Craven Arms road from Ludlow, and turn left on the B4368 to Little Brampton. Then take the right turn (B4385) to Lydbury North, and turn left into the estate at the Powis Arms
Carp Stock: A few carp to about 10lbs
Category: Few Carp
Other Species: Bream, roach, perch
Permits: Birmingham Anglers Association, 100Icknield Port Road, Rotton Park, Birmingham B16 OAP. Tel: 021-454 9111. 9.30am to 1.30pm, 7pm to 9pm, weekdays. (Members only)
Cost: About £13 a season, which includes all other BAA waters
BK Rating: Difficult, as there are few carp
Control: B.A.A.
Restrictions: No groundbait of any kind
W/A: Anglian
Comments: Not worth considering unless you want a general fishing day with the chance of a carp

Whitchurch Lake

Location: Near Whitchurch
Type and Size: Small lake
Carp Stock: Well stocked with carp to about 10lbs
Category: Mixed Fishery
Other Species: Usual coarse fish
Permits: From J E Windsor, Black Park, Whitchurch
Cost: £5 per season
Control: Private
BK Rating: Not known
W/A: Severn Trent

Withy Pool

Location: In the town of Telford
Type and Size: Medium sized town park lake
How to Find: Telford town park
Carp Stock: Carp to over 30lbs. Numbers not known
Category: Mixed Fishery
Other Species: General coarse fish. Catfish to over 20lbs
Permits: Dawley Anglers Club and Rod & Gun, 3 High Street, Dawley.
Cost: On application
BK Rating: Difficult
Control: Club
Restrictions: No night fishing. No boilies

W/A: Severn Trent
Comments: This lake could produce both big carp and catfish. Contact Mr A Buttery, of Dawley AC. Tel: Telford 592899

Woodcote Hall Pool

Location: Newport, near Telford
Type and Size: 3 acre estate lake
Carp Stock: Well stocked with carp to upper 20's
Category: Carp Water
Other Species: Roach, bream, rudd, perch and tench
Permits: Season tickets only. Tel: 0952 503550
Control: Private
BK Rating: Moderate
W/A: Severn Trent
Comments: Heavily fished water, said to be the best carp water in this area. Try Rod and Gun, 3 High Street, Dawley. There may possibly be some day tickets at £3 per day

SOMERSET

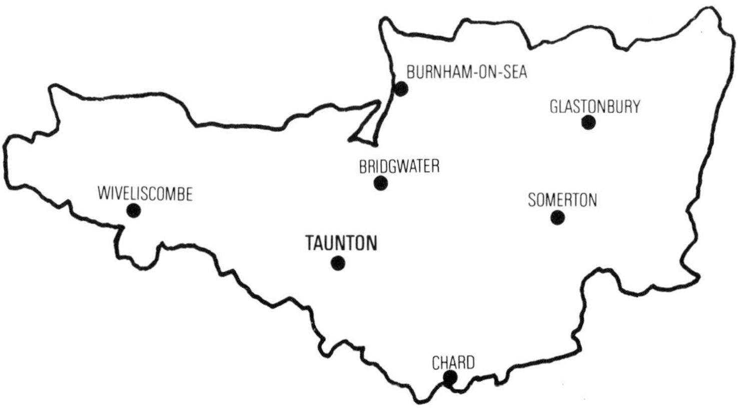

Apex Pond

Location: Burnham-on-Sea
Type and Size: Old pit of about 5 acres
How to Find: Go through Burnham-on-Sea and you will see the lake to the left of the road near houses
Carp Stock: Said to be well stocked with commons to about 6lbs
Category: Mixed Fishery
Other Species: Tench, rudd and pike
Permits: North Somerset Association of Anglers, and on the same tickets as Newton Pond and Hutton Pond. Secretary, R Newton, 64 Clevedon Road, Twickenham, Clevedon, Avon
Restrictions: No night fishing
Control: Club
BK Rating: Fairly Easy
W/A: Wessex
Comments: We cannot find out much about this water since it was drained and restocked by the local Council, but we think it might serve as a fun fishery

Bridgwater Bay Holiday Park A

Location: End of the Esplanade, Burnham-on-Sea
Type and Size: Small lake on holiday park
Carp Stock: Some mirror carp to 10 lbs+
Category: Mixed Fishery
Other Species: Roach, rudd, tench and bream
Permits: Residents only, weekly tickets from reception at low cost

Control: Private
Restrictions: No close season fishing allowed
BK Rating: Moderate
W/A: Wessex
Comments: Large holiday camp with lodges, chalets, apartments and caravans. All modern facilities, including outsoor heated swimming pool, boating lake, snooker and pool room, tennis courts, shops, bars etc. etc. Details and bookings from Hoseasons Holidays, Sunway House. Lowestoft NR32 3LT. Tel: 0502 500500

Bridgwater - Taunton Canal A

Location: Bridgwater to Taunton, exit 24 of the M5
Type and Size: Narrow canal
How to Find: See local maps
Carp Stock: Some carp, mostly doubles to over 20lbs
Category: Mixed Fishery
Other Species: General coarse fish
Permits: Local tackle shops in Bridgwater and Taunton. Bridgwater AA has some of the water
Cost: £1.50 per day in advance only
BK Rating: Difficult
Control: Club
W/A: Wessex
Comments: There are some big fish in this weedy canal. Near and between locks is often best. Could produce an upper 20. Self catering cottages on the banks of the canal. Tel: 0278 662783 (Mrs Day)

Combwich Pond

(pronounced Come-itch - or something similar!)

Location: Combwich, near Bridgwater
Type and Size: Old clay pit of about 25 acres
How to Find: From Bridgwater take the A39 Minehead road and turn right at the War Memorial, Cannington. After about 1¼ miles you will see a track on the right, opposite Bowlan Farm, which leads to the car park
Carp Stock: Well stocked with both commons and mirrors which are said to average more than 15lbs in weight. There are many upper doubles and a number of 20's, some of which are commons. Several lower 30's have been reported
Category: Carp Water
Other Species: Tench, roach, rudd, pike and many thousands of eels
Permits: Bridgwater Angling Association - same ticket as for Dunwear Ponds, from local tackle shops, Veals of Bristol, and the Secretary, 7 Webbers Way, Puriton, Bridgwater, Somerset
Cost: £11.50 per year, open to all
Control: Club - Bridgwater Angling Association
BK Rating: Very Difficult
Baits/Methods: All the most advanced baits, rigs and methods needed for this very hard water. Pastes and boilies are eaten by eels and it has been said that you may easily hook at least 100 eels per season, and lose many hooks in the snags and excessively irregular bottom of this lake, which was flooded at different times. Multiple (particle) baits are said to work best
W/A: Wessex

Comments: A very hard water where nearly all the success goes to long-stay carp specialists, although you can do a season there without catching a fish! If you do get one it is likely to be big, with a very good chance of a 20, though fish are reported 'going back' in 1991

Dunwear Ponds

Location: Dunwear Lane on the edge of the town of Bridgwater

Type and Size: Three clay pits known as the North Pond (about 4 acres); the South Pond (about 2 acres) and the Large Pond (about 20 acres)

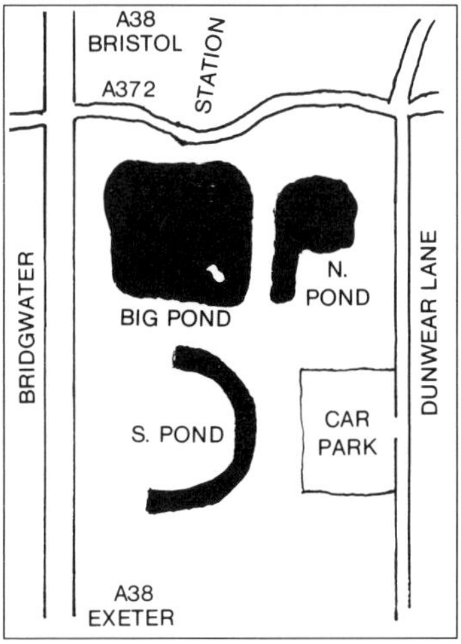

How to Find: Turn off the A38 at the traffic lights towards Bridgwater Station (Westonzoyland Road). After nearly a mile turn right into Dunwear Lane and the car park will be seen only 400 yards along the lane on the right hand side. This is the ONLY entrance to the lakes

Carp Stock: North Pond well stocked with carp to about 18lbs, although a fish of about 24lbs has been reported from this lake. South Pond contains a few carp but most are doubles, and there is one very big fish which has been caught more than once at over 30lbs. Large Pond has a big stock of commons to about 8lbs and a few mirrors, which are very hard to locate, to about 19lbs

Category: North Pond - Carp Water, South Pond - Mixed Fishery, Large Pond - Mixed Fishery

Other Species: Roach, rudd, tench, pike, bream

Permits: Season tickets for this club water of the Bridgwater Angling Association are obtainable from the Secretary, 7 Webbers Way, Puriton, Bridgwater, Somerset, or from local tackle shops in Bridgwater and from Veals Fishing Tackle, Old Market, Bristol. Membership is open to all

Cost: £11.50 per season which includes other waters

Restrictions: No entry to water by any roads other than from the car park. No fishing on north bank of Large Pond

BK Rating: North Pond - Moderate; South Pond - Moderate; Large Pond - Fairly Easy for the small commons. Difficult for the mirrors

Control: Club

Baits/Methods: Modern advanced carp rigs, methods and baits needed for most of these fish
W/A: Wessex
Comments: The Bridgwater club is an excellent club owning most of its own fisheries, but rules are strict, and anglers would do well to observe them. Best swim on the South Pond is the one next to the houses, past which you cannot go. This and the North Pond are hard fished by carp specialists, many of whom come from other parts of the country and spend days and nights in bivvies. Water is very busy during summer and crowded with children etc. Autumn fishing is much more peaceful. The Large Pond has islands and is split up by many reed beds which grow out into the lake along old, now flooded, paths. It is also very weedy with a thick growth of weed over most of the bottom. The club also has other ponds containing carp

Howley Street Pond

Location: Howley Street, near Chard
Type and Size: Half acre pond
Carp Stock: Some carp to about 10lbs
Category: Mixed Fishery
Other Species: Tench, bream, roach and perch
Permits: Day tickets from Chard Angling Centre, The Old Bakehouse, 2 Holyrood Street, Chard
Cost: £2
Control: Club
BK Rating: Not known
W/A: Wessex

Newtown Pond

Location: Centre of the town of Highbridge, west of A38
Type and Size: Clay pit of 7 acres
How to Find: Take the Burnham-on-Sea road from Highbridge, turn first left into housing estate; lake is on the left surrounded by houses
Carp Stock: 50 doubles, mostly mirrors. One or two lower 20's. 150 commons, mostly under 10lbs; fish said to be going back
Category: Carp Water/Mixed Fishery
Other Species: Pike, roach, rudd, bream, eels
Permits: Newsagent in Highbridge High Street, Veals of Bristol, Old Market, Bristol
Cost: Approximately £12.50 per season
Baits/Methods: Boilies and multiples. Normal carp legering methods and rigs
Control: Club. North Somerset Association of Anglers. Open to all
Restrictions: No night fishing between 10.30pm and 5.30am; one rod only; no floating crust
W/A: Wessex
BK Rating: Moderate
Comments: Town water quite noisy and busy, mostly 10-15 feet deep; little weed. Club Secretary: Mr R F Newton, 64 Clevedon Road, Tickenham, Clevedon, Avon, who will supply all information and possible details of day tickets

Oxenleaze Farm A

Location: Wiveliscombe
Type and Size: 2 farm ponds of an acre and ½ an acre
How to Find: From Taunton take the A361 (B3227) road west, where you will see a right turn to Wiveliscombe, by the Rock Inn to Waterrow - follow the fish sign for 4 miles
Carp Stock: Good number of carp to 20lbs
Category: Mixed Fishery
Other Species: Tench, roach, rudd and bream
Permits: Free fishing to those who stay in one of the six caravans on the site. Information from Mrs Rottenbury on 0984 23427 (caravan site open Easter until end of October). Day permits for non-residents
Control: Private
BK Rating: Moderate
W/A: South West - rod licences on sale at farm

Perry Street Pond

Location: Perry Street, near Chard
Type and Size: 1¼ acre matured pit
Carp Stock: Well stocked with carp, including a number of doubles to about 17lbs
Category: Mixed Fishery
Other Species: Tench, roach, rudd, bream and perch
Permits: Season tickets only from Chard Angling Centre, The Old Bakehouse, 2 Holyrood Street; Chard Cycle Centre, Holyrood Street
Control: Club
BK Rating: Difficult
W/A: Wessex
Comments: A pleasant little pond, but the doubles have been hooked a lot, and are not easy to catch

River Parrett A

Location: Upstream from Bridgwater
Type and Size: Short river
How to Find: Bridgwater to Somerton
Carp Stock: Unknown but commons caught recently to 21½lbs
Category: Few Carp
Other Species: Most coarse fish
Permits: Bridgwater Angling Club - local tackle shops
Cost: On application
BK Rating: Difficult due to location problems
Control: Club
W/A: Wessex
Comments: This river, the Huntspill, the King Sedgemoor Drain, and other rivers in the area all contain carp to about 25lbs - if you can find them! Try backwaters, mill pools, islands or any other features - and be prepared to do some walking! Try also the Milk Factory at Bason Bridge on the River Bure; Mark; and Edington. Holiday accommodation: self-catering lodges alongside River Huntspill, also bed and breakfast in main house with bar. Tel: 0278 781612 or 784264 for details and brochure

Viaduct Fishery

Location: Cary Valley, Somerton TA11 6LJ. Tel: 0458 74022
Type and Size: 3 acre lake
Carp Stock: Some carp to double figures
Category: Mixed Fishery
Other Species: Bream and tench
Permits: Restricted membership obtainable from Tim and Lisa Chapman at the address above. Write or phone for brochure
Cost: £3 per day; £2 - half day; £12 for 5 days; season - £35; weekday season - £20
Control: Private
BK Rating: Not known
W/A: Wessex
Comments: There is a lodge, where drinks and refreshments are sold, as well as fresh and smoked trout, and pick your own strawberries! There are also two trout fly lakes, and one novices any-method trout pond. The trout fisheries are open all the year; normal close season applies for the carp fishing. Best trout to date is 9lbs 3ozs

Walrow Ponds

Location: Near Bridgwater
Type and Size: Small pits
Carp Stock: Well stocked with carp to 10lbs or so
Category: Mixed Fishery
Other Species: Bream, roach, rudd, tench and perch
Permits: From local tackle shop. Secretary, Bridgwater AA. L A Williams, 7 Webbers Way, Puriton, Bridgewater TA7 8AS
Cost: About £11 per season, to cover all the other Bridgwater club fisheries, most of which contain carp
Control: Club
BK Rating: Easy
W/A: Wessex

Westhay Lake

Location: Between Westhay and Shapwick, off the B3151 road near Glastonbury
Type and Size: 3½ acre lake
Carp Stock: Well stocked with carp to 28lbs
Category: Mixed Fishery
Other Species: Tench, roach, rudd and crucians
Permits: All information and permits from Alan Tedder on 0278 456429
Cost: £4 per day; £3 per night
Control: Private
BK Rating: Not known
Comments: This new fishery opened on June 16th 1991. Many of the fish came from a water called The Beeches, near Bridgwater, which is now closed; breakfast and other services available. A 27 was reported in 1991

SOUTH GLAMORGAN (Wales)

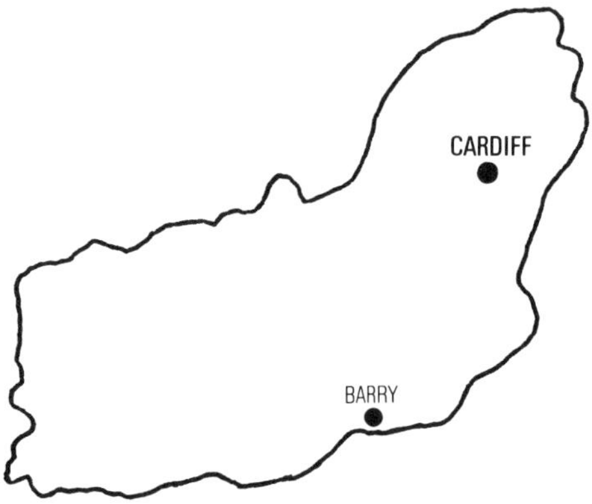

Barry Reservoir

Location: Barry Docks, Barry, near Cardiff
Type and Size: 5 acre shallow lake with reeds but little weed
Carp Stock: Well stocked with small commons, and a few double figure mirrors
Category: Mixed Fishery
Other Species: Eels, roach and rudd
Permits: Members only water of Glamorgan AC. Secretary: P Mason, 8 Denys Close, Dinas Powis, South Glamorgan
Cost: About £30 per season
BK Rating: Fairly Hard
Restrictions: No night fishing; no day tickets
W/A: Welsh

Cafarfatha Park Lake

Location: Brecon Road, Merthyr Tydfil (Mid Glamorgan)
Type and Size: Three acre town park lake with islands
Carp Stock: Well stocked with small carp, and a few upper doubles
Category: Mixed Fishery
Other Species: Eels, rudd and roach
Permits: Day tickets from bailiff on bank. Season tickets from local tackle shops
Cost: £1.50 per day; £10 per season
Restrictions: No night fishing; fishing from one bank only
BK Rating: Easy
W/A: Welsh

Hendre Lake

Location: Hendre Road, Cardiff, off the A48
Type and Size: Six acre town lake with island
Carp Stock: Quite well stocked with doubles to about 16lbs

Category: Mixed Fishery
Other Species: Roach, tench and bream
Permits: Day tickets from local tackle shop, in advance only. Night syndicate, members only
Cost: £1.50 per day; £12 per season
Control: Private
Restrictions: No night fishing for non-members
BK Rating: Easy
W/A: Welsh

Kenfig Lake

Location: Kenfig, between Port Talbot and Porthcawl
Type and Size: 90 acre lake
Carp Stock: Some carp to over 10lbs
Category: Mixed Fishery
Other Species: Pike, bream, tench, roach, rudd, brown and rainbow trout
Permits: Kinfig Hill and District AA. A Waite, 16 Marlas Road, Pyle, Glamorgan
Cost: £3 per day; £15 per season
Control: Club
BK Rating: Difficult, as this is a very big lake
W/A: Welsh

Marshfield Reens

Location: Near Cardiff
Type and Size: Small lake
Carp Stock: Well stocked with carp to over 10lbs
Category: Mixed Fishery
Other Species: Tench and some other coarse fish
Permits: Bute AA - season tickets from L V Powell, 176 Clare Road, Grangetown, Cardiff
Control: Club
BK Rating: Moderate
W/A: Welsh

Roath Park Lake

Location: Roath Park, Cardiff
Type and Size: Park Lake of about 4 acres
Carp Stock: Quite well stocked with carp to upper doubles
Category: Mixed Fishery
Other Species: Tench, roach, rudd
Permits: On bank
Control: Cardiff Corporation
BK Rating: Moderate
Restrictions: No night fishing
W/A: Welsh

SOUTH YORKSHIRE

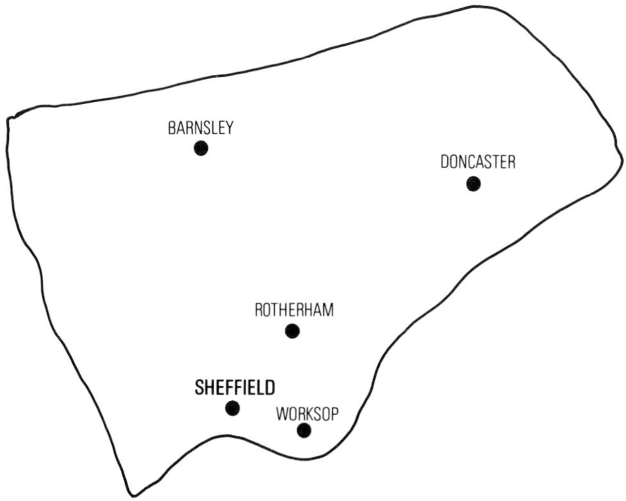

Askern Lake

Location: Askern, near Doncaster
Type and Size: Park Lake of 8 acres with an island
How to Find: Take the A19 from Doncaster to Askern. The lake is by the road on the right, in the town centre
Carp Stock: Lakes 1 and 2 contain a fair number of smaller carp. Lake 3 which is 8 acres, is well stocked with good carp to 29lbs
Category: Mixed Fishery
Other Species: Perch, roach, tench, crucians and pike
Permits: From bailiff on site
Cost: £1.10 per day, half price for juniors and OAP's. Boat hire at £2.15 for four hours
BK Rating: Moderate
Control: Council
Restrictions: No night fishing
W/A: Yorkshire
Comments: A busy town park lake, with tarmac banking which is very suitable for disabled anglers. Fishing allowed from boats

Bank End Coarse Fisheries

Location: Blaxton, near Doncaster
Type and Size: Two lakes of 4½ and 3½ acres
How to Find: Take the A614 Bawtry to Thorne road, then the B1396 from Blaxton. The lakes are on the right about 1½ miles from Blaxton
Carp Stock: These lakes were stocked in 1989 with carp to 12lbs
Category: Smaller lake - Carp Water; larger lake - Mixed Fishery
Other Species: Bream, tench, roach, rudd and perch
Permits: Day tickets on site
Cost: £2.50 per day
BK Rating: Insufficient information
Control: Private
Restrictions: No night fishing. No hemp or tares
W/A: Severn Trent
Comments: There are big tench and bream here, so every take will not be from a carp. Car parking on banks, with swims built to allow wheelchairs for the disabled

Beedom's Fishery

Location: South Yorkshire, undisclosed location
Carp Stock: Carp to well over 20lbs - at least five 20's and a thirty
Control: Club
Comments: Those who control this water do not want publicity, so no further details can be published. For information and an introduction to the controlling body, please contact Mr M A Beedom, 1 Martindale Walk, Carcroft, Doncaster DN6 8BX. Tel: Doncaster 330749

Blacker Dam

Location: Blacker Green Lane, Silkstone, near Barnsley, off the A628 Manchester road
Type and Size: Small attractive pond
Carp Stock: Thought to be quite well stocked
Category: Moderate
Other Species: Tench
Permits: Leeds and District ASA, members only but open to all - Secretary, Leeds and District ASA, c/o Leeds Anglers Club, Stoney Rock Lane, Leeds 9
Control: Club
W/A: Yorkshire

Bolton Brickponds

Location: Goldthorpe, Bolton-upon-Dearne, near Barnsley
Type and Size: 3 lakes, covering about 10 acres in all
How to Find: In Bolton-upon-Dearne, opposite the Council offices
Carp Stock: Well stocked with mirror and common carp to over 20lbs
Category: Mixed Fishery
Other Species: Pike, bream, tench, roach, perch, chub and trout
Permits: From the fishing hut on site, to be purchased before fishing. Only £3 per year, but day tickets needed in the trout season
BK Rating: Moderate

Restrictions: Night fishing by arrangement, but during the close season daytime only, and only using fly, worms, maggots or casters
Control: Community Miners Welfare
W/A: Yorkshire
Comments: Toilets on site. Good facilities for disabled anglers

Bullhole

Location: Barnby Dun, near Doncaster
Type and Size: Offcut of the River Dun, about 3½ acres in size
How to Find: Go through Barnby Dun towards the power station. The pond is on the left beside the banks of the Don
Carp Stock: Some carp to double figures
Category: Mixed Fishery
Other Species: Most coarse fish
Permits: Mr J Thornton. Tel: 0302 886126
Cost: £8.50 per year, which includes three other ponds
BK Rating: Difficult
Control: Club
W/A: Yorkshire
Comments: No close season

Campsall Country Park

Location: Campsall, Askern, near Doncaster
Type and Size: Clay pit of about 11 acres
How to Find: Take the A19 from Doncaster to Askern, then a left fork to Campsall. Turn left to the lake before the Sports Centre
Carp Stock: Stocked with carp to mid-doubles
Category: Mixed Fishery
Other Species: Bream, tench, perch and rudd
Permits: Day tickets on bank
Cost: £1.10, half price for juniors and OAP's
BK Rating: Not known
Control: Council
Restrictions: No night fishing
W/A: Yorkshire
Comments: This is a park fishery stocked in 1982. It is very deep and has an island. Many fishing platforms, and good for the disabled. Askern Miners Welfare actually control the water

Carlton Mill Pond

Location: Carlton-in-Lindrick, on the A609 just north of Worksop
Type and Size: 3 acre mill pond - enquire locally for exact venue
Carp Stock: Some carp to over 20lbs reported caught
Category: Mixed Fishery
Other Species: Usual coarse fish, including tench
Permits: Enquire locally or on bank - small local angling club, but we have no further details
BK Rating: Not known
W/A: Severn Trent

Crookes Valley Lake

Location: In the centre of Sheffield, at Crookesmoor
Type and Size: City park lake
Carp Stock: Some mirrors to about 12lbs
Category: Few Carp
Other Species: Tench, roach, perch and pike
Permits: On bank
Control: Sheffield City Council
BK Rating: Difficult as there are not many carp
W/A: Yorkshire
Comments: Flat concrete banks like many park lakes. Rowing boats etc

Cumwell Canal Pond

Location: Cumwell Lane, between Thurcroft and Bramley
Type and Size: 2 acres of canal-like open water
Carp Stock: Some carp to over 20lbs, number and sizes not known
Other Species: General coarse fish
Permits: Day tickets on bank at low cost
Control: Local council
Restrictions: No night fishing
BK Rating: Moderate
W/A: Yorkshire
Comments: Public area; a bit like a rubbish tip!

Cusworth Park Lakes

Location: Cusworth House, Cusworth, near Doncaster
Type and Size: Two estate lakes of about 4 acres each
How to Find: Take the A638 from Doncaster for about 1½ miles, and follow the signs for Cusworth Hall
Carp Stock: Well stocked with carp to 18lbs
Category: Mixed Fishery
Other Species: Crucians, roach, perch, rudd and tench
Permits: Day tickets on bank
Cost: £1.10 per day, half price for juniors and OAP's
BK Rating: Easy
Control: Council
Restrictions: No night fishing
W/A: Yorkshire
Comments: Fine country house and grounds, with museum. Toilet facilities, a picnic area and good for the disabled

Elsecar Reservoir

Location: Elsecar Park, Hoyland Nether, near Barnsley
Type and Size: Medium-sized reservoir
How to Find: Take junction 36 from the M1 to Hoyland, then follow the signs for Elsecar. Turn left at the T-junction, and at the Market Hotel turn right towards Wentworth
Carp Stock: Carp to over 20lbs
Category: Mixed Fishery, although possibly Few Carp
Other Species: Pike, bream, roach and tench

Permits: Day permits from bailiff on bank. Low cost, reduced prices for disabled and free to pensioners
BK Rating: Not known
Control: Elsecar Main Colliery Angling Society. Secretary: Mr W Turner, 14 Eaden Crescent, Hoyland, near Barnsley. Tel: Barnsley 746002
Restrictions: No night fishing. No fishing from the parkside foreshore
W/A: Yorkshire
Comments: Costs for these reservoirs and other waters in Yorkshire seem to be very low, so Yorkshire looks like a good county for anglers

Fleets Dam

Location: Smithies Lane, off the A61 one mile north of Barnsley
Type and Size: 10 acre attractive reed-fringed lake
Carp Stock: Well stocked with carp, about three years ago, and now caught to 10lbs
Category: Mixed Fishery
Other Species: Tench, roach, perch and pike
Permits: Day tickets on the bank
Cost: £3.50 for adults, £2.50 juniors; evening tickets from 4pm at £2.50. Season tickets £10
Control: Allan Hanson, Stanborough Fisheries. Tel: 0226 29579
Baits/Methods: Luncheon meat, sweetcorn and bread all work well, with standard methods, especially float fishing close in
BK Rating: Easy
W/A: Yorkshire
Comments: This is mainly a match fishery, with big weights taken, and many anglers are broken in carp whilst pole fishing. Most matches take place on Tuesdays, Wednesdays, Saturday and Sunday, on about half the lake

Graves Park Pond

Location: Left side of the A61, travelling south from Sheffield City centre
Carp Stock: A few carp to about 7lbs
Category: Few Carp
Other Species: Roach and perch
Permits: From bailiff on bank
Control: Sheffield City Council
BK Rating: Difficult
W/A: Yorkshire
Comments: Good for disabled anglers, with a cafe nearby

Hoyle Mill Dam

Location: Kinsley, Hemworth, near Pontefract. Find Hoyle Mill Road, near Hemsworth Water Park
Type and Size: Large lake
Carp Stock: Carp to double figures
Category: Mixed Fishery
Other Species: Roach, tench, bream, chub and big eels
Permits: Day tickets from bailiff on bank, at £2 each
Control: Hemsworth and District AA. Open to all. Details and membership from Stan Pollington, 2 Common Road, Kinsley, Pontefract. Tel: Hemsworth 612556
BK Rating: Not known
W/A: Yorkshire

Long Pond

Location: Barnby Dun, near Doncaster
Type and Size: Offcut from River Don, about half a mile long
How to Find: Near Thorpe Marsh power station, which is just across the canal through Barnby Dun
Carp Stock: Well stocked with carp to over 20lbs, and several thirties are rumoured to have been caught recently
Category: Mixed Fishery
Other Species: Most coarse fish
Permits: On the same permit as Bullhole - Mr I Thornton. Tel: 0302 886126
Cost: £8.50 per year, which includes three other ponds
BK Rating: Difficult
Control: Club
W/A: Yorkshire
Comments: No close season

Rother Valley Country Park

Location: Killamarsh, Sheffield
Type and Size: Public country park lake of about 20 acres
Carp Stock: Some carp stocked to about 2lbs
Category: Few Carp
Other Species: General coarse fish
Permits: Day ticket on bank at low cost
Control: Private
BK Rating: Very Difficult
W/A: Yorkshire
Comments: Many members of the public, boats and water-ski-iers; no night fishing

Roundwood Pond

Location: The Mill, Aldwalk, Rotherham
Type and Size: Mill dam of about 10 acres
Carp Stock: Quite a few doubles to about 20lbs
Category: Mixed Fishery
Other Species: Usual coarse fish
Permits: British Rail - try BR Staff Association, 8 Upper Belmont Road, St. Andrews, Bristol, or enquire from tackle shops in Rotherham
BK Rating: Moderate
W/A: Yorkshire
Comments: This water was stocked with about 50 good carp in the early 70's, and there could be some even better fish than the 20's reported caught

Sheffield Canal

Location: Tinsley, in the centre of Sheffield
Type and Size: Typical city canal
Carp Stock: The carp were put in 1979, and there are plenty of small fish, with the occasional double and 20
Category: Mixed Fishery
Other Species: Roach, pike, rudd and bream
Permits: Local club - enquire at tackle shops. Day tickets on bank in some areas
BK Rating: Moderate - Easy in the locks

W/A: Yorkshire
Comments: Usual problems associated with fishing in cities and towns - most of them caused by other people!

Thurnscoe Reservoir

Location: Opposite Hickleton Main Colliery, off the A635 Barnsley - Doncaster road at Thurnscoe
Type and Size: Small reservoir
Carp Stock: Fairly well stocked with carp, sizes not known
Category: Mixed Fishery
Other Species: Pike, roach, tench and bream
Permits: From bailiff on bank
Cost: About £2 per *season*
Control: Hickleton Main Angling Cub
BK Rating: Not known
W/A: Yorkshire

Underbank Reservoir

Location: Stocksbridge, Sheffield
Type and Size: 60 acre reservoir, very deep
Carp Stock: A few carp, some doubles and the odd 20
Category: Few Carp
Other Species: Trout and some coarse fish
Permits: Day tickets on bank at low cost
Control: Council
BK Rating: Very Difficult
Restrictions: No night fishing
W/A: Yorkshire

William De Windholme Lake

Location: On the A64 8 miles SE of Doncaster, between Hatfield Woodhouse and Bawtry
Type and Size: 10 acre lake
Carp Stock: Well stocked with carp between 5lbs and 15lbs
Category: Carp Water
Permits: Annual only from Neville Fickling, 27 Lodge Lane, Upton, Gainsborough DN21 5NW
Cost: £50 for 12 months
BK Rating: Easy
W/A: Severn Trent
Comments: Close season fishing allowed within NRA rules; a good water to learn on. Water sports centre, can be busy at weekends

Willow Garth Fishery

Location: Shaftholme Lane, Arksey, near Doncaster
Type and Size: 4 acre lake
How to Find: From Doncaster take the A19 to Bentley, then turn right onto Arksey Lane and Marsh Lane
Carp Stock: Well stocked with carp to mid-doubles

Category:	Carp Water
Other Species:	Roach, perch and tench, and stocked annually with rainbow trout
Permits:	Day tickets on bank
Cost:	£2 dawn till dusk; £1.30 4pm till dusk; £2.50 per night
BK Rating:	Moderate
Control:	Private
W/A:	Yorkshire
Comments:	Very pleasant water, sometimes heavily fished. Car park and refreshment bar. One side suitable for disabled anglers. Groundbait, keepnets and nuts as baits not allowed. No close season. Information from the owner, Keith Davis. Tel: Doncaster 974258

Wintersett Reservoir

Location:	Two miles from Crofton village in between Wakefield and Doncaster
Type and Size:	Wintersett is the small lake next to Wintersett Reservoir. The fishery also includes Cold Hindley Reservoir
How to Find:	Take the A638 Doncaster road from Wakefield. After about 2½ miles, take a right turn down Lodge Lane to Crofton village. The lakes are about two miles beyond the village
Carp Stock:	Quite well stocked with plenty of doubles, and mirrors to 27lbs
Category:	Mixed Fishery
Other Species:	Roach, perch, tench, bream and pike from the small Wintersett lake. Crucians from Cold Hindley
Permits:	From bailiff on bankside
Control:	Coal Industries Social Welfare Organisation
BK Rating:	Moderate
W/A:	Yorkshire

STAFFORDSHIRE

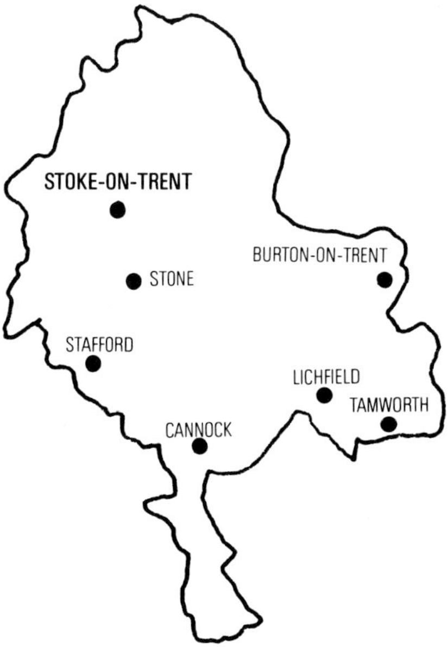

Amington (Pigs)

Location: Near Tamworth
Type and Size: 40 acre natural lake
How to Find: Near Shuttington village
Carp Stock: Well stocked with small carp, but fish up to possible 30lb
Category: Mixed Fishery
Other Species: General coarse fish
Permits: Birchmoor Angling Club. Secretary: Peter Mason, c/o Game Cock Inn public house. Tel: 0827 895144. Also day tickets available for small part of lake from Pritty Pigs public house on bank
Cost: £7 per year
Control: Club
Restrictions: No fishing from one bank
BK Rating: Easy for small fish, large fish - Difficult, due to quantity of small ones
W/A: Severn Trent
Comments: Lake formed by land subsidence and is mostly very shallow, river runs along one margin. Stalking best bet to sort out better fish

Canwell Pool

Location: Canwell estate
Type and Size: 5 acre estate lake
How to Find: Off the A453 Tamworth to Sutton Coldfield road
Carp Stock: Well stocked with carp to mid-20's
Category: Mixed Fishery
Other Species: General coarse fish
Permits: Sutton Coldfield AS. Secretary: Don Jones, Bricklyn House, Bulls Lane, Wishaw, Sutton Coldfield B76 9QN
Cost: £25 + possible joining fee
Control: Private
BK Rating: Fairly Hard
W/A: Severn Trent
Comments: There is a long waiting list to join SCAS. A very quiet and attractive water

Chasewater Lake

Location: Chasewater Park, Brownhills, Cannock
Type and Size: 20 acre lake
Carp Stock: Not many carp, but possibly a couple of 20's
Category: Few Carp
Other Species: Roach, rudd, bream, tench, perch and pike
Cost: About £2 per day
Control: Private
BK Rating: Very Difficult
W/A: Severn Trent
Comments: A public water, and very busy. Only worth a try if you fancy something really hard, as this is certainly not a carp water

Cudmore Fishery

Location: Whitmore, near the M6 and Newcastle-under-Lyme; the sign to the fishery will be seen 1½ miles from Whitmore on the Keele road
Type and Size: Two medium-sized man-made lakes
Carp Stock: Milo Pool - well stocked with carp to 20lbs; Avaco Pool has small carp
Category: Milo - Carp Only; Avaco - Mixed Fishery
Other Species: Chub, tench, roach and possibly some barbel
Permits: Day tickets on site, in advance only
Cost: £2.50 for two rods
Control: Cyril Brewster. Tel: 0782 680919
Restrictions: Lots....! No boilies, barbed hooks or hemp, no pole fishing (!); anglers must 'book in' and 'book out' even if they catch nothing
Baits/Methods: Sweetcorn and maggots, legered or float fished, and floaters also work well
BK Rating: Milo - Easy; Avaco - Moderate
W/A: Severn Trent
Comments: A new venue recently opened

Deep Hay Pool

Location: Near Leek
Type and Size: Two small pools
Carp Stock: Carp to about 15lbs

Category: Mixed Fishery
Other Species: Roach, rudd, bream and tench
Permits: Members only water of Leek and Morland Fishing Club. H Emery, 20 Osbourne Street, Leek; or enquire from local tackle shops
Restrictions: No day tickets; no night fishing
BK Rating: Moderate
W/A: Severn Trent

Ellenhall Pools

Location: Eccelshall, near Stone
Type and Size: 4 small farm pools
Carp Stock: Some carp, numbers and sizes not known
Category: Mixed Fishery
Other Species: Roach, tench, bream and perch
Permits: N Dale Tackle Shop, Albert Street, Stone
Control: Stone and District AS
BK Rating: Not known
W/A: Severn Trent

Fisherwick Fly Fishing Lakes

Location: Whittington, near Lichfield. Tel: 0543 472515/472934
Type and Size: The Long Stream (500 yards); the Pump Pool (¼ acre); the Small Pool (¼ acre)
Carp Stock: Well stocked with carp to double figures
Category: Mixed Fishery
Other Species: Roach and perch
Permits: On site at the address above - discounts for annual membership
Control: Midland Game Fisheries
BK Rating: Not known
W/A: Severn Trent
Comments: There are also three fly fishing lakes of 12 acres, 5 acres and 3 acres, and the Short Stream (fly fishing) - brown and rainbow trout in all these. Boats, tackle, rod licences, refreshments etc

Fradley Canal

Location: Burton-on-Trent
Type and Size: Small canal
How to Find: Near Burton-on-Trent
Carp Stock: Plenty of carp when located - stocked with 5,000 small carp in 1990
Category: Mixed Fishery
Other Species: General coarse fish
Permits: Enquire in local tackle shops
Cost: On application
BK Rating: Easy, when fish are located
Control: Club
W/A: Severn Trent
Comments: An early season catch last year was reported as 7 fish to 12lbs in 4 hours, on legered boilies, using a 4lb line. For information try Burton-on-Trent AA - D J Clark, 7 Denton Rise, Burton-on-Trent DE13 OQB

Hopton Pools

Location: Hopton, near Stafford
Type and Size: Small lakes
Carp Stock: Some carp, sizes not known
Category: Mixed Fishery
Other Species: Tench and other coarse fish
Permits: Day and weekly tickets - Izaak Walton (Stafford) AA - T H Babbs, 4 Fieldside, Wildwood, Stafford
Control: Club
BK Rating: Not known
W/A: Severn Trent

Serpentine Reservoir

Location: Knypersley, Stoke-on-Trent
Type and Size: Reservoir of 50 acres
How to Find: Knypersley is north of Stoke-on-Trent about half-way between Stoke and Congleton on the A527
Carp Stock: Not many carp in a very large water, but there are one or two big fish of well over 20lbs
Category: Few Carp
Other Species: General coarse fish
Permits: Cheshire Anglers' Association - members only. Secretary: G Brassington, 12 Highfield Drive, Nantwich, Cheshire
Control: Club
BK Rating: Very Difficult
W/A: Severn Trent
Comments: Waters of this kind, which are large and contain only a very few big carp, are only recommended for experienced and successful carp anglers prepared to spend very long periods without catching, for the sake of a very big fish

Shuttington Pool

Location: Near Tamworth
Type and Size: 11 acre natural lake
How to Find: Near Shuttington village
Carp Stock: Well stocked to mid-20's
Category: Mixed Fishery
Other Species: General coarse fish
Permits: Lambs Angling Club. Secretary: Mr Ghent, Hopleys, Ingram Pit Lane, Amington, Tamworth, Staffs B77 3JA. Tel: 0827 51033
Cost: £17 + £5 joining fee
Control: Club
Restrictions: See club book
BK Rating: Unknown
W/A: Severn Trent
Comments: May be a very long waiting list to join Lambs AC

Stowe Pool

Location: Lichfield
Type and Size: Town lake of 4 acres
How to Find: In the centre of Lichfield
Carp Stock: Some carp to over 20lbs
Category: Few Carp
Other Species: General coarse fish
Permits: Day tickets on bank
Cost: £1.50 per day approximately
Control: Council
BK Rating: Difficult
W/A: Severn Trent
Comments: A busy town lake

SUFFOLK

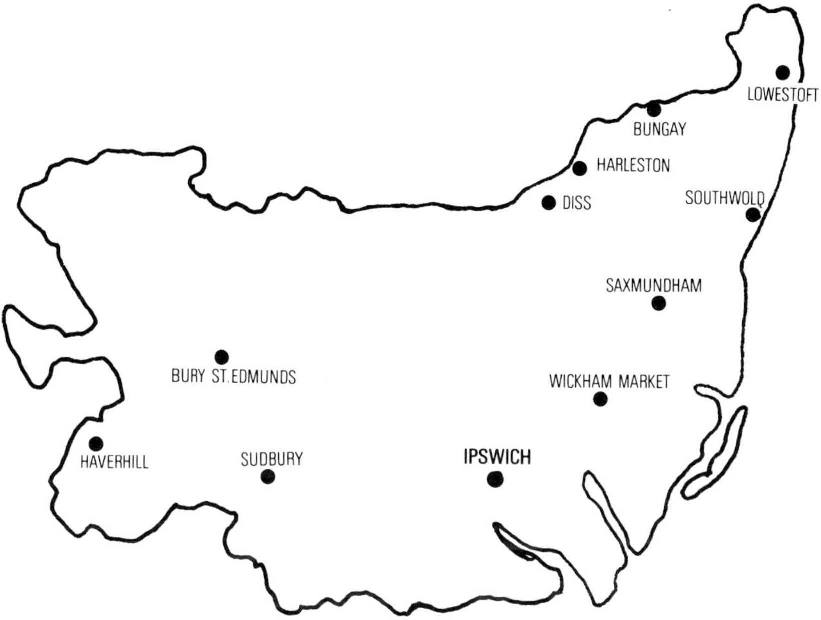

Barham Pits

Location: Claydon, near Ipswich
Type and Size: 2 pits of 20 acres and 4 acres
How to Find: At Barham, 5 miles north of Ipswich, off the A45 Ipswich-Norwich road; Pest House Lane
Carp Stock: Some good carp in both waters
Category: Mixed Fishery
Other Species: General coarse fish; big pike
Permits: Members only. Gipping Angling and Preservation Society. Membership from G Alderson, 19 Clover Close, Chantry Estate, Ipswich
Cost: About £20 - £25
BK Rating: Moderate
Control: Club
W/A: Anglian
Comments: The big lake is very attractive, with islands and bays. The club has other lakes and 10 miles of the River Gipping

Brandon Lake

Location: Close to the Little Ouse in Brandon, near Thetford
Type and Size: Man-made lake of about three acres
How to Find: In Brandon - Remembrance Park
Carp Stock: Some carp to double figures
Category: Mixed Fishery
Other Species: Roach, perch and bream
Permits: Day tickets before fishing from the Rod'n'Line tackle shop, Thetford. Tel: 0842 752930
Cost: £2 per day
BK Rating: Moderate
Control: Club
W/A: Anglian

Broome Pits

Location: Near Bungay, about a mile off the B1332 from Norwich
Type and Size: Four pits from one to four acres
Carp Stock: Mirrors to double figures
Category: Mixed Fishery
Other Species: Crucians, roach, pike and big bream
Permits: Day tickets on bank
Cost: 50p per day: £2.50 weekly
Control: Bungay Cherry Tree AC - membership at £10 per season open to all, including numerous other waters in the area. Details from the Secretary, Mr I Gosling, 37 St.Mary's Terrace, Bungay. Tel: Bungay 2982. Pit administrator is Mr R Patrick. Tel: Bungay 4371
BK Rating: Moderate
W/A: Anglian
Comments: The Club Secretary has a leaflet on these waters. The two bigger pits are about ten feet in depth about one rod length from the bank

Bures Lake

Location: Bures, near Colchester
Type and Size: Beautiful wooded gravel pit of 4½ acres
How to Find: Take the B1508 into Bures from Colchester, and after the river bridge turn right past the church and along the Nayland road; 500 yards further on you will see the LAA entrance sign and gate
Carp Stock: A small number of big carp to over 20lbs
Category: Few Carp
Other Species: Many big tench to 6lbs, bream to 8lbs, roach, rudd, perch and pike
Permits: A members only water of the London Anglers Association - no day or season tickets, so to fish you will have to join the LAA, or one of the affiliated clubs. Details from the LAA, Hoe Street, Walthamstow, London E7.
Cost: £15 a year, to include many other fine waters all over the country
Restrictions: Members only
Control: LAA
BK Rating: Difficult
W/A: Anglian
Comments: This water became well known to carp anglers some years ago when a carp of well over 30lbs was reported from it, though most carp anglers I have spoken to did not believe that the weight was genuine

Colston Hall Ponds

Location: Colston Hall, Dennington, near Harleston
Type and Size: Two irrigation reservoirs of about an acre each
How to Find: From Harleston take the B1116 to Dennington, and turn left onto the A1120. In two miles turn down a lane to Colston Hall
Carp Stock: The pond nearest the house contains some carp. The other is about 6ft deep and is well stocked with mirrors to double figures
Category: Pond near house - Mixed Fishery; Other Pond - Carp Only
Other Species: Tench and rudd in the Mixed Fishery pond
Permits: Members only water of the Framlingham and Dist AA. Open to all for an annual subscription of £9 (£5 juniors) with several other local ponds and fishing on the River Deben. Details from the Secretary, Mr Brian Finbow, Saxmundham Angling Centre, Market Place, Saxmundham. Tel: Saxmundham 3443
Control: Club
BK Rating: Moderate
Restrictions: Members only
W/A: Anglian

Diss Mere

Location: In the town of Diss
Type and Size: 4 acre mere
How to Find: Take the A140/A1066 from Norwich to Diss
Carp Stock: Some mirrors to double figures
Category: Mixed Fishery
Other Species: General coarse fish
Permits: Diss AC members only. Membership from 'Catch 22' Tackle shop, 23 Victoria Road, Diss. Tel: 3272
Cost: About £7 per year
BK Rating: Difficult
Control: Club
W/A: Anglian

Ditchingham Pit

Location: Bungay Common
Type and Size: 3 acre gravel pit
How to Find: Bungay Common, off the B1332 alongside the River Waveney
Carp Stock: Well stocked with carp to doubles
Category: Mixed Fishery
Other Species: General coarse fish
Permits: Bungay Cherry Tree AC members only. Membership from Mr I Gosling, 37 St Mary's Terrace, Bungay. Tel: 2982
Cost: About £10
BK Rating: Moderate
Control: Club
W/A: Anglian
Comments: Attractive lake. This club has much other fishing in the area

Flood Park

Location: Haverhill
How to Find: Opposite Sainsbury's superstore in Haverhill
Type and Size: 2½ acre clay pit
Carp Stock: About 50 fish to upper doubles
Category: Mixed Fishery
Other Species: Very large perch, roach, rudd and bream
Permits: Haverhill AC. Permits avaiable from J & A Tackle. £11 per season. £7 Juniors and OAP's free
BK Rating: Moderate
W/A: Anglian
Comments: Carp are doing well and twenties are expected soon

Glemsford Lake

Location: Near Sudbury and Long Melford
Type and Size: 3 gravel pits of 18, 14 and 3 acres
How to Find: Take the A1092 from Long Melford and then to Cavendish. The lakes are on the left, opposite Glemsford Road
Category: Few Carp
Other Species: General coarse fish
Permits: London Anglers Association - members only, open to all. Join through affiliated clubs or the LAA, Hoe Street, Walthamstow, London E17
Cost: About £12 a year
BK Rating: Difficult
Control: Club
Restrictions: No night fishing
W/A: Anglian
Comments: The LAA has many waters all over the south of England, including Bures Lake near Nayland, which contains a few 20lb carp

Great Lodge Farm Ponds

Location: Great Lodge Farm, Dennington, near Harleston
Type and Size: 4 small farm ponds on private estate
How to Find: Take the B1116 from Harleston to Dennington, then left onto A1120. In 2 miles turn right onto the B1120 and a mile further on turn right down a track to the farm
Carp Stock: Mirrors to doubles
Category: Mixed Fisheries
Other Species: General coarse fish
Permits: Framlingham and Dist AC. (members only). Open to all. Apply to the Secretary, Mr B Finbow, Saxmundham Angling Centre, Market Place, Saxmundham. Tel: 3443
Cost: About £9 a year
BK Rating: Moderate
W/A: Anglian
Comments: Membership also includes other local ponds and a stretch of the River Debden

Gunssons Lake

Location: White House Farm, Sibton
Type and Size: One acre pond
How to Find: Off the A120, south-west of Southwold
Carp Stock: Well stocked with mirrors to doubles
Category: Carp Water
Other Species: Some tench and bream
Permits: Season tickets only from Mr Kitson. Tel: Peasenhall 260
Cost: On application
BK Rating: Moderate
Control: Private
Restrictions: Season tickets and touring caravanners only
W/A: Anglian
Comments: Shallow, coloured water, mainly for touring caravanners

Gunton Hall Lake A

Location: Corton, near Lowestoft
Type and Size: Two acre lake
How to Find: From Lowestoft take the A12 towards Great Yarmouth: Gunton Hall is on the right, just before Corton
Carp Stock: Some mirrors to double figures
Category: Mixed Fishery
Other Species: Tench, roach, rudd
Permits: Day tickets from Reception at Hall - must be booked in advance. Summer season and winter season tickets
Cost: On application. About £4 a day
BK Rating: Moderate
Control: Gunton Hall. Tel: Lowestoft 720288
W/A: Anglian
Comments: This is a holiday centre; golf, tennis, archery and clay pigeon shooting for residents. For details telephone Gunton Hall. Attractive, weedy lake, quite shallow

Henham Dairy Pond

Location: Henham Park Estate, near Brampton
Type and Size: One acre estate lake only about 3 feet deep
How to Find: From Beccles take the A145 to Blythburgh. Go through Brampton and after 2 miles turn left into Henham Park Estate. The pond is on the left hand side
Category: Mixed Fishery
Other Species: Crucians, tench, roach and rudd
Permits: Day tickets from the farmhouse before fishing
Cost: Approximately £1 per day
Restrictions: No night fishing; one rod only; limited number of tickets
Control: Henham and District Angling Club (details from farm)
BK Rating: Easy
W/A: Anglian

Holmans Pits

Location: Northfield Farm, Southery, near Downham Market. The pits are on the left off the B1386 Southery road, and probably just in Norfolk!
Type and Size: Three shallow pits of one to three acres
Carp Stock: Some carp, sizes not known
Category: Mixed Fishery
Permits: Members only water of Kings Lynn AC. Membership £12 to include many other local waters, from the Secretary, Mr George Bear. Tel: Downham Market 387114
Other Species: Roach, rudd, bream, tench, perch and pike
Control: Club. Southery is is Norfolk, so the pits may also be Norfolk
Restrictions: Members only
BK Rating: Difficult
W/A: Anglian

Ickworth Lake

Location: Horringer, near Bury St. Edmunds, in the middle of the village
Type and Size: 5 acre estate lake
Carp Stock: Some carp, sizes not known
Category: Probably Few Carp
Other Species: Roach,rudd and tench
Permits: From bailiff on bank
Cost: £2 per day
Control: National Trust
BK Rating: Difficult
W/A: Anglian

Lakeside Caravan Park A

Location: Saxmundham
Type and Size: Three acre lake
How to Find: Find Harleston and take the B1116 to Framlingham, then the B1119 Saxmundham road. At Rendham you will see signs on the left to the caravan park and lake
Carp Stock: A good head of mirror carp to double figures
Category: Mixed Fishery
Other Species: Roach, bream, perch and tench
Permits: Day tickets from bailiff who calls round. Information from the Manager. Tel: 0728 3344
Cost: About £2 per day
Control: Caravan site
BK Rating: Moderate
W/A: Anglian
Comments: Campers and touring caravans welcome

Long Pond

Location: Stoke-by-Clare
How to Find: Alongside road between Cavendish and Clare
Type and Size: 2 acre clay pit
Carp Stock: Well stocked with fish to upper doubles
Category: Mixed Fishery
Other Species: Roach, rudd, crucians, bream and tench

Permits: Enquire locally
BK Rating: Easy
W/A: Anglian
Comments: An idyllic lake

Redgrave Lake

Location: Redgrave Park, Botesdale, near Norwich
Type and Size: Huge estate lake with open bank - wooded at the dam end
Carp Stock: Only a few, but some big ones
Category: Few Carp
Other Species: Many bream to 8lbs, tench, roach, perch, eels and pike to 25lbs
Permits: Members only water. Apply to Redgrave Park, Redgrave. Tel: 0379 898206
Cost: £29.50 per year
Control: Private
Restrictions: Members only - no day tickets
BK Rating: Difficult
W/A: Anglian

Reydon No.1 Pit

Location: Lakeside Park Development, near Southwold off the A1095
Type and Size: Three acre reed-fringed gravel pit
How to Find: Take the A1095 from Southwold, and after going over a bridge, turn into the Lakeside Park estate road. The car parking area is behind the pit.
Carp Stock: Some carp to 20lbs
Permits: Purdy's Newsagents, 31 High Street, Southwold. Tel: Lowestoft 724250. In advance only
Carp Stock: £2 per day
Control: Southwold and Dist. Freshwater Angling Preservation Society, Secretary, Mr Barry Reid. Tel: Lowestoft 518198
Restrictions: No night fishing. One rod only. No Sunday fishing. No fishing until 9am
BK Rating: Not known
W/A: Anglian
Comments: This lake is over 20ft deep in places. The club also has other waters. Half price for juniors. A new fishery has been constructed nearby, especially as a carp fishery, and known as Reydon No.4 Pit. Permits as above, and the water has been stocked with mirrors and commons to double figures

Roydon Sand Pit

Location: Roydon, near Diss
Type and Size: Little ¾ acre pit, 25 feet deep in places
How to Find: From Diss take the A1066 to Roydon. Just before the service station, turn left down a lane to the house
Carp Stock: Small carp
Category: Mixed Fishery
Other Species: Tench, rudd, crucians
Permits: From the house next to the pit; Mrs Alasia. Tel: Diss 4409
Cost: About £2 per day
BK Rating: Easy

Control:	Private
Restrictions:	Not known
W/A:	Anglian

Rushbrooke Lake

Location:	Near Bury St. Edmunds
Type and Size:	3 acre lake
How to Find:	Take the A45 from Bury towards Ipswich. In 2 miles turn right, then second right to Wellnethan. The lake is on the left
Carp Stock:	Carp to over 20lbs
Category:	Mixed Fishery
Other Species:	Tench, bream, roach
Permits:	Members only - yearly from N Bruton. Tel: Bury St. Edmunds 66074 or local tackle shops
Cost:	On application
BK Rating:	Moderate
Control:	Private
Restrictions:	No night fishing
W/A:	Anglian
Comments:	Membership also entitles members to fish West Stow Country Park, an 18 acre pit, which is a bird sanctuary (no night fishing) containing some carp to doubles - this water is near Lackford, off the A1101

Starfield Pit

Location:	Long Melford, near Sudbury
Type and Size:	Gravel pit about 6 acres
How to Find:	Take the A134 from Sudbury to Rodbridge Corner and turn left here towards Foxearth. Go through Liston and to the right of the chemical factory and take a track on the right through Liston Gardens. The pit is on the right at the bottom of the track
Carp Stock:	Quite well stocked with mirrors to double figure size
Category:	Mixed Fishery
Other Species:	Bream, roach and pike
Permits:	Day tickets in advance only from Mr N Mealham, 6 Springfield Terrace, East Street, Sudbury. Tel: Sudbury 77139. Season ticket/Club membership costs approximately £12 from the Club Secretary as above
Cost:	About £1.50 per day. Approximately £12 per season for club membership
Control:	Long Melford and District Angling Association
BK Rating:	Moderate
W/A:	Anglian
Comments:	Irregular shaped pit with some weed of 2 - 10 feet deep, with islands

The Deep Hole

Location:	Frostend, one mile from Wrentham, near Lowestoft
Type and Size:	Small clay pit between 14ft and 20ft deep
How to Find:	Take the A12 from Lowestoft, go through Wrentham, and turn right just before the Wangford Plough pub. Pit is one mile, on the right
Carp Stock:	Some mirrors to double figures
Category:	Possibly Few Carp

Other Species: Perch, chub, roach, rudd
Permits: Members only water of the Southwold and Dist. Freshwater Preservation Society. To join apply to the Membership Secretary, Mr Barry Reid, 19 Sussex Road, Lowestoft. Tel: Lowestoft 518198
Cost: £14 a year, and £8 joining fee (juniors half price), which includes 5 other ponds
Control: Club
Restrictions: Members only
BK Rating: Not known
W/A: Anglian

Thorpeness Mere

Location: Thorpeness, near Leiston
Type and Size: Huge lake with many islands
How to Find: Norwich - Bungay - Halesworth, then the A12 to Yoxford. Take the B1122 to Leiston, and the B1353 to Thorpeness
Carp Stock: Some commons to 10lbs
Category: Few Carp
Other Species: Roach, rudd, eels
Permits: Free (100 yards only)
Cost: None
BK Rating: Difficult
Control: Thorpeness Estate Office. Tel: Aldeburgh 3555
Restrictions: No fishing on most of the bank. No night fishing
W/A: Anglian
Comments: This is a 'children's playground' with 150 boats for hire - might do for a family day out. The lake is very shallow, only up to 2½ feet deep

West Stow Country Park

Location: Just off the A1101 Bury St. Edmunds - Mildenhall road. Just after the bridge over the River Lark, the country park will be seen on the right
Type and Size: 18 acre pit in a bird sanctuary. The lake has three islands and depths of up to 25ft
Carp Stock: Some double figure carp
Category: Probably Few Carp
Other Species: Tench, roach, perch, bream and pike
Permits: Members only. Permits from local tackle shops or from Mr N Bruton. Tel: Bury St. Edmunds 66074
Cost: £12 per year, juniors half price. Also includes Rushbrooke Lake
Control: Club
Restrictions: No night fishing
BK Rating: Not known
W/A: Anglian

Weybread Gravel Pits

Location: Weybread near Harleston, and quite near Waveney Valley Lakes
How to Find: Take the A140 from Norwich, and at Pulham Market take the B1134 to Harleston. Then take the road to Weybread and after crossing the river the pits will be seen on either side of the road
Type and Size: Five gravel pits, one of which is very big

Carp Stock:	The middle pit is very well stocked with mirrors; many are doubles and there are also some 20's. Club only pit is also well stocked with carp
Category:	Middle Pit - Carp Water
Other Species:	Crucians, roach, perch, tench, bream and pike
Permits:	Day tickets in advance only from G Denny, The Tackle Shop, Harleston. Tel: Harleston 852248; and the Cherry Tree public house in Harleston. Club membership Harleston and District Angling Club - details from tackle shop. Club Secretary: J Adamson, Yew Villa, Roydon,Diss - tickets
Cost:	Day tickets about £1.20 per day, which includes the 4 pits but not the small club carp water. Club membership £7 per year (small club pit plus several miles of the Waveney), and an EXTRA £8 a year to include all 5 pits and the river
Restrictions:	Club pit cannot be fished on a day ticket. Night fishing in all pits is for CLUB MEMBERS ONLY
BK Rating:	Moderate
Baits/Methods:	Advanced carp methods, baits and rigs usually needed for the larger carp
W/A:	Anglian
Comments:	Good gravel pit club fishery, with 20's possible. Worth joining the club for the small pit and the night fishing

White House Farm

Location:	White House Farm, Rendham
Type and Size:	Shallow half acre lake
Carp Stock:	Some mirrors to 10lbs
Category:	Mixed Fishery
Other Species:	Roach, perch, crucians, and small tench
Permits:	Mr Tate. Tel: Renham 485
Control:	Private
Restrictions:	No fishing, except for those parking touring caravans on the land
BK Rating:	Not known
W/A:	Anglian

Wickhambrook Lake

Location:	Wickhambrook, Suffolk
How to Find:	About 2 miles outside village towards Newmarket
Type and Size:	Narrow 2 acre clay pit
Carp Stock:	Very heavily stocked with carp to mid-doubles
Category:	Carp Water
Other Species:	A few roach, rudd and bream
Permits:	£7.50 on the bank per 12 hours for 2 rods
BK Rating:	Very Easy
W/A:	Anglian
Comments:	Very prolific, 100 pound catches common, ideal water for beginner

Wickham Market Reservoir

Location:	Near Wickham Market
Type and Size:	1½ acre lake
How to Find:	From Harleston, take the B1116 to Framlingham and Wickham Market. The lake is visible from the road, on the left just before the town
Carp Stock:	Some carp to double figures

Category: Mixed Fishery
Other Species: Roach, rudd, perch
Permits: Day tickets - Rod and Gun, Woodbridge. Tel: 03942 2377
Cost: On application - about £1.50 per day
BK Rating: Moderate
Control: Woodbridge Angling Club
Restrictions: Tickets in advance only. No night fishing
W/A: Anglian
Comments: Small weedy water

Wickham Skeith Mere

Location: Village common of Wickham Skeith
Type and Size: Small common pond
How to Find: A140 from Norwich to Stoke Ash (27 miles) then turn right to Wickham Skeith
Carp Stock: Well stocked with small carp
Category: Carp Water
Other Species: Small pike
Permits: Free
BK Rating: Easy
W/A: Anglian
Comments: A free fishery ideal for youngsters or the family. Shallow and weedy

SURREY

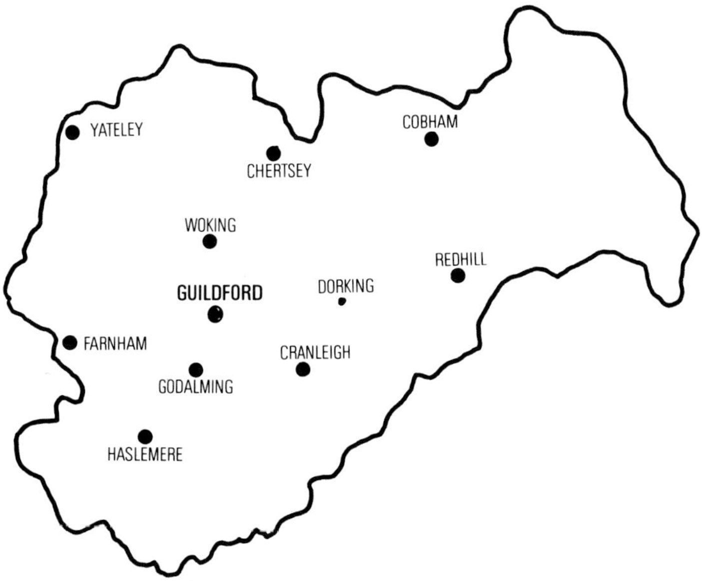

Ash Vale

Location: Lakeside Road, Ash Vale, Aldershot

Type and Size: Gravel pits. Lake 1 – 3 acres; Lake 2 – 1¼ acres; Lake 3 – 7½ acres

How to Find: From the A30 at Camberley, go to Frimley, then Frimley Green on the A321. After 3 miles take the Ash Vale road (A3013) then turn right onto Lakeside Road. The entrance to the fishery is under the railway bridge on the left

Carp Stock: Carp to 20lbs

Category: Mixed Fishery

Permits: Leisure Sport Angling, Thorpe Park, Staines Road, Chertsey, Surrey. Tel: Chertsey 64872. Season tickets only – no day tickets. Send for permit application form and enclose when sending in the form two passport size photographs of yourself. Ash Vale is included under 'unrestricted single water' permits. If you want to fish a number of Leisure Sport waters under this category, you can apply for a Group Water Permit to include all 21 of their waters

Cost: Single Water Permit, Ash Vale – About £14. Junior/OAP/disabled – £7, Group Water Permit for 21 venues (65 lakes and 15 stretches of river) – £29. Junior/OAP/disabled – £14.50

Restrictions: No fires, no camping, no radios, no bright lights. Night fishing is allowed

Other Species: Crucian carp, tench, roach, rudd, perch. Pike in Lake 1

Control: Leisure Sport

BK Rating: Moderate

W/A: Thames

Comments: Send to Leisure Sport for the rule and guide book. Rules are strict in Leisure Sport waters and you will lose your membership if you break them

Badshot Lea Pond

Location: Badshot Lea, Farnham
Type and Size: Small pond
How to Find: Badshot Lea is on the outskirts of Farnham, about 3 miles from the centre of town, north of the Hogs Back
Carp Stock: Heavily stocked with carp of 10lbs, with a few doubles
Category: Carp Water
Other Species: General coarse fish
Permits: Farnham Angling Society. Secretary: 70 Prince Charles Crescent, Farnborough, Hants
Cost: On application
Control: Club
BK Rating: Easy
W/A: Thames

Beaver Farm

Location: Off the A22 Eastbourne road, Newchapel, Lingfield, near East Grinstead
Type and Size: Two lakes - Snipe Lake (2½ acres) and West Lake (small)
Carp Stock: Snipe Lake well stocked with carp, sizes not known; West Lake also has carp
Category: Mixed Fisheries
Other Species: Pike, rudd, roach and tench
Permits: From Beaver Farm
Cost: £5 per day, second rod £2; under 15's and OAP's half price weekdays only
Control: Private
Restrictions: No night fishing (8am to sunset); no keepnets, no radios
BK Rating: Not known
W/A: Southern

Brittens Pond

Location: Jacobs Well, near Guildford
Type and Size: Old pond of about 4 acres, recently dredged and stocked
How to Find: Find Salt Box Road, Jacobs Well, Guildford, off the A320 towards Woking
Carp Stock: About 300 fish to 19½lbs, some doubles, mostly small fish. Many of the carp are commons
Category: Carp Water
Other Species: Roach, rudd, tench and crucians
Permits: Guildford Angling Society. Secretary: G Pank, 72 St. Phillips Avenue, Worcester Park, Surrey. Day tickets from Guildford Angling Centre. Tel: 0483 506333
Cost: £30 per season. Day tickets about £3 per day
Control: Guildford Angling Centre
BK Rating: Easy
W/A: Thames
Comments: A heavily fished water. No floating baits; no night fishing - dawn to dusk only. Barbless hooks, size 12 or larger. Unhooking mat compulsory. No carp to be retained

Broadwater Lake

Location: Near Godalming
Type and Size: Lake of about 10 acres
Carp Stock: Very heavily stocked with many carp. Huge bags of small carp to 8lbs possible. Some doubles up to 20lbs
Category: Carp Water
Other Species: General coarse fish
Permits: Godalming Angling Society. Secretary: A Johnson, 86 Peper Harrow Road, Godalming, Surrey. Very long waiting list though juniors should get in at once
Cost: On application
Control: Club
BK Rating: Easy
W/A: Thames
Comments: A very easy water for small carp; it is hard to get through the small fish to catch the bigger ones, which are there. Club membership is hard to obtain

Chertsey

Location: Thorpe Road, near Chertsey
Type and Size: Gravel pit, 4½ acres
How to Find: Take the M25 to Staines and turn off at the A30 roundabout onto the A320 Staines–Chertsey road. Go to Egham, then Chertsey and take the right turn to Thorpe at the small roundabout. The entrance is on the right just before the M3 flyover
Carp Stock: Not known – the Leisure Sport guide book reports 'carp in excess of 20lbs'. We will assume it to be...
Category: Few Carp
Other Species: Bream, perch, roach, pike
Permits: Season tickets only from Leisure Sport, Thorpe Park, Staines Road, Chertsey, Surrey. Tel: 64872
Cost: £20 per season. Juniors/OAP/disabled £10
Restrictions: No night fishing. No trespassing onto Thorpe Park property. No parking on M3. Cars must not be driven round lake
BK Rating: Difficult
Control: Leisure Sport Angling
W/A: Thames

Cobham Lake

Location: Cobham, near Walton-on-Thames
Type and Size: Small lake
Carp Stock: Well stocked with carp
Category: Mixed Fishery
Other Species: Pike, tench and bream
Permits: A members only water of Walton-on-Thames AS. Secretary: A Finlayson, 14 Harrow Road, West Bedfont, Feltham, Greater London
Cost: Season – £25
BK Rating: Not known
W/A: Thames

Cobham Manor Fishery

Location: Off the M25 at Cobham, near Woking
Type and Size: 8 acre estate lake, 12 to 16 feet deep
Carp Stock: Well stocked with commons and mirrors to 34lbs
Category: Mixed Fishery
Other Species: Tench, bream, roach, rudd and pike to 25lbs+
Permits: Jeff Cornell Fishing Developments, Charter House, 29a London Road, Croydon CRO 2RB - syndicate only
Cost: About £30
Control: Cornell Fishery Developments
Baits/Methods: High protein baits and boilies work well
Restrictions: No keepnets
BK Rating: Moderate
W/A: Southern
Comments: Attractive natural lake on private estate, yet only half an hour from London. Stream fed, with beautiful surroundings. Membership may include other carp waters

Cut Mill

Location: Elstead, near Farnham
Type and Size: Estate lake of about 7 acres
How to Find: Elstead is on the B3001 between Farnham and Milford
Carp Stock: About 200 carp, mostly doubles, and some twenties; lake record is 29lbs 12ozs
Category: Carp Water
Other Species: Mixed coarse fish
Permits: Farnham Angling Society - season tickets only. Secretary: 70 Prince Charles Crescent, Farnborough, Hants
Cost: About £20 per year plus a joining fee. Details on application
Control: Club
Restrictions: No long stay fishing - 48 hours maximum
Baits/Methods: You will need all the modern rigs, such as hair and bolt rigs and the most sophisticated baits and methods on this hard-fished carp water
BK Rating: Moderate
W/A: Thames
Comments: This is quite a well-known carp water and is heavily fished by carp specialists. It is sometimes hard to find a place to fish as there are only about 20 swims on the lake; there are many trees and a marshy area. Recommended mainly for experienced carp anglers. It is a pleasant and attractive lake

Cutt Mill House

Location: Between Guildford and Farnham
Type and Size: Beautiful 7 acre lake next to Farnham AA's well known Cutt Mill
Carp Stock: Well stocked with carp to over 30lbs
Category: Mixed Fishery
Other Species: Pike, tench, bream, roach, rudd and perch
Permits: In advance only from Mrs R Skinner, Cutt Mill House, Puttenham GU3 1BG. Tel: 0252 702229
Control: Private
BK Rating: Moderate

W/A: Thames
Comments: This water, always known to contain big carp, was only opened in 1990. It could produce some big fish

Firs Farm Lake

Location: Near Cranleigh
Type and Size: Newly dug lake of about 4 acres with two islands
How to Find: From Guildford take the A281 for 8 miles to a left turn into Wildwood Lane, then turn right at the T-junction into Knowle Lane. In a mile you will see the Firs Farm on the right
Carp Stock: Some small carp to about 7lbs - recently stocked
Category: Mixed Fishery
Other Species: Chub, perch, bream and some trout, as this was formerly a trout fishery
Permits: Day tickets on bank
Cost: £5 per rod, dawn till dusk; £3 for juniors, OAPs and the disabled
Control: W Welch. Tel: 0403 822878
Restrictions: No night fishing; no boilies
BK Rating: Not known
W/A: Thames

Frensham Great and Little Ponds

Location: Frensham, between Farnham and Aldershot
Type and Size: Big Pond is a very old, large lake of about 30 acres; Small Pond about 5 acres
Carp Stock: Both quite well stocked - the Big Pond did have carp in it until recently to well over 30lbs, but most of these fish died in the late 80's
Category: Mixed Fishery
Other Species: Most coarse fish
Permits: From the Creel, Station Road, Aldershot
Cost: Day - £3; season - £26 + £2 joining fee
Control: Farnham and District AS
BK Rating: Difficult
W/A: Southern

Goldsworth Water Park

Location: Goldsworth Park, Woking - off the A425 near Knaphill
Type and Size: 20 acre lake on a housing estate
Carp Stock: Some carp to doubles
Category: Few Carp?
Other Species: Roach, tench, bream, chub and perch
Permits: Day tickets on bank, dawn till dusk only
Cost: £3 for one rod, and £4.50 for two rods, with reductions for juniors, OAP's and the disabled; annual permits at £25, or £35 to include night fishing
Control: Woking Water Activity Centre; Head Bailiff Brian Rich. Tel: 0483 764836 after 6.30pm. Other details from Woking Tackle Shop
Restrictions: No night fishing on day tickets; no bloodworm (!); only 50 boilies per session (I expect they count them!)
BK Rating: Moderate to Difficult
W/A: Thames

Hungerford Lake

Location: Near Redhill, just off the M25
Type and Size: Medium sized lake, much used for match fishing
Carp Stock: Very heavily stocked with small carp to about 10lbs; hundreds in the 2-3lb range
Category: Carp Water
Other Species: Tench and roach
Permits: Local tackle shops
Control: Club, but we are not sure which - enquire locally
BK Rating: Very Easy - small carp caught on match tackle
W/A: Thames

Lodge Pond

Location: Off the A325 Farnham-Bordon road
Type and Size: Lake of about 3 acres
How to Find: Take the A325 from Farnham
Carp Stock: About 100 carp up to around 17lbs
Category: Carp Water
Other Species: General coarse fish
Permits: Farnham Angling Society. Some temporary membership (day) tickets from local tackle shops; day tickets on bank
Cost: £5 for 1 rod; £10 per 2 rods. Farnham AS membership about £22 per season plus an entry fee
Control: Club, Tel: 0420 89694 - T Tarling
BK Rating: Easy
W/A: Thames
Comments: A pleasant lake on Forestry Commission land

Newdigate

Location: New Barn Lane, Newdigate, near Dorking
Type and Size: Clay pits. Lake 1 - 8½ acres; Lake 2 - 3½ acres
How to Find: Take the A24 from Dorking, turn left onto Newdigate Road, then take left fork to T-junction in Newdigate village. Turn right, then first left at church. Bear left at next fork and the lakes are about 400 yards on the right, park in car park only
Carp Stock: Good catches of carp reported to 8lbs (Lake 2); 5½lbs (Lake 1). Much larger carp have been seen in Lake 1
Category: Carp Waters
Other Species: None listed in guide book
Permits: Season tickets only from Leisure Sport, Thorpe Park, Staines Road, Chertsey, Surrey. Tel: Chertsey 64872
Cost: £20 per season, junior/OAP/disabled - £10
Restrictions: Night fishing permitted. Usual rules apply. No swimming or boating
BK Rating: Easy. Guide book reports 'extremely good catches'
Baits/Methods: Normal carp methods and baits
Control: Leisure Sport Angling
W/A: Thames
Comments: Looks like a good water for some fairly easy catches of small carp, with the chance of something much bigger

Old Bury Hill

Location: Lake View, Old Bury Hill, Dorking
Type and Size: 12½ acre estate lake 200 years old, deep at one end, with lilies at the other
How to Find: Near Dorking, just off the A25 Dorking–Guildford road
Carp Stock: Plenty of mid-doubles; some good low 20's; best fish 30lbs
Category: Mixed Fishery
Other Species: Tench, bream, rudd, crucians, perch, roach, pike and zander
Permits: Day tickets on bank; season tickets - Lake View, Old Bury Hill, Dorking. Tel: Dorking 883621 (9am to 9pm) (Mike Ewin)
Cost: One rod £6; two rods £10; juniors £4 and £7 respectively
BK Rating: Moderate
Control: Private
Restrictions: No night fishing; no sacking; no particles
W/A: Thames
Comments: An attractive, fairly shallow lake. Large, hard boilies needed to avoid the big tench. Boats can be hired, but must be booked in advance. Refreshments and toilets on bank

Priory Lake

Location: Priory Farm, Nutfield
Type and Size: Lake of 2½ acres
Carp Stock: Well stocked with carp to doubles
Category: Mixed Fishery
Other Species: Rudd, perch, roach and tench
Permits: Day tickets on bank - Tuesdays only
Cost: £4.50 from 7am till dusk; £2.50 from 4pm
Control: Private
Restrictions: No night fishing; tickets limited on certain days; no wading and anglers must fish from allocated pegs
BK Rating: Easy
W/A: Thames
Comments: This is mainly a match water, but good carp are caught close to the bank, or by the islands

River Valley Fishery

Location: River Valley, Sandhurst Road, Yateley, Camberley
Type and Size: Gravel pit of 16 acres
How to Find: This lake is in the same road as Tri-Lakes and the Leisure Sport Lakes
Carp Stock: Well stocked with carp to 30lbs
Category: Mixed Fishery
Other Species: Rudd to 3½lbs; perch, pike, tench
Permits: On site. Day and night permits
Cost: About £2.50 per day; approximately £3.50 per night
BK Rating: Difficult
Control: Private
Baits/Methods: Usual carp baits and methods
W/A: Thames
Comments: Season tickets at about £25 for day; £35 for night. Very deep 47 year old lake, oldest in area, attractive with trees, bushes etc. For information telephone 0252 873865. There are also two smaller lakes and 1½ miles of the River Blackwater containing trout and chub

River Wey

Location: Byfleet and Wisley
Type and Size: Tributary of the River Thames
Carp Stock: Some fish to around 20lbs
Category: Few Carp
Other Species: Pike, dace, roach, chub, barbel, bream and perch
Permits: Byfleet AA - Mrs B Stilwell, 15 Rutson Road, Byfleet
Cost: £20 per season
Control: Club
BK Rating: Very Difficult
W/A: Thames

Send

Location: Send, near Woking
Type and Size: Two pits
Carp Stock: Well stocked with carp to over 30lbs
Category: Mixed Fishery
Other Species: Tench and perch
Permits: A members only water of Woking and District AA - new members welcome. Details from the Secretary: D Powell, Maymont, Guildford Road, Knaphill, Woking
Control: Club
Restrictions: Members only, though some guest tickets for members' friends
BK Rating: Very Difficult
W/A: Thames

TriLakes

Location: Yateley Road, Sandhurst
Type and Size: Two gravel pits of about 14 acres
How to Find: Take the Sandhurst road and turn into Yateley Road, at Yateley. Fishery is on the right just after the entrance to Yateley (Match Lake)
Carp Stock: Not very heavily stocked with carp, but there are a number of 20's and thirties, with the best mirror caught over 35lbs
Category: Mixed Fishery
Other Species: Tench, roach, rudd, perch, bream, chub, pike, trout
Permits: Must be obtained before fishing from the fishing hut by the entrance - £5 per rod per day. C Homewood, TriLakes, Yateley Road, Sandhurst. Tel: Aldershot 873191
BK Rating: Difficult
Restrictions: No night fishing - open 7am to sunset
W/A: Thames
Comments: This is a well-known commercial fishery which is often heavily fished, especially at weekends. It is quite a pleasant water with many trees and bushes around the banks, and with islands. There are toilets, and a shop which sells bait, drinks, snacks and sweets and a licensed restaurant. A number of very big carp are caught each season. Fishing continues during the close season under special rules. Although most anglers are not carp specialists, the lake is fished by hard-line, and some well-known carp anglers, in the hope of a thirty. Long spells without takes can be expected

Willow Pond

Location: Beaver Farm, A22 Eastbourne road, Newchapel, Lingfield, near East Grinstead. Tel: 0342 833144
Type and Size: Half acre specialist carp fishery
Carp Stock: Well stocked with carp, sizes not known
Category: Carp Only
Permits: Day tickets from Beaver Farm
Cost: £5 per day, second rod £2
Control: Private
Restrictions: No night fishing; no keepnets
BK Rating: Not known
W/A: Southern
Comments: Publicity from Beaver Farm gives no information on the sizes of the fish in their three ponds - there is a third one acre fishery on the farm which is stocked with perch, pike, bream and roach

Wisley Common Ponds

Location: Wisley and Ockham Commons, Wisley
Type and Size: Several small common ponds
Carp Stock: Quite well stocked with carp, mostly small
Category: Mixed Fisheries
Other Species: Pike, perch and roach
Permits: FREE fishing
BK Rating: Easy
W/A: Thames

Yateley

Location: Sandhurst Road, Yateley, near Camberley
Type and Size: 14 gravel pits varying in size from ¾ acre to 12 acres
How to Find: Take the A30 from London to Camberley, then the A327 to Yateley, and turn right at the Royal Oak public house onto Sandhurst Road. Entrance to the west lakes is on the left and the car park to the east lakes is on the right
Carp Stock: Most of the lakes contain good carp. Lake 11, known as the Match Lake, has plenty of doubles and 20's. Lake 12, known as the Copse Lake, has a small number of big carp including a 30 which has been caught at 35lbs. On the west side of the road, the Car Park Lake (Lake 9) has produced a fish of 42lbs, and the North Lake (Lake 4) contains a small number of large carp, including the 45.12 caught by Ritchie McDonald, which was the second biggest carp ever landed in this country
Category: Carp Waters/Mixed Fisheries
Other Species: Crucians, tench, roach, rudd, pike and bream
Permits: This is a Leisure Sport Angling Special Venue. Season tickets only available, and they are limited, and issued on a 'first come - first served' basis. Apply to LSA, Thorpe Park, Staines Road, Chertsey, Surrey. Tel: Chertsey 64872
Cost: £28 per season, juniors/OAP/disabled - £14
BK Rating: The waters vary but most must be regarded as Fairly Hard
Baits/Methods: Since these waters contain big fish, most of which have been caught a number of times, you will need all the most advanced carp fishing techniques and baits
Control: Leisure Sport Angling

W/A: Thames

Comments: Whilst some of these pits are really mixed fisheries, and some contain few carp, we have marked them as mainly carp waters, because of the huge size of some of the fish. Carp specialists fish these waters knowing that they may have very long waits, but may catch a very big fish. Because of the size of these fish, Yateley has become known as one of the top big carp fisheries in the country. It is fished by leading carp specialists, and in most cases long stay fishing and much patience is needed. Some of the lakes are actually just across the border in Hampshire

TYNE AND WEAR

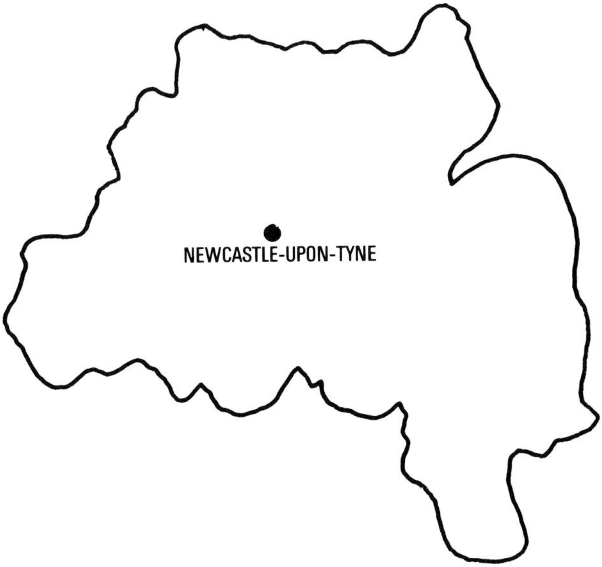

Fellgate Fishery

Location: Near Gateshead
Type and Size: Three acre lake
Carp Stock: Well stocked with commons, mirrors and leathers, doubles to 14lbs
Category: Mixed Fishery
Other Species: Dace, tench, roach, perch
Permits: Steve Sloan. Tel: 091-489 6919
Cost: About £2 per day
Control: Day ticket
Restrictions: No night fishing
BK Rating: Moderate?
W/A: Northumbrian

Halneby Lake

Location: 3 miles from Croft-in-Teesdale, Darlington
Type and Size: 5½ acre lake
Carp Stock: Very well stocked with carp to 15lbs
Category: Mixed Fishery
Other Species: Bream, roach and tench
Permits: Mr Walton. Tel: 0325 377335 – season tickets only
Cost: About £35 per season
Control: Private
BK Rating: Moderate
W/A: Northumbrian

Leazes Park Lake

Location: Leazes Park, near the football ground, Newcastle
Type and Size: Small public boating lake of about 2 acres in size, with an island
Carp Stock: Well stocked with carp to about 12lbs
Category: Mixed Fishery
Other Species: Roach and rudd
Permits: Day tickets from Roberts Tackle Shop, Newcastle
Control: Council
BK Rating: Moderate
W/A: Northumbrian

Stargate Pools

Location: In the centre of Newcastle
Type and Size: Two very small pools, which have heavy weed
Carp Stock: A few to over 20lbs
Category: Few Carp
Other Species: Roach, rudd and tench
Permits: None necessary - free fishing, with no restrictions
W/A: Northumbrian

WARWICKSHIRE

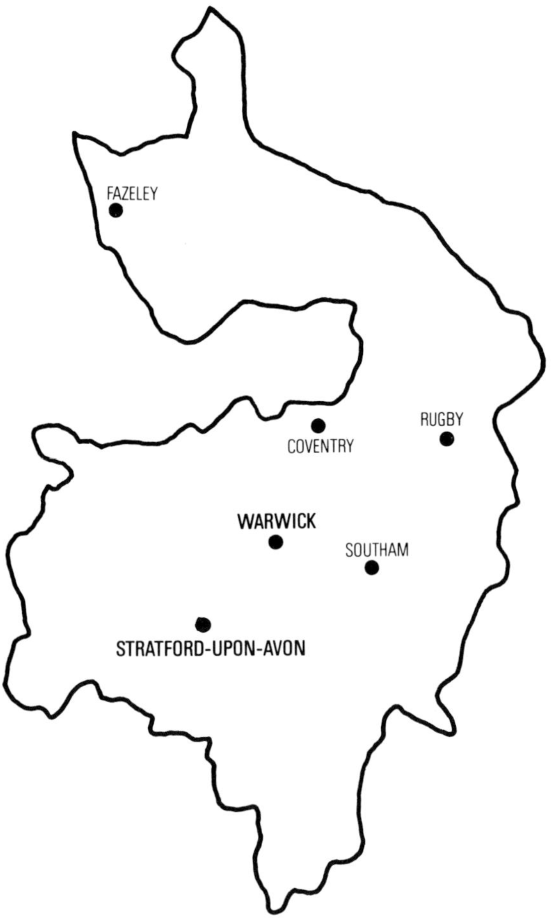

Bishops Bowl Lakes

Location: Bishops Itchington, Southam
Type and Size: 6 small pools
How to Find: Off the B4451 south east of Leamington Spa
Carp Stock: Dinosaur's Dip – small carp; Mitre Pool – some carp; Blue Pool – carp to 20lbs
Category: Mixed Fisheries
Other Species: General coarse fish, and some trout. Big pike, bream and tench
Permits: On site. Tel: 0926 613344

Cost: £3.50 per day approximately (6am to just after sunset); about £2 for a half day
BK Rating: Moderate
Control: Private
Restrictions: No night fishing
W/A: Severn Trent
Comments: Best known for its trout lake, but the ponds mentioned are worth a try for carp. Matured limestone quarries, now a Nature Reserve. Mitre Pool 40 feet deep in places. Very pleasant surroundings

Foxholes Fishery

Location: Crick, near Rugby
Type and Size: 3 lakes
How to Find: Off the A428 Rugby–Northampton road
Carp Stock: Some carp, sizes not known
Category: Mixed Fishery
Other Species: General coarse fish including tench
Permits: R Chaplin, Great Arbour Close, Kenilworth. Information also from Banks and Burr, 27 Claremont Road, Rugby
Cost: On application
BK Rating: Insufficient information
Control: Private
W/A: Severn Trent
Comments: Rugby Federation of Anglers also has some carp in Newbold Quarry (20 acres) near town centre. Tickets from Banks and Burr

Freemans Lake

Location: Wolvey, on the B4109 south of Hinckley
Type and Size: Small lake
Carp Stock: Heavily stocked with small carp, mostly commons
Category: Mixed Fishery
Other Species: Curcians, roach and big perch
Permits: Try tackle shops in Hinckley and Nuneaton
Control: Club
BK Rating: Easy
W/A: Severn Trent

Kingsbury Water Park, Gibsons Lake

Location: Fazeley, near Tamworth
Type and Size: Several old pits, one a specialist carp fishery of about 3 acres
How to Find: Follow the Tamworth road from Birmingham and take the road signposted 'Bodymoor Heath'. After one mile along this lane the fishery is on your left
Carp Stock: Few carp in some of the lakes. Carp lake well stocked with about 100 carp, plenty of doubles to over 20lbs
Category: Carp Water
Other Species: Tench, roach, rudd, bream, perch, pike
Permits: County Council Offices, Shire Hall, Warwick. No day tickets
Cost: Season tickets about £35 which cover 6 other gravel pits, including a good pike water
Control: County Council
BK Rating: Moderate
W/A: Severn Trent
Comments: This water has been developed as a carp fishery since 1980, and the fish are said to be still growing well. Quite a pleasant setting

Napton Reservoir

Location: Napton, near Southam, Coventry
Type and Size: Two lakes, 20 acres and 4 acres
How to Find: Take the A425 from Warwick to Southam and then to Napton
Carp Stock: Few but large. Mirrors to over 20lbs
Category: Few Carp
Other Species: Bream, roach, tench and perch
Permits: From bailiffs on bank
Baits/Methods: Normal carp methods and baits
Control: Club - Coventry and District Angling Association, Secretary: P O'Connor, 48 Loxley Close, Wood End, Coventry. Tel: Coventry 612880
BK Rating: Difficult
W/A: Severn Trent
Comments: Most of the bigger carp are caught from the smaller lake, but both have a reputation as hard waters, probably because the carp stock is not large

Newbold Quarry

Location: On the edge of Rugby, about 1½ miles from town centre
Type and Size: 25 acre quarry
Carp Stock: Well stocked with carp to double figures
Category: Mixed Fishery
Other Species: Tench and pike
Permits: From bailiffs on bank, or from Banks and Burr, 17 Claremont Road; C Donald, 155a Bilton Road
Cost: Day tickets £1; season tickets £12 (£2 juniors)
Control: Club; Rugby Federation of Anglers, G Lawrence, 53 Manor Road, Rugby
BK Rating: Moderate
W/A: Severn Trent

Warwick Canal

Location: South of Warwick
Type and Size: 12½ miles of Grand Union Canal
How to Find: South of Warwick and Leamington Spa
Carp Stock: Good carp in reasonable numbers
Category: Mixed Fishery
Other Species: General coarse fish
Permits: Royal Leamington Spa AA. E G Archer, 9 Southway, Leamington Spa, and from local tackle shops
Cost: Day tickets about £1
BK Rating: Moderate
Control: Club
Restrictions: Not known
W/A: Severn Trent
Comments: There are also some carp in the River Leam in this area – Leam AA, details from local tackle shops

Please remember – litter loses fishing.

Take any you find home with you.

IMPORTANT NOTE

All items advertised are exclusive Gold Label products and are only available from your Gold Label stockist.

Customer enquiries phone 021 373 4523

Terry Eustace

Gold Label Tackle

AVAILABLE AT GOOD TACKLE SHOPS

ASK YOUR DEALER FOR GOLD LABEL PRODUCTS

BERKLEY BIG GAME LINE

The ideal line for the big fish angler would ideally lay better on the spool and cast further than other lines; would check out very favourably against it's stated breaking strain and even better would withstand higher shock loads than other lines; would have greater abrasion resistance so that you could use it with confidence in weeds and snags and over gravel bars AND when you put it into a plastic container with either nothing, sand or mud on the bottom, would virtually disappear whilst other popular lines stood out very visibly. Should your line have all these qualities then you are already using Berkley Big Game Line. Whilst our preference is for the clear, some anglers asked if we could supply in green. We now have this available in 10lb, 12lb, 15lb and 20lb.

10lb Big Game by 1500 yards Ref 225
12lb Big Game by 1175 yards Ref 195
15lb Big Game by 900 yards Ref 196
20lb Big Game by 650 yards Ref 197
25lb Big Game by 595 yards Ref 198
30lb Big Game by 440 yards Ref 199
40lb Big Game by 370 yards Ref 200
50lb Big Game by 275 yards Ref 201

STAINLESS STEEL SQUARE SECTION BUZZER BARS

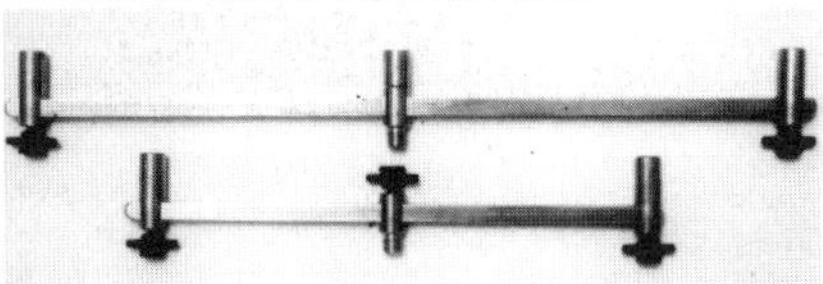

The obvious solution for perfect alignment with no roll pins or pegs so that stability is 100%, these are the ultimate buzzer bar. Single handed adjustment, even with buzzers on, is easy with the peg screws which lock so positively. Altogether the ultimate system.
10" 2 Rod Ref 218 15" 3 Rod Ref 219
Spare Square Bar Bankstick Adaptor Ref 221
Spare Square Bar Slider Ref 222

STAINLESS STEEL NEEDLES

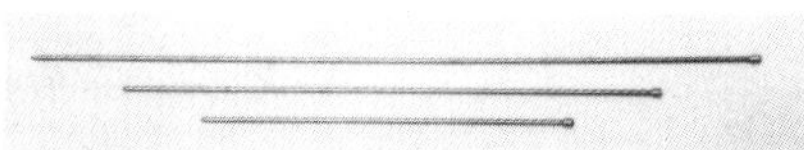

These needles are of robust 3/16" dia stainless steel. The caps are of a tear drop shaped brass stop which is more practical than a plastic cap.
12" Ref 235 18" Ref 236 24" Ref 237

STAINLESS STEEL ROD POD

Our Rod Pod is the ultimate in stability, is simple to set up and easy to adjust. It can be taken apart and stored in a matter of seconds. It is designed to take the 3/8" slim Stainless Banksticks which we also manufacture. The pod is supplied with or without an ariel holder which takes our square ariel bar. After having used inferior pods you will find it difficult to fault this ultimate rod pod system.
Ref 253 (without ariel holder)
Ref 227 (with ariel holder)

STAINLESS STEEL BANKSTICKS

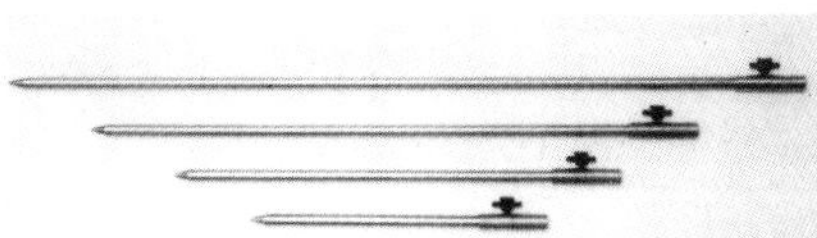

Slim, light and yet stronger than some models of comparable dimensions they look good and function perfectly. The Peg Screws allow positive locking with the minimum of pressure.
10" Adjustable Ref 242 20" Adjustable Ref 244
15" Adjustable Ref 243 25" Adjustable Ref 234

CAGE CLIMBER BODIES

With these climbers the isotope (not supplied) is clearly visible from any angle you look from. The slim stainless rods help to keep the weight down on the standard model and aid maximum visibility on both models.
Standard Body Ref 238
Heavy Body Ref 241

CARP BEADS

These shatterproof beads have smooth bores to eliminate problems of line wear. The hole diameter of the 5mm and 6mm allows the bead to sit over the swivel knot to avoid damage in this area when casting or playing a fish.
4mm Olive Ref 073
5mm Black Ref 074
6mm Brown Ref 075

SLIDER/KNOT BEADS

Beads on one side of the stem have large bores to allow the bead to sit over the swivel knot to protect it during casting. Beads on the other side of the stem are fine bored for use as back or float stops.
Ref 076

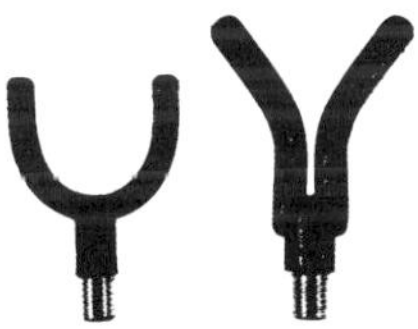

SUPER "U" REAR REST HEAD

The amount of money people spend on reels and pods and rods, then rest them on scruffy back rests. A really neat item of tackle.
Ref 043

SUPER "V" FRONT REST HEAD

As above but for use as a front rest.
Ref 044

BLACK ALLOY NET SPREADER

Ideal for replacing that cheap plastic one which broke so easily, hope it wasn't just as you were netting that big fish, or more sensibly for replacing it before it breaks!
Ref 038

POLYPOPS

They reckon mine are the biggest balls in the business! These are much larger than some of the pathetic polyballs which you would have trouble popping up a maggot with.
Ref 091

SPOOL CASE

This spool case holds up to three large spools (Shimano 4500 for example) and has a number of foam discs. There are sufficient foam spacers to pack between any number/size of spools.
Ref 033

FLOATER FLOATS

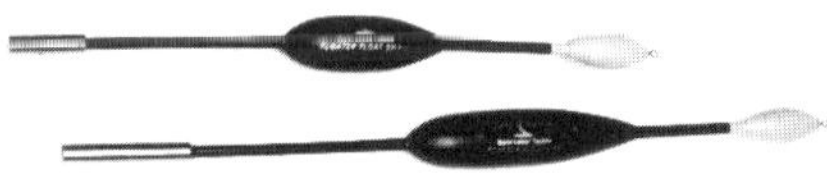

I was using the prototypes of these floats 10 years ago and since then nobody has put what I consider to be a model as good as my originals on the market. With these models, especially with free offerings in the same area, watch the float every time a swirl or movement in the area of the bait appears. As soon as the float tips over (at range it actually seems to sink) strike before the Carp ejects the bait.
Small Size Ref 071
Standard Size Ref 072

WEST MIDLANDS

Blackhills Lake

Location: Wombourne, off the B1477 just south of Wolverhampton - enquire locally for exact location
Type and Size: 4 acre lake on the edge of the golf course
Carp Stock: Very heavily stocked with small carp, and the occasional lower double
Category: Carp Water
Permits: Day tickets from the site office
Cost: About £2 per day
Control: Private
BK Rating: Easy
W/A: Severn Trent

Blackroot 20 Carp

Location: Sutton Park, near Birmingham
Type and Size: Estate lake of 12 acres
How to Find: Six miles north of Birmingham on the A38 road to Lichfield
Carp Stock: Quite well stocked with carp which includes several 20's and two fish over 30lbs each
Category: Mixed Fishery
Other Species: Good pike and other coarse fish
Permits: From bailiffs on bank
Control: Private
BK Rating: Very Difficult
W/A: Severn Trent

Bonehill Mill

Location:	Lichfield Street, Fazeley, Tamworth, B78 3QQ. Tel: 0827 288482
Type and Size:	Three lakes totalling 20 acres
How to Find:	Take the A5 to Tamworth and Fazeley village will be found just to the south of the town
Carp Stock:	Very heavily stocked with many small commons mostly in the 2-5lbs range, with the occasional double figure fish. Some 20's to 25lbs
Category:	Mixed Fisheries
Other Species:	Bream, roach, pike, perch
Permits:	Day tickets on bank
Control:	Private
Restrictions:	No night fishing; no nets or sacks; no groundbait, peanuts or tiger nuts; barbless hooks
BK Rating:	Easy
W/A:	Severn Trent
Comments:	Under new management - V Martin

Bracebridge Lake

Location:	Sutton Park, Birmingham, off the A38 Lichfield road
Type and Size:	4 acre park lake close to Blackroot 20
Carp Stock:	Few carp, but possibly some big ones
Category:	Few Carp
Other Species:	Tench, roach, bream and pike
Permits:	Day tickets from bailiff on bank
Cost:	About £2 per day
Control:	Private
BK Rating:	Very Difficult
W/A:	Severn Trent

Bridge Pool

Location:	Patshull Park, Wolverhampton
Type and Size:	Three acre lake next to the Great Lake at Patshull Park
How to Find:	Take the A454 from Wolverhampton, turn right to Pattingham; take the Burnhill Green Road and you will see the fishery on the right in 1½ miles
Carp Stock:	Quite well stocked with carp to doubles, many of which came from the Great Lake
Permits:	Day tickets from the lodge on site before fishing
Cost:	£2.50 per day; £1.50 for juniors - 7.30am till dusk
Control:	Patshull Park
BK Rating:	Moderate
Restrictions:	No night fishing; no groundbait or hemp
W/A:	Severn Trent
Comments:	Easy access for disabled anglers; good float fishing water, with sweetcorn as bait - 4 feet to 9 feet deep, and separated from the big lake by a narrow causeway

Calf Heath Reservoir

Location:	Junction 12 of the M6
Type and Size:	Reservoir of 50 acres
How to Find:	Come off the M6 at junction 12 and take the A5 road towards Telford

Carp Stock:	Stocked by the club with thousands of carp. Several 20's and a 30 have been reported recently
Category:	Carp Water
Other Species:	Some coarse fish
Permits:	Annual permit available from the bailiff's house on the A5 bank
Cost:	On application
Control:	Club
BK Rating:	Fairly Easy
W/A:	Severn Trent
Comments:	This water is being developed as a carp fishery and is not far from the centre of Birmingham

Church Pool

Location:	Patshull Park, Wolverhampton
Type and Size:	Old pit, about 12 acres
How to Find:	From Wolverhampton, take the A41 road west and then turn onto the A464. After the village of Tettenhall turn left to Pattingham. Here turn right to Patshull
Carp Stock:	Well stocked with mirrors and commons to 25lbs. Many of the bigger fish are commons - which is rare! Mixed Fishery but almost reaches Carp Water status
Category:	Mixed Fishery
Other Species:	Bream, roach and tench, all of which reach large sizes
Permits:	Lakeside Lodge Hotel, Patshull Estate. Tel: Pattingham 700100. Pattingham Anglers
Baits/Methods:	Modern advanced carp fishing methods. Recent summer success has been with floating pet foods such as Pedigree Chum Mixer. Boilies are also good, especially later in the year
Control:	Private. Day ticket
Restrictions:	No keepnets
BK Rating:	Moderate
W/A:	Severn Trent
Comments:	This water has not been open long and is producing fine catches of big carp to specialist carp anglers. It is in a very attractive setting but is quite hard fished. There are lilies and some weed, and some of the banks are tree-lined. The lake is over 15 feet deep in places. Good chance of a 20

Coleshill Pool

Location:	Coleshill, near Birmingham
Type and Size:	2 acre lake
Carp Stock:	Quite well stocked with carp to 14lbs
Category:	Mixed Fishery
Other Species:	Tench, roach and bream
Permits:	Telephone 021-351 1907
Control:	Private
BK Rating:	Not known, but used for match fishing
W/A:	Severn Trent

Cuttle Mill

Location: Wishaw, Sutton Coldfield, Birmingham (Cuttle Mill Lane)
Type and Size: Five acre lake, plus 2¾ acre coarse pool
How to Find: Off the A4091 towards Tamworth, near the National Golf Centre
Carp Stock: Very heavily stocked with many doubles and a few twenties. In 1985, 2,500 doubles and 100 twenties were reported; one or two possible thirties
Category: Carp Water. Long Pool is Mixed Fishery
Other Species: Tench and roach
Permits: Day tickets from the owner, Tony Higgins, at the above address. Tel: Tamworth 872253
Cost: £8.50 per day for two rods
Restrictions: No night fishing - fishing is from 7am till dusk and 7am to 7pm in winter. No barbed hooks. No keepnets. No seed, nut, bean or pea baits are allowed
Baits/Methods: Advanced carp rigs and methods needed. Recent successes have been on high protein boilies fished on the hair rig, and floating baits
Control: Private
BK Rating: Moderate
W/A: Severn Trent
Comments: This is one of the best known commercial carp fisheries in the country, where anglers have a good chance of landing 20's and probably 30's. Up to 10 doubles in a day have been reported, and as this is a commercial fishery it is obviously heavily fished. The house of the owner is right on the bank, and a small mill stream leads from the lake, which is in peaceful surroundings. Alongside the carp lake is another lake of 2¾ acres which is a Mixed Fishery. It contains plenty of carp to over 20lbs, and tench, roach, perch, chub, bream and dace. Details from the owners. Until recently Cuttle Mill was not open in the winter

Earlswood Lakes

Location: Earlswood, Birmingham
Type and Size: Three estate lakes - 85 acres in all
Carp Stock: Two of the lakes contain some carp; sizes not known
Category: Mixed Fishery
Other Species: Big eels, roach, perch, bream, pike and tench
Permits: From bailiff on bank
Control: Private - information from Mrs Palmer, The Bungalow, Valley Road, Earlswood, Birmingham. Tel: Earlswood 2436
BK Rating: Difficult
W/A: Severn Trent

Edgbaston Reservoir

Location: Reservoir Road, Rotton Park, Birmingham
Type and Size: 20 acre reservoir in the city
How to Find: Turn into Monument Street from the A456 Hagley road in Ladywood, south west Birmingham. Reservoir Road is the fifth turning on the left
Carp Stock: Some carp to 20lbs
Category: Few Carp?
Other Species: Roach, perch, bream and pike
Permits: Day tickets on bank
Cost: £1.30 (80p for unemployed)

Control: Birmingham City Council
BK Rating: Difficult
W/A: Severn Trent
Comments: Cafe and other town facilities

Fen Pools

Location: Pensnett, near Brierly Hill
Type and Size: 3 lakes, two quite large
How to Find: West Birmingham, near Dudley
Carp Stock: Some carp to over 20lbs, in Middle Pool and also some carp in Grove Pool
Category: Mixed Fishery
Other Species: Tench, bream and eels
Permits: On bank
Cost: Not known
Control: Private
BK Rating: Difficult
W/A: Severn Trent
Comments: Unpleasant surroundings, between a factory and a housing estate!

Heron Brook Fishery

Location: Near Wolverhampton, off the A41 near Tettenhall
Type and Size: Three acre lake with the River Penk flowing through the middle
Carp Stock: Some carp in the main lake, and the rest in the adjoining carp pool. These fish are mostly doubles
Category: Coarse Lake - Mixed Fishery; Carp Pool - Carp Only
Permits: Day tickets *in advance only* from Nigel Williams Fishing Tackle, Wolverhampton. Tel: 0902 744824 - phone call essential, or you may not be able to fish when you get there. Only 4 anglers a day on the Carp Pool
Control: Private
Baits/Methods: Boilies, luncheon meat and sweetcorn all do well on standard methods; floaters also take fish
BK Rating: Moderate
W/A: Severn Trent

Himley Island Pool

Location: Himley Park, Dudley
Type and Size: Small estate lake
How to Find: Himley Park, near Wombourne
Carp Stock: Well stocked with carp to 20lbs
Category: Mixed Fishery
Other Species: Tench, crucians, bream and roach
Permits: Beddows Tackle Shop, Wombourne. Day tickets and night syndicate vacancies
Cost: On application
Control: Private
BK Rating: Moderate
W/A: Severn Trent
Comments: Night carp syndicate members claim carp to mid-twenties

Lady Barbara's Pool

Location: Patshull Park, Pattingham, Wolverhampton
Type and Size: 6 acre estate lake, and very attractive
Carp Stock: Plenty of doubles and a few 20's
Category: Mixed Fishery
Other Species: Tench, roach, bream and eels
Permits: Season tickets from Pattingham AC only - enquire locally
Control: Club
Restrictions: No day tickets; no night fishing
BK Rating: Moderate
W/A: Severn Trent

Netherton Reservoir

Location: Housing estate in Dudley
Type and Size: 10 acre public lake, with water ski-ing and many boats
Carp Stock: Not many carp, but those reported caught were doubles
Category: Few Carp
Other Species: Mixed coarse fish
Permits: Day tickets on the bank at low cost
Restrictions: No night fishing
Control: Private
BK Rating: Very Difficult
W/A: Severn Trent

Packington

Location: Packington, near Meriden, Coventry
Type and Size: Two pits, Molands Mere and Gearys Level, totalling 35 acres
How to Find: Take the A45 from Birmingham and turn right at the sign for Maxstoke. Entrance is on your right
Carp Stock: Both waters are well stocked with doubles up to 28lbs
Category: Carp Water
Other Species: Large pike, roach, bream and rudd
Permits: Day tickets from the Lodge near the entrance before fishing. Season tickets. Tel: 021-742 2682
Cost: £3 per day, £60 per season
Control: Private
Restrictions: Night fishing for season ticket holders only
BK Rating: Fairly Hard
W/A: Severn Trent
Comments: Well-known water, quite heavily fished and publicised

Park Lime Pits

Location: Near Walsall
Type and Size: Small disused pits
Carp Stock: Some carp, number and sizes not known
Category: Mixed Fishery
Other Species: Bream, roach, perch and pike
Permits: Walsall and District AS - day and season tickets, 38 Lichfield Road, Bloxwich, Walsall
Cost: Cheap tickets

Control: Club
BK Rating: Not known
W/A: Severn Trent

Penns Hall Lake

Location: Sutton Coldfield, Birmingham
Type and Size: Long, narrow lake of about 10 acres
How to Find: Behind Penns Hall Hotel, Penns Lane, Sutton Coldfield
Carp Stock: Not many carp, doubles up to mid 20's
Category: Mixed Fishery
Other Species: Mostly bream and tench
Permits: Ansells Angling Club. Secretary: Mrs Rogers, Tel: 021-748 1200. Must join Ansells Sports and Social Club first
Cost: Ansells AC £14 per year, Ansells S & S Club £8 per year
Control: Private
BK Rating: Difficult, because small numbers of carp
W/A: Severn Trent
Comments: Town water, very popular with walkers

Pool Hall

Location: Lower Penn, near Wolverhampton
Type and Size: 25 acre lake
How to Find: Take the Wolverhampton to Bridgnorth road and follow the signs to Lower Penn
Carp Stock: Heavily stocked with many small carp, mostly commons, but a good number of doubles and twenties to 30lbs
Category: Carp Water
Permits: Day ticket on bank
Cost: About £3 for 24 hours
Control: Private
Baits/Methods: All types of carp fishing baits and methods will catch on this easy water
BK Rating: Very Easy
W/A: Severn Trent
Comments: Popular, heavily fished water

Salford Park

Location: In Birmingham, near Spaghetti Junction
Type and Size: 12 acre reservoir
How to Find: On the A38 towards the centre of Birmingham, close to junction 6 of the M6
Carp Stock: About 100 carp which average about 13lbs. There are several fish over 20lbs
Category: Mixed Fishery
Other Species: Roach, perch and tench
Permits: Day tickets available on bank
Cost: £1 per rod
Control: Council
Restrictions: No night fishing
BK Rating: Fairly Hard
W/A: Severn Trent
Comments: Hard fished and busy town fishery

Shatterford Fishery

Location: Arley, near Kidderminster
Type and Size: 3 small lakes
How to Find: Take the Bridgnorth road to Arley
Carp Stock: Eric's - some carp; Stuart's - carp to 20lbs; Knight's Folly - one acre lake stocked with doubles and contains fish to 25lbs+
Category: Eric's and Stuart's - Mixed Fisheries; Knight's Folly - Carp Only
Other Species: Mixed coarse fish in Eric's and Stuart's
Permits: On site - day tickets
Cost: On application
Control: Private
BK Rating: Moderate
W/A: Severn Trent
Comments: Knight's Folly is advertised as 'expecting to contain some very big carp'

Solo Loop

Location: Loop of the Birmingham canal, near Dudley Road Hospital
Type and Size: Narrow and quite attractive canal arm
How to Find: Take the A45 Dudley Road, left into Winson Green Road, past the prison, then right into Lodge Road, and turn into the entrance on the right past the hospital
Carp Stock: Some carp to double figures
Category: Few Carp
Other Species: Roach, bream, tench, gudgeon and perch
Permits: Day tickets on bank at 70p
Control: Fisherman's Friend Tackle Shop in Birmingham
BK Rating: Difficult
W/A: Severn Trent

Walsall Arboretum

Location: In the centre of Walsall
Type and Size: 4 acre lake with islands etc
Carp Stock: Some carp to upper doubles, but fish hard to find
Category: Few Carp
Other Species: Roach, bream and tench
Permits: Day tickets at the lake
Control: Private
BK Rating: Difficult
W/A: Severn Trent
Comments: A town lake not much fished for carp, but it could produce the odd good fish

WEST SUSSEX

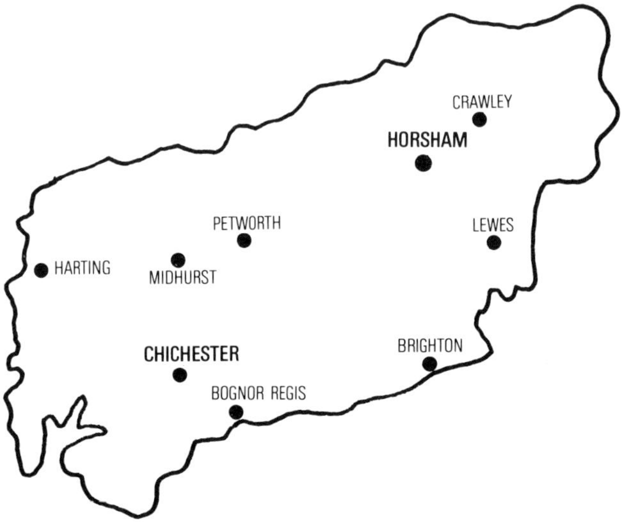

Buchan Park Fisheries

Location: Off the A246 Crawley to Horsham road, about 1½ miles from Crawley
Type and Size: Two lakes, one of which, Douster Pond, is about 5 acres and is very attractive, surrounded by trees and rhododendrons; this lake is 40 feet deep in places
Carp Stock: Well stocked with carp to doubles
Category: Mixed Fishery
Other Species: Bream, tench, roach, perch, pike, crucians and sunfish
Permits: Day tickets on bank
Cost: £3, or £2 in advance from Jack Frost Tackle, Crawley; or Ash Tackle, Horsham
Control: Crawley AS. Secretary: Mr Kichols, 24 Rillside, Furness Green, Crawley, West Sussex
Restrictions: No night fishing - dawn till dusk only
BK Rating: Moderate
W/A: Thames

Chichester Canal

Location: Near Chichester - runs from Chichester to Birdham Locks
Type and Size: Narrow disused canal about 10 miles long
Carp Stock: Well stocked with carp to about 10lbs, most of which are commons
Category: Mixed Fishery
Other Species: Tench, perch, pike and roach
Permits: Details from Mr Snook of Portsmouth and District AS, and also from Chichester Angling Association, Mr J Cooper, 'Jaspers', Coney Road, East Wittering, nr Chichester, West Sussex
Control: Club
BK Rating: Moderate

W/A: Southern
Comments: PM claims the distinction of having stocked this part of the canal between 1946 and 1949! At the age of 16, this was the first water where he caught carp in any quantity. At the time, the lower part of the canal, known as Birdham Locks, was separated from the upper part towards Hunston and Chichester by a dam, constructed when the top lock collapsed. Fish could not get into the upper part, as it was at a higher level. The upper part was said to be almost devoid of fish, since pollution from Chichester Canal Basin killed them during the 1939-45 war. The Birdham Locks section was packed with small commons, said by locals to be 'wildies', though I don't think they were! They had never been caught by 1946, as far as I know, as they were considered in those days to be 'uncatchable'. Once PM got them going on floating crust, which took 6 weeks, they were easy, and he caught up to 18 carp a day, mostly between 2lbs and 5lbs, with his best at 8lbs 3ozs. No-one else fished for carp. He put about 50 of these fish in the upper part of the canal, and is sure that the present stock descended from these fish, though he never fished the upper part of the canal. Later it was said that the Birdham Locks section was also polluted, and the fish had died, so whether there are still carp in the lower section we don't know - on the last visit a few years ago the water looked and smelt unpleasant, and there was no sign of any fish.... though carp are notoriously hardy...

Crayfish Farm

Location: Pound Hill, Crawley
Type and Size: Four acre lake
How to Find: Ordnance Survey Sheet No. 187; Reference 307 375
Carp Stock: Well stocked with carp; quite a number of doubles to about 23lbs
Category: Carp Only
Permits: The Owner, Old Hollow, Pound Hill, Worth, West Sussex. Season tickets only
Cost: About £150 per season
Control: Private syndicate
BK Rating: Easy
W/A: Southern
Comments: An attractive water, membership of which the owners were asking for £250 for the 1985 season, although it is rumoured that this will be down to £150 for 1991

Ditchling Pond

Location: Ditchling Common
Type and Size: Small pond on common land
How to Find: Take the B2112 from Haywards Heath towards Burgess Hill - pond is just before the B2113
Carp Stock: Small head of carp
Category: Few Carp
Other Species: General coarse fish
Permits: Free fishing
Cost: None
BK Rating: Insufficient information
W/A: Southern
Comments: Very weedy free fishery

Harting Coombe Pond

Location: Harting, near Petersfield
Type and Size: 4 acre woodland lake
How to Find: Enquire from Portsmouth AS Secretary
Carp Stock: Well stocked with carp, sizes not known
Category: Mixed Fishery
Other Species: Tench, roach, rudd, bream and pike
Permits: Portsmouth and District AS. Mr R Snook, 86 Carnarvon Road, Copnor, Portsmouth PO2 7NL. Tel: Portsmouth 662986
Cost: On application - new members about £45 per year
BK Rating: Not known
Control: Club
W/A: Southern

Hawkins Pond

Location: Hammer Pond Road, Horsham
Type and Size: Clay pit and former tin mine of 15 acres
How to Find: In the town of Horsham - find Hammer Pond Road
Carp Stock: Reasonable number of small carp, and about 30 doubles. Probably 3 carp to 28lbs, one of which is a common
Category: Mixed Fishery
Other Species: Big pike, tench, bream, roach, rudd, perch, chub
Permits: Horsham and District AA. Secretary: G Kempson, 11 Clarence Road, Horsham, West Sussex
Cost: About £28 a season - includes all club waters
Baits/Methods: All baits but floaters good in summer. Hair rig best
Control: Club
Restrictions: No night fishing except for permit holders - fishing is from 4am to 11pm. No prebaiting. No litter
BK Rating: Moderate
W/A: Southern
Comments: A beautiful lake surrounded by woodland. Average depth 8 feet

Ivy Lake

Location: Wyke, Chichester, just off the Chichester by-pass
Type and Size: 5 acre matured gravel pit
Carp Stock: Quite well stocked with carp, including some doubles and a few 20's
Category: Mixed Fishery
Other Species: Roach, rudd, bream, tench and crucians
Permits: Day tickets on bank
Control: Private - Tel: Chichester 787715
BK Rating: Moderate
W/A: Southern

Milton Mount Lake

Location: Three Bridges, Crawley
Type and Size: Small lake
How to Find: Off junction 13 of the M23
Carp Stock: Well stocked with carp
Category: Carp Water

Other Species: Some other coarse fish
Permits: Crawley AS. Mr Kichols, 24 Rillside, Furness Green, Crawley
Cost: Season tickets approximately £20. Some day tickets at about £2
BK Rating: Moderate
Control: Club
W/A: Thames
Comments: Crawley AS also has carp in Tittermus Lake, Roffey Park Lake, Colgate, Buchan Park Lake and New Pond (listed). It is rumoured that this lake has been closed, so you will need to check locally

Newells Lake

Location: Monks Gate, Horsham
Type and Size: Clay pit of 4½ acres
How to Find: Take the A281 from Horsham towards Brighton and after 3 miles the lake will be seen from the road
Carp Stock: Stocked in 1982 with 220 mirrors to 7lbs. Fish to 19lbs have been caught since
Category: Carp Water
Other Species: Tench, pike, roach and rudd
Permits: Season tickets only from the owner, Mr T Cotton, Newells Pond House, Newells Lane, Lower Beeding, Horsham. Tel: 040376 424
Cost: £30 per season
Baits/Methods: Boilies on hair and bolt rigs
Control: Private
BK Rating: Easy
Restrictions: No keepnets or sacks. No particle baits. No Kamatsu hooks
W/A: Southern
Comments: No weed, open water, with an average depth of about five feet. Several carp a day possible, mostly small fish. Anglers' hut provided with book to record catches

New Pond

Location: Pease Pottage, near Crawley
Type and Size: Small tree-lined lake
How to Find: Near Crawley, off the A23
Carp Stock: Some carp, to mid doubles
Category: Mixed Fishery
Other Species: General coarse fish
Permits: Crawley AS, Mr Kichols, 24 Rillside, Furness Green, Crawley
Cost: Season - about £28
BK Rating: Moderate
Control: Club - no day tickets
W/A: Thames
Comments: Crawley AS also has other waters containing carp. No keepnets

Nunnery Lake

Location: Wyke, Chichester; part of the Chichester gravel pits, just off the by-pass
Type and Size: 10 acre matured gravel pit, with very clear water
Carp Stock: Well stocked with small carp and doubles to about 20lbs
Category: Mixed Fishery

Other Species:	Roach, rudd, bream, pike and tench
Permits:	Day tickets on bank
Cost:	£3 per day
Control:	Club
BK Rating:	Moderate
W/A:	Southern
Comments:	A heavily fished water, and so not very easy to catch the fish, although they take well on the surface at times

Petworth Park

Location:	Petworth Park, Petworth
Type and Size:	Seven acre estate lake in the grounds of a stately home
Carp Stock:	A small number of carp to over 20lbs
Category:	Few Carp
Other Species:	A few big pike, tench, roach and perch
Permits:	Portsmouth and District AS. Mr R Snook, 86 Carnarvon Road, Copnor, Portsmouth PO2 7NL. Tel: Portsmouth 662986
Control:	Club
Restrictions:	Fishing 9am till dusk only. Only 20 anglers per day. Members of Portsmouth and District AC must book by telephone before fishing - details and phone number from Mr Snook or Petworth Park Estate Office
BK Rating:	Difficult
W/A:	Southern
Comments:	This is a very beautiful Estate, and the mansion is often open to the public; details from the Estate Office

Rivers Arun and Adur

Location:	Arun from Pulborough northwards, Adur from Henfield near Brighton northwards
Type and Size:	Some big carp
How to Find:	The Arun runs from Littlehampton through Arundel to Pulborough; and Adur from Hove northwards
Carp Stock:	Not known
Category:	Few Carp
Other Species:	General coarse fish
Permits:	Local angling clubs and tackle shops
Cost:	On application
Control:	Clubs, CALPAC has fishing on these rivers and others, also canals and lakes. Send SAE to CALPAC, 93 Chapel Way, Epsom Downs, Surrey KT18 5TD
BK Rating:	Very Difficult
W/A:	Southern
Comments:	As usual with rivers, location is the main problem. Try slower stretches, backwaters and bays. Carp to 20lbs+ have been taken in the middle and upper reaches of both rivers. Try also Pulborough AS. M Booth, 5 South Lane, Houghton, Arundel, West Sussex (Arun)

River Ouse

Location: Barcombe Mills, near Lewes
Type and Size: 33 mile long river
Carp Stock: A few good carp reported to about 20lbs, in the Barcombe Mills area, and possibly in other sections of the river
Category: Few Carp
Other Species: Sea trout (believe it or not!) and some big ones too; perch, bream, roach, dace, chub and pike
Permits: Old Mill Farm, Barcombe has day tickets. Other tickets from Ouse APS, Dr J L Cotton, Down End, Kingston Road, Lewes
Control: Private and Club
Restrictions: Some areas reserved for sea trout fishing; season tickets limited on club stretches
BK Rating: Very Difficult
W/A: Southern

Roosthole

Location: Hammer Pond Road, Horsham
Type and Size: Clay pit of 3½ acres
How to Find: The lake is in the town of Horsham, find Hammer Pond Road
Carp Stock: Quite well stocked with small carp and about 20 doubles, best fish 26lbs mirror
Category: Mixed Fishery
Other Species: Pike, bream, roach, rudd, perch
Permits: Season tickets from Horsham and District Angling Association. Secretary: G Kempson, 11 Clarence Road, Horsham
Cost: About £28 per year to include other club waters
Baits/Methods: Normal carp methods and all types of baits. Floaters work well
Control: Club
BK Rating: Very Difficult
Restrictions: No night fishing, fishing 4am till 11pm. Prebaiting banned. No litter
W/A: Southern
Comments: Very clear water and depths to 22 feet. Many snags. A peaceful lake, not heavily fished. Much larger carp are said to be in the water, but have not been caught, and the 22lb mirror has only been taken once in the last 5 years

Rother A.C. Lakes

Location: Near Midhurst
Type and Size: 3 lakes and River Rother
How to Find: Enquire locally
Carp Stock: Some carp
Category: Mixed Fisheries
Other Species: General coarse fish
Permits: Day tickets from Rice Bros, West Street; The Rother Inn, Lutener Road
Cost: Annual subscription about £10 with a £6 entry fee. Secretary: D Merritt, 17 Sandrock, June Lane, Midhurst
BK Rating: Insufficient information
Control: Club
W/A: Southern

Soake Pond

Location: Denmead, near Chichester
Type and Size: A very rich and attractive two acre lake
Carp Stock: A good number of carp to over 20lbs
Other Species: Roach, perch, pike, tench and rudd
Permits: Portsmouth and District AS. Mr R Snook, 86 Carnarvon Road, Copnor, Portsmouth PO2 7NL. Tel: Portsmouth 662986
Control: Club
BK Rating: Moderate
W/A: Southern
Comments: This water has been run as a specimen fishery for nearly 20 years, so it should contain some very big fish. All information from Mr Snook

Southern Leisure Centre

Location: Wyke, near Chichester
Type and Size: 3 fair sized gravel pits
How to Find: On the A27 from Chichester, to the south of the city
Carp Stock: Ivy, Nunnery and Triangle Lakes contains plenty of carp, up to upper doubles
Category: Mixed Fishery
Other Species: General coarse fish
Permits: On site. Tel: Chichester 787715
Cost: Approximately £2-£3 per day
Control: Southern Leisure Centre
BK Rating: Moderate
W/A: Southern
Comments: Very heavily fished in summer, and fishing can be difficult at times

Stemps Wood Pond

Location: On a farm near Bognor Regis
Type and Size: One acre farm pond in woodland
Carp Stock: Some commons, sizes not known
Other Species: Tench, rudd and crucians
Permits: Details from Mr R Snook, 86 Carnarvon Road, Copnor, Portsmouth PO2 7NL. Tel: Portsmouth 662986
Control: This pond is controlled by Bognor Regis AC, a member of the Hants and Sussex Anglers Alliance - details from Mr Snook above
BK Rating: Not known
W/A: Southern
Comments: A newly opened water, rebuilt and stocked from an overgrown derelict farm pond by the hard work of members of the Bognor club

Tilgate Park Lake

Location: Crawley
Type and Size: Estate type of lake of 10 acres
How to Find: Ordnance Survey Sheet No. 187. Reference: 278 345
Carp Stock: Many small commons and a few double figure mirrors to about 22lbs
Category: Mixed Fishery
Other Species: General coarse fish, including large pike
Permits: From park keepers on bank - day tickets at £4

Control: Council
Restrictions: No night fishing
BK Rating: Very Difficult
W/A: Thames
Comments: A 'public' water; windsurfers, canoeists and dog walkers. There is even said to be a ghost which joins you in your bivvy! You need to find out the movements of the carp for success, not too easy with a casual approach

Triangle Lake

Location: Chichester gravel pits, just off the by-pass
Type and Size: 6 acre pit
Carp Stock: Well stocked with carp to about 17lbs
Category: Mixed Fishery
Other Species: Roach, crucians, rudd, bream and pike
Permits: Day tickets on site at low cost
Control: Private
Baits/Methods: Quite hard fished water, so sophisticated methods and baits needed; fixed lead methods and pop-ups work well
BK Rating: Moderate
W/A: Southern

Wyke Lake

Location: On the Chichester by-pass
Type and Size: Gravel pit of about 8 acres
How to Find: From Bognor Regis, take the Chichester road and turn right towards Portsmouth at the roundabout just before Chichester. The lake will be seen on the right - it is the third lake along
Carp Stock: Quite well stocked with carp to mid-twenties
Category: Mixed Fishery
Other Species: Most other coarse fish to a good size
Permits: Chichester and District Angling Society. Membership Secretary: Mr C Few, Fisherman's Den, 5 Canada Grove, Bognor Regis, West Sussex. Season tickets only. Membership includes 3 other lakes and some stretches of river. The lakes all contain carp
Cost: £12 annual subscription plus a £10 entry fee. Juniors/OAPs about £6 entry fee and approximately £5 annual subscription. OAPs about £3 annual subscription only
Control: Club
BK Rating: Moderate
W/A: Southern
Comments: Chichester, Bognor Regis and Portsmouth clubs all have gravel pits in this area, most of which contain carp, including the Southern Leisure Centre. Enquire from tackle shops

WEST YORKSHIRE

Brookfoot Lake

Location: Brighouse, off the A6025 Brighouse-Elland road - parking at the Grove Motel
Type and Size: Small lake
Carp Stock: Well stocked with carp, to about 10lbs
Category: Mixed Fishery
Other Species: Rudd, tench, perch and roach
Permits: Day tickets from Calder Angling Supplies, Gooder Lane, Brighouse and Pondworks Angling Supplies, 364 Bradford Road, Bailiff Bridge, Brighouse
Control: Brighouse Angling Association. M Riley, 30 Ravenstone Drive, West Vale, Greetland, Halifax
BK Rating: Very Easy
Restrictions: No Sunday fishing; limited numbers
W/A: Yorkshire

Clayton Ponds

Location: Clayton Wood Road, Leeds
Type and Size: Two small ponds
How to Find: Off the Leeds ring road
Carp Stock: Some carp to double figures
Category: Few Carp
Other Species: Tench, roach, perch and big eels
Permits: Day and season tickets at low cost from Abbey Match Anglers, Commercial Road, Kirkstall, Leeds; and Headingly Angling Centre, Headingly
Control: Fox and Hounds Angling Club
BK Rating: Difficult
W/A: Yorkshire

Doe Park Reservoir

Location: Denholme, between Halifax and Keighley
Type and Size: 20 acre reservoir
How to Find: Take the A629 from Halifax towards Keighley, and the fishery is at Denholme, on the right hand side of the road
Carp Stock: Some carp, sizes not known
Category: Few Carp
Other Species: Bream, tench, roach, rudd, pike, chub and trout
Permits: Day tickets from the keeper's house at Doe Park, and from Richmonds, 110 Morley Street, Bradford
Cost: £2.20 per day
Control: Bradford City Angling Association. Secretary: H Briggs, 4 Brown Hill Close, Birkinshaw, Bradford, West Yorkshire
BK Rating: Difficult, as there are not many carp
Restrictions: No night fishing (starts 7am). Fishing is from June 1st until the end of February. Entrance only from the marked gates
W/A: Yorkshire
Comments: Bradford City AA issues tickets for other lakes, the canal and rivers

Flanshaw Dam

Location: Flanshaw Lane, Flanshaw, Wakefield
Type and Size: Tiny park pond of about half an acre
Carp Stock: Quite well stocked with carp to about 10lbs
Category: Mixed Fishery
Other Species: Bream, tench and roach
Permits: Day tickets from clubhouse on site. Low cost
Control: Wakefield Angling Club
BK Rating: Not known
W/A: Yorkshire

Flash Lane Pond

Location: Flash Lane, Wickersley, Rotherham
Type and Size: Small lake of about two acres
Carp Stock: Some carp to about 20lbs
Category: Few Carp
Other Species: Roach, rudd, tench and perch
Permits: Enquire from local tackle shops or ask on bank
Control: Small local club
BK Rating: Difficult
W/A: Yorkshire

Hemsworth Water Park

Location: Kinsley, near Wakefield
Type and Size: Large lake
Carp Stock: Some carp, numbers and sizes not known
Category: Mixed Fishery
Other Species: Bream, tench and roach
Permits: Low cost day tickets on site
Control: Hemsworth Water Park

BK Rating: Insufficient information
W/A: Yorkshire
Comments: Special stands for disabled anglers

Hill Top Reservoir

Location: Longlands Road, Hill Top, near Huddersfield
Type and Size: 11 acre reservoir
How to Find: Off the A62, seven miles south west of Huddersfield
Carp Stock: Some carp
Category: Few Carp
Other Species: Roach, perch, bream and pike
Permits: Day tickets from the Albion Inn, Longroyd Bridge, Slaithwaite
Control: Slaithwaite and District Angling Club
BK Rating: Difficult
W/A: Yorkshire

Horbury Quarry

Location: Horbury Junction, near Wakefield
Type and Size: 15 acres, very deep sand quarry
Carp Stock: Not many, but they go to upper doubles
Category: Few Carp
Other Species: Roach, bream, perch and pike
Permits: Season tickets only from Wakefield AC. Secretary: B D Harper, 29 Victoria Crescent, Horsforth, Leeds
Control: Club
BK Rating: Very Difficult
W/A: Yorkshire

Kettlethorpe Hall Lake

Location: Kettlethorpe Hall, near Wakefield
Type and Size: Small estate lake of about 2 acres, very attractive, with islands
Carp Stock: Heavily stocked with commons and mirrors average size about 4lbs, but possibly one or two of 10lbs or just over
Category: Carp Water
Other Species: Roach and pike
Permits: Season tickets from local tackle shops
Control: Wakefield AC. B D Harper, 29 Victoria Crescent, Horsforth, Leeds
BK Rating: Very Easy
Restrictions: No night fishing
W/A: Yorkshire
Comments: A good, easy water to start carp fishing on, in spite of the fact that it is hard fished

Kippax Pond

Location: Brigshaw Lane, Kippax, Leeds
Type and Size: Small marshland pond
Carp Stock: Very well stocked with numerous small carp
Category: Mixed Fishery
Other Species: Roach

Permits: Leeds and District ASA, members only, but open to all - The Secretary, Leeds and District ASA, c/o Leeds Angling Club, Stoney Rock Lane, Leeds 9
BK Rating: Easy
Restrictions: No night fishing
Control: Club
W/A: Yorkshire

Knotford Lagoon

Location: 1½ miles from Otley, near Leeds
Type and Size: Large lake
How to Find: The fishery is just off the A659 Otley-Pool road
Carp Stock: Not many carp, but a few large fish to well over 20lbs
Category: Few Carp
Other Species: Tench, roach, chub, perch and trout
Permits: Day tickets from Angling and Countrysports, Pool Road, Otley and Leeds tackle dealers
Control: Club
BK Rating: Very Difficult
W/A: Yorkshire

Leeds to Liverpool Canal

Location: Three miles between Lodge Hill Bridge and Swine Lane Bridge
Type and Size: Narrow canal
Carp Stock: Well stocked with carp, mostly small, but some to doubles
Category: Mixed Fishery
Other Species: Bream and roach
Permits: Members only water of Marsden Star AC, Colne (try local tackle shops for permits and details)
Cost: £12 per season, members only
Control: Club
BK Rating: Easy
W/A: Yorkshire

Magdale Dam

Location: Honley, near Huddersfield, off the A616 Huddersfield-Holmfirth road
Type and Size: Medium-sized dam
Carp Stock: Plenty of carp to double figures
Category: Mixed Fishery
Other Species: Crucians, perch and rudd
Permits: Apply to Peter Budd, 39 Derwent Road, Honley, near Huddersfield. Tel: Huddersfield 660258
Cost: £8 for the season, £4 for juniors. Free to registered disabled persons
Control: Holme Valley Piscatorials Association
BK Rating: Moderate
W/A: Yorkshire
Comments: This is a purpose-built fishery, with ramps and stands for disabled anglers. Club membership is open to all

New Miller Reservoir

Location: Off the A61 at Kettlethorpe, near Wakefield
Type and Size: About 70 acres, very pleasant but busy
Carp Stock: Not many carp, but some 20's
Category: Few Carp
Other Species: Most coarse fish, and some trout
Permits: Season tickets only, from local tackle shops
Control: Wakefield AC. B D Harper, 29 Victoria Crescent, Horsforth, Leeds
Restrictions: No night fishing
BK Rating: Super-Difficult
W/A: Yorkshire

Nostell Priory A

Location: Nostell Priory, near Wakefield
Type and Size: 3 lakes of 26 acres, 16½ acres and 10 acres
How to Find: Just of the A638 south of Wakefield
Carp Stock: All 3 lakes are well stocked with carp and fish of over 20lbs have been reported from all 3 lakes
Category: Mixed Fishery
Other Species: Bream, perch and pike to over 30lbs
Permits: Day tickets and season tickets from the fishery shop. Information from John Austerfield or Tony Frost on 0924 863562
Cost: £2.75 per day. £1.75 for half day, from 7am to 1pm or 1pm till dusk. Season tickets £30 for top or bottom of lake, or £60 for all three
Control: Private
BK Rating: Moderate
Restrictions: No keepnets; no night fishing
W/A: Yorkshire
Comments: In the ground of a stately home owned by the National Trust. Fishing shop on lakeside. Touring caravans and tents welcome on the adjacent 30 acre woodland park. Tel: 0924 863938

Nunroyd Pond

Location: Guiseley; Nunroyd Park, Guiseley - off the A65 Leeds–Ilkley road
Type and Size: Small park lake
Carp Stock: Some carp, sizes not known
Category: Few Carp
Other Species: Roach, tench
Permits: Membership from Abbey Match Anglers, Commercial Road, Kirkstall, Leeds
Control: Aireborough and District AA. Members only, open to all
BK Rating: Difficult
Restrictions: No night fishing. Barbless hooks
W/A: Yorkshire

Oulton Hall Pond

Location: Rothwell Sports Centre, off the M62 at junction 20, following the Rothwell–Oulton signs. In the grounds of Oulton Hall
Type and Size: New 1½ acre pond
Carp Stock: Plenty of commons and mirrors
Category: Mixed Fishery
Other Species: Crucians, bream, tench, roach, rudd, perch, gudgeon and pike
Permits: Day tickets from Rothwell Sports Centre, opposite the fishery
Control: Leeds City Council Leisure Services
BK Rating: Not known

Pastures Pit

Location: Allerton Bywater, just off the A639, between Castleford and Leeds, and close to the river
Type and Size: Shallow, 5 acre lake
Carp Stock: A very small number, though a common of over 30lbs has been reported
Category: Few Carp
Other Species: Most coarse fish
Permits: From tackle shops in Castleford and Leeds
Control: Private
BK Rating: Very Difficult
W/A: Yorkshire
Comments: No close season; very snaggy and difficult water

Pugney's Lake

Location: Crofton, near Wakefield
Type and Size: Very large, open park lake
How to Find: Take junction 39 from the M1, and at the roundabout take the Wakefield road, then the second right to Crofton; Pugney's Country Park
Carp Stock: Some carp, sizes not known
Category: Few Carp or possibly Mixed Fishery
Other Species: Bream, tench and perch
Permits: From reception at the entrance to the park – low cost day tickets
Control: Wakefield Metropolitan District Council
BK Rating: Not known
Restrictions: No night fishing
W/A: Yorkshire
Comments: There is windsurfing and sailing on the big lake. Club matches can be booked

Roberts Pond

Location: Behind Roberts Dye Works, Beechcliff, Keighley, off the Keighley to Skipton road
Type and Size: Small pond
Carp Stock: Some carp, number and sizes not known
Category: Probably Few Carp
Other Species: Bream, tench, roach, perch and pike
Permits: Keighley Angling Club, members only but open to all – Mr D Ward, 4 Compeigne Avenue, Keighley
Control: Club
W/A: Yorkshire

Roundhay Park Lakes

Location: Roundhay Park, 4 miles from Leeds
Type and Size: Two lakes, both of which contain some carp
Carp Stock: Some carp in both lakes, sizes not known
Category: Mixed Fishery
Other Species: Pike, perch, roach, tench, bream
Permits: Leeds and District AA. Secretary: G Copley, Anglers Club, Becket Street, Leeds 9
Cost: On application
BK Rating: Moderate
W/A: Yorkshire

Southern Washlands

Location: Outskirts of Wakefield
Type and Size: Two small lakes created by Wakefield District Council on a recently reclaimed site
Carp Stock: Some carp
Category: Mixed Fishery
Other Species: Bream, perch, roach and gudgeon
Permits: Day tickets from The Match Anglers Shop, off Westgate, Wakefield
Cost: £1.50 per day
Control: Wakefield MDC and Eastmoor AC - information on Eastmoor membership from Carl Young, 210 Stanley Road, Wakefield. Tel: 0924 373286
BK Rating: Not known

Sugden End Reservoir

Location: Crossroads, Keighley
Type and Size: Large reservoir
How to Find: Off the A60 Bradford–Skipton road
Carp Stock: Some big carp
Category: Mixed Fishery
Other Species: General coarse fish; large tench
Permits: Keighley AC. L Brocklesby, 11 Eelholme View Street, Keighley (information only)
Cost: Day tickets - about £2. Season - approximately £10. From local tackle shops
BK Rating: Moderate
Control: Club
W/A: Yorkshire
Comments: The Keighley club also has other waters containing carp

Ulley Country Park

Location: Near Rotherham, off the A618 Pleasley Road
Type and Size: Large reservoir, 30 acres and very deep
Carp Stock: Some carp, to mid-doubles
Category: Mixed Fishery
Other Species: Bream, roach, perch, pike and trout
Permits: Tickets from a vending machine in the car park (I expect they have robot bailiffs also!)

Control: Rotherham MBC. Information on 0709 365332
BK Rating: Very Difficult
Restrictions: No night fishing
W/A: Yorkshire
Comments: This is part of Ulley Country park, which is a nature reserve. Anglers leaving litter will be ordered by the rangers to leave the fishery; sailing on the lake

Wentworth Fishery–Greasborough Dam

Location: East Lodge, Greasborough
Type and Size: Two small estate lakes
How to Find: Take the B6089 from Rotherham and after Greasborough, turn left at East Lodge and the fishery is 300 yards
Carp Stock: Well stocked with carp to upper 20's
Category: Mixed Fishery
Other Species: Big bream and tench, roach, big perch and trout to 10lbs
Permits: Season tickets only. Applications in writing only to: Fitzwilliam Wentworth Amenity Trust, Estate Office, Clayfields Lane, Wentworth, Rotherham S62 7TD
BK Rating: Not known
Control: Estate
W/A: Yorkshire
Comments: A pleasant water with lilies and easy access. There is also a fly only trout lake on the site

Whitefields Reservoir

Location: Near Keighley
Type and Size: Reservoir
How to Find: Off the A60 Bradford–Skipton road near Keighley. Enquire at tackle shops
Carp Stock: Some carp in both waters
Category: Mixed Fisheries
Other Species: Tench, roach, perch, pike
Permits: Keighley AC. L Brocklesby, 11 Eelholme View Street, Keighley (information only)
Cost: Approximately £2 per day; about £10 per season. Tickets from local tackle shops
BK Rating: Moderate
Control: Club
W/A: Yorkshire
Comments: Large carp also in Sugden End Reservoir, Keighley AC

Workshop Lake

Location: Fairburn, off the A1 near Castleford
Type and Size: 4 acre snaggy lake
Carp Stock: Very well stocked with plenty of carp to low doubles, and possibly one or two 20's
Category: Mixed Fishery
Other Species: Usual coarse fish
Permits: Castleford and District AS. R Holmes, 1 Hope Street East, Castleford

Control: Club; season tickets only; night fishing for members only
BK Rating: Easy
W/A: Yorkshire

Workshop Ponds

Location: Charles Roberts Factory, Horbury Junction, near Wakefiled
Type and Size: Three acre weedy lake used as a water supply for the factory
Carp Stock: Quite well stocked to lower doubles
Category: Mixed Fishery
Other Species: Roach, rudd and bream
Permits: Charles Roberts Angling Club, hard to obtain - enquire locally
BK Rating: Moderate
W/A: Yorkshire
Comments: A heavily weeded works pond, attractive and used by match anglers

Yeadon Tarn

Location: Cemetery Road, Yeadon, between Bradford and Harrogate
Type and Size: Large lake
Carp Stock: Quite well stocked with carp to double figures
Category: Mixed Fishery
Other Species: Tench, roach, bream, trout
Permits: Day tickets from Abbey Match Anglers, Commercial road, Kirkstall, Leeds. Tel: 744562; The Sweet Shop, Albert Square, Yeadon and Tobacconist, High Street, Yeadon
Control: Aireborough and District Angling Association
Restrictions: No night fishing. No fishing from the Sailing Club jetty whilst sailing is taking place
Baits/Methods: Luncheon meat said be good for the bigger carp
BK Rating: Moderate
W/A: Yorkshire
Comments: Big open lake, used also for sailing. Level banks ideal for the disabled

WILTSHIRE

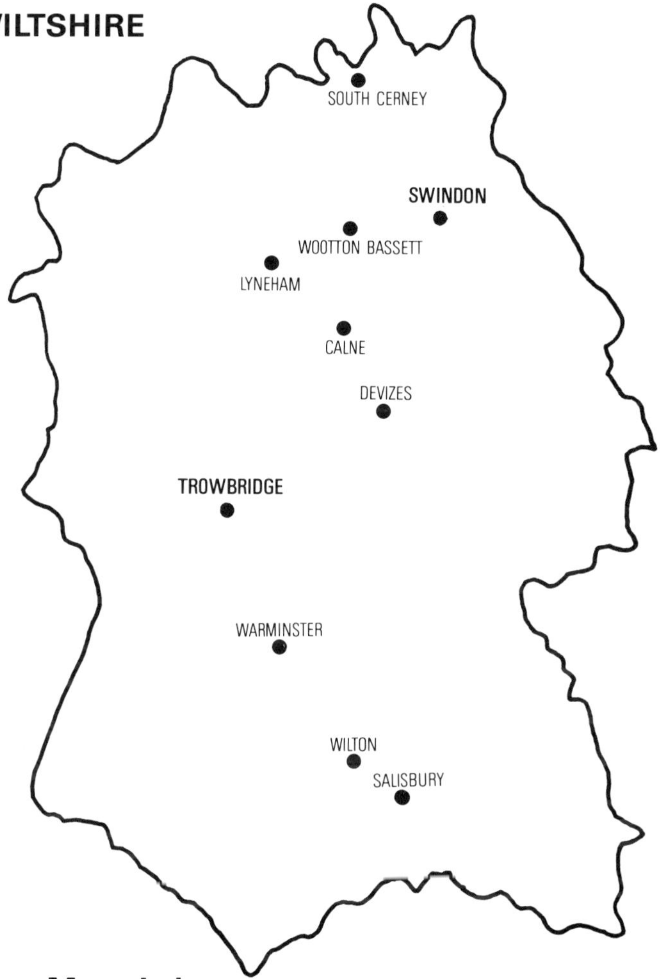

Barn Moor Lake

Location: Witherington Farm, Downton, Salisbury
Type and Size: 1½ acre lake
How to Find: Take the right hand Alderbury turn off the A36 Salisbury–Southampton road. Take the first right turn and the farm is three miles further on, on the right hand side
Carp Stock: Well stocked with mirrors to 10lbs, and commons to 15lbs
Category: Mixed Fishery
Other Species: Tench and roach
Permits: Day tickets from owner on bank
Cost: £3. 50 per day – half price for junior and OAP's
Control: Private
Restrictions: No keepnets; no boilies or high protein baits(!)
BK Rating: Moderate
W/A: Wessex

Bowood Lake

Location: Bowood, near Calne
Type and Size: 20 acre estate Lake
How to Find: Bowood Estate near Calne
Carp Stock: Some carp, including doubles
Category: Few Carp
Other Species: General coarse fish
Permits: Bowood Estate, Bowood, Calne
Cost: On application
BK Rating: Difficult
Control: Private
Restrictions: No fishing at the north end of the lake
W/A: Wessex
Comments: This beautiful lake contains big pike, and possibly a few big carp

Coate Water

Location: Coate Water Country Park, Marlborough Road, Swindon
Type and Size: Large old lake of about 70 acres
How to Find: Southern outskirts of Swindon
Carp Stock: Few original fish up to 23lbs. Recently stocked with a number of small carp. A 28 was caught in 1988
Category: Mixed Fishery
Other Species: Large bream, tench, roach, pike perch
Permits: On bank
Cost: £1 per day - season night tickets for Swindon residents
Control: Thamesdown Borough Council, Euclid Street, Swindon
BK Rating: Difficult
W/A: Thames
Comments: A big lake made famous by the writings of naturalist Richard Jefferies who lived on the bank. Boats and people - a 'public' water

Flamstone Cottage

Location: Bishopstone, near Salisbury
Type and Size: Small stream fed pool
How to Find: South West of Salisbury off the A354
Carp Stock: Well stocked with carp to 19lbs
Category: Carp Water
Other Species: Brown trout to 12lbs; tench, orfe, chub, roach and grayling - all large
Permits: Ealing Angling Centre. Tel: 081-567 3101
Cost: On application
Control: Private
Restrictions: Barbless hooks no larger than size 12, no keepnets
BK Rating: Easy
W/A: Wessex
Comments: An exclusive private specimen fishery. Standard baits. Carp by the island, near rushes

Hunters Moon Lodges A

Location:	Henford Marsh, Warminster
Type and Size:	Pleasant, small farmland lake
Carp Stock:	Said to be some carp, number and sizes not known
Category:	Mixed Fishery
Other Species:	General coarse fish, and some trout
Permits:	Fishing for residents only
Cost:	On application at reception
Control:	Private
BK Rating:	Not known
W/A:	Wessex
Comments:	There are a number of well eqipped timber built lodges for rent on the site round the lake. Prices vary from £125 to £300 per week. Booking details from Hoseasons Holidays, Sunway House, Lowestoft NR32 3LT. Tel: 0502 500500

Longleat

Location:	Longleat, near Warminster
Type and Size:	Large estate lakes
How to Find:	Off the Warminster - Frome road
Carp Stock:	Some carp to over 20lbs - stocked with 6,500lbs of small carp to 7lbs in 1990
Category:	Mixed Fishery
Other Species:	General coarse fish
Permits:	The Bailiff, Parkhill Cottage, Longleat Estate
BK Rating:	Moderate
Control:	Longleat Estate
Restrictions:	Not known
W/A:	Wessex
Comments:	Watch out for the 'Lions of Longleat!'

Lower Foxhangers A

Location:	Lower Foxhangers Farm, Rowde, Devizes, Wilts. Tel. 0380 828245
Type and Size:	This farm/guesthouse does not actually have its own fishing, but it is on the edge of the Kennet and Avon Canal, which contains some carp in this area
How to Find:	Take the A361 from Devizes, and the road to the farm will be seen on the right after a few miles
Carp Stock:	Canal contains plenty of common and mirror carp to about 20lbs
Category:	Mixed Fishery
Other Species:	Roach, perch, tench, crucian carp
Permits:	Devizes Angling Association, Secretary, T.W. Fell, 21 Cornwall Crescent, Devizes
Cost:	Day and weekly tickets on application, and also from local tackle shops
BK Rating:	Fairly Hard
Control:	Club
W/A:	Wessex
Comments:	Bed and Breakfast accommodation at the farm, with good facilities - £28 per night for two. There are also four mobile homes to rent close to the canal, each of which sleeps four, and costs from £110 per week to £160 per week according to the time of year. Enquire from Colin and Cynthia Fletcher at the farm

Old Warden Castle

Location: Near Tisbury
Type and Size: Castle lake
How to Find: Tisbury, near Wilton; off the A30 six miles west of Wilton
Carp Stock: Some carp
Category: Mixed Fishery
Other Species: General coarse fish
Permits: Tisbury AC, P Lever, 1 Maypole Bungalow, Ansty, Tisbury
Cost: On application
BK Rating: No information
Control: Club
Restrictions: Not known
W/A: Wessex

Petersfinger Lakes

Location: Two miles east of Salisbury just off the A36 Warminster road
Type and Size: Two large estate lakes in nature reserve
Carp Stock: Well stocked with good carp to 24lbs, including commons and mirrors
Category: Mixed Fishery
Other Species: Bream to 8¾lbs, tench, perch and pike
Permits: Salisbury and Dist. Angling Club (members only). Membership Secretary, 29 New Zealand Avenue, Salisbury, Wilts SP2 7JX
Cost: £43 plus £10 registration fee - reduced prices for local OAP's, juniors and members' wives
Control: Club
BK Rating: Moderate
W/A: Wessex
Comments: This well known and very pleasant fishery is partly surrounded by trees and the surrounding nature reserve is owned by the club

Rowde Lake

Location: In the village of Rowde, near Devizes
Type and Size: Small pond of about an acre
Carp Stock: Fairly well stocked with carp to lower doubles
Category: Mixed Fishery
Other Species: General coarse fish, including large crucians
Permits: From house at lake, which is a caravan site
Cost: Day tickets to about £1 per day
Control: Private
BK Rating: Easy
W/A: Wessex

Silverlands Lake

Location: Lacock, near Chippenham
Type and Size: 5 acre open gravel pit
How to Find: Off the A350 between Chippenham and Melksham
Carp Stock: In the past, very few to 26lbs, but was restocked in 1987 - a 26 pounder was reported in late 1990
Category: Mixed Fishery
Other Species: Tench, roach, bream, pike

Permits: Robs Tackle, 22 Marshfield Road, Chippenham
Cost: Day and night - approximately £3.00; season about £45
Control: Private
Restrictions: Night fishing now allowed
BK Rating: Moderate
W/A: Wessex
Comments: A long walk - nearly a mile! - across fields. PM's 25¼ caught here in 1971, is now dead - and the walk nearly killed him too!!A 27 was reported from here in 1991. (Late news is that you can now drive to within 50 yards of the lake).

Steeple Langford Lakes

Location: Steeple Langford, near Warminster
Type and Size: Gravel pits
How to Find: Off the A36 ten miles north west of Salisbury
Carp Stock: Well stocked with carp to over 20lbs
Category: Carp Water
Other Species: General coarse fish
Permits: From bailiff on site. Salisbury and District AC, R W Hillier, 29 New Zealand Avenue, Salisbury
Cost: On application
BK Rating: Difficult
Control: Club
Restrictions: Not known
W/A: Wessex
Comments: Salisbury AC also has other good carp waters

Tockenham Reservoir

Location: Tockenham, near Lyneham
Type and Size: Reservoir of 8 acres, recently dredged
How to Find: Off the main Lyneham - Wootton Bassett road. Turn left just outside Lyneham. Down land about 150 yards on right
Carp Stock: Stocked with about 600 carp of 2 - 4lbs and about 30 bigger fish to 20lbs. Good head of doubles including commons
Category: Carp Water
Other Species: Tench, bream, roach
Permits: Bristol and District Amalgamated Anglers, membership open to all: Season only. Secretary, J Parker, 16 Lansdowne View, Kingswood, Bristol BS14 4AW
Cost: About £15 per season
Restrictions: No night fishing
Baits/Methods: Normal carp fishing methods, boilies and floaters
Control: Club
BK Rating: Easy
W/A: Wessex
Comments: A very pleasant club water but hard fished especially during the summer. Carp harder to catch as season progresses. Stock fish said to be growing well and now averaging about 8lbs in weight

Wick Water

Location: Near South Cerney
Type and Size: Gravel pit of 7 acres
How to Find: Take the Cerney Wick road from South Cerney and turn right onto the Spine Road at the first crossroads. Wick Water is on the left shortly after the turn
Carp Stock: About 100 carp to low twenties
Category: Mixed Fishery
Other Species: General coarse fish
Permits: South Cerney Angling Club. Secretary, Fisherman's Rest, Broadway Lane, South Cerney (Send SAE)
Cost: £13 per season
Restrictions: No night fishing
Control: Club
BK Rating: Fairly Hard
W/A: Thames

Wootton Bassett Lake

Location: Wootton Bassett, near Swindon
Type and Size: Small pond of about 1 acre
Carp Stock: Quite well stocked with carp to low doubles
Category: Mixed Fishery
Other Species: General coarse fish
Permits: Wootton Bassett Angling Club; members only, and you will need to live in the Wootton Bassett area. Secretary, T Strange, 15 Shakespeare Road, Wootton Bassett, Swindon, Wilts.
Control: Club
BK Rating: Easy
W/A: Thames

EUROPEAN SECTION

On our last revision, we resisted the temptation to start listing waters in other European countries but during the last three years so many anglers have been fishing for carp in these countries that we decided to start a small European section.

Needless to say, information has been hard to obtain, and we are very grateful to those who have helped, especially to Bill Turner, Allan Parbery, and Sven Heininger who supplied the section on Germany.

If you know of any waters in any other country you would like listed please let us know about them in time for the next edition of this book.

We would urge all those who go to fish in other countries to remember that *they* are the foreigners, and that they should behave well at all times. Buy all the licences, and keep to all laws and rules; this way, you will help to give English anglers a good name. In some European countries, laws and rules are especially strict, and may be enforced by armed police and rangers.

Already some English carp anglers have become unpopular in France, especially at Lake Cassien, where many English anglers have ignored the rules, and have been caught and had their tackle confiscated. They have also upset local anglers, and have caused trouble in other ways. We have a picture of huge piles of 'English' litter left by English anglers at Lake Cassien, whilst in Holland, the Dutch, who are some of the most pleasant and friendly people we have ever met, already have a bad opinion of some English anglers, and are reluctant to have them on their waters. This especially applies to the lakes, where, so we are told by the Dutch, English anglers often 'bivvy up' for days, weeks, and in some cases, even for months, thus spoiling the fishing for the locals, and often drinking too much and behaving like English football hooligans.

If you cannot behave, and keep to all rules and laws when fishing abroad, you should not go to other countries; if you do, be well-behaved and friendly to local people and anglers, and you will help to restore the good name of English anglers – don't forget, it is *their* country, and whether or not you agree with their laws and rules, you *must* accept them and keep to them whilst you are there. Many fish in European countries are killed and eaten for food (just as English anglers kill sea fish and eat them!) and some English anglers even kill pike in England without even the excuse that they are to eat. If it is the custom to kill fish for food, then it is best to say nothing about it, however much you dislike the idea.

HOLLAND

You *must not fish* anywhere in Holland unless you hold a 'Sportvisakte', the national licence which enables you to fish the whole year with two rods. You can fish most Dutch waters with this alone. It can be purchased at all Post Offices and most tackle shops. It only costs about £4 per year. For private waters, you may need another permit, from the club which controls it, or the person who owns the water. If you see the sign 'Verpacht Viswater' the water is *private* and you must get another permit. There is no close season in Holland.

Night fishing is normally allowed by law during June, July and August. On many waters you cannot night fish in the other months. Some clubs allow night fishing outside the months listed.

The small private lakes in Holland rarely contain the big fish, and as they are private you should *not* fish this type of water. Many of the big Dutch carp are caught in canals and rivers, and as these are also the most heavily stocked carp waters in Holland, it is these you should fish.

FRANCE

You must have a French National Licence, available from all fishing tackle shops to fish nearly all waters in France. Some are private and an extra permit will be required. Night fishing is not allowed by law on nearly every water in France, although there are a few exceptions. Many of the successful and well known English anglers who caught big fish at Lake Cassien 'made their names' with 50, 60 and 70 pounders which shouldn't be 'counted' because they were caught at night, whilst the anglers were breaking the law - make sure you don't do the same!

BELGIUM

A Government National Licence is essential to fish nearly all waters. Generally no night fishing but some night fishing is allowed on private waters and there is no close season

GERMANY

German anglers have to take a long written examination to obtain a fishing licence, but this is waived for foreigners. A Government licence is normally obtained by all before fishing - this costs about £6 a year from Post Offices. There is no night fishing by law although owners of private waters can allow it, and many fish are killed and eaten. German rules and laws in relation to angling are very strict, so make sure you know what they are and that you keep to them. However, one law that you might choose to break is that *all* fish caught must be killed - the Green Party has managed to get laws passed that fishing is a cruel sport and all fish should be killed and not tortured by returning them alive! Most German anglers, unless fishing for food, do not agree with this law and return the fish alive; the choice is yours!

BELGIUM

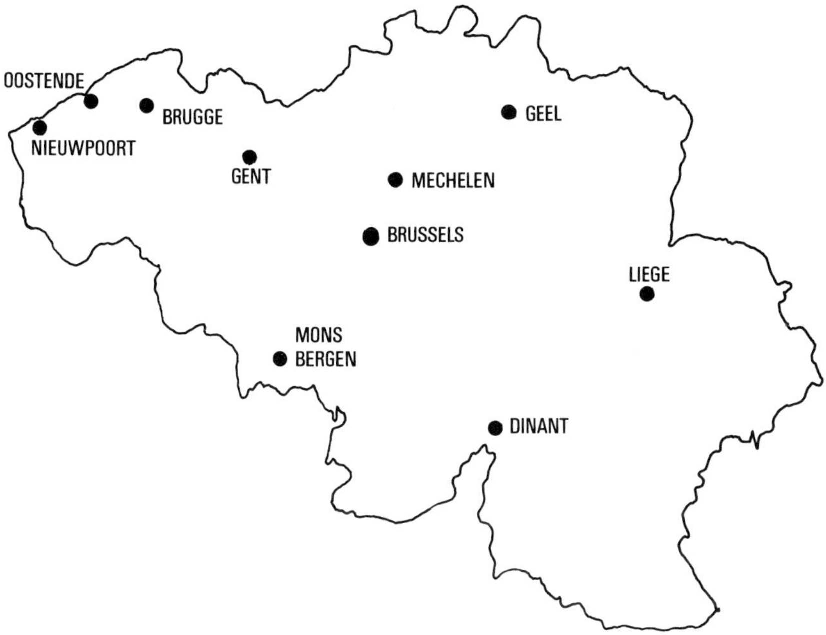

Eghlegemvyver

Location: Hombeek, near Mechelen, a city about 40 miles north of Brussels

Type and Size: 92 acre rectangular sandpit

How to Find: Take the motorway from Ostend to Gent, then the road marked 'Brussels'. Near Brussels follow the ring road, and take the Mechelen exit. At Mechelen take the Hombeek exit

Carp Stock: Plenty of small carp, and a good number of 20's; best mirror taken was 31lbs and the best common 30lbs

Category: Mixed Fishery

Other Species: Pike to 41lbs, bream and big eels

Permits: On site

Cost: Day tickets £1.50 per rod; season - £18

Control: Private

Restrictions: You can only normally fish from March to the end of September, but the Chairman, Mr R Van Lint, may be able to give permission for fishing at other times. Night fishing only allowed at weekends in May and June

Comments: This big lake is not far from the pleasant city of Mechelen, and is not a long drive - nearly all motorway - from the port of Ostend

Steve White with a 22.6 from Hotel Gehrove, near Geel, Belgium

Hotel Gehrove

Location: One mile from Geel, which is 20 miles east of Antwerp
Type and Size: Four lakes
Carp Stock: Heavily stocked with carp to over 30lbs
Permits: Day and night tickets available on the bank
BK Rating: Easy
Comments: The third lake is usually the best, with a good chance of catching many fish

Kalkaert

Location: Between Middelkerke and Oostende
Type and Size: Chalk pit of about 20 acres
How to Find: Follow the coast road from Calais to Ostend
Carp Stock: Fairly heavily stocked with carp to 38lbs
Category: Mixed Fishery
Other Species: Big bream (to which our Belgian correspondent adds '... and I know that carp anglers love them!')
BK Rating: Moderate
Control: Private
Permits: On site
Restrictions: Long stay fishing not allowed, though you may be able to make an arrangement with the bailiff, to stay longer; night fishing allowed (which is rare in Belgium)
Comments: Can be fished the whole year, but it is a busy camping site

Montreal

Location: In the outskirts of the city of Mechelen, which is about 40 miles north of Brussels
Type and Size: Pleasant town park lake of 5 acres, very busy at most times
Carp Stock: Said to be the most heavily stocked water in Belgium, with up to 10 doubles caught in a day, and plenty of twenties and smaller carp
Category: Mixed Fishery
Other Species: Roach and bream
Permits: Enquire locally, possibly from the restaurant called Montreal, which is on the banks of the lake
Control: Local club - day tickets issued
BK Rating: Very Easy (though PM had a blank there when he fished for a day in January!)
Comments: Plenty of members of the public, dog walkers and water birds, but an attractive, heavily stocked lake where you can hardly fail to catch - or so we're told!

Plassendaalse Vaart

Location: Near Nieuwpoort, in the Ostend area
Type and Size: Big canal, but the best carp area is near the sluices at Nieuwpoort
How to Find: Take the Nieuwpoort road, close to the coast from Calais or Ostend
Carp Stock: Well stocked with carp to all sizes; best caught so far was 47lbs(!)
Category: Mixed Fishery
Other Species: Roach, rudd, bream and eels
Permits: Government licence from any Post Office
Cost: £6 per season
Control: Government
BK Rating: Moderate
Restrictions: Night fishing during June, July and August only
Comments: Rod pods needed for the hard banks. Not a pleasant environment with many tourists. There are many similar canals in Belgium, of which this is a typical example; the canals go from the coast to Brussels, out towards the German border and back via Antwerp to Brugge (Bruges)

Vossem

Location: Near Zaventem, the Brussels airport
Type and Size: Town park lake of about 45 acres
How to Find: From Brussels take the Zaventem road, and follow the signs to Vossem
Carp Stock: Many very small carp, with a few big ones to 30lbs
Category: Carp Water
Other Species: Some coarse fish
Permits: On site
Cost: £5 per day
Control: Private
BK Rating: Very Easy for the small fish, but Difficult for the big ones
Restrictions: No night fishing
Comments: Long range fishing not necessary - the closer you fish, the bigger fish you are likely to catch

Watersportbaan

Location: Gent, which is south east of Bruges towards Brussels, and is on the motorway
Type and Size: Not very large, long and narrow like a canal
Carp Stock: Heavily stocked with carp, including plenty of 20's
Category: Mixed Fishery
Other Species: Most coarse fish
Permits: Government licence at £6 from any Post Office
Control: Government
Restrictions: No night fishing
BK Rating: Fairly Hard

FRANCE

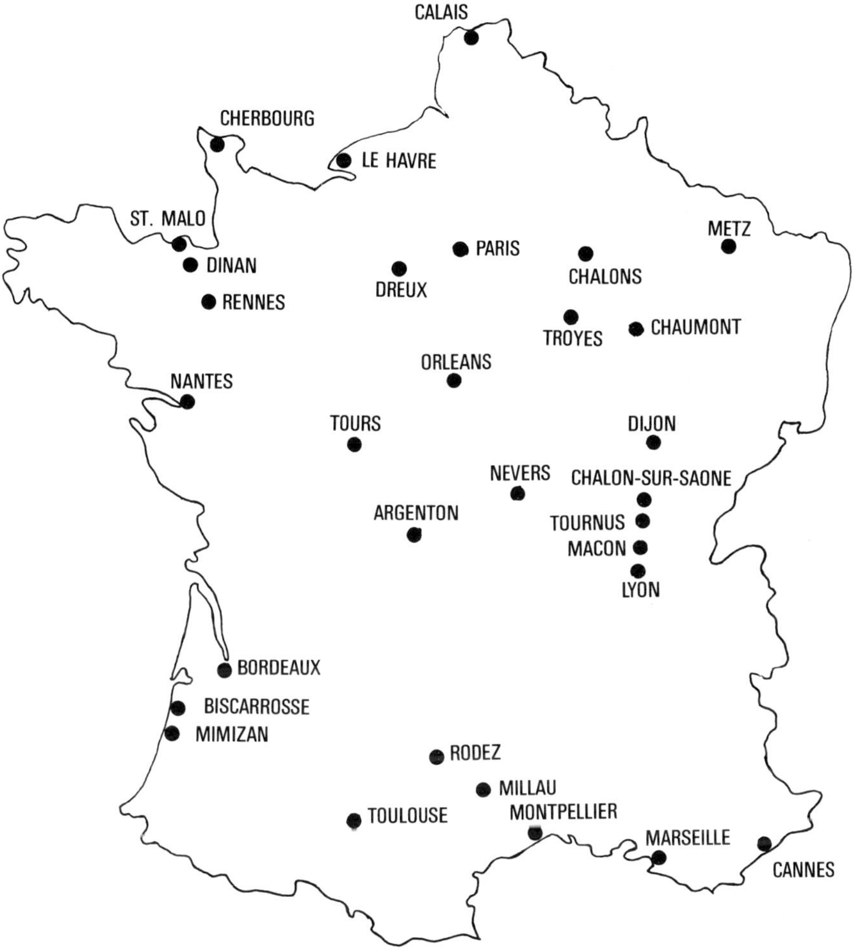

Blois Lake

Location: Near Blois, 16 miles south west of Orleans
Type and Size: Natural lake of about 30 acres
How to Find: From Blois take the 765 road south towards Romorantin. About 3 miles out of Blois turn left towards Barcieux. Before entering the village, take the second dirt track on the right, a rough track which leads to the lake
Carp Stock: Quite heavily stocked with doubles and twenties
Permits: From tackle shops in the Market Square at Blois; French national licence
BK Rating: Easy
Comments: A good fun water, not suited to the ultra-serious specimen hunter. Crayfish and snaggy areas full of trees can be a problem

Chalet Lake A

Location: Metz, 20 miles south of St. Avold
Type and Size: Horseshoe-shaped lake of about 18 acres
Carp Stock: Heavily stocked with carp to 31lbs
Category: Mixed Fishery
Other Species: Koi to 20lbs, grass carp to 33lbs, catfish to 48lbs
Permits: In advance from 'Carp Fishers Abroad', Rose Cottage, Roddington Heath, near Shrewsbury, Shropshire SY4 4RB. Tel: 0952 770771
BK Rating: Moderate
Comments: Chalet available on the lake with cooking facilities, toilet etc. A very attractive lake, with fast growing stocks and plenty of twenties

Boulet in Brittany produced this mid-twenty for Allan Parbery

Etang de Biscarrosse et Parentis

Location: Biscarrosse, close to the west coast about 40 miles south west of Bordeaux. Shown on all road maps
Type and Size: Dammed river forming a huge reservoir of several thousand acres. Sandy bottomed lake used for drinking water
Carp Stock: Quite well stocked with long lean commons to about 40lbs, plenty of 20's
Permits: French National licence from local tackle shops
BK Rating: Moderate
Comments: This water is partly on an air force base, and is regularly patrolled at night by military police

Etang de Boulet

Location: Feins, about 20 miles north of Rennes in northern France
Type and Size: Dammed river forming a very large, wedge-shaped lake
How to Find: The lake is on the D20, just off the N175 between Rennes and Mont St. Michel
Carp Stock: Lightly stocked with carp averaging over 20lbs; English anglers have had carp to at least 47lbs
Permits: Available from the cafe at Feins - French national licence
BK Rating: Difficult
Comments: A huge boom prevents windsurfers from entering the lake margins, but also causes problems where it is anchored to the bottom. Deeper areas produce the better fish. Hard boilies recommended because of crayfish. There was a fish kill in 1990, but it is still worth fishing

Etang Tremelin

Location: Near Rennes, in Brittany
Type and Size: Lake of over 100 acres
How to Find: At Montfort, west of Rennes, take the D30 to Iffendic, then the D61 south towards Phelan. The lake is 1½ miles from Iffendic
Carp Stock: Lightly stocked with carp to 50lbs, average 20lbs
Permits: On site
BK Rating: Moderate
Comments: A holiday-type complex, and quite busy at times. Other water sports take place, but there is a fishing only area

Bob Baldock, Kevin Maddocks and Allan Parbery with three twenties from Fishabil Lake, Brittany. This was part of a catch in excess of over 950 pounds of carp in three days fishing. All the fish were taken on KM Maestro Bird Spice and Honey boilies and are featured in the 'Euro Carp Quest' video.

You might encounter one of these monster catfish of 200 pounds plus at Fishabil!

Fishabil A

Location: Loscouet-sur-Meu, Brittany

Type and Size: Originally a dammed stream built by monks, but in 1990 the lake was increased in size to about 80 acres and the stream diverted. Most of the water is shallow, only 3-6 feet deep.

How to Find: Close to Rennes - as you approach Lascouet-sur-Meu the Fishabil centre is clearly signposted

Carp Stock: Originally there were only a few carp present to about 30lbs but in 1990 more than 35 tons of fish was stocked and most of these were carp. The majority are 15-25lbs with the occasional 30 and 40. One or two of over 50lbs have also been put in!

Permits: Available from the office on site. This is a private water so the normal French national licence is not required. Cost is £24 for 24 hours for 4 rods - a bit expensive but this water is only about an hour's drive from the ferry at St. Malo. Petrol costs are low, and there are no toll roads on this route.

Category: Mixed Fishery

Other Species: Catfish from Russia to over 200lbs have been stocked, with a number of 50-80 pounders; pike, zander, tench and black bass.

BK Rating: Easy

Comments: Late in 1989 Fishabil S.A. purchased the property with the intention of creating a first class fishery, with no expense spared. Bore holes were drilled to obtain high quality water, and as the lake is privately owned it is one of the very few in France which you can legally night fish. The lake is managed by carp angler Raphael Farragi, who speaks good English and is extremely helpful to visitors. High quality accommodation is available by the lakeside, there is a tennis court, an anglers' cinema, horse riding and a coffee shop (no cooked meals).

In 1991 Fishabil was the scene for the highly acclaimed 'Euro Carp Quest' video, featuring Kevin Maddocks, Allan Parbery and Bob Baldock. In three days more than 900lbs of carp including many 20's were caught and anyone contemplating a visit would find the video extremely helpful.

To book a room in advance write to: Fishabil, Le Lac, 22230 Loscouet-sur-Meu, Brittany, France. Tel: 010 33 96252766.

La Puisaye

Location: Normandy, northern France
Type and Size: Small estate lake
Carp Stock: Well stocked with big carp to 51lbs
Category: Mixed Fishery
Other Species: Grass carp and catfish
Permits: Jean Louis Bunel, 35 Boulevard Arago, 75031 Paris. Tel: 010 331 43366821
BK Rating: Not known
Comments: Night fishing is allowed

Lac de Chambon

Location: Eguzon, near Argenton-sur-Creuse
Type and Size: Dammed section of the River Creuse, several hundred acres
Carp Stock: Lightly stocked, fish to over 40lbs have been caught
Permits: French national licence, available from tackle shops
BK Rating: Difficult
Comments: The best areas are supposed to be where the river opens out into the lake. The depth fluctuates and some banks are steep

Lac de Chaumont

Location: East of the E17 road, just south of St. Dizier, between Chalons and Chaumont
Type and Size: Natural looking lake of over 100 acres
Carp Stock: A good head of doubles and twenties, and there are certain to be fish of over 45lbs, though little is known of bigger fish
Permits: Available from the tackle shop in Chaumont; normal French national licence is needed
BK Rating: Moderate
Comments: As with all large waters, fish location is important, as they do tend to shoal. Multiple baits work well. Other water sports take place on this big lake

Lac de la Chaume

Location: About 30 miles south of Argenton-sur-Creuse
Type and Size: Lake of about 150 acres
How to Find: Follow the N20 south of Argenton, then take the D70 eastwards to Jeux. Half a mile from Jeux turn right down a track which leads to the lake
Carp Stock: Fairly heavily stocked with fish from about 20lbs to over 40lbs
Other Species: Coarse fish and some catfish
Permits: Available from the Mairie (Town Hall) at Azerables - about £12 for 24 hours with three rods
BK Rating: Easy to Moderate
Comments: Night fishing is permitted. Closed between November and March. Used for other water sports, but these are not a serious problem

Lac de Pres de St. Jean (Lake Zup)

Location: In the centre of Chalon-sur-Saone
Type and Size: Town park lake of about 60 acres
Carp Stock: Lightly stocked with carp to 40lbs, with 30's not uncommon. Stock also includes 'Mamur Carp' to about 100lbs, average weight about 10lbs
Permits: From Jackie Greset's tackle shop in the town. This is the only public water where you can night fish in France, and you must request a free night permit when obtaining your licence
BK Rating: Difficult
Comments: No boats present; has an overrated reputation, but it does give you somewhere to night fish legally when you are in the area

Allan Parbery and Ken Bishop with typical low twenties from Lake Salagou

Lac de Salagou

Location: West of Montpellier, in the south of France

Type and Size: A dammed river forming an irregular-shaped lake about 4 miles in length

How to Find: Turn off the A9/E15 motorway at the southern, last, Montpellier exit. Follow the signs for Millau/Lodeve on the 109 road. Just past the junction with the E9 (5 miles before Le Lodeve) you will see the signposts to the lake

Carp Stock: Heavily stocked with thousands of commons and mirrors. The average size is 20lbs, with plenty of twenties and thirties. Some 40's and a chance of a fifty. Full potential not known

Other Species: Large trout, bream, pike and zander

Permits: French national licence from the tackle shop just over the first bridge as you enter Lodeve

BK Rating: Easy to Moderate

Comments: Location is very important in this huge water. Mussels are a problem, and some areas are very snaggy. Other places have shelving bottoms which are 'stepped' and these have proved diffiuclt to fish. Hard boilies such as Maestros, are recommended, popped up. A boat is very useful – take your own if possible, as they are very expensive to hire, and are not designed for carp anglers! Most of the lake is accessible from tracks. The ground is very rocky, making bivvy erection difficult. Because of the many snags, a good supply of terminal tackle is essential. Several videos featuring this lake are available

Lac de St. Cassien

Location: About 10 miles west of Cannes and the Mediterranean coast

Type and Size: Dammed streams forming a lake of about 1,500 acres, which is made up of three sections, south, north and west arms. Depths to 60 feet in the west and south arms, and more than 100 feet in the north arm

How to Find: The lake is close to the north side of the E80/A8 motorway and is shown on all road maps

Carp Stock: Lake Cassien probably holds more big carp than any other lake in the world. Thirty pounders are 'small' by Cassien standards, with 40's, 50's and 60's being the target. Several carp over 70lbs have been caught, and there is little doubt that carp approaching 90lbs exist in the lake. It was first stocked in 1964, and fish of a good size are put in every year

Category: Carp Water

Other Species: A few catfish and one, estimated to weigh about 150lbs, was caught by English angler Johnny Allen; also tench, pike and black bass

Permits: From Chez Pierre's restaurant on the banks of the southern arm, or from tackle shops in Cannes. Normal French licence required

BK Rating: Difficult

Comments: As far as English anglers are concerned, this mecca of carp waters was 'discovered' by Kevin Maddocks and Paul Regent in September 1984. Most English anglers who visit Cassien feel that they have to break the rules to catch fish. Night fishing is against the law and the French authorities have found it necessary to employ *armed* rangers to stop visitors from breaking the rules. Most people, if careful, get away with night fishing, but many have been caught and had their tackle confiscated.

Shortly after the lake was 'discovered' by Kevin Maddocks and Paul Regent, hundreds of English anglers visited the lake, and some historic catches were made.

The English were followed by the Dutch (as usual!) and then the Germans. In recent years the fishing has become much harder and now the water receives much less pressure. The next few years will see only the more serious and dedicated carp anglers visiting the water, and more big catches will be made – but the best time has gone! For full details on Cassien, including an aerial photograph of the lake, see the book 'Carp Fever' by Kevin Maddocks

Lac de St. Croix

Location: About 80 miles north of the Mediterranean coast, and north west of Cannes

Type and Size: A huge lake of more than 10,000 acres, formed by the damming of the River Verdon

Carp Stock: Lightly stocked with some very large fish, which have been caught to over 60lbs. Potential unknown

Permits: French national licence from tackle shops

BK Rating: Difficult

Comments: Very busy with holidaymakers. Lots of snags, but lots of potential also

Lac de Vouglans

Location: Close to the Swiss border, north west of Lyon

Type and Size: The dammed River Ain, about 20 miles long

How to Find: Take the N78 from Chalon-sur-Saone to Lons Le Saunier, and after 15

	miles you will see the north end of the lake
Carp Stock:	Lightly stocked with some very big carp – commercial fishermain claim carp to 90lbs!
Permits:	French national licence from tackle shops
BK Rating:	Difficult
Comments:	Lots of snags and very steep banks in places. It is advisable not to fish until carp are located, and although it is difficult you could get a very big fish

La Darce

Location:	Macon, on the Saone
Type and Size:	This 'lake' is part of the River Saone, and is over 40 acres in size
How to Find:	Going south, go through Macon on the main road. Just before the end of the town turn left into the industrial estate
Carp Stock:	Variable, as this depends on conditions in the river. When the river is highly coloured and fast, it is quite common for hundreds of carp to enter the Darce, and this also happens at spawning time, so the Darce always contains carp to over 40lbs – sometimes a few, sometimes many hundreds!
Other Species:	Catfish to over 100lbs
Permits:	French national licence from tackle shops
BK Rating:	Moderate
Comments:	Not a very attractive place as it is in the middle of an industrial estate, but many of the fish are commons of over 30lbs. Multiple (particle) baits work well

Allan Parbery with a 30 pound common from La Darce at Macon

La Fert Vidame

Location: Puissay, west of Dreux, in Normandy
Type and Size: Dammed stream of about 12 acres
How to Find: Turn off the N12 at Verneuil, which is between Dreux and Alecon. Head south for about 5 miles to La Ferte Vidame
Carp Stock: Fairly heavily stocked with many doubles, quite a few twenties, some thirties and an occasional forty
Other Species: Some coarse fish, including grass carp to 30lbs
Permits: Available on site, or from J L Bunel's tackle shop in Paris
BK Rating: Easy
Comments: Night fishing is allowed, and the French licence is not required, as this is a private water. A nice looking lake, where the average angler can catch some good fish

Les Ormes A

Location: Near Dinan, Brittany
Type and Size: Small pit of less than 10 acres
Carp Stock: Heavily stocked with doubles, and the occasional twenty
Permits: On site, but only for those who stay at the camp site
BK Rating: Easy
Comments: Ideal family venue, busy at times

Lyon Canal

Location: In the big city of Lyon
Type and Size: Large canal used by huge barges and tankers
How to Find: The Lyon ring road passes over this canal which runs from the River Saone to the River Rhone
Carp Stock: Heavily stocked and although the full potential is unknown, many thirties are caught
Permits: French national licence from tackle shops in Lyon
BK Rating: Easy
Comments: This is a water for the adventurous, who don't mind boat traffic and human beings. Location is easy, as the carp congregate in groups and some very big fish can be seen

Merceuil

Location: Four miles south of Beaune, between Dijon and Chalon-sur-Saone
Type and Size: Gravel pit of about 40 acres
How to Find: Turn off the A6/E15 motorway at Beaune, and head east on the D970. Follow signs to Bligny-les-Beaunes. The lake is alongside the motorway about 4 miles out of Beaune
Carp Stock: Lightly stocked with carp to over 35lbs
Permits: Available from Jackie Greset's shop in Chalon-sur-Saone (alongside the river a little downstream of the road bridge). French national licence required
BK Rating: Fairly Hard
Comments: Mussels and crayfish a problem. The old river course in the centre of the lake is productive. Very hard boilies (such as KM Maestros) necessary to beat the crayfish

Mimizan

Location: Mimizan, close to the west coast, 60 miles south west of Bordeaux
Type and Size: Dammed river forming a lake of more than 200 acres
Carp Stock: Quite well stocked with long, lean commons to over 30lbs, with plenty of 20's
Permits: Local tackle shops; French national licence
BK Rating: Moderate
Comments: Strictly controlled, as it is near an air force base, and so is patrolled at night

Pareloup

Location: Between Rodez and Millau
Type and Size: Dammed streams which form a huge reservoir, several miles across, and 1,800 acres in extent
How to Find: The lake is about 3 miles to the south of the 911 road between Rodez and Millau - take the D993 towards Salles Curan
Carp Stock: A good head of low doubles, some 20's, 30's and 40's and a reported 57 pounder
Permits: French national licence from the tackle shop in Millau
BK Rating: Moderate
Comments: Location is of paramount importance - don't bother to fish until you spot carp; mussels and crayfish a bit of a problem. Boat recommended - an ideal water for the pioneering big fish man

River Loire

Location: The Loire runs from the Lyon area northwards through Roanne and Nevers, and then west through Orleans (60 miles south of Paris), Tours, Angers, and out to the sea at Nantes
Type and Size: A medium-sized river about 400 miles in length, quite fast flowing, and fairly shallow in places, especially in its upper reaches. There are several power stations on the banks
Carp Stock: Most areas contain carp. The best part of the river is the 150 miles stretch from Decize to Blois. Carp bigger than 30lbs are often caught from the Decize, Fourchambault, St. Laurent and Gien areas
Other Species: Most European species, including catfish to more than 100lbs
Permits: French national licence from tackle shops
BK Rating: Easy - once the fish are located
Comments: The areas near the power stations, especially at Gien and St. Laurent des Eaux, produce a lot of good fish over 30lbs. Unlike most French rivers, boilies are readily acceptable by the Loire carp. It is worth noting that one or two of the lakes alongside the river hold carp of over 40lbs

River Lot

Location: This excellent carp water is more than 100 miles long and runs into the River Garonne about 45 miles south of Bordeaux
Type and Size: The river is dammed in several sections, and water levels vary considerably
How to Find: There are many good areas on this river, but one of the most popular is near St. Geniez d'Olt - follow the signs to Cabanac village
Carp Stock: Very heavily stocked with carp including many big commons. Plenty of doubles, twenties and thirties, and certainly some fish over 40lbs

Permits: French National licence from local tackle shops, such as Serges, 4 Place du Marche, St. Geniez
BK Rating: Easy to Moderate
Comments: Often the carp form in large groups so location is important. Large beds of boilies and cooked particles have been very successful. A boat is recommended, and these can be hired in Cabanac. The Lot is featured in two videos: Dave Plummer's 'French Carp Fishing' and Mick Hall's film

River Saone

Location: From just north of Dijon to Lyon, at its confluence with the Rhone
Type and Size: River about 100 miles long and 200–400 yards wide; slow flowing with depths of 20–25 feet in the middle
Carp Stock: Good stock of singles, doubles and twenties along the whole length. Carp to over 60lbs have been caught, and it is believed that this river holds a French record
Category: Mixed Fishery
Other Species: Most European coarse fish, including many catfish to 150lbs
Permits: Local tackle shops; French national licence
BK Rating: Moderate
Comments: For big fish, location is vitally important. One of the best areas is in the town of Chalon-sur-Saone, close to the islands and barge moorings. Here many large carp well over 50lbs have been caught. Boilies not successful at first, and you need to bait heavily with sweetcorn and other multiple baits, whilst introducing boilies. Large barges frequent this river, but don't present a problem. Serious approach and commitment needed for success on this river. The Saone was one of the areas fished during the making of the video 'Cat Fever', featuring Kevin Maddocks and Bob Baldock

River Seille

Location: This river is about 40 miles long and runs into the River Saone at Tournus, between Chalon and Macon
Type and Size: A medium-sized river which in its lower reaches is some 30 yards wide, with an average depth of about 10 feet
Carp Stock: Heavily stocked with mid-doubles and a good sprinkling of thirties. The river record is supposed to be 59lbs, but the largest authenticated fish we know of is 42lbs
Other Species: Most European species, and catfish to well over 100lbs
Permits: French national licence from tackle shops
BK Rating: Moderate
Comments: One of the best stretches is between the Pont Seille and Ratanelle road bridges, especially in the areas of fallen trees. This river is very susceptible to flooding so always have another water you can fish so you don't go all the way there for nothing

River Seine

Location: Runs from Troyes, through Paris, and out to the sea at Le Havre
Type and Size: Very large river up to a quarter of a mile wide, with varying depths
Carp Stock: Carp are found almost anywhere in the Seine, but certain areas produce the bigger fish. Fish of over 80lbs have been caught, and the French record came from the river, near Fontainebleu – a common of 84lbs!

Permits: French national licence from local tackle shops
BK Rating: Moderate
Comments: For big fish local knowledge must be sought - carp of 50–60lbs are not uncommon in some areas. Heavy baiting with particles at first whilst boillies are introduced is recommended, as many of the fish have never seen boilies; the river carries a lot of boat traffic. A good spot is at Fault Yonne near Monteraux. There are several warm water outlets here, and the winter fishing is quite good

A magnificent 63 pound common from the River Seine

Sennecey

Location: Between Chalon-sur-Saone and Tournus
Type and Size: The lake is over 40 acres in size, and is the largest of a group of three lakes
How to Find: Turn off the A6/E15 motorway at Chalon. Head south along the N6, which runs parallel to the motorway, to the town of Sennecey. The lakes are clearly signposted in the town
Carp Stock: Lightly stocked with carp to over 40lbs
Permits: Available from Cafe de Laives near the church in Laives; day and year permit available
BK Rating: Difficult
Comments: Became well known some years ago and subsequently received a lot of angling pressure. One English angler had three forties in a weekend, but nowadays it is not much fished. Crayfish and mussels a problem

Sorigny

Location: About 8 miles south of Tours
Type and Size: Natural lake of about 40 acres
How to Find: Take the N10 road heading south from Tours to the village of Sorigny. As you leave town follow the sign for camping/caravan site – the lake is part of the site
Carp Stock: A reasonable head of commons and mirrors averaging nearly 20lbs. There are quite a few twenties with the occasional thirty
Permits: Permission must be obtained from the camp site
BK Rating: Moderate
Comments: Water sports take place, but this doesn't spoil your chances of catching. At one time you could only obtain a permit if you were staying on the site, but this rule has now been relaxed

Richard Tring with a 35.8 mirror from one of the lakes at Chalon-sur-Saone (Tailly)

Tailly

Location: 4 miles south of Beaune, between Dijon and Chalon-sur-Saone
Type and Size: Two gravel pits of about 30 acres and 10 acres
How to Find: Turn off the A6/E15 motorway at Beaune, and head south on the D970. The lakes are either side of the road about 4 miles from Beaune, just past the Meursault turn
Carp Stock: The larger lake has a very good head of carp to 47lbs, including many twenties; the smaller lake contains fewer carp to just over 20lbs
Permits: French national licence from Jackie Greset's tackle shop at Chalon-sur-Saone
BK Rating: Moderate

Comments: Local anglers have been moving fish around these lakes to confuse visitors! Hard boilies needed to beat the numerous crayfish. The small lake has many snags. The large lake is shallow at one end, with a small island at the deeper end, and the island shelf is most productive

Ville Franche A

Location: Near Montpon, 40 miles east of Bordeaux
Type and Size: Two lakes of 30 acres and 5 acres
How to Find: Leave the E70 road, which runs from Bordeaux to Perigeux, at Montpon, then south to Ville Franche. The lakes and camp site are clearly signposted as you enter the village
Carp Stock: The small lake is well stocked with small carp to mid-doubles. The larger lake is lightly stocked with fish up to 40lbs
Permits: Day tickets from the camp site
BK Rating: Small lake - Easy; larger lake - Difficult
Comments: Ideal place to take a family and also enjoy some carp fishing. Boats and swimming allowed on the larger lake, where there is a man-made beach. Very busy at times

GERMANY

by Sven Heininger

Atichkanal

Location: Off the A2/A39 near Braunschweig
Type and Size: Big canal much used by boats
Carp Stock: Well stocked with carp to 35lbs
Category: Mixed Fishery
Other Species: Most coarse fish, including pike and zander
Permits: In advance only from Restaurant Gerhard Dolsner, Weinberg 8, 3303 Vechelde
Cost: £4 per week - three rods
BK Rating: Moderate
Baits/Methods: Best method is a fixed lead with a pop-up hair rigged bait such as dog food

A superb 29 pounder caught by top German carp angler Sven Heininger, who wrote this section of the book

Bostalsee

Location: Between Hunsruck and Pfalz, in Saarland, south west Germany
Type and Size: Huge gravel pit of 350 acres
Carp Stock: Some carp from 10 to 18lbs
Other Species: Perch, tench, eels, trout, zander and other coarse fish
Permits: German national licence and day and weekly ticket on bank
Cost: £3 per day and £14 per week
BK Rating: Difficult
Comments: Two rods only; no fishing from December 15th to January 31st. Very busy with campers and swimmers

Dechsendorfer Weiher

Location: Between Nürnberg and Erlangen, in Bavaria, South Germany
Type and Size: Large pit, about three quarters of a mile in length
How to Find: Off the A3 Nürnberg to Wurzburg road
Carp Stock: Well stocked with carp, most of which are under 10lbs
Category: Mixed Fishery
Other Species: Tench and perch
Permits: Sportamt Erlangen, Fahrstree 18, Eerlange. Tel: 09131 86590
Cost: £4 per day
Restrictions: Two rods only
BK Rating: Easy
Baits/Methods: Boilies best at present

Dümmer

Location: Take the B51 from Osnabruck to Diepholz, near Niedersachen, North Germany
Type and Size: Very big lake, several miles square, and only about five feet deep
Carp Stock: Not many, but some very big ones
Category: Few Carp
Other Species: Perch to 6lbs, pike to 36lbs, a few tench and many eels
Permits: The tackle shop Bödeker/Hüde, or Friedrich Kemper, Steinstreet 19, 2840 Diepholz. Tel: 05541 3329
Cost: £3 per day
BK Rating: Super-Difficult
Comments: The best chance is boat fishing and boats can be hired for £3 an hour. Only for the dedicated specialist carp hunter as the fish are few and very hard to locate

Ellertshäuser Reservoir

Location: Unterfranken, between Würzbürg and Schweinfurt
Type and Size: Huge reservoir
Carp Stock: Well stocked with carp to 20lbs
Category: Mixed Fishery
Other Species: Tench, zander and trout
Permits: Bernd Müller, Zum See 10, 8721 Fuchstadt, Unterfranken

Cost: £5 per day
BK Rating: Insufficient information
Comments: The best water in Unterfranken, and a very pleasant area

Griebnitrsee

Location: In the middle of Berlin
Type and Size: Large town lake
Carp Stock: Many commons and mirrors to 25lbs
Category: Carp Water
Other Species: Bream, roach, eels and pike
Permits: Tickets from the fishing club Shöneberg, Islandrellistret 56, 1000 Berlin 46
Cost: £15 for 6 months
BK Rating: Easy
Comments: Two rods only; German national licence essential

Happurger Reservoir

Location: Abbochtal, between Deckersberg, Houbirg and Reicheneck in the Franken area of Bavaria, South Germany
Type and Size: 150 acre reservoir
Carp Stock: A few carp to 18lbs
Category: Few Carp
Other Species: Tench, zander, big trout, roach and eels
Permits: From the Town Hall in Happurg
Cost: £5 per day
BK Rating: Difficult
Comments: Much sailing and windsurfing in summer

Hopfensee

Location: Hopfen am See, Bavaria, South Germany
Type and Size: Big lake about half a mile across
Carp Stock: Well stocked with carp to 40lbs
Category: Mixed Fishery
Other Species: Tench, bream, roach, pike, zander, perch and eels
Permits: German fishing permit, and a £3 day ticket from the Hanpt tackle shop nearby
BK Rating: Difficult
Baits/Methods: Most fish are caught by float fishing with sweetcorn
Comments: Very snaggy water with island. Boat needed to catch the carp; a very pleasant lake

Kemnoder See

Location: Off the A43 motorway between Witten Herbede and Hattingen, in Nordheinwestfalen, North Germany
Carp Stock: Not many carp
Category: Few Carp
Other Species: Bream, roach, pike, zander and perch

Permits: ASV Bochum, Ruhr 1935; the tackle shop Simmerman Bochum, Herner Street 363. Tel: 0234 551679
Cost: £2 per day
BK Rating: Difficult

Kölner Seen-Platte

Location: Off the A4 from Aachen to Köln (Cologne), Nordheinwestfalen, North Germany
Type and Size: Huge lake
Carp Stock: Well stocked with commons to 18lbs
Category: Mixed Fishery
Other Species: Perch, pike to 33lbs, tench and grass carp
BK Rating: Very Difficult
Comments: You will need to enquire locally how to get permits to fish this lake, as we were not able to find out

Landgrafenweiher

Location: Fichtilgebirge, near Warmensteinach
Type and Size: Large gravel pit
Carp Stock: Quite well stocked with carp which average 6–8lbs. Some bigger fish to about 20lbs
Category: Mixed Fishery
Other Species: Grass carp, pike, zander, bream and catfish
Permits: From the house at the lake in Warmensteinach
BK Rating: Easy
Restrictions: No baiting with boilies, fish food or particles

Mossandl-Weiher

Location: Between Mamming and Dingolfing, near Regensburg in Bavaria, South Germany
Type and Size: Gravel pit of about 60 acres
Carp Stock: Well stocked with mirrors and commons to about 20lbs
Category: Mixed Fishery
Other Species: Pike and zander
Permits: Restaurante Fischwirt, 8388 Mamming, and Dingolfing tackle shop, Obere Stadt 52, Dingolfing. Tel: 08731 2404
Cost: £10 per week
Restrictions: No night fishing, but boat fishing is allowed
BK Rating: Moderate

Niedermooser See

Location: Hessen, in the centre of Germany, between Giessen and Eulda
Type and Size: 90 acre gravel pit
Carp Stock: Heavily stocked with commons to about 20lbs, and mirrors to 25lbs
Category: Mixed Fishery
Other Species: Tench, pike, eels, zander, trout and most other coarse fish
Permits: From the Campingrestaurante at the lake
Cost: £4 per day; £24 per week

Control: ASV Lauterbock, Lindenstrasse 4, 6420 Lauterbach
BK Rating: Moderate
Comments: A big lake also used for sailing

Niederwaldsee

Location: Near Frankfurt, between Nanheim and Gross Gerau
Type and Size: Big gravel pit
How to Find: Take the A67 from Frankfurt to Darmstadt, then the road to Gross Gerau
Carp Stock: Well stocked with small commons to 15lbs, and mirrors to 30lbs
Category: Mixed Fishery
Other Species: Pike, tench, chub, roach, bream, perch, eels and zander
Permits: Day tickets should be purchased from the tea shop at the lake. The tickets only cover 12 hours - night fishing not allowed
Cost: £3 per day
Control: Club
BK Rating: Small fish - Easy; big ones - Very Difficult
Baits/Methods: Advanced carp fishing rigs, methods and bait are needed at this lake for the big carp. Boilies and sweetcorn are very successful
Restrictions: No night fishing, two rods only
Comments: Restaurant and disco at the lake; camping in summer; car park

River-dam Quitrdorf

Location: Sachsen, near Dresden, on the Polish border in what used to be East Germany
Type and Size: Huge reservoir of about 2,000 acres
Carp Stock: Well stocked with commons and mirrors; water record is 38lbs
Category: Mixed Fishery
Other Species: Grass carp, tench and zander
Permits: Permits from the camping area in Kollm
Cost: £4 per day; £12 per week; boat hire £2 per day - two rods only
BK Rating: Moderate

River Rhein

Location: West Germany, near the French border
Type and Size: Huge European river
Carp Stock: Many carp under 10lbs, but the record is 48lbs
Category: Mixed Fishery
Other Species: Pike to 35lbs, zander to 30lbs and big catfish
Permits: German national rod licence *and* a weekly permit, bought locally
Cost: £10 per year
Control: Water police!
BK Rating: Easy, if you can locate the fish
Baits/Methods: Boilies catch the big fish. You need powerful rods, heavy leads, and line of 15lb+ breaking strain - and at least 200 metres of it, in case you hook one of the big catfish
Comments: Not a river for beginners to fish

Schnackensee

Location: Near the town of Gunzenhausen, Bavaria, South Germany
Type and Size: Eight acre lake
How to Find: The lake is about 25 miles south of Nürnberg
Carp Stock: Well stocked with plenty of doubles, and some bigger fish. Lake record is 44lbs
Category: Mixed Fishery
Other Species: Many catfish to 150lbs (see Kevin Maddocks' book 'Catfish'), grass carp to 70lbs, pike, zander and 'Mamur Carp' to 70lbs
Permits: Day ticket on bank
Control: Private - Werner Vogel
BK Rating: Easy
Cost: £8 for 2 rods; £6 per day for caravans and £3 for tent or bivvy
Baits/Methods: Modern, advanced rigs, methods and baits needed
Comments: A pleasant, heavily stocked water producing hundreds of carp each week; can be very busy at weekends. Night fishing not allowed

Werrstalsperre

Location: Between the towns of Eschwege, Kassel and Gottingen, in Hessen, central Germany
Type and Size: Huge gravel pit
How to Find: Take the A7 from Salsgitter to Kassel and then the B7 to Eschwege
Carp Stock: Carp to 20lbs
Category: Mixed Fishery
Other Species: Zander, rudd, bream and roach
Permits: Fremden Verkelswerein (FVV) Eschwege - 3440 Eshwege
BK Rating: Moderate
Comments: Float fishing is the best method here

HOLLAND

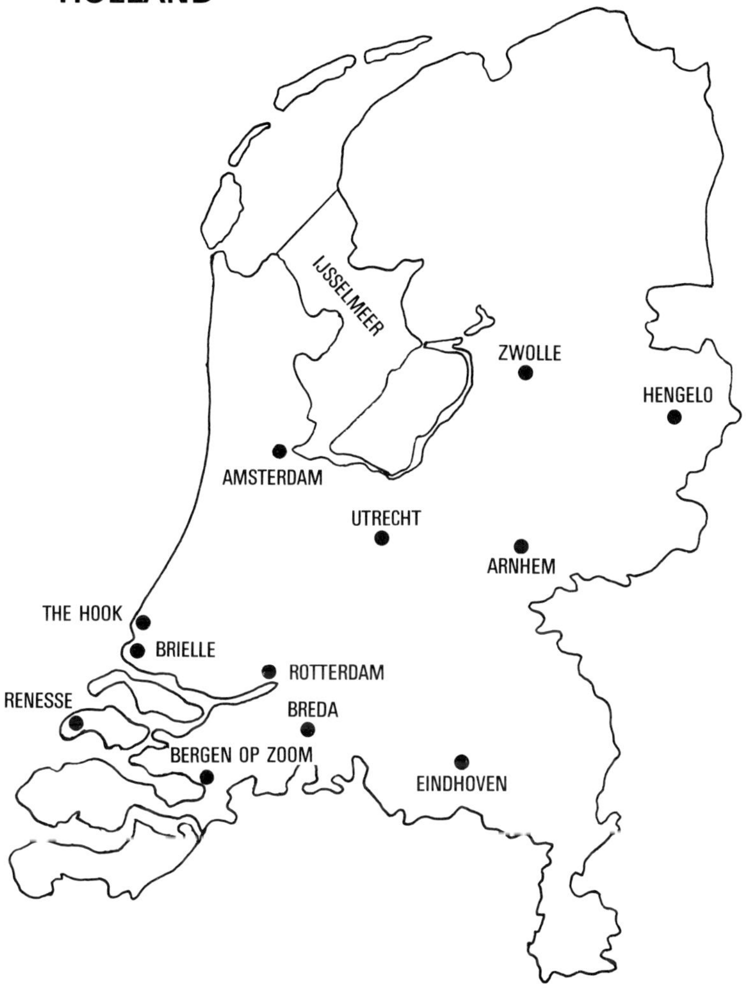

Barge and Jetty Lake and Complex

Location: Knieuwkoop, about an hour's drive from the Hook of Holland

Type and Size: Barge and Jetty Lakes about 1½ acres each. The main complex is about 150 acres, made up of many small lakes

Carp Stock: Jetty Lake is heavily stocked with carp from 15 to 30lbs, including some big commons. Barge Lake also heavily stocked with carp to mid-twenties

Permits: In advance only from: Carp Fishers Abroad, Rose Cottage, Roddington Heath, Shrewsbury, Shropshire SY4 4RB. Tel: 0952 770771

BK Rating: Easy to Moderate

Comments: Secure clubhouse with cooking and toilet facilities. A guide to the best fishing areas is provided and Carp Fishers Abroad has other waters

Brielle Moat

Location: 15 miles west of Rotterdam, very near the coast
Type and Size: Moat round the old town of Brielle
Carp Stock: Quite heavily stocked, including several 20lb commons
Permits: Available from 'local bar' or tackle shops
BK Rating: Moderate
Comments: A very well known fishery, which is heavily fished at times

Little Milahna

Location: Bergen op Zoom, 20 miles west of Breda
Type and Size: Town lake of about 8 acres
How to Find: In the town of Bergen op Zoom
Carp Stock: Very heavily stocked with some twenties
Permits: From the tackle shop in the town, or at the camp site nearby
BK Rating: Very Easy
Comments: An ideal water to take the family; several camp sites nearby

Molengat and Ovensgat Lake

Location: Rossum, near Utrecht
Type and Size: Two lakes of about 7 acres
How to Find: Take the A2 and the N322 to Rossum (between Utrecht and den Bosch)
Carp Stock: Carp to at least 35 pounds
Permits: Available from cafe named 'Waalzicht' in Rossum, cost approximately 5 guilders per day and 60 guilders for a year
BK Rating: Moderate
Comments: Very nice waters with potential of some very big fish. The nearby river also holds carp

Molenwiel

Location: Near Nederasselt, between Wychen and Druten
Type and Size: 6 acre lake
Carp Stock: Fish to at least 35 pounds, quantity unknown
Permits: Day tickets available from grocer's shop 'Van der Stappen' in Nederasselt, cost: 3 guilders, or 60 guilders per year
BK Rating: Moderate
Comments: A good quality water holding some very big carp – full potential unknown

Renesse

Location: 30 miles south west of Rotterdam, on the coast
Type and Size: 5 acre lake
Carp Stock: Well stocked with carp, and lots of twenties
Permits: Available on site at £6 per year
BK Rating: Very Easy
Comments: A good place to take the family; many camp sites close by

Rijnkanaal

Location: Amsterdam area, where there are many other canals, all containing carp
Type and Size: If you thought the Twente was big, you ought to see this one!
Carp Stock: Heavily stocked with plenty of big carp
Category: Mixed Fishery
Other Species: Most coarse fish
Permits: Compulsory Sportvisakte, the national licence obtainable from Post Offices; you MUST NOT fish in Holland without this licence - no other permit required. Covers two rods for a year at low cost
BK Rating: Difficult, unless the fish can be located when it is quite easy
Comments: No close season. Many big fish lost when line is cut on freshwater mussels, so you need line heavy enough and of the right type to combat this problem.
NB. The new Dutch record of 52lbs was caught from a river, and most of the biggest Dutch carp are found in rivers and canals; for this reason we strongly recommend anglers to fish the canals and rivers and not the Dutch lakes, which often are private and do not contain the biggest carp. Night fishing only allowed in June, July and August

River Ijssel

Location: Flows into the Ijsselmeer, near Zwolle, from above Arnhem
Type and Size: Big European river
Carp Stock: Well stocked with plenty of 20's and thirties along the whole stretch of the river, and considered to be one of the best carp waters in Holland
Category: Mixed Fishery
Other Species: Many, including grass carp to over 50lbs
Permits: National licence essential - do NOT fish until you have bought one from any Post Office. The Sportvisakte cover two rods for a year, at very low cost. No other permits needed
BK Rating: Carp hard to locate, as in most big rivers, but not too difficult to catch once they are found
Comments: A very good bet for big carp, but with the usual problems to be found in big rivers

River Maas

Location: Flows through Holland, and becomes the Meuse in Belgium and France. Maastricht to just north of Breda
Type and Size: Huge European river, hundreds of miles in length
Carp Stock: Very heavily stocked with big carp - the Dutch record of over 52lbs was caught from here in May 1991
Category: Mixed Fishery
Other Species: Most coarse fish including some you may never have seen!
Permits: National licence, the Sportvisakte, must be obtained before fishing. This is available from Post Offices at low cost, and it covers two rods and the whole year - no close season
BK Rating: Difficult, due to location problems and the strong currents in this big river
Comments: Try to take local advice to find out where carp are being caught. Night fishing only allowed in June, July and August

Gary Delyster with a Dutch common of 36 pounds

The Ijsselmeer

Location: North Holland, north of Amsterdam
Type and Size: Huge inland sea, once salt water, 40 miles long and about 25 miles across and separated from the sea only by the Afsluitdijk, a 12 mile dam built by the Dutch and one of the world's greatest engineering feats
Carp Stock: Very well stocked with carp, most of which are huge and immensely long wildies which go to well over 20lbs
Category: Mixed Fishery
Other Species: Most European coarse fish
Permits: You must have the official Government licence, the Sportvisakte, obtained from Post Offices at low cost, and valid for two rods for a year. No other permits needed
BK Rating: Very Difficult, though some huge catches have been made when the fish are located
Comments: No close season. Best areas are around Amsterdam and Flevoland. Try to get help from someone who knows the area, and may know where carp are caught. When I stood at the middle of the dam, two years ago, the waves on this 'lake' were several feet high, with spray breaking over my head

T. Luytelaar

Location: Mariahout, near Eindhoven
Type and Size: Lake of about 3 acres
How to Find: Take the N266 and N272 to Lieshout and from there to Mariahout
Carp Stock: Heavily stocked with carp to 30 pounds, mainly commons
Other Species: Big grass carp
Permits: Day tickets available in the village of Mariahout and the address and directions are explained on a signpost at the lake
BK Rating: Easy
Comments: A very peaceful and quiet place to fish

Twentekanaal

Location: Hengelo area, by the warm water outlet
Type and Size: Huge canal, about 80 metres across
Carp Stock: Heavily stocked with many big carp to nearly 40lbs
Category: Mixed Fishery
Other Species: Most coarse fish
Permits: You will need a Sportvisakte, which is a national licence - you *must not* fish in Holland without this licence, which can be bought at all Post Offices and most tackle shops. The licence is annual, covers two rods and costs only about £4 for a year - there is no close season in Holland. You can fish most other Dutch waters with this licence, and no other permits, the exceptions being where a club has the rights, which is usually indicated by the sign 'Verpacht Viswater'
BK Rating: Very Difficult
Comments: This is one of the most famous and pressurised fisheries in Europe, especially as it fishes so well in the winter, due to the warm water. It is wide and very deep, and the boats are of ocean-going size, and will disturb your swim for half an hour after they pass. Best fishing is at night, and the most sophisticated methods and rigs are needed - PM had a blank here too - though nothing at all was caught during the day whilst he was there, although a number of good fish were taken during the night.. after he had left for England! Night fishing only allowed in June, July and August. Steam rises from the water in winter!

Zuiderdiep

Location: Much searching of the map of the Netherlands has not been able to show us where this canal is, so you'll have to enquire when you get there
Type and Size: Small, closed down canal with no boats
Carp Stock: Well stocked with carp to 35lbs
Category: Mixed Fishery
Other Species: Most European coarse fish
Permits: Sportvisakte, the national licence, essential; do *not* fish before obtaining this cheap, compulsory licence from any Post Office - it covers two rods, and the whole year, as there is no close season. You will also need an *extra* permit for this private canal; details locally or from notices by the canal
Control: Club
BK Rating: Moderate
Comments: This pleasant canal is heavily fished, which is not surprising as it is unlike most Dutch canals, being club controlled, and having no boat traffic... if you find out where it is, please let us know..!

HINDERS

Bird Seed Manufacturing Specialists
Importers Specialists Particles

The Finest quality Products are on display and available for immediate despatch or collection. All items throughout this price list are in stock and not just available to special order, therefore enabling you to select your particular flavours and bait at your leisure, but without a long wait for delivery. If however you are unable to visit us in person we will be pleased to despatch your requirement via our mail order service. For bulk orders, delivery can be arranged throughout the country.

- Tiger Nuts
- Small Red Kernels
- Medium Kernals 50/60
- Extra Large Kernels
- Pine Nuts
- Whole Brazil Nuts
- Broken Brazils
- Almonds
- Hazel Nuts
- Cashews
- Pistachios
- Hemp (standard)
- Hemp ($3^1/_2$)mm
- Tares (Chinese)
- Tares (Polish)
- Red Dari
- White Dari
- Buckwheat
- Groats
- Pinhead Oatmeal
- French Maize (deep yellow)
- Red Rape
- Black Rape
- Paddy Rice
- Whole Oats
- Barley
- Wheat
- Striped Sunflower
- Safflower
- Panicum Millet
- Japanese Millet
- White Millet
- Linseed
- Red Millet
- Flaked Maize
- Layers Mash
- Bran
- Moth Beans
- Black-eyed Beans
- Adzuki Beans
- Red Kidney Beans
- Maple Peas
- Mini Maples
- Dun Peas
- Sweet Lupins
- Blue Peas
- Chick Peas
- Haricot Beans
- Tic Beans
- Mung Beans
- Pinto Beans
- Soya Beans
- Lima Beans
- Salmon Fry Crumb (02)
- Trout Pellets No. 4/6
- Crushed Hemp
- Maize Flour
- Semigrueso RRR
- Paprika
- Carophyll red

FLOATERS

- Chum Mixer
- Mini No. 1
- Maxi No. 2
- Top Mix

TRADE ENQUIRIES WELCOME

KRYSTON PRODUCTS

AMBIO FEEDING TRIGGER – the ultimate additive 125ml £3.53 500ml £11.20

ANISEED FLAVOURING 10ml bottle £2.00

▪ BIRD FOOD INGREDIENTS ▪

SUPER SEGGO takes bird food ingredients one step further – this excellent ready-ground product will make the bird food bait of your dreams. The make-up and consistency is perfect for holding large amounts of liquid additives and should be used for up to 70% of your base mix. SUPER SEGGO ANALYSIS IS AS FOLLOWS:

ADDED PER KG:

Vitamin A – 19.500I.U.	Vitamin D3 – 2.000 I.U.	Vitamin E – 30mg	Vitamin K3 – 2.2mg
Vitamin B1 – 12mg	Vitamin B2 – 38mg	Pantothenic Acid – 55mg	Choline Chlonde – 475mg
Niacin – 100mg	Vitamin B6 – 1.75mg	Vitamin B12 – 0.075mg	Folic Acid – 6.8mg
Biotin – 0.38mg	Vitamin C – 4mg	Calcium – 0.9%	Phosphorous – 0.4%
Sodium – 0.05%	Magnesium – 125mg	Manganese – 80mg	Zinc – 58mg
Iron – 29mg	Cobalt – 18mg	Copper – 5mg	Iodine – 1.2mg
DL Methionine – 500mg	L-Lysine – 1.150mg	Selenium – 0.1mg	

"MYSTIC" Hooded sweatshirts £16.50 T-shirts £6.50.

CIPRO

SOLE U.K. DISTRIBUTORS

For the Specialist Carp Angler

These **ETHYL ALCOHOL FLAVOURS** are not only the best acceptable solvent for carp. They do more. For instance they will give you a smell for at least 12 hours in summer and winter.

We have designed these high quality tried and tested ETHYL ALCOHOL FLAVOURS with the specialist carp angler in mind. Taste them and see for yourself.

THESE FLAVOURS ARE WINNERS.

Banana Royal	pH. 5.3	Watermelon	pH. 5.2
Butter-Caramel	pH. 5.1	Strawberry Fort	pH. 2.8
Cream	pH. 5.5	Real chocolate	pH. 5.5
Pineapple	pH. 5.6	Peanut	pH. 4.4
Pistache	pH. 5.4	Spice Mix	pH. 5.1
Raspberry	pH. 3.7	Apricot	PH. 6.1
Nougat	PH. 4.2		

Colours available:
RED, YELLOW, ORANGE, and PINK

HINDERS, Ermin Street, Stratton St. Margaret, Swindon SN3 4NJ
Tel. (0793) 825372/822145/822692/828961 Fax. (0793) 824725

Open Mon-Sat, 8.30am – 5.30pm ▪ Ample Free Parking ▪ We look forward to seeing you soon or contact BRYAN on (0793) 828961 or 822145 Fax. (0793) 824725

MAIL ORDER – For mail order please send cheques or postal orders including postage payable to: Hinders of Swindon to the address above

Index

UK WATERS

EUROPEAN WATERS

BELGIUM

FRANCE

GERMANY

HOLLAND

Waters Questionnaire

Please insert name of contact..
Tel (...........) .... who can verify details

Name: ....

Location: ....

Type and Size: ....

How to Find: ....

Carp Stock: ....

Other Species: ....

Permits: ....

Control: ....

Cost: ....

Restrictions: ....

Baits/Methods: ....

Comments: ....

Please insert name of contact..
Tel (...........) .... who can verify details

Name: ....

Location: ....

Type and Size: ....

How to Find: ....

Carp Stock: ....

Other Species: ....

Permits: ....

Control: ....

Cost: ....

Restrictions: ....

Baits/Methods: ....

Comments: ....

Please return to:

FREEPOST Beekay Publishers
Withy Pool
Henlow Camp
Bedfordshire
SG16 6EA